普通高校"十三五"规划教材·会计学系列

会计英语

徐海峰 ◎ 编　著

清华大学出版社
北京

内 容 简 介

《会计英语》全书分 3 个部分共 12 章,全面地介绍财务报告、成本管理和投融资管理基本核心知识,注重知识的实用性及内在联系,各章相互独立又有机结合,形成一个完整的会计英语体系。本书将理论知识、现实世界、课内例题和课后测试融为一体,书后还附有主要财务报表的中英文对照,便于读者使用。

本书可供高等院校会计、财务管理、资产评估等专业作为本科教材,也可供财务与会计从业人员自学和培训使用,是广大读者学习地道的会计专业英语表述和实务操作的一本理想书籍。

本书封面贴有清华大学出版社防伪标签,无标签者不得销售。
版权所有,侵权必究。举报:010-62782989,beiqinquan@tup.tsinghua.edu.cn。

图书在版编目(CIP)数据

会计英语/徐海峰编著. —北京:清华大学出版社,2018 (2021.7重印)
(普通高校"十三五"规划教材·会计学系列)
ISBN 978-7-302-49831-5

Ⅰ. ①会… Ⅱ. ①徐… Ⅲ. ①会计－英语－高等学校－教材 Ⅳ. ①F23

中国版本图书馆 CIP 数据核字(2018)第 042848 号

责任编辑:梁云慈
封面设计:汉风唐韵
责任校对:王荣静
责任印制:沈 露

出版发行:清华大学出版社
　　　　网　　址:http://www.tup.com.cn, http://www.wqbook.com
　　　　地　　址:北京清华大学学研大厦 A 座　　　邮　　编:100084
　　　　社 总 机:010-62770175　　　　　　　　　　　邮　　购:010-62786544
　　　　投稿与读者服务:010-62776969,c-service@tup.tsinghua.edu.cn
　　　　质量反馈:010-62772015,zhiliang@tup.tsinghua.edu.cn
印 装 者:三河市龙大印装有限公司
经　　销:全国新华书店
开　　本:185mm×260mm　　　印　张:21.75　　　字　数:501 千字
版　　次:2018 年 3 月第 1 版　　　　　　　　　印　次:2021 年 7 月第 4 次印刷
定　　价:49.00 元

产品编号:078429-02

前 言

随着经济全球化的发展,会计作为国际通用"商业语言"的功能日益凸显。目前,全球已有超过120个国家和地区采用与国际财务报告准则(International Financial Reporting Standards, IFRS)等效趋同的准则作为本国企业财务报告标准,降低了不同国家和地区间的信息获取及分析成本,提高不同国家和地区公司间的会计信息可比性,进而促进资源区域性的优化配置。中国全球市场经济地位的不断提升,也促使会计在经济发展中扮演越来越重要的角色,这必然对会计与财务等相关专业的学生和从业人员提出更高的要求。本教材基于"专业+英语=职业胜任"的理念,期望帮助会计专业高校学生和相关专业的从业人员提升综合职业能力。本教材的特色如下:

1. 实用性强。为方便教学和自学使用,每章开篇列示学习目标和本章简介,正文中清晰标识出重点概念,结合生动的例题和案例与知识点无缝连接,章后附有本章小结、核心词汇、自测题及答案。在调动学生学习积极性的同时强化对关键知识的消化和理解,达到学以致用的目的。

2. 体系合理。涵盖财务会计、管理会计和财务管理三部分的核心知识,共12章,各章相互独立又有机结合,形成一个完整合理的体系。系统阐述会计基本理论、财务报告、成本管理、投融资和资产运营管理等基本专业知识,满足读者全面学习财会知识、适应对外交流和实务工作的需要。

3. 多维支持。为满足教学和自学的需要,不仅在每章中提供丰富的训练题型,包括单选题、判断题、分析题和业务题,有效帮助读者理解重要知识点,还提供与教材配套的立体化教学资源,包括PPT、财务报表中英文对照和相关阅读资料等。通过多元化的学习资源,向读者提供支持并展现地道专业英语,充分体现国际会计的最新变化。

全书3个部分,共12章。第1部分为财务会计篇,包括第1章至第6章,具体内容为会计概论、会计循环、资产负债表、损益表、现金流量表和财务报表分析。第2部分为管理会计篇,包括第7章至第9章,具体内容为成本与价格、本—量—利分析和预算编制。第3部分为财务管理篇,包括第10章至第12章,具体内容为资本投资决策、融资和营运资金管理。

一本好的教材的出版,凝结着作者、出版者的辛苦付出。本书的出版得到了清华大学出版社的大力支持,尤其是梁云慈编辑的耐心沟通和宝贵意见,深表感谢。特别感谢大连大学经济管理学院的支持,还要感谢我的学生孙艳玲和任倩的协助。

本书可供高等院校会计、财务管理、资产评估专业作为本科教材,也可供财会从业人员自学和培训使用,是广大读者学习地道的会计专业英语表述和实务操作的一本理想书籍。

由于编者水平有限,书中不妥之处在所难免,殷切期望同仁和广大读者不吝赐教,批评指正。

徐海峰

2017年11月23日

Contents

Part 1 Financial Accounting

CHAPTER 1 Introduction to Accounting 3

   1.1 Accounting information and decision making 4
   1.2 Financial accounting and management accounting 6
   1.3 Globalization of accounting 8
   1.4 The Conceptual Framework for Financial Reporting 10
   1.5 Professional ethics in accounting 13
   SUMMARY 15
   KEY TERMS 16
   SELF-EVALUATION ACTIVITIES 17

CHAPTER 2 Business Transactions 19

   2.1 Identifying business transactions and events 19
   2.2 The accounting equation and Double-entry system 22
   2.3 The accounting worksheet 24
   2.4 Journals and ledgers 28
   2.5 The trial balance 32
   2.6 Accounting errors 33
   SUMMARY 34
   KEY TERMS 36
   SELF-EVALUATION ACTIVITIES 37

CHAPTER 3 Balance Sheet 40

   3.1 Nature and purpose of the balance sheet 40
   3.2 The definition and recognition of asset, liability and equity 44
   3.3 Disclosure of elements on the balance sheet 49
   3.4 Format and presentation of the balance sheet 56
   3.5 Measurement of various assets 58
   3.6 Accounting policy choices, estimates and judgements 64

3.7　Potential limitations of the balance sheet ······ 67
SUMMARY ······ 68
KEY TERMS ······ 71
SELF-EVALUATION ACTIVITIES ······ 73

CHAPTER 4　Statement of Profit or Loss ······ 80

4.1　Purpose of measuring financial performance ······ 80
4.2　Accounting concepts for financial reporting ······ 83
4.3　Effect of accounting policy choices, estimates and judgements on financial statements ······ 89
4.4　Measuring financial performance ······ 92
4.5　Applying recognition criteria to income and expenses ······ 96
4.6　Presenting the statement of profit or loss ······ 99
4.7　The statement of comprehensive income ······ 104
4.8　The statement of changes in equity ······ 105
SUMMARY ······ 108
KEY TERMS ······ 111
SELF-EVALUATION ACTIVITIES ······ 112

CHAPTER 5　Statement of Cash Flows ······ 115

5.1　The purpose and usefulness of a statement of cash flows ······ 115
5.2　The main features of the statement of cash flows ······ 119
5.3　Preparing the statement of cash flows ······ 124
5.4　Explanation of the statement of cash flows ······ 130
SUMMARY ······ 131
KEY TERMS ······ 132
SELF-EVALUATION ACTIVITIES ······ 132

CHAPTER 6　Analysis of Financial Statements ······ 135

6.1　Assist financial statements users to make decisions ······ 136
6.2　Analytical methods ······ 138
6.3　Profitability analysis ······ 149
6.4　Asset efficiency analysis ······ 153
6.5　Liquidity analysis ······ 156
6.6　Capital structure analysis ······ 158
6.7　Market performance analysis ······ 161
6.8　Ratio interrelationships ······ 163
SUMMARY ······ 167

KEY TERMS	170
SELF-EVALUATION ACTIVITIES	171

Part 2   Management Accounting

CHAPTER 7   Costing and Pricing … 179

7.1	Role of cost information	179
7.2	Classification of costs	181
7.3	Cost allocation	183
7.4	Product cost of inventories	191
7.5	Pricing methods	197
SUMMARY		200
KEY TERMS		201
SELF-EVALUATION ACTIVITIES		202

CHAPTER 8   Cost-volume-profit Analysis … 204

8.1	Cost behavior	204
8.2	Break-even analysis	207
8.3	Contribution margin ratio	211
8.4	Operating leverage	213
8.5	Relevant concepts for decision making	216
SUMMARY		226
KEY TERMS		227
SELF-EVALUATION ACTIVITIES		228

CHAPTER 9   Budgeting … 231

9.1	Strategic planning and budgeting	231
9.2	Budgeting progress and types	233
9.3	Master budget	236
9.4	Cash budget	241
SUMMARY		246
KEY TERMS		246
SELF-EVALUATION ACTIVITIES		247

Part 3 Financial Management

CHAPTER 10 Capital Investment 253

10.1　The nature and scope of investment decisions 253
10.2　Accounting rate of return 256
10.3　Payback period 258
10.4　Net present value 259
10.5　Internal rate of return 264
10.6　Practical issues in making decisions 268
SUMMARY 271
KEY TERMS 272
SELF-EVALUATION ACTIVITIES 272

CHAPTER 11 Financing the Business 275

11.1　Sources of internal finance 275
11.2　Sources of external finance 278
11.3　Providing long-term finance for small businesses 287
SUMMARY 289
KEY TERMS 290
SELF-EVALUATION ACTIVITIES 290

CHAPTER 12 Managing Working Capital 292

12.1　Definition of working capital 292
12.2　Managing inventories 294
12.3　Managing receivables 303
12.4　Managing cash 309
12.5　Managing trade payable 316
12.6　Working capital problems of small businesses 318
SUMMARY 320
KEY TERMS 322
SELF-EVALUATION ACTIVITIES 322

Appendix 324

Main References 335

目　录

第1篇　财务会计

第1章　会计概述 3
1.1　会计信息与决策 4
1.2　财务会计与管理会计 6
1.3　会计全球化 8
1.4　财务报告概念框架 10
1.5　会计职业道德 13
本章小结 15
关键词汇 16
自测题及答案 17

第2章　会计循环 19
2.1　明确交易和事项 19
2.2　会计等式和复式记账 22
2.3　会计工作底稿 24
2.4　日记账和分类账 28
2.5　试算平衡 32
2.6　会计差错 33
本章小结 34
关键词汇 36
自测题及答案 37

第3章　资产负债表 40
3.1　资产负债表概述 40
3.2　资产、负债和所有者权益的确认 44
3.3　资产负债表要素的披露 49
3.4　资产负债表格式与列报 56
3.5　资产的计量 58
3.6　会计政策选择、估计和判断 64

3.7 资产负债表的局限性 ⋯⋯⋯⋯⋯⋯⋯⋯⋯⋯⋯⋯⋯⋯⋯⋯⋯⋯⋯⋯⋯⋯⋯⋯⋯⋯⋯⋯ 67
本章小结 ⋯⋯⋯⋯⋯⋯⋯⋯⋯⋯⋯⋯⋯⋯⋯⋯⋯⋯⋯⋯⋯⋯⋯⋯⋯⋯⋯⋯⋯⋯⋯⋯⋯ 68
关键词汇 ⋯⋯⋯⋯⋯⋯⋯⋯⋯⋯⋯⋯⋯⋯⋯⋯⋯⋯⋯⋯⋯⋯⋯⋯⋯⋯⋯⋯⋯⋯⋯⋯⋯ 71
自测题及答案 ⋯⋯⋯⋯⋯⋯⋯⋯⋯⋯⋯⋯⋯⋯⋯⋯⋯⋯⋯⋯⋯⋯⋯⋯⋯⋯⋯⋯⋯⋯⋯ 73

第4章 损益表 ⋯⋯⋯⋯⋯⋯⋯⋯⋯⋯⋯⋯⋯⋯⋯⋯⋯⋯⋯⋯⋯⋯⋯⋯⋯⋯⋯⋯⋯⋯⋯⋯⋯ 80

4.1 损益表概述 ⋯⋯⋯⋯⋯⋯⋯⋯⋯⋯⋯⋯⋯⋯⋯⋯⋯⋯⋯⋯⋯⋯⋯⋯⋯⋯⋯⋯⋯⋯ 80
4.2 财务报告中的重要概念 ⋯⋯⋯⋯⋯⋯⋯⋯⋯⋯⋯⋯⋯⋯⋯⋯⋯⋯⋯⋯⋯⋯⋯⋯ 83
4.3 会计政策选择、估计和判断对财务报告的影响 ⋯⋯⋯⋯⋯⋯⋯⋯⋯⋯⋯⋯⋯⋯ 89
4.4 经营成果的计量 ⋯⋯⋯⋯⋯⋯⋯⋯⋯⋯⋯⋯⋯⋯⋯⋯⋯⋯⋯⋯⋯⋯⋯⋯⋯⋯⋯ 92
4.5 收入和费用的确认 ⋯⋯⋯⋯⋯⋯⋯⋯⋯⋯⋯⋯⋯⋯⋯⋯⋯⋯⋯⋯⋯⋯⋯⋯⋯⋯ 96
4.6 损益表的列报 ⋯⋯⋯⋯⋯⋯⋯⋯⋯⋯⋯⋯⋯⋯⋯⋯⋯⋯⋯⋯⋯⋯⋯⋯⋯⋯⋯⋯ 99
4.7 综合收益表 ⋯⋯⋯⋯⋯⋯⋯⋯⋯⋯⋯⋯⋯⋯⋯⋯⋯⋯⋯⋯⋯⋯⋯⋯⋯⋯⋯⋯⋯ 104
4.8 所有者权益变动表 ⋯⋯⋯⋯⋯⋯⋯⋯⋯⋯⋯⋯⋯⋯⋯⋯⋯⋯⋯⋯⋯⋯⋯⋯⋯⋯ 105
本章小结 ⋯⋯⋯⋯⋯⋯⋯⋯⋯⋯⋯⋯⋯⋯⋯⋯⋯⋯⋯⋯⋯⋯⋯⋯⋯⋯⋯⋯⋯⋯⋯⋯ 108
关键词汇 ⋯⋯⋯⋯⋯⋯⋯⋯⋯⋯⋯⋯⋯⋯⋯⋯⋯⋯⋯⋯⋯⋯⋯⋯⋯⋯⋯⋯⋯⋯⋯⋯ 111
自测题及答案 ⋯⋯⋯⋯⋯⋯⋯⋯⋯⋯⋯⋯⋯⋯⋯⋯⋯⋯⋯⋯⋯⋯⋯⋯⋯⋯⋯⋯⋯⋯ 112

第5章 现金流量表 ⋯⋯⋯⋯⋯⋯⋯⋯⋯⋯⋯⋯⋯⋯⋯⋯⋯⋯⋯⋯⋯⋯⋯⋯⋯⋯⋯⋯⋯⋯ 115

5.1 现金流量表概述 ⋯⋯⋯⋯⋯⋯⋯⋯⋯⋯⋯⋯⋯⋯⋯⋯⋯⋯⋯⋯⋯⋯⋯⋯⋯⋯⋯ 115
5.2 现金流量表的结构 ⋯⋯⋯⋯⋯⋯⋯⋯⋯⋯⋯⋯⋯⋯⋯⋯⋯⋯⋯⋯⋯⋯⋯⋯⋯⋯ 119
5.3 现金流量表的编制 ⋯⋯⋯⋯⋯⋯⋯⋯⋯⋯⋯⋯⋯⋯⋯⋯⋯⋯⋯⋯⋯⋯⋯⋯⋯⋯ 124
5.4 现金流量表信息披露 ⋯⋯⋯⋯⋯⋯⋯⋯⋯⋯⋯⋯⋯⋯⋯⋯⋯⋯⋯⋯⋯⋯⋯⋯⋯ 130
本章小结 ⋯⋯⋯⋯⋯⋯⋯⋯⋯⋯⋯⋯⋯⋯⋯⋯⋯⋯⋯⋯⋯⋯⋯⋯⋯⋯⋯⋯⋯⋯⋯⋯ 131
关键词汇 ⋯⋯⋯⋯⋯⋯⋯⋯⋯⋯⋯⋯⋯⋯⋯⋯⋯⋯⋯⋯⋯⋯⋯⋯⋯⋯⋯⋯⋯⋯⋯⋯ 132
自测题及答案 ⋯⋯⋯⋯⋯⋯⋯⋯⋯⋯⋯⋯⋯⋯⋯⋯⋯⋯⋯⋯⋯⋯⋯⋯⋯⋯⋯⋯⋯⋯ 132

第6章 财务报表分析 ⋯⋯⋯⋯⋯⋯⋯⋯⋯⋯⋯⋯⋯⋯⋯⋯⋯⋯⋯⋯⋯⋯⋯⋯⋯⋯⋯⋯⋯ 135

6.1 财务报表分析目的 ⋯⋯⋯⋯⋯⋯⋯⋯⋯⋯⋯⋯⋯⋯⋯⋯⋯⋯⋯⋯⋯⋯⋯⋯⋯⋯ 136
6.2 财务报表分析方法 ⋯⋯⋯⋯⋯⋯⋯⋯⋯⋯⋯⋯⋯⋯⋯⋯⋯⋯⋯⋯⋯⋯⋯⋯⋯⋯ 138
6.3 盈利能力分析 ⋯⋯⋯⋯⋯⋯⋯⋯⋯⋯⋯⋯⋯⋯⋯⋯⋯⋯⋯⋯⋯⋯⋯⋯⋯⋯⋯⋯ 149
6.4 营运能力分析 ⋯⋯⋯⋯⋯⋯⋯⋯⋯⋯⋯⋯⋯⋯⋯⋯⋯⋯⋯⋯⋯⋯⋯⋯⋯⋯⋯⋯ 153
6.5 偿债能力分析 ⋯⋯⋯⋯⋯⋯⋯⋯⋯⋯⋯⋯⋯⋯⋯⋯⋯⋯⋯⋯⋯⋯⋯⋯⋯⋯⋯⋯ 156
6.6 资本结构分析 ⋯⋯⋯⋯⋯⋯⋯⋯⋯⋯⋯⋯⋯⋯⋯⋯⋯⋯⋯⋯⋯⋯⋯⋯⋯⋯⋯⋯ 158
6.7 市场绩效分析 ⋯⋯⋯⋯⋯⋯⋯⋯⋯⋯⋯⋯⋯⋯⋯⋯⋯⋯⋯⋯⋯⋯⋯⋯⋯⋯⋯⋯ 161
6.8 财务比率间的联系 ⋯⋯⋯⋯⋯⋯⋯⋯⋯⋯⋯⋯⋯⋯⋯⋯⋯⋯⋯⋯⋯⋯⋯⋯⋯⋯ 163
本章小结 ⋯⋯⋯⋯⋯⋯⋯⋯⋯⋯⋯⋯⋯⋯⋯⋯⋯⋯⋯⋯⋯⋯⋯⋯⋯⋯⋯⋯⋯⋯⋯⋯ 167
关键词汇 ⋯⋯⋯⋯⋯⋯⋯⋯⋯⋯⋯⋯⋯⋯⋯⋯⋯⋯⋯⋯⋯⋯⋯⋯⋯⋯⋯⋯⋯⋯⋯⋯ 170

自测题及答案 171

第2篇 管理会计

第7章 成本与价格 179

7.1 成本信息的作用 179
7.2 成本的分类 181
7.3 成本的分配 183
7.4 成本的计算 191
7.5 定价方法 197
本章小结 200
关键词汇 201
自测题及答案 202

第8章 本—量—利分析 204

8.1 成本性态 204
8.2 保本点分析 207
8.3 边际贡献率 211
8.4 经营杠杆 213
8.5 决策中的成本应用 216
本章小结 226
关键词汇 227
自测题及答案 228

第9章 预算编制 231

9.1 战略规划与预算 231
9.2 预算的程序与种类 233
9.3 全面预算 236
9.4 现金预算 241
本章小结 246
关键词汇 246
自测题及答案 247

第3篇 财务管理

第10章 资本投资决策 253

10.1 投资决策概述 253
10.2 投资回报 256

10.3 投资回收期法 ⋯⋯⋯⋯⋯⋯⋯⋯⋯⋯⋯⋯⋯⋯⋯⋯⋯⋯⋯⋯⋯⋯⋯⋯⋯⋯⋯⋯⋯⋯⋯⋯⋯⋯⋯⋯ 258
10.4 净现值法 ⋯⋯⋯⋯⋯⋯⋯⋯⋯⋯⋯⋯⋯⋯⋯⋯⋯⋯⋯⋯⋯⋯⋯⋯⋯⋯⋯⋯⋯⋯⋯⋯⋯⋯⋯⋯⋯⋯ 259
10.5 内涵报酬率法 ⋯⋯⋯⋯⋯⋯⋯⋯⋯⋯⋯⋯⋯⋯⋯⋯⋯⋯⋯⋯⋯⋯⋯⋯⋯⋯⋯⋯⋯⋯⋯⋯⋯⋯⋯ 264
10.6 投资决策方法的应用 ⋯⋯⋯⋯⋯⋯⋯⋯⋯⋯⋯⋯⋯⋯⋯⋯⋯⋯⋯⋯⋯⋯⋯⋯⋯⋯⋯⋯⋯⋯⋯ 268
本章小结 ⋯⋯ 271
关键词汇 ⋯⋯ 272
自测题及答案 ⋯⋯⋯⋯⋯⋯⋯⋯⋯⋯⋯⋯⋯⋯⋯⋯⋯⋯⋯⋯⋯⋯⋯⋯⋯⋯⋯⋯⋯⋯⋯⋯⋯⋯⋯⋯⋯⋯ 272

第 11 章 融资 ⋯⋯⋯⋯⋯⋯⋯⋯⋯⋯⋯⋯⋯⋯⋯⋯⋯⋯⋯⋯⋯⋯⋯⋯⋯⋯⋯⋯⋯⋯⋯⋯⋯⋯⋯⋯ 275

11.1 内部融资 ⋯⋯⋯⋯⋯⋯⋯⋯⋯⋯⋯⋯⋯⋯⋯⋯⋯⋯⋯⋯⋯⋯⋯⋯⋯⋯⋯⋯⋯⋯⋯⋯⋯⋯⋯⋯⋯ 275
11.2 外部融资 ⋯⋯⋯⋯⋯⋯⋯⋯⋯⋯⋯⋯⋯⋯⋯⋯⋯⋯⋯⋯⋯⋯⋯⋯⋯⋯⋯⋯⋯⋯⋯⋯⋯⋯⋯⋯⋯ 278
11.3 小企业长期融资 ⋯⋯⋯⋯⋯⋯⋯⋯⋯⋯⋯⋯⋯⋯⋯⋯⋯⋯⋯⋯⋯⋯⋯⋯⋯⋯⋯⋯⋯⋯⋯⋯⋯ 287
本章小结 ⋯⋯ 289
关键词汇 ⋯⋯ 290
自测题及答案 ⋯⋯⋯⋯⋯⋯⋯⋯⋯⋯⋯⋯⋯⋯⋯⋯⋯⋯⋯⋯⋯⋯⋯⋯⋯⋯⋯⋯⋯⋯⋯⋯⋯⋯⋯⋯⋯⋯ 290

第 12 章 营运资金管理 ⋯⋯⋯⋯⋯⋯⋯⋯⋯⋯⋯⋯⋯⋯⋯⋯⋯⋯⋯⋯⋯⋯⋯⋯⋯⋯⋯⋯⋯⋯ 292

12.1 营运资金概述 ⋯⋯⋯⋯⋯⋯⋯⋯⋯⋯⋯⋯⋯⋯⋯⋯⋯⋯⋯⋯⋯⋯⋯⋯⋯⋯⋯⋯⋯⋯⋯⋯⋯⋯⋯ 292
12.2 存货管理 ⋯⋯⋯⋯⋯⋯⋯⋯⋯⋯⋯⋯⋯⋯⋯⋯⋯⋯⋯⋯⋯⋯⋯⋯⋯⋯⋯⋯⋯⋯⋯⋯⋯⋯⋯⋯⋯ 294
12.3 应收账款管理 ⋯⋯⋯⋯⋯⋯⋯⋯⋯⋯⋯⋯⋯⋯⋯⋯⋯⋯⋯⋯⋯⋯⋯⋯⋯⋯⋯⋯⋯⋯⋯⋯⋯⋯⋯ 303
12.4 现金管理 ⋯⋯⋯⋯⋯⋯⋯⋯⋯⋯⋯⋯⋯⋯⋯⋯⋯⋯⋯⋯⋯⋯⋯⋯⋯⋯⋯⋯⋯⋯⋯⋯⋯⋯⋯⋯⋯ 309
12.5 应付账款管理 ⋯⋯⋯⋯⋯⋯⋯⋯⋯⋯⋯⋯⋯⋯⋯⋯⋯⋯⋯⋯⋯⋯⋯⋯⋯⋯⋯⋯⋯⋯⋯⋯⋯⋯⋯ 316
12.6 小企业营运资金管理 ⋯⋯⋯⋯⋯⋯⋯⋯⋯⋯⋯⋯⋯⋯⋯⋯⋯⋯⋯⋯⋯⋯⋯⋯⋯⋯⋯⋯⋯⋯⋯ 318
本章小结 ⋯⋯ 320
关键词汇 ⋯⋯ 322
自测题及答案 ⋯⋯⋯⋯⋯⋯⋯⋯⋯⋯⋯⋯⋯⋯⋯⋯⋯⋯⋯⋯⋯⋯⋯⋯⋯⋯⋯⋯⋯⋯⋯⋯⋯⋯⋯⋯⋯⋯ 322

附录 ⋯⋯ 324

参考文献 ⋯⋯⋯⋯⋯⋯⋯⋯⋯⋯⋯⋯⋯⋯⋯⋯⋯⋯⋯⋯⋯⋯⋯⋯⋯⋯⋯⋯⋯⋯⋯⋯⋯⋯⋯⋯⋯⋯⋯ 335

Part 1

Financial Accounting

CHAPTER 1

Introduction to Accounting

LEARNING OBJECTIVES

After studying this chapter, you should be able to:
- 1.1 understand the importance of accounting and its role in decision making
- 1.2 explain the differences between financial accounting and management accounting
- 1.3 discuss the globalization of accounting
- 1.4 outline the Conceptual Framework and identify the qualitative characteristics of financial information
- 1.5 outline the role of accounting professional ethics in business decision making

Why do I need to learn accounting and finance? What is accounting's role in business decision making? These questions and more will be answered in the first chapter of this textbook. People in all walks of life rely on accounting information to make daily decisions concerning the allocation of scarce resources. For example, a middle-aged couple may rely on accounting information to make investment decision on their pension plan; a student might use budgeting tools to help fund an overseas trip to Europe at the end of his university year; and knowledge of costs could help a company quote for a job on a large-scale order. All of these would benefit from accounting information to help them make the best decision.

The role of the accountant is continually evolving and comprises a lot more than just the basic preparation of financial statements and the traditional work areas of management and financial accounting. Accountants can work in exciting new growth areas such as carbon accounting, water accounting and sustainability accounting.

In addition to explaining the importance of accounting information in decision making, this chapter outlines the globalization of financial reporting, the Conceptual Framework for Financial Reporting(Conceptual Framework).

In recent years, the responsibilities of the accounting profession have changed dramatically. The Enron Corporation and Arthur Andersen financial scandal at the start of the millennium resulted in major changes to public expectations of the accountant. These raised questions about the role of accounting information and/or the integrity of the financial reporting.

1.1 Accounting information and decision making

The word account derives from the Latin words "ad" and "computend", which mean "to reckon together" or "to count up or calculate". **Accounting** can be defined as the process of identifying, measuring, recording and reporting economic information about an entity to a variety of users for decision-making purposes. Accounting is often viewed as an information system.

The first component of this definition is the process of identifying business transactions. A business transaction is an event that affects the financial position of an entity and can be reliably measured and recorded. **Business transactions** include such events as withdrawals of cash by the owner(s), payment of wages and salaries, earning of revenue, purchase of raw materials, capital contribution by owners, incurring of interest on a bank loan and payment of quarterly GST (goods and services tax).

The second component is the measuring of information, which refers to the analysis, recognition and classifying of business transactions. This component identifies whether transactions will belong to economic information, how transactions will affect the entity's position, and groups together similar items such as expenses and income. Throughout the accounting period, individual assets, expenses, income, equity and liabilities will be grouped (classified) together to summarize the information. For example, land, buildings, machinery, equipment and vehicles will be grouped together under the subheading "property, plant and equipment".

The third component is the recording of information. For example, the contribution of capital by the owners will be recorded in journals as increasing the cash at bank (asset) of the entity and increasing the capital (equity) of the entity. This core method is double-entry system.

The final component is the communication of relevant information through accounting reports, such as the statement of profit or loss and the balance sheet, for decision-making purposes for the various users. For example, the total of the property, plant and equipment account will be reported on the balance sheet. The different users require accounting information for making important decisions such as whether to invest in a business, what type of business structure would be appropriate, whether the entity should continue to manufacture a product or outsource this process to another entity, and whether the entity has the resources to pay debts on time. All these decisions involve making the most of the scarce resource — money. The process of accounting assists users in the allocation of this scarce resource.

The practices of accounting and bookkeeping date back to ancient civilizations in China, Egypt, Greece and Rome, where families had kept personal wealth to record their receipts and payments. The title "Father of accounting" belongs to Italian mathematician Fra Luca Pacioli who, in 1494, produced *Summa de Arithmetica, Geometrica, Proportioni et Proportionalita*, which included chapters based entirely on how to record business transactions using a double-entry system. Table 1.1 summarizes the process of accounting information system.

TABLE 1.1 The process of accounting

Identifying	Measuring	Recording	Reporting
Transactions that affect the entity's financial position are taken into consideration. They must be able to be reliably measured and recorded.	This stage includes the analysis, recognition and classifying of business transactions.	This stage applies the skills of double-entry system to record transactions in journals.	Accounting information is communicated through various reports such as statements of profit or loss, balance sheets and statements of cash flows.

Accounting information is an important part of our everyday decision-making process, as summarized by this excerpt in AICPA Report (American Institute of Certified Public Accountant Report).

> *People in every walk of life are affected by business reporting, the cornerstone on which our process of capital allocation is built. An effective allocation process is critical to a healthy economy that promotes productivity, encourages innovation, and provides an efficient and liquid market for buying and selling securities and obtaining and granting credit.*

Prospective and current investors, employees, consumers, regulatory bodies, government authorities and financial institutions are just some of the many individuals and groups who are interested in accounting information and require accounting to help them make decisions relating to the allocation of scarce resources.

Individuals and entities need accounting information to assist in making decisions, such as planning a business, and subsequently capital investment decisions. Accounting information is designed to meet the needs of both **internal users** and **external users** of accounting information. Accounting information is extremely valuable to an entity's owner or management (i.e. internal users). It is used to help owner(s)/managers achieve the following.

- Make decisions concerning the operations of the business entity. The information owners or managers require is usually detailed enough to assist them in initial management planning processes.
- Evaluate the success of the business entity in achieving its objectives. This is done by comparing the performance of the business entity against budgets and assessing how well employees have achieved their set targets.
- Weigh up various alternatives when investing the resources of the business entity.

External users (**stakeholders**) include such parties as shareholders, suppliers, banks, consumers, taxation authorities, regulatory bodies, all of whom have their own information needs. They have a "stake" or interest in the performance of the entity.

Table 1.2 summarizes the accounting information required by different stakeholders for their decision making.

TABLE 1.2 Stakeholders and the accounting information they need to make decision

Stakeholder	Accounting information and decision making
Shareholders	Information to determine the future profitability of the entity, to assess the future cash flows for dividends and the possibility of capital growth of investment.
Banks	Information to determine whether the entity has the ability to repay a loan.
Suppliers	Information to determine an entity's ability to repay debt associated with purchases.
Employees	Information concerning job security, the potential to pay awards and bonuses, and promotional opportunities.
Consumers	Information regarding the continuity of the entity and the ability to provide the appropriate goods and services.
Government authorities	Information to determine the amount of tax that should be paid and any future taxation liabilities or taxation assets.
Regulatory bodies	Information to determine whether the entity is abiding by regulations such as the Corporations Act and taxation law.
Community	Information to determine whether the entity is contributing positively to the general welfare and economic growth of the local community.
Special interest groups	Information to determine whether the entity has considered environmental, social and/or industrial aspects during its operations.

1.2 Financial accounting and management accounting

In a typical accounting degree, you will study both financial accounting and management accounting. **Financial accounting** is the preparation and presentation of financial information for all types of users to enable them to make economic decisions regarding the entity. Financial statements will suit a variety of different users, such as the management of the entity, investors, suppliers, consumers, banks, employees, government bodies and regulatory authorities.

General purpose financial statements (**reports**) are prepared to meet the information needs common to users who are unable to command reports to suit their own needs, while **special purpose financial statements** (**reports**) are prepared to suit a specific purpose and do not cater for the generalized needs common to most users. For example, a bank might demand, as part of a loan agreement, that a borrowing organization provide information about its projected cash flows. General purpose financial statements is governed by **generally accepted accounting**

principles (**GAAP**), which provide accounting standards for preparing financial statements. Financial accounting is also guided by rules set out in the Corporations Act and the Listing Rules of the national Securities Exchange.

Financial accounting is traditionally based on historical figures that stem from the original transaction; for example, the purchase of a building for $500 000 would be shown in the financial statement (the balance sheet) as an asset of $500 000. Even though the $500 000 may not reflect the current market value of the building, the building is still shown at its **historical cost**, which is the original amount paid for the asset.

The **financial statements** consist of the entity's statement of cash flows, balance sheet and statement of profit or loss (for companies, the statement of profit or loss and other comprehensive income and the statement of changes in equity). The **statement of cash flows** reports on an entity's cash inflows and cash outflows, which are classified into operating, investing and financing activities. The **statement of profit or loss** reflects the profit of the entity for a specified time period. (Profit is the excess of income over expenses for a period.) An entity's assets, liabilities and its equity at a point in time are reported in the **balance sheet** (also called the statement of financial position).

Management accounting is a field of accounting that provides economic information for internal users, i.e. owner(s) and management. The core activities of management accounting include formulating plans and budgets and providing information to be used in the monitoring and control of different parts of the entity.

Management accounting reports are bound by few rules and are therefore less formal. Because management accounting reports suit the needs of management, they can provide any level of detail. For example, if the human resources manager requires information on the number of employees who have opted to make additional superannuation contributions, then a report can be produced. Management accounting reports must be up to date and can be prepared at any time for any period. For example, a sales manager in the entity may demand information on the current day's sales by the end of that day.

Obviously, there are differences between financial accounting and management accounting, but there will be an interaction between financial accounting and management accounting, because management accounting will provide economic information for internal users that is then reflected in the financial accounting statements for external users. Modern management accounting systems tend to provide managers with information that is relevant to their needs rather than what is determined by external reporting requirements. Financial reporting cycles, however, retain some influence over management accounting and managers are aware of expectations of external users.

The main differences between financial accounting and management accounting are summarized in table 1.3.

TABLE 1.3 Differences between financial accounting and management accounting

	Financial accounting	Management accounting
1. Regulations	Bound by GAAP. GAAP are represented by accounting standards, the Corporations Act, and relevant rules of the accounting association and other organizations.	Much less formal and without any prescribed rules. The reports are constructed to be of use to the managers.
2. Timeliness	Information is often outdated by the time the statements are distributed to the users. The financial statements present a historical picture of the past operations of the entity.	Management reports can be both a historical record and a projection, e.g. a budget.
3. Level of detail	Most financial statements are of a quantitative nature. The statements represent the entity as a whole, consolidating income and expenses from different segments of the business.	Much more detailed and can be tailored to suit the needs of management. Of both a quantitative and a qualitative nature.
4. Main users	Prepared to suit a variety of users including management, suppliers, consumers, employees, banks, taxation authorities, interest groups, investors and prospective investors.	Main users are the owner(s)/managers in the entity, hence the term management accounting.

1.3 Globalization of accounting

Even though most business entities are SMEs (small and medium-size enterprises), larger entities have become bigger, more diversified and multinational. As entities become more diversified and multinational, they require more complex accountancy and auditing services. Accountants must ensure that they remain up to date with the local GAAP and global accounting standards. Currently, more than 120 countries worldwide prepare their financial statements following global accounting standards. These accounting standards are known as **International Financial Reporting Standards (IFRS)** that issued by IASB (International Accounting Standards Board). The Real World, "Why adopt IFRS?", highlights the advantages of having one set of high-quality accounting standards.

REAL WORLD

Why adopt IFRS?

Today, the world's financial markets are borderless. Companies (including small companies) seek capital at the best price wherever it is available. Investors and lenders seek investment opportunities wherever they can get the best returns commensurate with the risks involved. To assess the risks and returns of their various investment opportunities, investors and lenders need financial information that is relevant, reliable and comparable across borders.

The amounts of cross-border investment are enormous. To illustrate:
- the Organization for Economic Co-operation and Development (OECD) estimates that worldwide Foreign Direct Investment (FDI) outflows in 2013 were US $1 281 trillion. The historically highest level was in 2007 (US $2 170 trillion)
- cross-border ownership of stocks and bonds amounts to many trillions of US dollars. For example, foreign ownership of US equities, corporate bonds and treasuries amounted to nearly US $14 trillion in 2013. And US investors held over US $9 trillion of foreign corporate stocks and bonds in 2013.

The use of one set of high quality standards by companies throughout the world improves the comparability and transparency of financial information and reduces financial statement preparation costs. When the standards are applied rigorously and consistently, capital market participants receive higher quality information and can make better decisions.

Thus, markets allocate funds more efficiently and firms can achieve a lower cost of capital.

A comprehensive review of nearly 100 academic studies of the benefits of IFRS concluded that most of the studies "provide evidence that IFRS has improved efficiency of capital market operations and promoted cross-border investment".

Source: Pacter, P 2015, *IFRS® as global standards: a pocket guide*, International Financial Reporting Standards Foundation, London, www.ifrs.org/Use-around-the-world/Documents/IFRS-as-global-standards-Pocket-Guide-April-2015.PDF.

Some new, more complex, environment has brought new challenges for managers and other users of accounting information. Their needs have changed and both financial accounting and management accounting have had to respond. To meet the changing of globalization accountants and information users have been a radical reviewer of the kind of information to be reported.

The changing business environment has given a clear framework and principles upon which to base financial accounting reports. Various attempts have been made to clarify the purpose of financial accounting reports and to provide a more solid foundation for the development of accounting rules.

1.4　The Conceptual Framework for Financial Reporting

With the EU (European Union) listed companies' adoption of IFRS in 2005, it was necessary to adopt the IASB's Framework for the Preparation and Presentation of Financial Statements (Framework). The IASB and the FASB (Financial Accounting Standards Board) undertook a joint project on the conceptual framework. The purpose of the joint project was to "develop an improved common conceptual framework that provides a sound foundation for developing future accounting standards". In 2010, the IASB issued a revised document titled Conceptual Framework for Financial Reporting (Conceptual Framework). This document supersedes the Framework and is yet to be fully adopted in Australia. However, this text will focus on the new Conceptual Framework.

The **Conceptual Framework** applies to entities that are required to prepare general purpose financial statements. As noted earlier in the chapter, general purpose financial statements are financial statements intended to meet the information needs common to users who are unable to command the preparation of statements tailored to suit their information needs. General purpose financial statements are in contrast to special purpose financial statements, which are prepared to suit a specific purpose and do not cater for the generalized needs common to most users. The components of the Conceptual Framework are as follows.

The objective of financial reporting

According to the Conceptual Framework:

The objective of general purpose financial reporting is to provide financial information about the reporting entity that is useful to existing and potential investors, lenders and other creditors in making decisions about providing resources to the entity.

Qualitative characteristics of financial reports

The two **fundamental qualitative characteristics** of financial reports are relevance and faithful representation. The four **enhancing qualitative characteristics** are comparability, verifiability, timeliness and understandability.

Fundamental qualitative characteristics

Relevance

The characteristic of relevance implies that the information should have predictive and confirmatory value for users in making and evaluating economic decisions.

Faithful representation

The characteristic of faithful representation implies that financial information faithfully represents the phenomena it purports to represent. This depiction implies that the financial information will be complete, neutral and free from error.

The relevance of information is affected by its nature and materiality. Information is material if omitting it or misstating it could influence decision making. A financial report should include all information which is material to a particular entity.

Enhancing qualitative characteristics

Comparability

The characteristic of comparability implies that users of financial statements must be able to compare aspects of an entity at one time and over time, and between entities at one time and over time. Therefore the measurement and display of transactions and events should be carried out in a consistent manner throughout an entity, or fully explained if they are measured or displayed differently.

Verifiability

The characteristic of verifiability provides assurance that the information faithfully represents what it suggests that it is representing.

Timeliness

The characteristic of timeliness means that the accounting information is available to all stakeholders in time for decision-making purposes.

Understandability

The characteristic of understandability implies that preparers should present information in the most understandable manner to users, without sacrificing relevance or reliability. "Financial reports are prepared for users who have a reasonable knowledge of business and economic activities and who review and analyze information diligently".

Cost constraint on financial information

The benefits of providing financial information, such as improved effectiveness and efficiency of decision making by users, should outweigh the costs of providing it. Cost is the major constraint on the provision of financial information. The costs of providing financial information include those associated with the collecting, processing, verifying, disseminating and storing of financial information.

Definition and recognition of the elements of financial statements

The Conceptual Framework establishes definitions of the elements of financial statements—assets, liabilities, equity, income and expenses — and specifies criteria for their inclusion in financial statements. These definitions will be explained in more details in chapters 3 and 4 of this textbook.

Assets

Assets are defined as "a resource controlled by the entity as a result of past events and from which future economic benefits are expected to flow to the entity". Examples of assets for a business include cash, inventories, investments, plant and equipment, goodwill and intangible assets.

Liabilities

Liabilities are defined as "a present obligation of the entity arising from past events, the settlement of which is expected to result in an outflow from the entity of resources embodying economic benefits". Examples of liabilities for a business include borrowings, trade payables, revenue received in advance, provisions and current tax payable.

Equity

Equity is defined as the residual interest in the assets of the entity after deducting its liabilities. Equity is increased through the contributions of owners, and the excesses of the entity's income over its expenses. Equity is decreased by excesses of expenses over income and distributions to owners. Equity includes capital contributions, reserves and retained earnings. For a sole trader and a partnership, the equity will be in the form of capital (owners contributions).

Income

Income is defined as "increases in economic benefits during the accounting period in the form of inflows or enhancements of assets or decreases of liabilities that result in increases in equity, other than those relating to contributions from equity participants". Income includes revenue, interest, and dividend income from investments in other entities.

Expenses

Expenses are defined as "decreases in economic benefits during the accounting period in the form of outflows or depletions of assets or incurrence of liabilities that result in decreases in equity, other than those relating to distributions to equity participants". Expenses include sales and marketing expenses, rent expense, finance costs and salaries, and so on.

Although accounting information were required to help internal and external users make their decisions, for decision-making purposes, other relevant business factors in addition to accounting information need to be considered. For example, if a potential investor was considering purchasing shares in a company, they would spend some time analyzing the financial statements of the company (i.e. looking at accounting information). To make an informed judgment, they would also need to consider other sources of information, such as the company's percentage of market share, how long the company has been in existence and the company's social and environmental policies (if any). When making investment decisions, investors are increasingly evaluating a company's social and environmental credentials as well as its financial situation.

Additionally, users of accounting information need to consider carefully a number of limitations of the information provided, especially in the financial statements. These limitations include the time lag in the distribution of the information to the various users, the historical nature of accounting information and the subjective nature of the financial statements.

1.5 Professional ethics in accounting

There are new opportunities for today's accounting graduates. But accounting professionals need to safeguard the interests of their clients and employers and be responsible for the public at large. Some scholars defined ethics as a set of rules which will encourage a minimum standard. They argue that an approach that goes beyond the rules is needed to encourage a culture that leads to high ethical behavior. There are five fundamental principles espoused to guide a member's decision making which are summarized below.

- Integrity

Be straightforward, honest and sincere in your approach to professional work.

- Objectivity

Do not compromise your professional or business judgment because of bias, conflict of interest or the undue influence of others.

- Professional competence and due care

Perform professional services with due care, competence and diligence. Carry out your professional work in accordance with the technical and professional standards relevant to that work. Maintain professional knowledge and skill at a level required. Refrain from performing any services that you are not competent to carry out unless assistance is obtained.

- Confidentiality

Respect the confidentiality of information acquired in the course of your work and do not disclose any such information to a third party without specific authority unless there is a legal or professional duty to disclose it. Refrain from using confidential information acquired as a result of the professional engagement to your advantage or the advantage of third parties.

- Professional behavior

Conduct yourself in a manner consistent with the good reputation of the profession and refrain from any conduct that might bring discredit to the profession.

A background in accounting is beneficial for people working in various positions in an entity. There are many well-known accounting techniques that will be discussed later in the text that are extremely important for management to understand and implement.

Table 1.4 Illustrates some opportunities for accountants.

Commercial Manager — Manufacturing
Fantastic opportunity to make a difference and drive change. A positive, high performing work environment. Build a future with this growing business.

Audit Manager
- Network of International gurus + industry influencers to expand your knowledge
- Large grants to support your choice in personal and professional development
- Design and execute planned audits, manage WIP, scheduling, debtors + ledgers.

Audit Manager. Assist within the expansion & development of the client base. Transparent environment, time in lieu. World class technology & leaders.

Senior Tax Accountant
- A Leading National Firm
- Genuine Career Progression
- Friendly, Supportive & Professional Team Environment

Join a leading national firm that boasts a culture that values each individual employee as an essential part of the team!

Forensic Accountant — Senior Analyst
Fantastic role for Audit/Insolvency CA looking to move into forensic accounting. Full training, great clients and leading firm with opportunities galore.
Accounting > Forensic Accounting & Investigation

SAP Solution Specialist — Accounting Background
Handling a variety of training, product and presales support activities. Candidate should have a functional understanding of SAP-FI/CO moudle.

EXAMPLE 1.1

Accounting Professional Ethic

SITUATION You are currently the auditor for the Healthcare Centre. It values your audit each year and your suggestions for improving its internal control and accounting systems. It has engaged you to undertake some consultancy services for its information system upgrade. Do you take on the engagement?

DECISION Independence is a key attribute of auditing services. Not only do you have to be in fact, but independent in appearance. Taking on the consultancy may impair your independence. It would result in you auditing a system you helped to install. The engagement may also impair your integrity and objectivity in the eyes of the investors and members of the healthcare centre that you are auditing. An audit is an independent check on behalf of those investors and members. This could also lead to a breach of professional behavior as it may not be seen to enhance the reputation of the profession. A choice would need to be made between continuing to be an auditor and taking on the consultancy engagement. Prior to accepting the consultancy engagement you would need to ensure that you comply with the principle of competence and due care. You should not take on the engagement if you do not have the expertise in the area.

SUMMARY

1. Explain the definition of accounting.

Accounting can be defined as the process of identifying, measuring, recording and reporting economic information about an entity to a variety of users for decision-making purposes. Accounting is often viewed as an information system.

2. Outline the importance of accounting and its role in decision making by various users.

Accounting information is an important part of the information used by individuals and entities in decision making regarding investment and other business opportunities. The internal users (i.e. management) use accounting information to make decisions concerning sales mix, which products to make or buy, and opportunities for expansion. Stakeholders (e.g. suppliers, consumers, banks, shareholders and regulatory bodies) require accounting information to help decide whether to lend money to the entity, whether to invest in the entity and whether to purchase goods from the entity.

3. Explain the differences between financial accounting and management accounting.

Management accounting concerns the creation of reports for use by management in internal planning and decision making. The management accounting reports are much less formal than financial accounting reports as they are not bound by regulatory requirements. The reports can also be tailored to suit the needs of management. There is no time lag with management reports, so they are up to date. Financial accounting provides information for the use of external parties so that they can make economic decisions about the entity. Financial accounting is bound by generally accepted accounting principles (GAAP). There is usually a time lag from the date of the report to when it is distributed to the various users. The financial accounting information is concise as unnecessary detail is disclosed in the notes to the financial statements. The users of financial statements include suppliers, consumers, banks, investors and regulatory bodies.

4. Discuss the globalization of accounting.

In recent years, entities have become larger, more diversified and multinational. Currently, two-thirds of US investors own shares in foreign entities that report their financial information using IFRS. Over 120 countries worldwide have now adopted IFRS and, in years to come, the rest of the world will most likely adopt a single set of high-quality accounting standards that will meet the needs of all users.

5. Evaluate the role of the Conceptual Framework and illustrate the qualitative characteristics of financial statements.

The Conceptual Framework is designed to assist in the preparation and presentation of financial statements, to guide the standard setters in developing future accounting standards, and to help users interpret information in the financial statements. It specifies the objective of financial statements, their desirable qualitative characteristics, and the definition and recognition of elements in the financial statements. The two fundamental qualitative characteristics of financial statements are relevance and faithful representation. The enhancing qualitative characteristics are comparability, verifiability, timeliness and understandability. Cost is a constraint on financial reporting.

6. Know the use of accounting professional ethics.

Professional ethics are widely used in business to communicate a respect for the public good. The fundamental principles are integrity, objectivity, professional competence and due care, confidentiality and professional behavior. The application of accounting professional ethics helps accountants to identify the issues and clarify thoughts when making a business decision.

KEY TERMS

Accounting　会计

Asset　资产

Balance sheet　资产负债表

Business transactions　公司(经济)业务

Comparability　可比性

Enhancing qualitative characteristics　辅助的(会计信息)质量特征

Equity　所有者权益

Expenses　费用

External users　外部信息使用者

Faithful representation　如实反映

Financial accounting　财务会计

Financial statements　财务报告

Fundamental qualitative characteristics　基本的(会计信息)质量特征

General purpose financial statements　通用目的财务报告

Generally accepted accounting principles（GAAP）　公认会计准则

Historical cost　历史成本

Income　收入

Internal users　内部信息使用者

International Financial Reporting Standards（IFRS）　国际财务报告准则

Liability　负债

Listed company　上市公司

Management accounting　管理会计

Materiality 重要性
Professional ethics 职业道德
Profit 利润
Relevance 相关性
Special purpose financial statements 特殊目的财务报告
Stakeholders 利益相关者
Statement of financial position 资产负债表
Statement of cash flows 现金流量表
Statement of profit or loss 利润表
Timeliness 及时性
Understandability 可理解性
Verifiability 可验证性

SELF-EVALUATION ACTIVITIES

Single choice questions

1. Which are the key qualitative characteristics of accounting information? (   )
    (a) Comparability and relevance.
    (b) Understandability and comparability.
    (c) Relevance and Understandability.
    (d) Faithful representation and understandability.
    (e) Relevance and faithful representation.

2. If you wanted to establish the level of payments received from customers during a particular period, the financial report that you would peruse would be: (   )
    (a) The Balance Sheet.
    (b) The Statement of Cash Receipts.
    (c) The Statement of Profit or Loss.
    (d) The Cash Flow Statement.
    (e) All of the above.

3. Which of the following statements is correct in relation to management accounting? (   )
    (a) The preparation of management accounting reports is heavily regulated.
    (b) Management accounting reports are intended to satisfy the decision needs of a multitude of users.
    (c) Management accounting reports can consider future performance as well as past performance.
    (d) Management accounting reports are typically produced on an annual basis.
    (e) Management accounting reports only communicate information that can be

quantified in monetary terms.

4. Which is the term used to describe a present resource controlled by the entity raised from past events? (　　)

(a) Expense　　(b) Asset　　(c) Income　　(d) Liability

(e) Equity.

5. Financial reports are prepared for users who have a reasonable knowledge of business and economic activities and who review and analyze information diligently. Which quality of accounting information does this Sentence mean? (　　)

(a) Faithful representation　　(b) Relevance

(c) Verifiability　　(d) Comparability

(e) Understandability.

Answer to self-evaluation activities

1. e　2. d　3. c　4. b　5. e

CHAPTER 2

Business Transactions

LEARNING OBJECTIVES

After studying this chapter, you should be able to:
- 2.1 describe the characteristics of business transactions and event
- 2.2 explain the accounting equation process of the double-entry system of recording
- 2.3 prepare an accounting worksheet and simplified financial statements
- 2.4 identify how journals and ledger accounts are applied in accounting information system efficiently and effectively
- 2.5 apply debit and credit rules to record simple transactions of the business
- 2.6 prepare a trial balance
- 2.7 detect errors in transaction recording and investigate the origin of the errors.

In this chapter we will learn the typical characteristics of business transactions and identify the differences between business transactions, personal transactions and business events. It provides examples of business transactions and illustrates the concept of duality as applied to the accounting equation. Then it illustrates the process of recording business transactions. An introduction to recording in journals and ledgers is also provided with an explanation and illustration of the trial balance. Common errors involved in recording transactions, such as transposition errors, are described with accompanying illustrative examples at the end of the chapter.

2.1 Identifying business transactions and events

Business transactions are occurrences or exchanges of resources between the entity and another entity or individual which affect the assets, liabilities and owners' equity items in an entity. A business transaction is recorded in the accounting information system when there has been an exchange of resources between one business and another person or business, and where that exchange can be reliably measured in monetary terms and occurs at arm's length distance. An **arm's length distance transaction** can be described as where the parties are dealing from equal bargaining positions, neither party is subject to the other's control or dominant influence, and the transaction is treated with fairness, integrity and legality. If it is discovered by a taxing authority, the absence of an arm's length transaction may result in additional taxes incurred from transfer at less than fair market value.

Every type of entity (sole proprietor, partnership, company and trust) must keep records of its business transactions separately from any personal transactions of the owner(s). This is known as the **entity concept**, and it means that the owner of a business should not include any personal assets on the entity's **balance sheet**, as this statement must reflect the financial position of the business alone. For this reason, the balance sheet is also known as the **statement of financial position**. The entity concept also applies to the personal expenditures of the owner, which should not be included in the entity's expenses in the **statement of profit or loss**, as this statement must reflect the financial performance of the business alone. Personal expenditures of the owner that involve the business entity's funds are known as **drawings**.

For every business transactions that occur, there must be evidence provided of these transactions, and the transaction must be measurable in monetary terms. The evidence can come from a number of source documents. **Source documents** are the original documents verifying a business transaction, such as sales invoices, purchase orders and bills.

Business transactions

The frequency and type of daily business transactions will vary greatly among entities. Some entities will have hundreds of transactions every day — small, large, cash and credit business transactions. Consider large company every day, thousands of transactions would be recorded. Some transactions would involve very small sums of money, while others would represent large purchases or sales. Some of transactions would involve the exchange of cash for goods or services — known as **cash transactions**, but some would be classified as **credit transactions**, where an amount will be paid or received at a later date. Typical transactions for entities include:

- contribution of capital by owner(s)
- payment of wages
- receipt of bank interest
- payment of GST
- purchase of equipment
- payment of accounts payable
- sale of goods to customers
- provision of services to clients
- purchase of accounting software
- charging interest on overdue accounts receivable
- withdrawal of capital
- repayment of short-term loan to financial institution

- cash purchases of office supplies
- payment for advertising.

Personal transactions and business events

It is important to distinguish between business transactions, personal transactions and business events. Business transactions involve an exchange of goods between an entity and another entity or individual. **Personal transactions** are transactions of the owners, partners or shareholders that are unrelated to the operation of the business. Such transactions are not classified as business transactions because they do not involve an exchange of goods between the business entity and another entity. For example, if the owner purchases a new car for home use, this is unrelated to the operations of the business entity and is therefore not classified as a business transaction. However, if the owner withdraws business funds to purchase the car for home use, it does become a business transaction. The withdrawal of cash for personal use will be recorded as drawings and so will not be included in the business expenses.

Business events are occurrences that have the potential to affect the entity in some way, but will not be recorded as business transactions until an exchange of goods occurs between the entity and an outside entity or individual. Examples of such business events include negotiations between the entity and other entities or individuals. For example, if the entity negotiates a bank loan for the purchase of a new property, this will not be recorded as a loan by the entity until the loan is paid out to the business entity. Similarly, if the entity negotiates for a new employee to commence work from June, and signs a contract for him or her to start at that time, no transaction is recorded for wages until the employee has completed the first week, fortnight or month of work.

Many business entities now use accounting software to keep a record of their daily transactions such as cash and credit purchases, cash and credit sales, withdrawals by the owner and capital contributions. The real world "Kingdee accounting software for small businesses" outlines one of the software options that can help small businesses keep track of their daily business transactions.

REAL WORLD

Kingdee accounting software for small businesses

Now, most business entities use accounting software to keep a record of their daily transactions such as cash and credit purchases, cash and credit sales, withdrawals by the owner and capital contributions. Kingdee produces a number of software products for all different types of business entity use. Kingdee Essentials is an exciting new online accounting software tool popular for new and smaller

> businesses. It features a "cloud" accounting service that has a number of important and necessary functions including payroll management. This allows for collaboration to take place with other entities such as accountants and lawyers without all parties being in the same place! It's easy to set up, provides a more accurate view of cash flow and makes tax obligations easier by storing bills and invoices in the business accounts. The real-time invoice tracking function allows control of the sales process and, with additional software and credit card can be made at any time in any place.

2.2 The accounting equation and Double-entry system

The **accounting equation** expresses the relationship between the assets of the entity and how the assets are financed. **Assets** are resources controlled by the entity. They can be financed by outside fund providers, which are classified as **liabilities**, or through inside funds, known as **equity**. The liabilities and equity represent the claims against the entity's assets. For example, if an enterprises has assets totaling $5 million and liabilities of $3.6 million, the amount of equity must be $1.4 million. We can see this illustrated in the accounting equation as:

$$\text{Assets (A)} = \text{Liabilities (L)} + \text{Equity (E)}$$
$$\$5\,000\,000 = \$3\,600\,000 + \$1\,400\,000$$

The concept of duality

The concept of **duality** is important to understand the effect of business transactions on an entity's performance and position. This simply means that every business transaction will have a dual effect. For example, the purchase of a new office building through a bank loan will increase an asset (the building) and increase a liability (the loan):

$$\text{Assets (A)} = \text{Liabilities (L)} + \text{Equity (E)}$$
$$\uparrow \text{Office Building} = \uparrow \text{Loan}$$

The financial statement known as the balance sheet is based on the accounting equation. The balance sheet reports the entity's assets, liabilities and equity. Its common format is to show assets net of liabilities (net assets), which are represented by the equity of the entity. We can also expand the equity section of the accounting equation to show the impact of the income earned and the expenses incurred by the entity, which will determine the entity's profit or loss for the reporting period. Recall from chapter 1 that **income** is inflows or other enhancements, or decreases of liabilities, which result in an increase inequity during the reporting period. **Expenses** are decreases in economic benefits that result in a decrease in equity during the reporting period. The profit (loss) will be added (subtracted) to opening equity in the equity section of the balance sheet. Income increases equity and expenses reduce equity. Therefore, incorporating income and expenses into the accounting equation is illustrated as follows:

Balance sheet　　　　　　　**Statement of profit or loss**

Assets (A) = Liabilities (L) + Equity (E)　　　Income (I) – Expenses (E)

Further:

Income (I) increases Equity (E)

Expenses (E) decrease Equity (E)

Therefore:

Assets (A) = Liabilities (L) + Opening Equity (E) + Income (I) – Expenses (E)

Double-entry system of recording

The following examples (2.1 to 2.3) illustrate the analysis of business transactions using the accounting equation.

EXAMPLE 2.1

Analysis of business transactions (capital contribution)

Jack recently set up his own basketball coaching academy. He contributes $20 000 of his personal savings into a business bank account under the name of ABC company. The impact of the initial transaction is that the business will have assets of $20 000 in cash and also $20 000 in equity, which represents $20 000 owed to the owner, Jack. This would be shown as an increase in the cash account and an increase in the equity account. At this stage there are no liabilities against the assets. Note that the total of the assets always equals the claims on the assets.

The accounting equation would record the impact of the transaction as follows:

Assets (A) = Liabilities (L) + Equity (E)

↑ Cash $20 000 = 　　$0　　+ ↑ Capital $20 000

EXAMPLE 2.2

Analysis of business transactions (asset purchase)

ABC purchases a new mobile phone for $500 in cash. The iPad will be classified as an item of office equipment for the business. Therefore, this transaction will result in the cash account going down by $500 and the office equipment account going up by $500.

Assets (A)　　=　　Liabilities (L) + Equity (E)

↓ Cash $500

↑ Office equipment $500

Note that this transaction affects only the asset side; it has no impact on the liability and equity side (the claims against the assets). The effects on the asset side cancel each other out.

Note also that transactions result in changes of accounts on one or both sides of the equation.

EXAMPLE 2.3

Analysis of business transactions (income earned)

ABC sends an invoice to Basketball Club for providing coaching services totalling $3 000. Basketball Club will have 30 days' credit. Basketball Club will be recorded as an accounts receivable and the services rendered will be shown as income:

Assets (A) = Liabilities (L) + Equity (E) + Income (I) − Expenses (E)

↑ Accounts receivable　　　　　　　　　　↑ Coaching fees
　　　$3 000　　　　　　　　　　　　　　　　$3 000

Note that the $3 000 of income recorded increases profit, thereby increasing equity. Hence, the accounting equation remains in balance.

2.3　The accounting worksheet

The accounting worksheet summarises the duality associated with each of the business transactions. All the business transactions of the entity can be entered into the worksheet. This is especially useful when there are a large number of transactions to be analysed. If we kept analyzing each transaction using just the accounting equation, it would be quite cumbersome to summarise the impact of all the transactions over a certain period. This could lead to errors that would ultimately affect the financial statements. Once the transactions have been entered into the worksheet, we can total the individual columns of the worksheet and use them as the basis for preparing the financial statements.

The following transactions occurred for ABC during the month of September 2020. The first step in preparing the worksheet is to understand the effect of each business transaction on the accounting worksheet.

Date	Transaction	Effect on accounting equation
2020		
September 1	Jack contributed $20 000 cash to the business bank account	↑ cash $20 000 ↑ equity $20 000
3	The business purchased a mobile phone for $500 cash	↑ office equipment $500 ↓ cash $500 Note: Do not record individual asset items. Here record it as a category of assets (office equipment).
4	The business sent an invoice to Basketball Club for services rendered $3 000	↑ accounts receivable $3 000 ↑ income $3 000.

Continued

Date	Transaction	Effect on accounting equation
2020		
5	The business banked cash received from coaching services of $10 000.	↑ cash $10 000 ↑ income $10 000
7	The business paid rent of $1 000	↓ cash $1 000 ↑ rent expense $1 000
8	The business negotiated with a contractor to perform 80 hours of work over the next two weeks for Hi Club	This event isn't a business transaction, as there is no exchange of resources between the business and another entity or individual.
9	The business banked cheques received for coaching services provided of $5 000	↑ cash $5 000 ↑ income $5 000
10	The business paid salaries to part-time staff of $2 200	↓ cash $2 200 ↑ salaries expense $2 200
12	The business paid $1 800 for office furniture.	↓ cash $1 800 ↑ office furniture $1 800.
14	The business paid $450 for electricity	↓ cash $450 ↑ electricity expense $450
15	The business invoiced $3 800 for coaching services.	↑ accounts receivable $3 800 ↑ income $3 800
16	The business paid mobile phone charges of $280.	↓ cash $280 ↑ phone expense $280
17	The business paid $2 000 for website development	↓ cash $2 000 ↑ marketing expense $2 000
19	Jack purchased a camera for home use for $300 from his personal credit card.	This event is a personal transaction, not a business transaction. It should not be recorded in the books.
20	The business bought an office desk on credit for $1 400.	↑ office furniture $1 400 ↑ accounts payable $1 400.
21	The business banked $500 for coaching services to school.	↑ cash $500 ↑ income $500
25	The business bought a computer for $6 000 for cash.	↑ office equipment $6 000 ↓ cash $6 000.
28	Business use a bank loan to purchase equipment for $50 000 to be repaid in five years.	↑ cash $50 000 ↑ bank loan $50 000.

Once we understand the effect of each transaction on the accounting equation, we can enter the transactions into the accounting worksheet. Example 2.4 contains a worksheet with all the transactions of ABC for September 2020. It is designed around the columns that represent the type of accounts affected by each transaction. Typical columns included in a worksheet are cash, accounts receivable, equipment, motor vehicle, accounts payable, bank loan and capital. The column headings will change, depending on the nature of the business entity. Two worksheet accounts will be affected for each transaction. Consider the transaction on 1 September 2020 as an example; the two accounts affected are the business cash account and the capital account. The $20 000 is recorded in the cash column, with a corresponding entry of $20 000 in the capital column. Both these amounts are recorded as positives because they increase the accounts. When the business makes a payment out of the cash account, as done in the transaction on 14 September, the balances of both the cash account and the profit or loss account will be decreased. After each transaction, the worksheet should remain balanced.

These two examples affect both sides of the accounting equation. However, certain transactions will result in entries to only one side of the equation. Consider the transaction on 3 September, when the business purchases a mobile phone for cash. This transaction results in changes of two asset accounts, with the cash account decreasing and the office equipment account increasing. There is no overall change to the asset side of the worksheet resulting from this transaction, and no entries are made on the liability and equity side.

EXAMPLE 2.4

Worksheet for ABC

Sep 2020	Cash	Accounts receivable	Office furniture	Office equipment	Accounts payable	Bank loan	Capital	Profit or loss
1	20 000						20 000	
3	(500)			500				
4		3 000						3 000
5	10 000							10 000
7	(1 000)							(1 000)
8	No transaction							
9	5 000							5 000
10	(2 200)							(2 200)
12	(1 800)		1 800					
14	(450)							(450)
15		3 800						3 800
16	(280)							(280)
17	(2 000)							(2 000)

Sep 2020	Cash	Accounts receivable	Office furniture	Office equipment	Accounts payable	Bank loan	Capital	Profit or loss
19	No transaction							
20			1 400		1 400			
21	500							500
25	(6 000)			6 000				
28	50 000					50 000		
Total	71 270	6 800	3 200	6 500	1 400	50 000	20 000	16 370

When all the transactions have been entered into the worksheet, each of the columns should be summed, and the total of the asset columns should be the same as the total of the liability and equity totals. We can now prepare the statement of profit or loss and balance sheet from this summarized information, based on the column totals at the bottom of the worksheet (see example 2.5).

EXAMPLE 2.5

Statement of profit or loss and balance sheet for ABC

Statement of profit or loss for one month ending 30 September 2020		
Income		
Coaching fees		$22 300
Expenses		
Website development	$2 000	
Wages	2 200	
Telephone	280	
Rent	1 000	
Electricity	450	5 930
Profit		**$16 370**
Balance sheet as at 30 September 2020		
Assets		
Current assets		
Cash	$71 270	
Accounts receivable	6 800	$78 070

Continued

Non-current assets		
Office furniture	3 200	
Office equipment	6 500	9 700
Total assets		87 770
Liabilities		
Current liabilities		
Accounts payable		1 400
Non-current liabilities		
Bank loan		50 000
Total liabilities		51 400
Net assets		36 370
Owner's equity		
Capital —Jack		20 000
Profit		16 370
Total equity		36 370

2.4 Journals and ledgers

Under the concept of duality every transaction has a dual effect. Analysing each transaction by using the accounting equation is not appropriate for a large number of transactions. Instead, the journal or ledger should be used.

The journal

A **journal** is a book that records each business transaction shown on the source documents in chronological order. The journal entry will consist of the transaction date, the name of the two accounts affected by the transaction, and whether each account is debited or credited. Transactions that occur frequently can be recorded in separate journals. For example, businesses that deal mainly in cash will have a cash receipts journal and a cash payments journal. A business dealing with credit will also have a credit sales journal and a credit purchases journal.

Now let us use the journal to record the first transaction for ABC for the month of September 2020 (see example 2.6).

EXAMPLE 2.6

Journal entry for ABC

The transaction recorded in the journal below represents a contribution of $20 000 cash by the owner (Jack) on 1 September 2020. Cash is debited because the debit represents an increase in cash, and capital is credited because this represents an increase in equity.

Date	Name of account	Dr	Cr
1/9/20	Cash	$20 000	
	Capital—Jack		$20 000

The ledger

A **ledger** is an account that accumulates all the information about changes in specific account balances. It can be used in place of a journal, or it can be used to record the summarised information from a journal. For example, if you use special journals to record similar transactions such as cash receipts or cash payments, then you will post the totals from these journals to the ledger account. There will be a separate ledger account for each item affected by the transaction, and each account will have a debit side and a credit side. The debit side is the left side and the credit side is the right side of the ledger account. The advantage of recording in a ledger rather than in a journal is that it allows us to summarise all the transactions affecting that ledger account.

Chart of accounts

A **chart of accounts** is a listing of the ledger account titles and their related numbers and/or alpha number, and is maintained in both a manual or computerised system like Kingdee. A chart of accounts assists in locating ledger accounts efficiently and identifies whether the entity is a sole trader, partnership or company. A chart of accounts should be flexible enough to cater for expansions of accounts as the business grows. As you can see in Appreciation Basketball Coaching's chart of accounts in table 2.1, each number has not been assigned, which allows for the insertion of new accounts in the future.

TABLE 2.1   Example of chart of accounts

Chart of accounts	
Assets (100-199)	
Cash at bank	100
Accounts receivable	110
Office furniture	120

Continued

Chart of accounts	
Office equipment	130
Liabilities (200-299)	
Accounts payable	200
Bank loan	210
Equity (300-399)	
Capital —Jack	300
Drawings —Jack	310
Income (400-499)	
Coaching fees	400
Expenses (500-599)	
Wages	500
Website development	510
Telephone	520
Rent	530
Electricity	540

Let us now use the ledger to record the original capital contribution made by Jack (see example 2.7). Note the number reference in the right-hand corner of the T account.

EXAMPLE 2.7

Ledger entry

Cash at bank

1/9 Capital — Jack $20 000	

Capital —Jack

	1/9 Cash at bank $20 000

This transaction shows the capital contribution by the owner, Jack, of $20 000 cash. It is recorded by a debit to the cash account (an asset account) and a credit to the capital account (an equity account).

Rules of debit and credit

The debit and credit rules that we have applied are summarised in table 2.2. Remember that debits and credits are opposites of each other, so whichever rule is applied to one, the opposite rule must be applied to the other.

TABLE 2.2 Debit and credit rules

	Increase	Decrease
Debit	• Assets • Expenses	• Equity • Income
Credit	• Liabilities • Equity • Income	• Assets • Expenses

Let us now look at ABC's business some transactions as further examples of double entry accounting using journal entries.

3/9 ABC purchased $500 office equipment and paid cash.

Date	Name of account	Dr	Cr
3/9	Office equipment	$500	
	Cash		$500

4/9 The business sent an invoice for services rendered for $3 000.

Date	Name of account	Dr	Cr
4/9	Accounts receivable	$3 000	
	Service fees		$3 000

5/9 The business received $10 000 from coaching services.

Date	Name of account	Dr	Cr
5/9	Cash	$10 000	
	Services fees		$10 000

7/9 The business paid rent of $1 000 for September.

Date	Name of account	Dr	Cr
7/9	Rent expense	$1 000	
	Cash		$1 000

When recording the transaction in the ledger, the description identifies the corresponding ledger entry. Instead of using journals, we could record the transactions in the ledger account:

Cash

1/9	Capital — N Cash	$20 000	3/9	Office equipment	$500
5/9	Coaching fees	10 000	7/9	Rent	1 000
			30/9	Balance c/d	28 500
		$30 000			$30 000
1/10	Balance b/d	$28 500			

Accounts receivable

4/9	Coaching fees	$3 000			

Office equipment

3/9	Cash	$500			

Capital —Jack

			1/9	Cash	$20 000

Coaching fees

			4/9	Accounts receivable	$3 000
			5/9	Cash	$10 000
					$13 000

Rent expense

7/9	Cash	$1 000			

Examine the cash ledger account. It has been balanced at the end of the period by subtracting the side with the smallest balance from the side with the highest balance. The resulting amount is a cash balance of $28 500 on 30 September. This amount is c/d (carried down) to the start of the next period. On 1 October, the balance has been b/d (brought down), and this provides the opening balance for the new period.

Note that similar rules apply to the debits and credits as they do to the accounting equation: there will be dual effects for every transaction. For debits and credits, each transaction will have at least one debit and at least one credit. For example, for the transaction on 3 September, it would be incorrect to record the transaction by debiting office equipment and debiting cash. First, we have not recorded a debit and a credit. Second, according to the debit and credit rules, a debit to cash will increase the asset cash account, and that is not what we want to do — we want to decrease the cash account! This is achieved by crediting the account.

2.5　The trial balance

The **trial balance** is a list of ledger account balances that is prepared at the end of the period. It is prepared to assist in the preparation of the financial statements and to check the accuracy of the ledger or journal entries. However, the trial balance will not detect all recording errors. Any errors that are made to both accounts affected by the transaction will not be detected by the trial balance. For example, if rent paid of $1 000 is incorrectly recorded as $10 000 both in the rent and cash accounts, both sides of the trial balance will still be equal. Care must be taken to double-check that the correct accounts are being recorded for each transaction.

The trial balance has two columns: a debit column and a credit column. Example 2.8 shows the trial balance after recording all transactions as at 7 September.

EXAMPLE 2.8

Trial balance for Appreciation Basketball Coaching

Appreciation Basketball Coaching Trial Balance as at 7 September 2020		
Name of account	Dr	Cr
Cash	$28 500	
Accounts receivable	3 000	
Office equipment	500	
Capital – Jack		$20 000
Coaching fees		13 000
Rent expense	1 000	
Total	**$33 000**	**$33 000**

The totals of the debit side and the credit side are shown at the bottom of the trial balance. Both sides are equal at $33 000. If the trial balance did not balance, we would then need to retrace the transactions to identify if we have followed the double-entry rules and not made any errors that were discussed earlier in the chapter (such as transposition errors or single-entry errors).

2.6 Accounting errors

Sometimes the asset side of the accounting equation might not balance with the claims side (the liabilities and equity) of the accounting equation. This could be evident through the preparation of a worksheet, trial balance or balance sheet, and it could occur for a number of reasons. The main technique for rectifying the situation is to double-check every transaction entered and ensure that the duality rules have been followed. The most common errors are single-entry errors, transposition errors and incorrect entry.

Single-entry error

The concept of duality must be applied to every transaction. If only one effect of the business transaction is entered, this will cause both sides of the accounting equation to be out of balance. A single-entry error arises when only one part of a transaction is entered. For example, if a payment of wages of $2 000 were recorded only as a decrease in bank, it would cause the asset side to be lower than the claims side. This transaction would decrease cash for $2 000 and at the same time decrease profit or loss for $2 000 (to record the expense of wages).

Transposition error

A transposition error occurs when two of the digits recorded in the transaction are transposed (switched). Imagine that office equipment of $9 500 is purchased for cash, and $5 900 is shown as a decrease to the cash account but $9 500 is mistakenly shown as an increase to the office equipment account. As we can see, the last two digits have been transposed. This can be identified as a transposition error because the difference of $3 600 is divisible by 9.

Here are two examples: a business bought stationery for $541 and recorded it as a decrease of $514 to cash and a decrease of $541 to profit or loss. The difference is divisible by 9. The business banked takings of $3 650 and recorded the takings as $3 560 income. The difference is 90, and this amount is divisible by 9.

Incorrect entry

Another common error is to incorrectly record a business transaction as two increases (or decreases) to one side of the equation, or an increase on one side and a decrease on the other. All of these situations will also cause the equation (and therefore the worksheet) to be out of balance. Here are some examples.

1. The entity records advertising expense $2 000 as a decrease to cash and an increase to profit or loss of $2 000. This error will cause the claims side to be $4 000 greater than the assets side.

2. The entity purchases office equipment for $5 000 cash and records the transaction as a decrease to cash of $5 000 and a decrease to office equipment. This will result in the asset side being $10 000 less than the claims side.

3. The owner withdraws cash $1 000 and records the transaction as an increase in cash of $1 000 and a decrease in equity. The correct entry would be to decrease cash and decrease equity. The result of this error is that the asset side will be $2 000 higher than the claims side.

SUMMARY

1. Describe the characteristics of business transactions.

A business transaction involves the exchange of resources between an entity and another entity or individual, and must be at arm's length distance.

2. **Differentiate between a business transaction, a personal transaction and a business event.**

Business transaction to be recognised there must be an exchange of resources between an entity and another entity or individual (e.g. the purchase of office equipment for cash).

Personal transactions do not involve an exchange of goods between the entity and another party. Similarly, no exchange of resources takes place when a business event occurs, such as when the contract of a new employee is being negotiated or when the entity is being advised that the loan interest rate will increase from 1 July in the current year. These two events will become business transactions at some later stage when the exchange of resources takes place.

3. **Explain the accounting equation process of the double-entry system of recording.**

The accounting equation expresses the relationship between the assets controlled and owned by the entity, and the claims on those assets — whether it is by outside funds (known as liabilities) or through inside funds (known as the equity of the business). The expanded accounting equation includes the profit or loss of the entity, which is represented by the entity's income less expenses.

4. **Identify the impact of business transactions on the accounting equation.**

Every business transaction will have a dual effect. As a result, the accounting equation remains in balance after each business transaction is recorded in the journals or ledgers of the entity.

5. **Prepare an accounting worksheet and simplified financial statements.**

The accounting worksheet summarises the duality associated with each of the business transactions. The column totals provide the basis for the preparation of the financial statements. The information in the profit or loss column will be used to prepare the statement of profit or loss, and the profit or loss will be transferred to the equity section of the balance sheet at the end of the reporting period. The information in the asset, liability and equity columns will form the basis of the balance sheet.

6. **Identify how journals and ledger accounts apply in accounting information system efficiently and effectively.**

Accounting information can be captured efficiently and effectively through the use of journals and ledger accounts. Frequent transactions such as cash receipts and cash payments are recorded in separate journals. Ledger accounts can be used in place of a journal, or to record the summarized information from the journal. Both journals and ledger accounts summarise and classify the information, thereby enabling the financial statements to be more easily prepared.

7. **Apply debit and credit rules to record simple transactions of the business.**

A debit entry is used to increase assets and expenses, and to decrease liabilities, equity and revenue. A credit entry is used to increase liabilities, equity and income, and to decrease assets and expenses. Each journal or ledger entry will consist of a debit entry and a credit entry to at least two separate accounts.

8. Explain the purpose of a trial balance.

A trial balance assists in the preparation of the financial statements and checks the accuracy of the ledger or journal entries. If the trial balance does not balance, then the preparer needs to retrace the transactions to ensure that the double-entry rules were correctly followed and the correct amounts were entered.

9. Detect errors in transaction analysis and investigate the origin of the errors.

The common recording errors are transposition errors, single-entry errors and incorrect entry. Transposition errors are easily identified if the difference between the total assets and total claims on those assets (liabilities plus equity) is divisible by 9.

KEY TERMS

Accounting equation 会计等式
Arm's length distance transactions 日常交易
Asset 资产
Balance sheet 资产负债表
Business events 企业(经济)事项
Business transactions 企业(经济)业务
Cash transactions 现金交易
Chart of accounts 会计科目表
Credit transactions 信用交易
Drawings 提取现金
Duality 复式(记账)
Entity concept 主体概念
Equity 权益
Expenses 费用
Income 收入
Journal 日记账
Ledger 分类账
Liability 负债
Personal transactions 个人(私人)交易
Single-entry error 单式记账错误
Source documents 原始凭证
Statement of financial position 资产负债表
Statement of profit or loss 损益表
Transposition error 数位错误
Trial balance 试算平衡表

SELF-EVALUATION ACTIVITIES

2.1 Matching

_____ ① Business transactions

_____ ② Duality

_____ ③ Accounting equation

_____ ④ Trial balance

_____ ⑤ Journal

A. Describes how every business transaction has at least two effects on the accounting equation.

B. The relationship between the assets controlled by the entity and the claims on those assets.

C. An accounting record in which transactions are initially recorded in chronological order.

D. Occurrences that affect the assets, liabilities and equity items in an entity and must be recorded.

E. A list of ledger account balances prepared at the end of the period.

2.2 Determine the missing entries.

Current assets	Non-current assets	Current liabilities	Non-current liabilities	Capital	Income	Expense
$5 000	$9 000	$6 000	$1 400	$3 000	A	$5 000
7 000	5 000	2 000	3 000	2 000	26 000	B
21 000	61 000	9 000	12 000	C	60 100	41 000

2.3 From the following financial information on the business of Graceville Professional Services (owner—Tom), prepare a worksheet and extract a statement of profit or loss for the period ending 31 December 2020 and a balance sheet as at 31 December 2020.

December 5 Owner, Tom, contributed $200 000 into the entity.

8 Purchased office furniture for cash $460.

9 Received from Black $1 340 for services.

10 Paid electricity account $130.

11 Paid rent on building $2 400.

12 New neon sign purchased for entity on credit for $1 750.

14 Collected cash fees from clients $1 300.

15 Paid wages to office executive assistant $790.

16 Tom injected another $10 000 into the entity.

17 Sent invoice to a client for services provided $1 800.

19　　Received full payment on invoice of 17 December.

21　　Received an invoice from CBD electronics for new office computer $1 356.

Answer to self-evaluation activities

2.1　Matching

① D　　　② A　　　③ B　　　④ E　　　⑤ C

2.2　Determine the missing entries.

A = (8 600)　B = 21 000　C = 41 900

2.3　Worksheet

Dec 2016	Cash	Accounts receivable	Office furniture	Equipment	Accounts payable	Capital	Profit or loss
5	200 000					200 000	
8	(460)		460				
9	1 340						1 340
10	(130)						(130)
11	2 400						2 400
12				1 750	1 750		
14	1 300						1 300
15	(790)						(790)
16	10 000					10 000	
17		1 800					1 800
19	1 800	(1 800)					
21				1 356	1 356		
Total	$210 660	$0	$460	$3 106	$3 106	$210 000	$1 120

Statement of profit or loss for December in 2020

Graceville Professional Services Statement of profit or loss for one month ending 31 December 2020		
Income		
Fees revenue		$4 440
Expenses		
Electricity	$130	
Wages	790	
Rent	2 400	3 320
Profit		**$1 120**

Balance sheet at the ending 31 December 2020

Graceville Professional Services Balance sheet as at 31 December 2020		
Assets		
Current assets		
Cash		$210 660
Non-current assets		
Office furniture	460	
Equipment	3 106	3 566
Total assets		**214 226**
Liabilities		
Current liabilities		
Accounts payable		3 106
Total liabilities		**3 106**
Net assets		**211 120**
Equity		
Capital —Tom		210 000
Profit		1 120
Total equity		**211 120**

CHAPTER 3

Balance Sheet

LEARNING OBJECTIVES

After studying this chapter, you should be able to:
3.1 identify the nature and purpose of the balance sheet
3.2 master the important concepts and recognition about asset, liability and equity
3.3 describe the disclosure about asset, liability and equity on the balance sheet
3.4 discuss the measurement of various assets and liabilities on the balance sheet
3.5 understand the accounting policy choices, estimates and judgements on financial statements
3.6 discuss the limitations of the balance sheet.

The focus of this chapter is the financial statement that depicts the financial position of an entity at a point in time: the balance sheet (or the statement of financial position). The balance sheet lists an entity's assets, liabilities and equity at a particular point in time. Simplistically, the assets can be thought of as items that the entity owns, the liabilities and equity representing the external and internal claims on those items respectively. The purpose of this chapter is to examine in more detail the nature and purpose of the balance sheet. It will explore the definition, recognition, measurement, classification and disclosure criteria applied to assets, liabilities and equity reported on the balance sheet. The presentation of the balance sheet and potential limitations associated with using financial numbers on the balance sheet will also be discussed.

3.1 Nature and purpose of the balance sheet

There are major four financial statements in a entity. They are balance sheet (also referred to as statement of financial position), statement of profit or loss (also known as income statement and included as part of a statement of comprehensive income), statement of changes in equity, and statement of cash flows. In this chapter we will pay attention to the balance sheet.

Financial reporting obligations

Before learning the balance sheet, a broader discussion of the reporting obligations of entities is necessary. The previous chapter introduced the business Appreciation Basketball Coaching (ABC). What financial statements does ABC have to prepare? How does this differ from the financial statements that a listed company has to prepare? What are the rules and regulations that govern the preparation of financial statements prepared by entities?

Entities that are structured as companies (incorporated entities) generally have a legal obligation to prepare financial statements. These entities must prepare financial statements with a relevant regulatory body. For example, a listed company has legal obligation to prepare and lodge financial statements. Similarly, legislative obligations exist for some public sector entities, such as hospitals and schools, to prepare financial statements to discharge their accountability to the public.

For other entities, such as partnerships and sole traders, it is not legally required to prepare financial statements as the businesses are not separate legal entities from their owners. A business such as ABC is not required to prepare financial statements. However, for taxation purposes, records of the operations of the business are required so that the owner can fulfill his taxation obligations. Further, if the owner(s) wanted to sell the business as a going concern, potential purchasers would wish to view financial statements. A lender to the business may also demand financial statements to assess the entity's ability to service debt obligations, when providing new, or renewing existing, financing facilities. Financial statements should also assist the owner to assess the financial position and performance of the business.

General purpose and special purpose financial statements

Entities required to prepare financial statements may have to prepare general purpose financial statements or special purpose financial statements. What is the difference between general purpose financial statements and special purpose financial statements? Statements that are purported to be general purpose financial statements must be prepared in accordance with generally accepted accounting principles (GAAP), whereas special purpose financial statements can be prepared without adhering to GAAP. GAAP is a set of rules and practices that guide financial reporting.

As the conceptual framework (paragraph OB6) states: general purpose financial reports do not and cannot provide all the information that existing and potential investors, lenders and others creditors need. Those users need to consider pertinent information from other sources, for example, general economic conditions and expectations, political events and political climate, and industry and company outlooks.

Special purpose financial statements can be contrast with general purpose financial statements, which are provided to meet the information demands of particular users and which are not required to comply with accounting standards. In this textbook we considered general purpose financial statements.

A country's GAAP is usually specified in accounting standards. Accounting standards detail specific recognition, measurement, presentation and disclosure requirements applicable to various types of transactions. Historically, accounting standards varied by country. For example, China issued Chinese accounting standards that were different from the accounting standards issued in the United States, Japan, Germany and Australia. As markets have become increasingly borderless, considerable progress has occurred in developing a set of acceptable international accounting standards — International Financial Reporting Standards (IFRS). IFRS particularly focus on for-profit entities and are issued by the International Accounting Standards Board (IASB). Most countries, more than 120 jurisdictions have adopted or converged their domestic standards with IFRS. Countries adopting IFRS include Australia, South Africa and all European Union countries. Countries substantially converging their domestic standards with IFRS include China and India. Notable countries that have not adopted or substantially converged their standards to IFRS are the United States and Japan.

A set of public sector accounting standards — International Public Sector Accounting Standards (IPSAS) — issued by the International Public Sector Accounting Standards Board, are also available for jurisdictions to adopt. Are there different versions of IFRS to use when preparing general purpose financial statements? The IASB has issued IFRS as well as IFRS for Small and Medium-sized Entities (IFRS for SMEs). IFRS for SMEs simplifies some of the recognition and measurement rules, omits topics not relevant to SMEs and reduces disclosure requirements. The use of IFRS or IFRS for SMEs when preparing general purpose financial statements depends on whether an entity has public accountability.

Entities with public accountability must prepare general purpose financial statements using IFRS. Public accountability is applicable to entities with securities, debt or equity that are traded in a public market, or entities that hold assets in a fiduciary capacity as their main business activity. For example, a listed company is subject to public accountability. IFRS for SMEs are available for use by small and medium-size entities that are not subject to public accountability but do publish general purpose financial statements.

Nature and purpose of the balance sheet

A primary objective of a for-profit entity is the generation of profits and a strong financial performance. To generate profits, or to provide services, entities need to invest in productive assets. Assets are items controlled by an entity that provide the entity with future economic benefits. Value creation can also occur if the assets in which an entity invests appreciate in value. Decisions concerning the acquisition and sale of assets are referred to as investing decisions.

The acquisition of assets requires financing, which may be provided by external parties

(e. g. lenders) and/or internal parties (e. g. the owners). The external claims on the entity's assets are termed liabilities. The internal claims on the entity's assets are referred to as equity. The mix of debt and equity financing an entity chooses reflects its financing decisions.

The balance sheet is a financial statement that details the entity's assets, liabilities and equity as at a particular point in time — the end of the reporting period. A balance sheet can be prepared more frequently than on an annual basis — indeed, it can be prepared as at any date. However, common practice is to prepare the balance sheet semi-annually or annually as at the end of the reporting period.

Recall from chapter 2 that the accounting equation specifies that the entity's assets equal the sum of the entity's liabilities and equity. The duality system of recording business transactions means that the business transactions have a dual effect on the accounting equation such that the equation remains in balance after the recording of each transaction. This is why a balance sheet, prepared as at any point in time, will always balance.

An example of a balance sheet for ABC is reproduced as example 3.1. The assets of the business as at 30 September 2020 are $87 770. The external claims on the assets at this date, the liabilities, are $51 400 and the equity, the internal claim on the entity's assets, is $36 370. Thus, the assets ($87 770) equal the liabilities ($51 400) plus the equity ($36 370). Net asset refers to the assets less the liabilities. As assets less liabilities equal to equity, net asset equals equity. For ABC, the net assets are $36 370, representing the assets of $87 770 less the liabilities of $51 400.

Analysing a balance sheet enables users to make a preliminary assessment as to the financial position of the entity. For example, ABC commenced the business with an investment of $20 000. As at 30 September 2020, Jack has invested in some office furniture and equipment only. ABC has $71 270 cash in the bank and is unlikely to face liquidity issues in the short term. As the business grows, the investment and finance decisions will be reflected on the balance sheet. For example, if ABC purchases ball machines and uses cash to finance the acquisitions, the cash balance will reduce and ball machines will appear as assets of ABC. Alternatively, if ABC purchases a mini bus to transport junior players and it is financed by a loan, assets of ABC will increase and liabilities will increase. By reviewing the balance sheet, a user may make a preliminary assessment of the economic condition of the entity by identifying the types of assets in which the entity invests and the entity's use of liabilities relative to equity to finance the assets, by appreciating the types and terms of liabilities used to finance the assets and the sources of equity used to fund assets, and by assessing the entity's financial solvency.

EXAMPLE 3.1

A balance sheet

Appreciation Basketball Coaching (ABC) Balance sheet as at 30 September 2017		
Assets		
Current assets		
Cash	$71 270	
Accounts receivable	6 800	$78 070
Non-current assets		
Office furniture	3 200	
Office equipment	6 500	9 700
Total assets		$87 770
Liabilities		
Current liabilities		
Accounts payable		1 400
Non-current liabilities		
Bank loan		50 000
Total liabilities		51 400
Net assets		$36 370
Owner's equity		
Capital — J Cash		20 000
Profit		16 370
Total equity		$36 370

3.2 The definition and recognition of asset, liability and equity

The financial conceptual frameworks address matters such as the objective of financial statements, the assumptions underlying financial statements and the qualitative characteristics of financial statements, define the elements of financial statements (assets, liabilities, equity, income and expenses) and identify the recognition criteria to be applied to the elements. They also guide the development of accounting standards. As is the case with the globalisation of accounting standards, conceptual frameworks are also converging. The IASB issued an exposure draft in May 2015 and in this chapter will be on the proposed revised definitions.

Asset definition

The asset definition in the revised Conceptual Framework is "*an asset is a present economic resource controlled by the entity as a result of past events*" where an economic resource is a right that has the potential to produce economic benefits. The essential characteristics for an asset are:

1. a present economic resource
2. the resource must be controlled by the entity
3. the resource must be as a result of a past event.

Present economic resource

An economic resource is a right that has the potential to produce economic benefits. The rights can be established by contract or legislation, or arise from a constructive obligation of another party. In principle, each of an entity's rights is a separate asset. However, for accounting purposes, related rights tend to be treated as a single asset. For example, the following rights may arise from legal ownership of a property: the right to use the property and the right to sell the property.

For the economic resource to have the potential to produce economic benefits, it is only necessary that the economic resource already exists and that there is at least one circumstance in which it will produce economic benefits. There is no requirement that it be certain, or even probable, that the resource will produce economic benefits. The provision of benefits can take the form of having goods and services desired by customers available for sale. It can also take the form of being able to satisfy human wants.

Control

An entity must control the item for that item to be considered an asset and recognised on the balance sheet. Legal ownership is synonymous with control; however, legal ownership is not a necessary prerequisite for control. The concept of control refers to the capacity of the entity to benefit from the asset in the pursuit of its objectives, and to deny or regulate the access of others to the benefit.

To illustrate this concept, consider an entity that arranges to lease an asset required for its manufacturing process. The lessee (the entity) pays the lessor (the owner of the asset) a monthly rental. The lease contract specifies that the lease can be cancelled by the lessor with one month's notice. In this scenario, the entity is able to use the asset but it does not have control of the asset, given that the lessor can cancel the contract. It is the lessor who controls access to the asset. What if the contract was non-cancellable and the lessee had the right to purchase the asset at the end of the lease contract at a predetermined price? In this situation, it is most likely that the lessee controls the asset even in the absence of legal ownership. Other examples of assets where control is present in the absence of legal ownership include licences and management rights.

Past event

Another criterion necessary for an item to be defined as an asset is the existence of a past event that has resulted in the entity controlling the asset. Most assets are generated as a result of an exchange transaction, non-reciprocal transfers or discoveries. Consider an office building that is to be used as a rental property. The first two asset definition criteria are satisfied, as the building creates future economic benefits in the form of rental income, and the entity owns the building. If the building is purchased, an exchange transaction has occurred and the requirement that there be a past event is satisfied. If the building is bequeathed to the entity, a non-reciprocal transfer (a past event) is also deemed to have occurred. If the entity is in the process of finding a suitable property and has enlisted the services of a commercial real estate agent to assist in the task, the past event criterion is not satisfied as no exchange has occurred yet. The building is not considered an asset until this exchange has occurred.

Liability definition

The liability definition in the revised Conceptual Framework is "*a present obligation of the entity to transfer an economic resource as a result of past events*". The essential characteristics of a liability are:

1. a present obligation
2. to transfer an economic resource
3. a result of past events.

Present obligation

An essential element of the liability definition is a present obligation to another entity, even if the entity cannot be identified. A legal contractual obligation clearly creates a present obligation; however, the "obligation" for accounting definition purposes is more far-reaching than a legal obligation — it extends to the entity having no practical ability to avoid the transfer. The obligation can arise as a result of a duty to do what is fair, just and right; or it can arise if a particular set of facts creates valid expectations in other parties that the entity will satisfy the obligation.

If an entity has no realistic alternative to settling the obligation, the obligation would be deemed a present obligation. For example, if an entity has entered into a binding non-cancellable contractual arrangement to purchase equipment from a manufacturer and subsequently cancels the order, a liability will exist. The contract creates a legal obligation for the entity, and the entity will need to honour that obligation in the form of damages for breach of contract.

Transfer an economic resource

An entity's obligation to transfer an economic resource must have the potential to require the entity to transfer an economic resource to another party. Transferring economic resources is associated with adverse financial consequences for the entity. For example, accounts payable involve future sacrifices of economic benefits because the entity must remit cash to the supplier in the future. Similarly, a bank loan is a liability, as the entity must transfer an economic resource in the form of cash payments for interest and loan repayments to service the loan. The transfer does not necessarily have to be a cash sacrifice. For example, the requirement to transfer goods constitutes the transfer of an economic resource.

Past event

Another essential element for a liability is the existence of a past event. The event resulting in the future sacrifice of economic benefits must have occurred. Consider an entity that has contracted a company to undertake a major overhaul of its machinery. Until the overhaul is performed (the past event), there is no present obligation for the entity to pay the contractor and so the liability definition is not satisfied.

One of the contentious issues in financial reporting has been how lease financing should be addressed in financial reporting. If an entity leases assets, should the leased assets be recorded as assets and the future lease obligations as liabilities? The reporting of leased assets is covered by an accounting standard. Currently, the accounting treatment depends on the contractual terms of the lease and whether the substantial risks and benefits associated with the assets transfer from the lessor to the lessee. If they do, the leased assets are recorded as assets and must be amortised. Correspondingly, the lease obligations are recorded as liabilities. If the substantial risks and benefits associated with the assets remain with the lessor, lease financing has no balance sheet implications. The lease payment is recorded as an expense in the statement of profit or loss. This is why lease financing is referred to as "off balance sheet financing".

Equity definition

The remaining element of the balance sheet to discuss is equity. Equity is defined in the Conceptual Framework as *"the residual interest in the assets of the entity after deducting all its liabilities"*. The revised Conceptual Framework does not propose to alter this definition.

The definition means that equity cannot be determined without reference to assets and liabilities. The definition is such that the entity's assets less liabilities (that is, net assets) at a particular point in time equal its equity. The equity balance represents the owner's (or owners') claims on the assets of the entity. Equity is a difficult concept to define independently of assets and liabilities.

Equity section of a balance sheet contains many different items. For example, one item within the equity section of the balance sheet is contributions made by the owner(s). The term given to the funds contributed by owner(s) is share capital for a company, or contributed capital for a partnership or sole trader. Retained earnings, also referred to as "unappropriated earnings" or "undistributed profits", are another equity item. Retained earnings are the cumulative profits made by an entity since it commenced operation that have been retained in the entity for reinvestment rather than distributed to the owner(s).

Recognition to assets, liabilities and equity

Only items that meet the definition of an asset, a liability or equity can be recognised in the balance sheet. The term recognition refers to recording items in the financial statements with a monetary value assigned to them. Therefore, "asset recognition" or "liability recognition" means that the asset or liability is recorded and appears on the face of the balance sheet with its amount included in totals in the relevant statement.

Central to the recognition principle is that items can be measured in monetary terms. This is referred to as the monetary concept. As money is the language used to quantify items recognised in the financial statements, if items cannot be assigned a monetary value, then they cannot appear on the balance sheet. It is recognition that links the elements in financial statements — assets, liabilities, equity, income and expenses — and hence the financial statements.

There are no definitive rules to assist the decision of whether an item should be recognised. The recognition decision requires judgment. The factors to consider when making a recognition decision are as follows.

- **Uncertainty**: if it is uncertain whether an asset exists, or is separable from goodwill, or whether a liability exists. For example, customer relationships are not contractual and therefore uncertainty exists as to whether these are assets or whether they are separable from the business as a whole.
- **Probability**: if an asset or a liability exists, but there is only a low probability that an inflow or outflow of economic benefits will result. For example, an entity is being sued for a claimed act of wrong doing but the probability of having to pay damages is assessed as low.
- **Measurement uncertainty**: if a measurement of an asset or a liability can be obtained, but the level of measurement uncertainty is high, impacting the relevance of the information. For example, the economic benefits are derived from business reputation that the reasonableness of the estimation is questionable.

If due to uncertainty or unreliable measurement an asset or liability is not recognised, an entity always has the option to disclose information concerning the asset or liability in the notes to the accounts supporting the financial statements. The term "contingent" is often used to describe such assets or liabilities. For example, an entity may be embroiled in a court case, resulting in a contingency being disclosed in the entity's notes to the accounts.

REAL WORLD

Apple's contingent liabilities

In its 2014 statements, Apple identified contingent liabilities relating to unfavourable results of legal proceedings, such as being found to have infringed intellectual property rights. Technology companies, including many of Apple's competitors, often enter into litigation, alleging patent infringement or other violations of intellectual property rights. Also, patent holding companies seek to monetise patents they have purchased or otherwise obtained. As Apple has grown, the intellectual property rights claims against it have increased, and may continue to increase. In particular, the company's cellular enabled products compete with those of mobile communication and media device companies that hold significant patent portfolios, and the number of patent claims against Apple has significantly increased. The company is vigorously defending infringement actions in a number of US jurisdictions and before the US International Trade Commission, as well as internationally in various countries. The plaintiffs in these actions frequently seek injunctions and substantial damages.

Source: *Apple* 2014, *annual report*, *p.* 262.

3.3 Disclosure of elements on the balance sheet

The presentation and disclosure of financial information is designed to communicate information to users in an effective and efficient manner, which enhances the qualitative characteristics of relevance, faithful representativeness, understandability, and comparability.

The balance sheet details recognised assets, liabilities and equity as at a particular date. Relevant information is also conveyed through disclosures accompanying the financial statements. Accounting standards exist that prescribe the presentation and disclosure requirements for financial statements. In this section, we will explore some of the key presentation and disclosure requirements applicable to the balance sheet.

Small entities with no public accountability, such as ABC, are not required to comply with accounting standards. This means that they are unconstrained in the preparation of their financial statements. A small business operation such as ABC would not have raised equity or debt capital from the public and would not have investors and shareholders who depend on financial statements to monitor and assess their investment decisions. Some entities with no public accountability voluntarily adopt presentation and disclosure practices required by accounting standards.

Current and non-current assets and liabilities

When preparing a balance sheet, assets and liabilities should be presented in a current/non-current format unless an alternative presentation, such as listing the assets and liabilities in order of their liquidity, provides information that is more relevant and reliable. The distinction between current assets and non-current assets is based on the timing of the future economic benefits. Similarly, the distinction between current liabilities and non-current liabilities is based on the timing of the expected future sacrifices. If the economic benefits (outflow of resources) attached to the asset (liability) are expected to be realised within the next reporting period (assumed to be 12 months), the asset (liability) is categorised as current. However, if the economic benefits (outflow of resources) attached to the asset (liability) are expected over a period extending beyond the next reporting period, a non-current categorisation is appropriate.

To illustrate the current/non-current classification concept, consider an entity that has inventory available for sale. The inventory would be categorised as a current asset, as the entity would expect to sell the inventory and receive the cash within the next 12-month period. In contrast, the entity's machinery used to produce the inventory will generate economic benefits beyond the next reporting period and, accordingly, would be categorised as a non-current asset. If an entity secures a term loan in 2014, with the loan maturing in 2019, the portion of the loan that is to be repaid within the next 12 months would be classified as a current liability, whereas the loan payments beyond the next 12 months would be classified as a non-current liability.

Disclosure of assets, liabilities and equity

On the balance sheet, assets are classified according to their nature or function. This means that the asset classifications can reflect an asset's:

- liquidity
- marketability
- physical characteristics
- expected timing of future economic benefits
- purpose

Liabilities and equity are classified according to their nature. The following factors could be used to classify liabilities:

- liquidity
- level of security or guarantee

- expected timing of the future sacrifice
- source
- conditions attached to the liabilities.

Classification of equity items on the balance sheet can be based on their origin or source (that is, contributions from owners or retained earnings), and/or the rights attached to the item.

Assets

The various asset classes disclosed on the balance sheet for a large entity are as follows.

- **Cash and cash equivalents** — the cash resources that an entity has on hand at a particular point in time. Generally, you would not expect the cash amount to be substantial as cash generates low returns relative to productive assets.
- **Trade and other receivables** — the cash the entity expects to receive from parties that owe it money. This class is often called trade receivables, **trade debtors or accounts receivable.**
- **Inventories** — the supplies of raw materials to be used in the production process (in the case of a manufacturing firm), work-in-progress and/or the finished goods that the entity has available for sale. The term "stock" can be used interchangeably with "inventories".
- **Non-current assets** classified as held for sale — a group of assets that the entity plans to dispose of as a group in a single transaction.
- **Investments accounted for using the equity method** — this class of asset will appear only if the entity owns enough shares in another entity to enable it to exert significant influence (not control) over the other entity's decision making. This amount on the balance sheet represents the cost of the shares acquired plus any share of the other entity's profits, less any dividends that the entity has received from the other entity.
- Other financial assets — a **financial asset** is any asset that is cash, a contractual right to receive cash or another financial asset, a contractual right to exchange financial instruments with another entity under conditions that are potentially favourable, or an equity instrument of another entity. Items included in this category are investments in shares. Often the other financial assets category includes derivative financial assets. However, sometimes the derivative financial assets are separately listed. A **derivative financial asset** is a financial asset whose value depends on the value of an underlying asset, reference rate or index.
- **Property, plant and equipment** — items of property, plant and equipment controlled by the entity. This classification includes land, buildings, machinery and other items of plant and equipment.
- Deferred tax assets — accounting rules are used to determine accounting profit, and

taxation rules are used to derive taxable income. Differences in the two sets of rules can give rise to expected taxation benefits that satisfy the asset definition and recognition criteria.

- **Agricultural assets** — living animals or plants such as grapevines, trees in a plantation, dairy cattle, fruit trees and sheep (also known as biological assets).
- **Intangible assets** — assets do not have to be in physical form. An intangible asset is a non-monetary asset without physical substance. Intangible assets are identifiable in the sense that they are able to be individually identified, measured and recognised. Examples of identifiable intangible assets include trademarks, brand names, patents, rights, agreements, development expenditure, mastheads and licences.
- **Goodwill** — this is classified as an unidentifiable intangible. Goodwill can be recognised on the balance sheet only if it is acquired. The goodwill acquired is calculated as the excess of the consideration paid for a business over the fair value of the net assets acquired at the date of acquisition. Effectively, goodwill represents an amount the acquirer is paying for things such as an established client base, reputation, operational synergies and control. For example, in 2014 Facebook acquired WhatsApp for US $22 billion. As the price paid exceeded WhatsApp's net assets of approximately US $6.7 billion, Facebook recognised goodwill associated with this acquisition of $15.3 billion.

EXAMPLE 3.2

Goodwill determination

On 1 July 2019, Vocation acquired 100 per cent of the issued share capital of Endeavour College of Natural Health (ECNH), one of higher education and vocational training in the health and wellness sector. The acquisition sought to significantly strengthen Vocation's position in the higher education market, broaden its educational offering by providing further exposure to the growing health and wellness sector, and deliver an established and high-quality national campus footprint which would significantly improve the consolidated entity's overall geographic exposure.

Source: *Information from Vocation, preliminary final report* 2019, *p.* 26.

Step 1: Determine the purchase consideration.

1. What is the purchase consideration? This is the purchase price paid by Vocation for ECNH:

$$\$82\ 944\ 000$$

Step 2: Determine the fair value of the net assets acquired.

2. Determine the fair value of net assets acquired (fair value of assets acquired less the fair value of any liabilities acquired):

$$\$34\ 002\ 000$$

Step 3: Calculate goodwill.

3. Calculate goodwill as the purchase consideration less the fair value of net assets acquired:

$$\$82\,944\,000 - \$34\,002\,000 = \$48\,942\,000$$

Liabilities

The various liability classes disclosed on the balance sheet for a large entity are as follows.

- Trade and other payables — the cash expected to be paid to entities or individuals to whom money is owed. This class is often called **trade payables**, **trade creditors** or **accounts payable**.
- Borrowings — debt funding that requires interest payments. It is useful for users to be able to identify and separate the entity's liabilities requiring periodic servicing in the form of interest payments from the liabilities that do not involve regular interest payments.
- Tax liabilities — differences in the accounting and taxation rules used to determine accounting profit and taxable income respectively can result in the entity having future tax obligations.
- **Provisions** — qualify as liabilities on the basis of satisfying the definition and recognition criteria. However, they are recorded as a liability subcategory on the basis that there is greater uncertainty in the amount or timing of the sacrifice of economic benefits relative to other liabilities.
- Other financial liabilities — a financial liability is any liability that is a contractual obligation to deliver cash or another financial asset to another entity or a contractual obligation to exchange financial assets or financial liabilities with another entity under conditions that are potentially unfavourable to the entity. Often the other financial liabilities category includes derivative financial liabilities. However, sometimes the derivative financial liabilities are separately listed. A derivative financial liability is a financial liability whose value depends on the value of an underlying security, reference rate or index.

Another example of what we will see on balance sheets in the future is carbon liabilities. There is currently no accounting standard governing reporting of carbon liabilities; however, some entities are voluntarily disclosing and measuring carbon-related information.

REAL WORLD

AGL's carbon liabilities

Under the Clean Energy Act, AGL and a number of its subsidiaries incurred direct carbon liabilities arising from emissive facilities (primarily electricity generation), participation in joint ventures and the embodied emissions associated with natural gas supply to customers. In FY 2014, AGL had 17 "liable entities" within its corporate group, with liabilities totalling 24.6 million tCO2e. At the fixed price of $24.15 per tonne, the cost of this liability is $595 million.

In June 2014, AGL acquitted its interim liability for the FY 2014 compliance year, which was equivalent to approximately 75 per cent of the liability incurred during the year. AGL surrendered a total of 18.8 million eligible carbon units, including almost 725 000 Australian Carbon Credit Units registered under the Carbon Farming Initiative, thereby discharging its obligations under the scheme. The remaining 25 per cent of the FY 2014 liability is due to be acquitted before 2 February 2015.

Source: Orton, F 2014, "*AGL's FY2014 carbon liabilities*" *AGL Energy Sustainability Blog*, 31 October.

Equity

Depending on the entity structure, the terminology and equity classifications appearing on the balance sheet will vary among entities. For example, in the case of ABC, a sole operator business, the equity comprises capital that the owner, Jack, has contributed plus profits generated by the business since its commencement less any drawings. Not dissimilar to a smaller entity, the equity of a company is categorised into three components on its balance sheet:

- share capital (contributed equity)
- retained earnings (retained profits)
- reserves.

Share capital (also called issued capital or contributed equity) refers to the capital contributions to the entity made by the owners of the entity. For listed company, when shares are subsequently transacted in the market, the capital of the company does not change — the company receives no money from this transaction because the transaction involves the exchange of shares that are already on issue between investors. An entity's share capital changes when the company makes a new issue of shares through a public or private issue or via employee share plans. For entities that are not companies, such as ABC, capital usually takes the form of a cash injection and is referred to as contributed capital.

A contribution of capital does not necessarily have to take the form of cash. Entities may receive a capital contribution in the form of plant and equipment. For example, when establishing a company, the vendor might contribute a property to the business in exchange for shares, or an individual starting their own business may contribute equipment.

Retained earnings (also called retained profits or un appropriated profits) represent the sum of the entity's undistributed profits, being the profits the entity has generated since its inception that have not been distributed in the form of dividends or transferred to reserve accounts. Consider the following. Owners contribute $100 000 to commence a business. During the first year of operations, the entity reports a loss of $40 000. In year 2, a profit of $10 000 is recorded, increasing to $50 000 in year 3. Year 4's profits are $80 000, and a $20 000 dividend is distributed to the owners. A $110 000 profit is reported in year 5, and the entity increases the dividend to $30 000 and transfers $20 000 to a general reserve account. Table 3.1 shows the balance that would appear in the retained earnings as at the end of the reporting period. At the end of year 5, the retained earnings are $140 000, comprising the sum of the five years of profits, being $210 000 (- $40 000 + $10 000 + $50 000 + $80 000 + $110 000) less the $50 000 dividends distributed over this time, less the $20 000 transfer to the general reserve account.

TABLE 3.1 Concept of retained earnings

	Statement of profit or loss		Distribution of profits		Equity section of balance sheet		
Year	Profit or loss	Dividends	Transfer to general reserve	Retained earnings at end of period	Contributed capital	Retained earnings	General reserve
1	$(40 000)			$(40 000)	$100 000	$(40 000)	
2	10 000			(30 000)	100 000	(30 000)	
3	50 000			20 000	100 000	20 000	
4	80 000	$20 000		80 000	100 000	80 000	
5	110 000	30 000	$20 000	140 000	100 000	140 000	$20 000

Reserves are a component of equity that is difficult to define because they are accounts that can be created in a number of ways. Fundamentally, reserves represent the funds that are retained in the entity, in addition to retained profits. Examples of "reserves" that an entity may have include, but are not limited to, asset revaluation surplus, capital reserve, and foreign currency translation reserve. A revaluation surplus will arise if an entity is using fair value rather than cost to measure its long-term assets such as property. The reserve reflects the increase in the fair value of the long-term assets. This increase is not a revenue item, hence it is not part of retained earnings. Rather, the transaction involves increasing the asset and increasing the reserve account in recognition that additional funds are available to the owners as a result of this valuation adjustment. A capital reserve can be created by transferring funds from retained earnings to the capital reserve. This is signalling that the entity is isolating funds for the purpose of future capital investment.

A simple way of thinking about reserves is that they represent changes to an entity's assets and liabilities, other than through what is captured in the capital contribution and retained earnings components of the balance sheet.

3.4　Format and presentation of the balance sheet

The balance sheet can be presented in a number of ways. A T-format is often used by smaller entities, whereas a narrative format tends to be used by larger entities. A T-format lists the assets on one side (left-hand side), and the liabilities and equity on the other (right-hand side). A narrative format presents the assets, liabilities and equity down the page. Examples of the narrative format were presented in example 3.1. While it is usual to list the assets first, with current assets listed before non-current assets, followed by the liabilities, with current liabilities listed before non-current liabilities, and then the equity section, there is no requirement to do so.

It is usual practice to present the balance sheet for the previous reporting period in addition to the current reporting period. Known as comparative information, it allows users to see how the entity's financial position has changed from the previous period to the current period. When comparing the figures for the current and previous years, users should familiarise themselves with the entity's accounting policies to ensure that a change in accounting policy is not the reason for the change in the reported figures. Whether the figures on the balance sheet are expressed in whole dollars, or thousands or millions of dollars, is at the discretion of the entity. The entity should clearly identify on the statement the monetary value reported.

For companies which have investments in other companies that give them control of those entities' financial and operating policies, it is necessary to prepare financial statements for the group. Financial statements presented for the group are referred to as consolidated financial statements or group financial statements. Thus, the consolidated balance sheet would be reporting the combined assets, liabilities and equity for the parent entity and the controlled entities as a single economic entity with inter-company transactions eliminated.

A parent entity is an entity that controls another entity. A controlled entity is referred to as a subsidiary entity. A fundamental consideration as to whether or not power exists is the extent of voting rights. Having more than half of the voting power in another entity is normally regarded as having power. However, even if less than 50 per cent of the voting power is held, an entity may still be regarded as controlling another entity if it has powers to govern the financial and operating policies of the entity. For example, an entity may have a number of its directors on the board of another entity and therefore may have majority voting rights on the board of directors.

The group balance sheet for a listed company is illustrated in table 3.2. It is presented in a narrative format and reports the group's assets, liabilities and equity as at 30 June 2020. Note that the assets equal the liabilities plus equity.

CHAPTER 3 Balance Sheet

TABLE 3.2 Consolidated balance sheet

		Consolidated	
	Notes	2020	2019
		$'000	$'000
Current assets			
Cash and cash equivalents		49 131	43 445
Trade and other receivables	9	81 480	70 745
Inventories	10	478 871	458 625
Other current assets	14	7 416	5 332
Total current assets		**616 898**	**578 147**
Non-current assets			
Plant and equipment	12	176 208	181 564
Deferred tax assets	13	17 363	14 909
Intangible assets	14	84 541	85 218
Other financial assets		3	3
Total non-current assets		**278 115**	**281 694**
Total assets		**895 013**	**859 841**
Current liabilities			
Trade and other payables	15	325 604	302 979
Provisions	16	40 585	36 840
Other current liabilities	17	4 566	4 111
Current tax liabilities		9 474	8 184
Other financial liabilities		107	79
Total current liabilities		**380 336**	**352 193**
Non-current liabilities			
Borrowings	18	139 461	179 653

	Notes	Consolidated 2020 $'000	Consolidated 2019 $'000
Provisions	19	6 073	8 699
Other non-current liabilities	20	25 664	24 638
Other financial liabilities		—	25
Total non-current liabilities		**171 198**	**213 015**
Total liabilities		**551 534**	**565 208**
Net assets		**343 479**	**294 633**
Equity			
Contributed equity	21	56 521	58 383
Reserves	22	17 636	16 265
Retained earnings		269 322	219 985
Total equity		**343 479**	**294 633**

3.5 Measurement of various assets

Assets and liabilities on the balance sheet assigned by dollar value are referred to as the carrying amount or book value. What we need to assess is how carrying amounts are determined. Recall that equity is defined as the residual interest in the assets of the entity after all its liabilities have been deducted. As such, equity is not directly measured. The measurement of equity is the carrying value of all recognised assets less the carrying value of all recognised liabilities.

A number of measurement systems are used in financial reporting and these are discussed in the revised Conceptual Framework. Examples of alternative measurement systems for assets and liabilities, and the corresponding income and expense items, include historical cost and current value. The measurement principles discussed here relate to the International Financial Reporting Standards (IFRS) requirements.

Measurement principles

Historical cost is an entry value as it reflects the value in the market in which the entity acquires the asset or incurs the liability. Historical cost is:
- for an asset — the cash or cash equivalents paid to acquire the asset
- for a liability — the amount of proceeds received in exchange for the obligation.

Current cost is also an entry value. It reflects the cash or cash equivalents that would have to be paid to replace the asset, or the undiscounted amount of cash or cash equivalents that would be required to settle the obligation at measurement date.

Current value measures provide monetary information about assets and liabilities (and income and expenses) using information that is updated to reflect conditions at measurement date. Compared to the previous measurement date, current values may have increased or decreased. There are a number of current value measurement bases. The two current value measurement bases are fair value and value-in-use for assets and the fulfillment model for liabilities.

Fair value is defined as the price that would be received to sell an asset or paid to transfer a liability in an orderly transaction between market participants at the measurement date. A fair value is determined by considering various factors including estimates of future cash flows and their timing and uncertainty, the time value of money, and liquidity. Fair value is an exit value as it represents the perspective of market participants. If there is an active market, the fair value of an item will be observable and verifiable. For a liability it would be the settlement value required for payment in the normal course of business. In the absence of an active market, valuation models are required to determine fair value. For example, a cash flow-based measurement model could be used, with the asset measured as the present discounted net cash flows associated with the asset and a liability measured as the present discounted value of the future net cash flows that are expected to be required to settle the liabilities in the normal course of business.

The value-in-use and fulfillment models are used for determining the value of the asset and liability to the entity. Value-in-use represents the present value of the cash flows that an entity expects to derive from the continuing use of an asset and its ultimate disposal. Fulfillment value applies to liabilities and is the present value of the cash flows that an entity expects to incur to satisfy a liability. As the valuation models are entity specific, the assumptions factored into the models are entity specific rather than market based.

Given that the basis for measurement can be historical cost or current value (with options in each category), the question arises as to what is the preferred measurement basis. The Conceptual Framework discusses advantages and disadvantages associated with each of the measurement bases, noting that the measurement basis selection is context specific and should be determined with reference to the desirable qualitative characteristics of financial information — relevance, faithful representation, comparability, verifiability and understandability.

At acquisition date, the historical cost and fair value should be fairly equivalent. However, the fair value and cost value of an item can diverge as time passes. Take the example of a property purchase. An entity pays $1 000 000 for a property. At acquisition date, the $1 000 000 represents the property's historical cost and its fair value. Three years later, the property's cost price remains at $1 000 000. However, due to a property boom, its fair value based on the estimated selling price is $1 500 000. For financial reporting purposes, this presents a problem: subsequent to initial recognition, should the property be reflected on the balance sheet at its original cost, its cost adjusted for changing prices associated with the inflation rate, or its fair value?

Unless the accounting rules require otherwise, it is common to leave physical assets and liabilities at their historical cost, or historical cost adjusted for depreciation in the case of assets, in the balance sheet. However, where a measurement choice exists, some entities elect to use fair value. This means that not all items on a balance sheet are recorded using the same measurement basis.

REAL WORLD

Why fair value is the rule

Fair value accounting, the practice of market-based measurement of assets and liabilities, has been on the increase. This increase is a large step away from the tradition of keeping books at historical cost. Subsequently, this has implications across the business world as the accounting basis (fair value or historical cost) affects investment choices and management decisions, with consequences for aggregate economic activity.

Fair value accounting is supported on the basis that it makes accounting information more relevant, while historical cost accounting is considered more conservative and reliable. The rise of fair value accounting could be the result of financial theory, notably the idea that financial markets are efficient and their prevailing prices are reliable measures of value, becoming more prevalent in academic accounting research (from the 1980s onwards) — with the shift seeming to change opinions on the relative advantages of historical cost and fair value.

The International Financial Reporting Standards use fair value extensively — such as in goodwill impairment testing and financial asset and employee stock option assessment — despite claims that fair value accounting led to suspicious practices before the 1929 Wall Street crash and the Global Financial Crisis in 2008.

Source: Ramanna, K 2013, "Why 'Fair Value' is the rule", *Harvard Business Review*, March; Australian Government Australian Accounting Standards Board 2011, *Fair Value Measurement*, AASB Standard, September.

Measuring receivables

The carrying amount of receivables on the balance sheet is the expected cash to be received (the cash equivalent). This is the amount owing, less an allowance (provision) for amounts expected to be uncollectable. The term "allowance for doubtful debts" (also referred to as "provision for impairment" or "provision for doubtful debts") refers to the amount estimated to be irrecoverable. An entity makes an assessment as to the estimated irrecoverable amount based on objective evidence. A review of individual receivables and an examination of the age of the debtors may be useful in assessing the uncollectability of debts.

On the balance sheet, receivables are usually shown at their net amount (that is, gross value less allowance for doubtful debts), with details of the gross value and the allowance for doubtful debts disclosed in the notes to the accounts.

Measuring inventory

The accounting standards prescribe that the carrying amount of inventory must be **the lower cost or net realisable value**. Measuring the cost or net realisable value of inventory is a particular issue for retail and manufacturing entities, but not service entities as they do not manufacture or sell inventory. The process for determining the cost price of a retailer or manufacturing firm's inventory depends on the inventory system that the entity is using. There are two types of accounting systems to record inventory — a **perpetual inventory system** and a **periodic inventory system**.

Using a perpetual system, when inventory is purchased, an asset account (inventory) is increased with dual entry being a reduction in cash or an increase in accounts payable depending on whether the inventory was purchased for cash or on credit. When inventory is sold, the entity can identify the specific inventory that was sold (e.g. by the barcode). The accounting entry reduces the inventory account by the cost price of the inventory sold with the dual entry being to increase an expense account — the cost of sales. Further, at the point of sale, the entity records the sales proceeds as an increase in revenue with the dual entry being to increase cash or accounts receivable depending on whether the transaction was for cash or on account. Given how the purchase and sale of inventory is recorded using a perpetual system, an entity will always have a record of the cost price of its inventory and the cost of the goods sold at any point in time.

In contrast, a periodic system of recording inventory does not keep a detailed record of the inventory on hand and the cost of the inventory sold. Using this system of recording inventory, when inventory is purchased, an expense account (purchases) is increased with the dual entry being a reduction in cash or increase in accounts payable depending if the purchase was for cash or on credit. When inventory is sold, sales revenue is increased and either cash increased (if the transaction is for cash) or accounts receivable increased (if the transaction is on account). Thus, while an entity will know its purchases and sales, it does not keep a continuous record of its inventory on hand and the cost of the inventory sold. To determine the inventory on hand, it is necessary for an entity to do a stock take at the end of the reporting period. The stock take will identify the inventory on hand (in quantities) but the entity will not necessarily know the particular cost price of that inventory given that inventory items can be purchased multiple times during the year at different cost prices. Hence, if using a periodic system to record inventory, a cost flow assumption is needed to determine the cost price of the inventory on hand.

While advances in technology mean that it is becoming more feasible to track individual inventory items, many entities do not operate such systems. When inventory is not being tracked through from purchase to point of sale, an entity is using a periodic inventory system. Under a periodic system there is no running balance of the inventory on hand or the cost price of the inventory sold. Hence, an assumption about the inventory flow is necessary to determine the inventory on hand and the cost of inventory sold. There are only two cost flow assumptions permitted by IFRS: **first-in, first-out** (**FIFO**); or **weighted-average**. A method known as **last-in, first-out** (**LIFO**) is not permitted.

The FIFO cost flow assumption assumes that the items sold are the ones that have been in inventory the longest (so the unsold items are the ones that have been purchased most recently). The weighted-average cost flow assumption calculates a weighted-average cost of inventory purchased and on hand at the start of the period, and applies this to the number of units sold (unsold). The LIFO cost flow assumption assumes that the items sold are the ones that have been in inventory the least amount of time (hence the unsold items are the ones that have been in inventory for the longest period of time). The cost assigned to the inventory under the FIFO and weighted-average methods for an entity using a periodic inventory system is demonstrated in example 3.3.

EXAMPLE 3.3

Inventory cost flow assumptions

FIFO method

Inventory purchases	Inventory sales	Cost of sales
200 units @ $44 (month 1) = $8 800	685 units =	200 units @ $44 (from month 1 purchases) = $8 800
210 units @ $45 (month 3) = $9 450		210 units @ $45 (from month 3 purchases) = $9 450
175 units @ $48 (month 7) = $8 400		175 units @ $48 (from month 7 purchases) = $8 400
200 units @ $46 (month 12) = $9 200		100 units @ $46 (from month 12 purchases) = $4 600
Total purchases 785 units ($35 850)		
Closing inventory 100 units @ $46 = $4 600		**Total cost of sales = $31 250**

Weighted-average method

The weighted-average method involves summing the total cost of purchases of a particular item of inventory for the period and any opening inventory, and dividing this by the number of units acquired and on hand at the start of the period.

Inventory purchases	Weighted cost	Cost of sales
200 units @ $44 (month 1)	8 800	
210 units @ $45 (month 3)	9 450	
175 units @ $48 (month 7)	8 400	
200 units @ $46 (month 12)	9 200	
Total 785 units at a cost of $35 850	$35 850/785 = $45.67	685 units @ $45.67 = $31 284

The **net realisable value** is the expected selling price less the expected costs associated with getting the inventory to a saleable state, plus the costs of marketing, selling and distribution. Consider an entity that has inventory on hand at the end of the reporting period that cost $4 600. The entity has to ensure that recording the inventory at its cost price would not state the inventory at an amount higher than its net realisable value. If the inventory's net realisable value is assessed at $3 500 due to some of the inventory being obsolete, the carrying amount of the inventory on the balance sheet would have to be $3 500, as this is lower than the cost price. The asset, inventory, would have to be reduced by $1 100. The dual effect of reducing the inventory is to record an expense (inventory write-down) that increases expenses, reduces profit and therefore reduces equity. Thus, assets have decreased and equity has decreased. If the net realisable value is assessed at $6 000, the inventory's carrying amount remains at its cost price given the rule that the carrying value is the lower of cost price or net realisable value.

Measuring non-current assets

All non-current assets with limited useful lives (depreciable assets) must be depreciated. Land is not required to be depreciated. Depreciation (the term "amortisation" is used for non-physical non-current assets such as intangibles and also for leased assets) is the allocation of the depreciable amount of adepreciable asset over its estimated useful life. The concept of depreciation is illustrated in chapter 4. **Accumulated depreciation** refers to the total depreciation charges for an asset from its acquisition to the end of the reporting period. The carrying amount of depreciable assets on the balance sheet is their cost (or fair value) less the accumulated depreciation.

In general, each class of non-current assets can be carried at either cost, written-down cost or fair value. There are some notable exceptions.

- Goodwill cannot be revalued upwards and must be tested at least annually for

impairment.
- Identifiable intangibles such as brand names can be revalued upwards only if an active and liquid market exists.
- Financial instruments are measured at their fair value.
- Agricultural assets are measured at their fair value less costs to sell.

Non-current assets carried at cost or written-down cost must not have a carrying amount that is greater than their recoverable amount. The recoverable amount of an asset is the higher of its expected fair value less costs of disposal, and value in use. Value in use refers to the present value of the expected future cash flows associated with the use and subsequent disposal of the asset. This means that the carrying amount must be compared with the recoverable amount; if the latter is lower, the asset is deemed impaired. The asset's carrying amount must be reduced to its recoverable amount, and an impairment loss (an expense) will be recognised immediately in the statement of profit or loss. The impact of the need to write down assets if their recoverable amounts are less than their carrying amounts is highlighted in the real world.

Because measurement choices exist, an entity should identify its measurement basis for various asset and liability classes in the accounting policy note. The measurement method will affect the carrying amount of assets. It is important for users of financial statements to be aware of the measurements employed, especially when making comparisons intra-entity and inter-entity.

3.6 Accounting policy choices, estimates and judgements

An entity is required to prepare general purpose financial statements in compliance with accounting standards. The financial statements for many listed entities are available from the entities' websites. When preparing financial statements in compliance with accounting standards, such as IFRS, the accounting standards provide preparers with choices. Therefore, most items in the financial statements involve the exercise of judgement and estimations on behalf of preparers. Users of financial statements need to appreciate that accounting flexibility and discretion exist, and to consider the potential impact this has on reported information in the balance sheet and statement of profit or loss.

This chapter will explore some of the permissible choices in the recording of transactions and estimations and judgements required by preparers. Accounting choices applied to the recognition and measurement of elements in the financial statements are referred to as accounting policies. This is why an analysis of an entity's accounting policies is important. There are numerous accounting rules that permit choices. Examples include the alternative methods of costing inventory, the measurement of property, plant and equipment subsequent to its acquisition, the method for calculating depreciation, and the treatment of development expenditure as an asset (known as capitalisation) or as an expense.

Examples of estimations that affect the values reported on the balance sheet include the impairment of accounts receivable, the costs associated with a well-planned and documented business restructure, and the liabilities related to employee benefits (e.g. long service leave and sick leave entitlements). When reviewing financial statements, a user must be cognisant of the particular accounting policies used, and of financial numbers that involve preparer estimations. Many accounting policy choices are transparent, as accounting standards require disclosure of such choices. However, entities are not obliged to detail all estimations used to derive various financial statement elements. For a listed entity, the accounting policy disclosures are usually in the first few notes accompanying the financial statements.

TABLE 3.3 Examples of accounting policy choices and accounting estimates

Examples of accounting policy choices	Examples of accounting estimates
• Method of depreciation.	• Useful life of depreciable assets.
• Method of inventory costing.	• Impairment of assets.
• Method of valuing property, plant and equipment.	• Employee benefits (e.g. long service leave).
• Capitalising or expensing development expenditure.	• Residual value used in depreciation calculations.

REAL WORLD

Notes to financial statements of a listed company at the financial year ended

1. Summary of Significant Accounting Policies

The principal accounting policies adopted in the preparation of these financial statements are set out below. These policies have been consistently applied to all the years presented, unless otherwise stated. For the purpose of preparing the consolidated financial statements, the company is a for-profit entity.

(a) **Basis of preparation**

These general purpose financial statements have been prepared in accordance with national Accounting Standards.

(i) *Compliance with IFRS*

The consolidated financial statements also comply with International Financial Reporting Standards (IFRS) as issued by the International Accounting Standards Board (IASB).

These financial statements have been prepared under the historical cost convention, except for financial assets and liabilities (including derivative instruments), and certain classes of property, plant and equipment measured at fair value.

(ii) *Critical accounting estimates*

The preparation of financial statements requires the use of certain critical accounting estimates. It also requires management to exercise its judgement in the process of applying the company's accounting policies. The areas involving a higher degree of judgement or complexity, or areas where assumptions and estimates are significant to the financial statements, are disclosed in note 2.

2. Critical Accounting Estimates and Judgements

Estimates and judgements are continually evaluated and based on historical experience and other factors, including expectations of future events that may have a financial impact on the entity and that are believed to be reasonable under the circumstances.

(a) Critical accounting estimates and assumptions

The company makes estimates and assumptions concerning the future. The resulting accounting estimates will, by definition, seldom equal the related actual results. The estimates and assumptions that have a significant risk of causing a material adjustment to the carrying amounts of assets and liabilities within the next financial year are discussed below.

Impairment of goodwill and other intangible assets

The company tests annually whether goodwill and other intangible assets have suffered any impairment. The recoverable amounts of cash generating units have been determined based on value-in-use calculations. These calculations require the use of assumptions. Refer to note 14 for details of these assumptions and the potential impact of changes to the assumptions.

(b) Critical judgements in applying the entity's accounting policies

Inventories

The net realisable value of inventories is the estimated selling price in the ordinary course of business less estimated costs to sell. The key assumptions require the use of management judgement and are reviewed annually. These key assumptions are the variables affecting the expected selling price. Any reassessment of the selling price in a particular year will affect the cost of goods sold.

Employee entitlements

Management judgement is applied in determining the following key assumptions used in the calculation of long service leave at balance date:
- future increases in wages and salaries;
- future on-cost rates; and
- experience of employee departures and period of service.

Share-based payments expense

At each reporting date the Company estimates the number of equity instruments expected to vest in accordance with the accounting policy stated in note 1. The number of equity instruments that are expected to vest is based on

> management's assessment of the likelihood of the vesting conditions attached to the equity instruments being satisfied. The key vesting conditions that are assessed are earning per share targets and required service periods. The impact of any revision in the number of equity instruments that are expected to vest is recognised as an adjustment to the share based payments expense in the reporting period that the revision is made and is disclosed in note 5.

3.7 Potential limitations of the balance sheet

The balance sheet details the entity's assets, liabilities and equity as at a particular point in time, usually at the end of the reporting period. If the business is cyclical, the position purported by the balance sheet may not necessarily be representative of the position at other times during the reporting period. For example, due to the peak retail Christmas period, the balance sheet for a retail business with a December end of reporting period may be different if compared to a June end of reporting period balance sheet for the same entity.

The balance sheet does not reflect the entity's value. The reasons why a balance sheet is not a reflection of an entity's value include the following.

1. Items creating value for the entity might not be recorded on the balance sheet. Entities may have items that generate economic benefits or involve future obligations that fail the definition and/or recognition criteria. For instance, entities cannot recognise internally generated goodwill on the balance sheet. For many entities, their employees are a valuable resource, but employees are not recognised as assets on the balance sheet.

2. Assets can be measured using different measurement systems and many are recorded at their written-down cost.

3. Even if a single measurement system is applied (i.e. historical cost), no consideration is given to differences in cost prices due to changes in the purchasing power of money. For example, if historical cost is the measurement basis, land acquired in 2014 for $100 000 would be aggregated with land acquired in 2020 for $1 000 000, and the value assigned to land on the balance sheet would be $1 100 000. If the entity elected to value the land at its fair value, independently assessed at $2 000 000, the same land could be recognised on the balance sheet at $2 000 000.

4. Preparation of the balance sheet involves choices, assumptions and estimations on behalf of the manager or preparer of the statement. We have just seen how the choice of measurement for land would affect the value recognised on the balance sheet. As another example, consider an entity with accounts receivable totalling $50 000. Identifying that 1 per cent of the accounts are impaired would reduce the carrying amount of the accounts receivable to $49 500. However, increasing the impairment to 5 percent of the total amount owed would

reduce the carrying amount of the accounts receivable on the balance sheet to $47 500. This is just one example of how applying different choices, assumptions and estimations will alter the financial numbers on the balance sheet.

5. The preparation of financial statements requires the use of certain critical accounting estimates. It also requires management to exercise its judgement in the process of applying the company's accounting policies. Estimates and judgements are continually evaluated and based on historical experience and other factors.

6. The balance sheet is essentially a historical representation, whereas expected future earnings and growth potential often influence value.

SUMMARY

1. Identify the financial reporting obligations of an entity.

The reporting obligations of an entity vary depending on the nature of the entity. Entities with public accountability are required to prepare general purpose financial statements in accordance with approved accounting standards.

2. Explain the nature and purpose of the balance sheet.

The balance sheet lists the entity's assets, the external claims on the assets (the liabilities) and the internal claim on the assets (the equity). The balance sheet reports the entity's financial position at a point in time. The financial position of the entity refers to the entity's:

- economic resources (assets)
- economic obligations (liabilities)
- financial structure
- financial solvency

3. Understand asset definition and apply the asset definition criteria.

The essential characteristics of an asset are:

- a present economic resource
- the resource must be controlled by the entity
- the resource must be as a result of a past event.

The item does not have to be tangible or exchangeable to be regarded as an asset. An entity can always disclose information about items that fail the definition criteria in the notes to the accounts.

4. Understand liability definition and apply the liability definition criteria.

The essential characteristics of a liability are:

- a present obligation
- to transfer an economic resource
- a result of past events.

A legal obligation is a liability; however, a non-legal obligation may also be a liability. An entity can always disclose information about items that fail the definition criteria in the notes to the accounts.

5. Discuss the definition and nature of equity.

Equity is the residual interest in the assets of the entity after the liabilities have been deducted. The equity balance represents the owner's or owners' claims on the entity's net assets. The equity on the balance sheet comprises capital that has been contributed by owners, and gains (or losses) accruing to the entity that are undistributed.

6. Apply the recognition criteria to assets, liabilities and equity.

The term recognition refers to recording items in the financial statements with a monetary value assigned to them. Therefore, "asset recognition" or "liability recognition" means that the asset or liability is recorded and appears on the face of the balance sheet with its amount included in totals in the relevant statement. It is recognition that links the elements in financial statements — assets, liabilities, equity, income and expenses — and hence the financial statements. The linkage between the statements arises because the recognition of one element (or a change in one element) requires the recognition of an equal amount in one or more other elements (or changes in one or more other elements) as per the accounting equation. There are no definitive rules to assist the decision of whether an item should be recognised. The recognition decision requires judgement. The overarching consideration when deciding to recognise an asset or a liability (and any related income, expenses or changes in equity) is whether the recognition provides financial statement users with relevant information about the asset or the liability and about any income, expenses or changes inequity, a faithful representation of the asset or the liability and of any income, expenses or changes in equity, and information that results in benefits exceeding the cost of providing that information. Factors of uncertainty and unreliable measurement may result in non-recognition. An entity always has the option to disclose information concerning items not recognised.

7. Describe the format and presentation of the balance sheet.

The balance sheet is usually presented in a narrative format or a T-format. A balance sheet in narrative format lists the assets, liabilities and equity in a column format. The T-format lists the assets on one side, with the liabilities and equity on the other side. It is usual for the balance sheet to report the financial figures for the current period and the corresponding previous reporting period. If an entity has subsidiary entities, then the balance sheet reports the consolidated entity results.

8. Describe the presentation and disclosure requirements for elements on the balance sheet.

Assets and liabilities are assigned either a current or non-current classification on the basis of when the economic benefits (sacrifices) are expected to occur. If the benefits (sacrifices) are expected to occur within 12 months of the end of the reporting period or within the entity's operating cycle, a current classification is appropriate. For assets (liabilities) where the benefit (sacrifice) is expected to occur beyond the next 12 months or operating cycle, a non-current classification results. Within the current and non-current sections, assets and liabilities are classified according to their nature or function.

Typical asset classifications include cash; receivables; inventories; investments; property, plant and equipment; intangibles; tax assets; and other assets.

Typical liability classifications include payables, interest-bearing liabilities, provisions, and tax liabilities.

The equity classifications on the balance sheet are capital (contributed equity), reserves, retained earnings.

A breakdown of the items within the various classifications is usually included in the notes to the accounts. The terms given to various elements on the balance sheet, and the extent to which entities aggregate elements for the purposes of balance sheet disclosure, vary according to the entity structure.

9. Discuss the measurement of various assets and liabilities on the balance sheet.

Numerous measurement systems can be used to measure elements on the balance sheet. These include historical cost and current value. The overarching consideration for selecting a measurement basis is the usefulness of information for users' decision making. At the time of acquisition, historical cost reflects an item's fair value. Subsequent to acquisition, receivables are recorded at their expected cash equivalent and inventory is measured at the lower of cost and net realisable value.

Property, plant and equipment can either remain at their cost price or be revalued regularly to fair value. Regardless, the carrying amount of an asset must not exceed its recoverable amount. If it does, the asset is impaired and must be written down. There are some asset classes (such as agricultural assets and derivative financial instruments) where accounting rules specify that the assets must be recognised at their fair value. Non-current assets with limited lives must be depreciated.

Goodwill cannot be revalued and identifiable intangible assets can only be revalued if an active and liquid market exists. Goodwill and intangible assets must be tested for impairment at least annually. The value assigned to such assets on the balance sheet is their cost or revalued amount, less the accumulated depreciation charges, less any impairment charges. It is important for a user to identify the basis for measuring assets and liabilities on the balance sheet.

10. Outline the effect of accounting policy choices, estimates and judgements on financial statements.

Even when preparing financial statements in compliance with accounting standards, preparers are given accounting choices and are required to use estimations and judgements. Users of financial statements need to appreciate that accounting flexibility, discretion and incentives exist that may affect preparer's choices, estimations and judgements, and therefore they need to be aware of the impact of these choices, estimations and judgements on the financial information reported.

11. Discuss the limitations of the balance sheet.

When analysing the financial numbers on the balance sheet, it is necessary to consider issues associated with the preparation of the statement that potentially limit the inferences made. The balance sheet is a historical snapshot of the entity's economic resources and obligations at a point in time only, and this may not be representative of its resources and obligations throughout the reporting period. Further, the balance sheet does not represent the value of the entity. This is due to the existence of assets and liabilities that are not reported on the balance sheet and the measurement systems used to recognise assets and liabilities. Finally, the definition and recognition of items on the balance sheet involve management choices, estimations and judgements.

KEY TERMS

Accounting policies 会计政策
Accumulated depreciation 累计折旧
Agricultural assets (biological assets) 生物资产
Allowance for doubtful debts 坏账准备
Asset 资产
Balance sheet 资产负债表
Carrying amount (book value) 账面值
Cash and cash equivalents 现金及现金等价物
Classes 分类
Comparative information 对比信息
Conceptual Framework 概念框架
Contingent 或有负债
Contributed capital 注册资本
Current assets 流动资产
Current cost 当期成本
Current liabilities 流动负债
Depreciable assets 可折旧资产
Depreciation 折旧
Derivative financial 衍生金融
Derivative financial liability 衍生金融负债
Duality 复式(记账)
Equity 所有者权益

Fair value　公允价值
Faithful representation　真实列报
Financial asset　金融资产
Financial liability　金融负债
Financing decisions　融资决策
First-in, first-out（FIFO）　先进先出法
Fulfillment value　可实现价值
General purpose financial statements　通用目的财务报告
Generally accepted accounting principles（GAAP）　公认会计原则
Goodwill　商誉
Group（economic entity）　集团（经济体）
Historical cost　历史成本
Identifiable intangible assets　可辨认无形资产
Impairment　减值准备
Intangible assets　无形资产
Inventories　存货
Investing decisions　投资决策
Investments accounted for using the equity method　权益法下的投资核算
Last-in, first-out（LIFO）　后进先出法
Liability　负债
Liquidity　流动性
Monetary concept　货币计量概念
Net realisable value　可变现净值
Non-current assets　非流动资产
Non-current liabilities　非流动负债
Operating cyclelength　经营周期
Paid-up share capital　实缴股本
Parent entity　母公司
Periodic inventory system　定期盘存制
Perpetual inventory system　永续盘存制
Property, plant and equipment　固定资产
Provisions　准备金
Public accountability　公共责任
Receivables　应收款
Recognition　确认
Recoverable amount　可回收金额
Reporting entity　报告主体
Reserves　公积金

Retained earnings 留存收益

Share capital 实收资本

Special purpose financial statements 特殊目的财务报告

The lower cost or net realisable value 成本与可变现净值孰低法

Trade payables(**trade creditors or accounts payable**) 应付账款

Trade receivables(**trade debtors or accounts receivable**) 应收账款

Value in use 使用价值

Weighted-average 加权平均法

SELF-EVALUATION ACTIVITIES

3.1 Single choice questions

1. Which of the following phrases is not an essential characteristic of an asset?(   )

    (a) It must have resulted from a past transaction or event;

    (b) It must be legally owned by the business;

    (c) There must be expected future economic benefits provided;

    (d) The business must have control over the benefits provided by the asset;

    (e) None of the above, i.e. all are essential characteristics.

2. Which of the following statements is incorrect?(   )

    (a) Balance Sheets are useful in assessing the financial structure of a business;

    (b) A Balance Sheet provides a clear picture of business profitability;

    (c) Business liquidity can be judged from the information contained in Balance Sheet;

    (d) Balance Sheets shows details of owner's equity, liabilities and assets;

    (e) Financial statement users can make judgements about a business' asset mix by investigating its Balance Sheet.

3. A business resource that is expected to be consumed or converted to cash within the next operating cycle or 12 months from the Balance Sheet date is known as a:(   )

    (a) Non-current liability;

    (b) Non-current asset;

    (c) Current asset;

    (d) Current liability;

    (e) Reserve.

4. If a business sold inventory to a customer for $4000, and that inventory had cost $2 500, which of the following statement is correct?(   )

    (a) The inventory has been sold at a profit and this will increase the owner's equity;

    (b) The inventory has been sold at a loss and this will increase the owner's equity;

    (c) The inventory has been sold at a profit and this will decrease the owner's equity;

    (d) The inventory has been sold at a loss and this will decrease the owner's equity;

(e) The inventory has been sold at a profit but there is no effect on the owner' equity.

5. The conservatism/prudence convention holds that: (   )

(a) Personal bias in financial reports should be reduced as possible;

(b) It is prudent to account for inflation when preparing the financial reports;

(c) Assets should only be included in the Balance Sheet if they are owned by the business;

(d) Financial reports should err on the side of caution;

(e) It is not possible to include current market valuations in the Balance Sheet.

3.2　True or false

1. The accounting equation may be stated as "assets equal liabilities plus owner's equity".   (   )

2. One of the key characteristics of an asset is that it involves a present obligation to an external party.   (   )

3. The collection of money from a debtor will cause total assets to increase.   (   )

4. If owner's equity is $43 000, current assets are $25 000, non-current liabilities are $235 000, and non-current assets are $55 000, then current liabilities must be $27 000.   (   )

5. A new business purchasing inventory for $88 000 and selling 80% of it for $105 600 will record a profit of $35 200 and stock on hand of $17 600.   (   )

3.3　The following is a list of account balances for Babala Pty Ltd for the financial year ended 31 May 2019 and 31 May 2020.

Account	31 May 2020 $	31 May 2019 $
Plant and equipment	25 124	22 136
Goodwill	5 245	4 020
Cash and cash equivalents	18 000	23 500
Accounts payable	23 241	20 557
Accounts receivable	20 120	19 852
Deferred tax assets	9 154	8 687
Deferred tax liabilities	15 356	14 524
Prepayments	6 859	5 274
Short-term borrowings	9 254	8 697
Long-term borrowings	14 652	14 328
Brand names	4 350	4 350
Licences	8 658	8 658
Issued capital	28 654	24 562
Inventories	6 854	5 277

Continued

Account	31 May 2020 $	31 May 2019 $
Provisions for employee benefits (short-term)	9 642	7 246
Patents	2 400	3 542
Provisions for employee benefits (long-term)	8 198	5 469
Land and buildings	32 725	29 865
Accumulated depreciation — land and building	12 585	14 249
Accumulated depreciation — plant and equipment	5 684	3 245
Accumulated amortisation — brand names	2 864	1 468
Accumulated amortisation — patents	1 142	985
Accumulated amortisation — licences	3 568	2 500
Accumulated amortisation — software development cost	3 458	2 468
Other current assets	7 684	8 579
Retained earnings	9 184	25 262
Current tax liabilities	6 845	5 248
Software development cost	7 154	7 068

Required

a. Prepare a narrative classified balance sheet for Babala Pty Ltd as at 31 May 2019 and 31 May 2020.

b. Comment on Babala Pty Ltd's liquidity and financing.

3.4 Dan, the owners of Household Pty Ltd intend to sell their business. To facilitate the sale, the owners have prepared the following balance sheet for prospective purchasers as at 30 April 2020. You are interested in purchasing the business, and take the balance sheet to your accountant for advice.

Household Pty Ltd Balance sheet as at 30 April 2020	
Assets	
Cash	$3 000
Accounts receivable	14 000
Inventory	43 000
Prepayments	2 000
Plant and equipment	28 000
Goodwill	29 000

Continued

Total assets	**119 000**
Liabilities	
Accounts payable	9 000
Loan	14 000
Net assets	**$96 000**
Equity	
Capital	60 000
Profit	36 000
Total equity	**96 000**

Notes to the accounts:

1. The entity also has a $10 000 bank overdraft.

2. The entity has borrowings of $100 000, on which it pays $14 000 (as shown on the balance sheet) in interest and loan repayments per annum.

3. The capital of $60 000 represents the original capital contributed by the owners. It does not include subsequent capital injections.

4. The profit of $36 000 is the reported profit for the current reporting period.

5. The inventory is measured at cost price.

6. The goodwill represents the figure that was necessary to "balance" the balance sheet.

7. The plant and equipment is at cost.

Required

a. Discuss at least five errors or divergences from acceptable accounting practices revealed.

b. List three limitations of the balance sheet.

Answer to self-evaluation activities

3.1 Single choice questions

1. b   2. b   3. c   4. a   5. d

3.2 True or false

1. T   2. F   3. F   4. F   5. T

3.3 Solution

a. Narrative classified balance sheet

Babala Pty Ltd Balance sheet as at 31 May		
	2020 $	2019 $
Assets		
Current assets		
Cash and cash equivalents	18 000	23 500
Accounts receivable	20 120	19 852
Inventories	6 854	5 277
Prepayments	6 859	5 274
Other current assets	7 684	8 579
Total current assets	**59 517**	**62 482**
Non-current assets		
Property, plant and equipment	39 580	34 507
Intangible assets	16 775	20 217
Deferred tax assets	9 154	8 687
Total non-current assets	**65 509**	**63 411**
Total assets	**125 026**	**125 893**
Liabilities		
Current liabilities		
Accounts payable	23 241	20 557
Short-term borrowings	9 254	8 697
Current tax liabilities	6 845	5 248
Provisions for employee benefits (short-term)	9 642	7 246
Total current liabilities	**48 982**	**41 748**
Non-current liabilities		
Long-term borrowings	14 652	14 328
Deferred tax liabilities	15 356	14 524
Provisions for employee benefits (long-term)	8 198	5 469
Total non-current liabilities	**38 206**	**34 321**
Total liabilities	**87 188**	**76 069**
Net assets	**37 838**	**49 824**
Equity		
Issued capital	28 654	24 562
Retained earnings	9 184	25 262
Total equity	**37 838**	**48 824**

b.

- Liquidity refers to an entity's ability to meet its short-term financial commitments. A preliminary assessment of the company's liquidity can be made by comparing the assets that the company can readily convert into cash (that is, cash, receivables and inventories) to the short-term cash demands on the company (that is, payables and short-term borrowings).

- Looking at Babala Pty Ltd's balance sheet in 2019 and 2020, the company's liquid assets (that is, cash, receivables and inventories) have decreased by $3 655 ($48 629 in 2019 compared to $44 974 in 2020). On the other hand, its short-term commitments (that is, payables and short-term borrowings) have increased by $3 241 ($32 495 in 2020 compared to $29 254 in 2019). It should be recognised that inventories may take some time to sell and are not as liquid as cash.

- For the time being, Babala Pty Ltd appears to be able to repay its short-term commitments when they fall due, as the balance sheet data show that its liquid assets exceed its short-term commitments in 2017. However, if the trend of decreased liquid assets and increased short-term commitments continues, Babala Pty Ltd may have a liquidity problem in the future, which means the company may have difficulty paying its short-term liabilities.

- Babala Pty Ltd has financed more of its assets in 2020 with liabilities relative to 2019. Total liabilities in 2020 represent 70 per cent of total assets. In 2019, 60 per cent of assets were financed with liabilities.

3.4 Solution

a. The errors or divergences from acceptable accounting practices include the following.

- The balance sheet does not provide information regarding the categorisation of the assets and liabilities as current and non-current. Furthermore, no subtotals for such items are detailed.

- Goodwill can be recognised only if it is purchased. Heyday Pty Ltd should not be recognizing any internally generated goodwill.

- The inventory is measured at cost price. Inventory should be measured at the lower of cost or netrealisable value. Having the inventory at cost price is acceptable providing that the cost of the inventory is higher than the net realisable value.

- No allowance for doubtful debts is provided.

- Assets with limited useful lives must be depreciated, so the plant and equipment should be recorded at its cost less accumulated depreciation.

- The balance of retained earnings should be reflected on the balance sheet, rather than just the current year's profit being included in the equity section.

- The $10 000 bank overdraft satisfies the liability definition and recognition criteria, and should be included on the balance sheet as a current liability.

- The capital contribution should be the sum of all contributions to the business by the owners, rather than restricted to the contributions originally made.
- The borrowings of $100 000 should appear as a liability on the balance sheet.

b. First, the balance sheet is a historical snapshot of the entity's economic resources and obligations at a point in time only and the snapshot presented may not be representative of that at other times of the year. Second, it does not purport to show the value of the entity due to the existence of assets and liabilities that are not reported on the balance sheet, and fair value not being the measurement systems used to recognise all assets and liabilities. Third, the definition and recognition of items on the balance sheet involves management choices, estimations and judgements.

CHAPTER 4

Statement of Profit or Loss

LEARNING OBJECTIVES

After studying this chapter, you should be able to:

4.1 explain the purpose and importance of measuring financial performance

4.2 understand the difference between accrual accounting and cash accounting

4.3 outline the effect that accounting policy choices, estimates and judgements can have on the financial statements

4.4 discuss the definition, classification and recognition criteria of income and expenses

4.5 identify presentation formats for the statement of profit or loss

4.6 explain the nature of the statement of comprehensive income and statement of changes in equity

4.7 discuss the relationship between the statement of profit or loss, the balance sheet, the statement of comprehensive income and the statement of changes in equity.

In this chapter, we discuss how a business generates profits from its available resources during a specified time period. The profit is presented in a financial statement that is referred to as the "statement of profit or loss". Other terms used to describe this statement are "income statement" and the "statement of financial performance". It is an overall assessment of the financial performance of an entity. Then we explain the statement of comprehensive income and the statement of changes in equity. The statement of comprehensive income commences with the profit or loss for the reporting period, as reported in the statement of profit or loss, and includes other income and expense items that are required by accounting standards to be taken directly to equity. The statement of changes in equity explains movements in equity, hence assets and liabilities, from the beginning to the end of the reporting period.

4.1 Purpose of measuring financial performance

Profit or loss, a measure of financial performance, is an important item in financial statements. Profit reflects the outcome of an entity's investment and financing decisions. An entity should periodically report its performance to enable internal and external users to make informed decisions. The profit or loss will inform internal decisions such as the entity's pricing of goods and services and the need to review cost structures. The profit or loss will inform external decisions such as whether or not to invest in, or lend to, the business. An entity that generates losses rather than profits is not sustainable.

Jack commenced a sole trader business ABC (see example 4.1). ABC's financial statements after one month of operations were provided as an example of financial statements for a small business. The statement of profit or loss of ABC reproduced as example 4.1. The statement of profit or loss identifies that the business has generated a profit of $16 370 for the one-month period ended 30 September 2020. Assuming the financial information for September 2020 is representative, the profit suggests that the owner, Jack, is operating a financially viable business with fees from coaching exceeding the expenses associated with delivering the coaching. A lender would be reasonably confident in the ability of the business to support a small loan to purchase ball machines. It would be useful to compare the profit this month to that of future months to better evaluate the performance of the business. Comparing the profit with the equity and the assets in the business used to generate the profit will allow Jack to better assess the success of his business.

EXAMPLE 4.1

A statement of profit or loss

ABC Statement of profit or loss for the month ending 30 September 2020		
Income		
Coaching fees		$22 300
Expenses		
Marketing	$2 000	
Wages	2 200	
Telephone	280	
Rent	1 000	
Electricity	450	5 930
Profit		$16 370

A financial objective of an entity is to create value for its owners. For a company listed on a securities exchange, the value creation (or lack thereof) is generally evidenced by movements in the company's share price. For business entities with no observable share price, value creation is realised when the business is sold. The two aspects that determine value creation are return and risk, with higher risk meaning higher return. The **statement of profit** or loss** reflects the accounting return for an entity for a specified time period. The accounting return is formally referred to as the profit or loss of the entity.

A business sustainable operation is important. Sustainability considerations often factor into the risk and return analysis. While many entities aim for profit maximisation, the importance of sustainable business practices means that decisions may be made that are not necessarily profit maximising, but are beneficial for the environment or the community. More recently, the concept of integrated reporting has emerged. Integrated reporting conveys information on how an entity's strategy, governance, performance and prospects lead to the creation of value. It must also be remembered that a profit objective is not relevant for all entities. Many entities are not for-profit entities.

The reported profit figure is also not a measure of the cash that the entity has accumulated during the period, as income and expense recognition is not contingent upon cash being received or paid. According to the Conceptual Framework for Financial Reporting, " **income**" is defined as:

Increase in economic benefits during the accounting period in the form of inflows or enhancements of assets or decrease in liabilities that result in an increase in equity, other than those relating to contributions from equity participant.

The definition of "income" encompasses both **revenue** and **gains**.
- revenue arising in the ordinary course of activities (e.g. sales, fees and dividends)
- gains (e.g. gains on disposal of non-current assets, and unrealised gains on revaluing assets).

While some gains are recognised in the statement of profit or loss, other gains are taken directly to equity, depending on the prescribed accounting treatment stated in various accounting standards. For example, property, plant and equipment (PPE) assets can be measured at their fair value. In electing to measure such assets at fair value, any value increase is an unrealised gain and increases the revaluation surplus in the equity section of the balance sheet, rather than being included as income in the measurement of profit or loss for the reporting period. Other gains, such as the gain on disposal of PPE, are required to be recognised as income and included in the determination of profit or loss.

Given that revenue is a subset of income, the terms "revenue" and "income" will both appear throughout the discussions. Do not let this confuse you. Remember that revenue is the term that applies to income arising in the ordinary course of an entity's activities.

Periodic determination of an entity's profit or loss is necessary because users need to assess the profitability of an entity throughout its life. It is common practice for an entity to prepare a statement of profit or loss for a 12-month period to the end of its reporting period, often 30 June. Large companies are subject to statutory reporting requirements and are required to prepare a statement of profit or loss for a 12-month period in addition to producing and lodging a semi-annual statement. However, a statement of profit or loss can be produced for management for any period of time (e.g. monthly or quarterly). More frequent profit determination and reporting provides timely information for managers, enabling them to assess performance against budgets and react to undesirable profit trends.

REAL WORLD

Qantas in profit turn around through low oil price

Qantas has turned around the financial woes of recent years with a full-year after-tax profit of $557 million announced. The result is a huge lift from last year's loss of $2.8 billion and the strongest profit recorded by the company since the global financial crisis. The company's transformation program has contributed to the upsurge in profit. This program involved the loss of 5 000 jobs, substantial cost savings (particularly through lower oil prices) and repaying more than $1 billion in debt.

The profit result announced is most likely going to be larger than that of Virgin, Singapore, and Air New Zealand and Etihad combined. Qantas is still in the process of completing the transformation, with rationalisation in areas where technology is changing business processes, such as call centres, still to occur.

In light of the strong result, Qantas delivered a $505 million capital return to shareholders. Investors responded positively, with Qantas shares rising half a per cent to $3.78.

Source: Hall, E 2015, *Qantas in profit turn around through low oil price*, *The World Today*, 20 August, www.abc.net.au/worldtoday/content/2015/s4296880.htm.

4.2   Accounting concepts for financial reporting

When discussing the statement of profit or loss, it is important to appreciate what is meant by the term "reporting period", and to understand the distinction between cash accounting and accrual accounting.

The reporting period

As discussed previously, parties with an inherent interest in the financial performance of an entity need to be informed on a regular basis as to the profit or loss generated by the entity. Management need to have timely information as they need to make informed decisions such as the price to charge for an entity's products. The financial statements assume that an entity is a going concern, but the life of the entity is divided into arbitrary reporting periods, also known as accounting periods. For external reports, the convention is that the arbitrary reporting period is yearly, and so the entity prepares financial statements at the end of each 12 months (not necessarily a calendar year). For internal reports, managers may divide the life of the business into time periods of less than one year. The reporting period to which the statement of profit or loss relates should be prominently displayed.

REAL WORLD

Financial reporting requirements of public hospitals

Public hospitals and health services are required to provide monthly data on an accrual basis to the State Government of Victoria, Department of Health. The information to be submitted is the statement of profit or loss, balance sheet, performance indicators, monthly cash flow statement, notes and Chief Executive Officer's comments. This information provides the Department with information to monitor the industry and evaluate the performance and viability of such entities.

Source: *State Government of Victoria* 2013, *Accounting and financial policy in Victoria's public hospitals*

Accrual accounting versus cash accounting

Accounting standards require that financial statements are prepared on the basis of **accrual accounting**, as distinct from **cash accounting**. Accrual accounting is a system in which transactions are recorded in the period to which they relate, rather than in the period the entity receives or pays the cash related to the transaction. This means that the reported profit or loss based on the accrual system is the difference between income and expenses for the period. This is not synonymous with cash.

A cash accounting system, in contrast, would determine cash profit or loss as the difference between the cash received in relation to income items and the cash paid for expenses for the period. Under an accrual basis of accounting, the entity does not have to receive cash associated with a transaction for that transaction to be regarded as income, so cash received in the reporting period may not result in income being recognised. Similarly, the entity does not have to pay cash for that transaction to be regarded as an expense, so cash paid in the reporting period may not result in the recognition of an expense. Accrual accounting involves recognising the income and expense transactions when they occur, not when cash is paid or received.

The purpose of accrual accounting is to better reflect the performance of the entity for a reporting period. The timing of cash payments and cash receipts has the potential to distort performance in a period if a cash basis of accounting is used to measure financial performance. Therefore, an entity required to comply with accounting standards must prepare its financial statements on an accrual basis. Entities not required to comply with accounting standards, such as many small businesses, may prepare their financial statements on a cash basis.

We will illustrate the concept of accrual accounting versus cash accounting, consider examples to ABC company. ABC's business transactions for September 2020 were recorded in the accounting worksheet in examples in chapter 2. The transactions described below relate to the reporting period ended December 2020.

Recognising income without receiving cash (accrued income)

ABC conducted a holiday clinic for a basketball club on 20 December 2020. The club was invoiced $800 for the coaching clinic by ABC, but as at 31 December 2020 (the end of the reporting period) the invoice had not been paid. In recording the transaction in ABC's accounting worksheet, the asset account, accounts receivable (i. e. debtors), would be increased by $800 and income (coaching fees) in the profit or loss column would be increased by $800, thereby increasing profit and hence equity. It is appropriate to recognise the $800 in the accounts as income in December, because ABC conducted the clinic and rendered the services in December. The income has been earned even though it has not been received in cash — it is accrued income.

Accrued income is income that has been earned but not received in cash. The club will not pay the invoice until January 2021. If ABC was operating a cash accounting system, there would be no transaction recorded in December 2020. No income would be recognised in ABC's accounts in relation to this invoice for the month ended 31 December 2020, because no cash has been received for the services rendered. Under a cash system, the income will be recognised in January 2021 when ABC receives the $800 cash from the club. In January 2021, the entry in the accounting worksheet under a cash system would be to increase an asset (cash) by $800 and increase income (coaching fees) in the profit or loss column by $800.

Receiving cash but not recognising income (income received in advance)

ABC is commissioned in December 2020 to conduct a four-week intensive training for players to take place in January 2021. ABC receipts an up-front payment of $1 200, which is deposit in bank by ABC. The transaction recorded by ABC is to increase an asset account (cash) and increase an income account (coaching fees). However, as at 31 December 2020 (the end of the reporting period), ABC has not commenced the training sessions. The sessions will not be conducted until January 2021. Under a cash accounting system, income of $1 200 would be recognised in ABC's accounts for December 2020 because the money has been received by ABC.

Under an accrual accounting system, no income in the current reporting period should be recognised in ABC's accounts because ABC had not rendered any services in December 2020. To reflect this in the accounts, it is necessary to do an adjusting entry. The initial recording of the transaction has resulted in income being overstated by $1 200 for December 2020. The adjusting entry necessary would be to reduce income by $1 200, thereby reducing profit and hence equity.

The dual nature of the transaction would be reflected with a corresponding entry recognising that the business has a liability at the end of the reporting period as it owes. This liability is income received in advance (being cash received for goods or services not yet provided) related to the coaching program. In January 2021, when ABC conducts the training, the liability would decrease and the income would be recognised.

Recognising an expense without paying cash (accrued expense)

ABC uses a mobile telephone for business purposes. At the end of the reporting period, being 31 December 2020, ABC had not paid for the December telephone charges, estimated to be $50. This account will be paid in January 2021. Under a cash accounting system, no expense would be recognised in ABC's accounts in relation to the December mobile telephone charges as no payment has been made to the mobile telephone service provider. Under a cash system, this would be recorded as an expense in the month that it is paid (i.e. January 2021).

Under an accrual accounting system, the expense associated with December mobile telephone usage would be recognized in ABC's accounts because the coach had been using the mobile telephone during December. An adjusting entry at the end of December 2017 is required to record the expense. The transaction would be recorded by increasing expenses by $50, thereby reducing profit and hence equity.

The corresponding entry to keep the accounting equation in balance is to record a liability at the end of December 2020. This liability is an accrued expense, being the December mobile phone charges owed by ABC to the provider of the mobile telephone service. When ABC pays the mobile phone bill in January 2021, the liability will decrease and an asset account (cash) will decrease.

Paying cash but not recognising an expense (prepaid expense)

ABC paid a $240, 12-month premium for public liability insurance at the start of December 2020. The transaction recorded is a decrease in an asset account (cash) and an increase in an expense account (insurance) that reduces profit and hence equity. Under a cash accounting system, an expense of $240 would be recognised in the statement of profit or loss at the end of the reporting period of 31 December 2020 because the premium has been paid.

Under an accrual accounting system, it is necessary to consider what expense has been incurred in December 2020. ABC has received the benefit for only one month of the insurance premium as at end of December. Therefore, the expense recognised in December would be 1/12 of the annual premium (1/12 of $240 = $20). Given how the transaction was initially recorded, an increase in expense of $240, the expense for December is overstated. An adjusting entry is needed. The transaction to be recorded to adjust the accounts is to reduce the expense from $240 to $20, a decrease of $220.

Further, the dual nature of this transaction would be reflected in ABC's accounts, with a corresponding entry recognising that ABC has an asset at the end of December representing the unused insurance premium. This asset is a prepaid expense or prepayment, being the amount paid in cash and recorded as an asset until the conomic benefits are used or consumed. The prepayment is the $220 of insurance premium for the next 11 months that had already been paid for by ABC.

The preceding transactions have used timing differences to distinguish between the accrual and cash concepts of profit or loss that arise under the accrual and cash systems of accounting respectively. If an entity reported its profit or loss at the end of its life rather than periodically throughout its life, there would be no difference between the accrual and cash concepts of profit. For example, assume that ABC's business had a life of two years. As illustrated in table 4.1, the income and expenses recognised over the two-year life would be identical despite the accrual and cash profit figures being different in the reporting periods ended 31 December 2020 and 31 December 2021. This is because timing transactions reverse over the life of the entity.

TABLE 4.1 Accrual and cash profits compared

	Reporting period ended December 2020	Reporting period ended December 2021	Over the two years
Accrual-based profit Income recognised	$800 for coaching fees	$1 200 for coaching fees	$2 000
Expenses recognised	$50 mobile phone $20 insurance	$220 insurance	$290
Accrual profit (loss) for period (income less expenses)	$730	$980	$1 710
Cash-based profit Income recognised	$1 200 coaching fees received in advance	$800 received for coaching fees provided in 2017	$2 000
Expenses recognised	$240 insurance premium paid	$50 mobile phone account paid	$290
Cash profit (loss) for period	$960	$750	$1 710

Depreciation

There are other expenses recognised under accrual accounting that do not involve cash flows. For example, **depreciation** and **amortisation** are expenses recognised in the statement of profit or loss that do not involve any outflow of cash. All property, plant and equipment assets must be depreciated and certain intangible assets must be amortised. Depreciation (amortisation) is the systematic allocation of the cost of a tangible (intangible) asset over its useful life. Depreciation (amortisation) expense recognises that the asset's future economic benefits have been used up in the reporting period. Depreciation and amortisation do not represent the reduction in the asset's market value from the start to the end of the reporting period. This is another reason why profit or loss does not represent the change in an entity's value from the start to the end of the reporting period.

Consider the following example of how depreciation can be calculated. An entity purchases a car for $40 000, with an estimated useful life of four years and expected residual value of $8 000. If assume that the benefits of using the car will be derived evenly over its useful life, then the straight-line depreciation method is used. Other depreciation methods are discussed later in this chapter. Straight-line depreciation results in the same depreciation expense being recorded each year for the asset's useful life. Straight-line depreciation is calculated using the equation below.

$$\begin{aligned} \text{Annual depreciation expense} &= \frac{\text{Cost of asset} - \text{Expected residual value}}{\text{Asset's expected useful life (years)}} \\ &= \frac{\$40\ 000 - \$8\ 000}{4\ \text{years}} \\ &= \$8\ 000 \end{aligned}$$

The annual depreciation expense to be recognised in the statement of profit or loss is $8 000. The transaction would be recorded by increasing an expense (depreciation) and increasing accumulated depreciation. Accumulated depreciation is the account used to capture the total depreciation that has been charged to statements of profit or loss for a particular asset. The accumulated depreciation account is referred to as a contra account. In the balance sheet, the accumulated depreciation account is deducted from the relevant asset account. Thus, when recording depreciation expense, the dual nature of the transaction is represented by an expense account increasing, thereby reducing profit and hence equity, and the contra account, accumulated depreciation, increasing, thereby reducing assets. The asset account, cash, is unaffected by the recording of depreciation expense.

Referring back to the example, after one year, the carrying amount of the car reported in the balance sheet is $32 000. The $32 000 represents the car's cost price ($40 000) less the accumulated depreciation expense ($8 000). The $32 000 is not necessarily equivalent to the market value of the car at the end of the reporting period, so the financial statements do not reflect the change in the car's market value. In the second year, another $8 000 depreciation expense is recognised in the statement of profit or loss. Hence, after two years the carrying amount of the car reported in the balance sheet is $24 000, being the car's cost price ($40 000) less the accumulated depreciation, which is now $16 000. The $16 000 accumulated depreciation amount is the sum of the depreciation expense for the car in year 1 and year 2. After four years, the accumulated depreciation is $32 000 being four years of an annual depreciation charge of $8 000. At the end of year four, the carrying amount of the car is $8 000, being its cost price ($40 000) less the accumulated depreciation ($32 000). Thus, at the end of the asset's useful life, in this example four years, the asset's carrying value is its residual value. This accumulated depreciation represents the asset's future economic benefits that have been used up in the four years since its purchase.

4.3 Effect of accounting policy choices, estimates and judgements on financial statements

Preparing financial statements in compliance with the accounting standards, the accounting standards provide preparers with choices. Further, estimations and assumptions are necessary. Users of financial statements need to appreciate that accounting flexibility and discretion exist, and they need to consider the potential impact this has on the quality of the reported financial information.

Just as some of the permissible choices in the recording of transactions and estimations and judgements required by preparers of balance sheets were explored in chapter 3, in this section we focus on the pertinent elements of the statement of profit or loss where similar considerations may be required. Earlier in this chapter we discussed the straight-line method of depreciation; however, this is not the only depreciation method permitted under approved accounting standards. An entity can select the straight line, diminishing balance or units of production depreciation method. The method selected should be representative of the pattern by which the asset's benefits are expected to be consumed. Further, when selecting the depreciation method, estimates and judgements need to be made in relation to the asset's useful life and residual value.

Consider an asset that is purchased for $30 000 at the start of the reporting period and has an estimated useful life of three years, with $3 000 residual (salvage) value. Employing **straight-line depreciation** (where the annual depreciation on the asset is the same each year), an expense of $9 000 would be recognised in the statement of profit or loss for each of the next three reporting periods. Using the calculation formula provided above, the annual depreciation expense is the asset's cost price less residual value divided by the useful life ((($30 000 − $3 000)/3 years). If the asset is acquired part way through a reporting period, the annual depreciation is pro-rata. For example, if the asset was purchased at the start of the seventh month of the reporting year, the depreciation expense for that reporting period would be $4 500 ($9 000 annual depreciation charge ×6 months/12 months).

The **diminishing balance depreciation** method assumes that the economic benefits of using the asset will decrease over its useful life. Consequently, depreciation expense is higher in the asset's earlier years relative to later years. Diminishing balance is calculated by applying a constant percentage to the asset's carrying amount at the start of each reporting period. Assume the asset is depreciated using a 50 per cent diminishing balance depreciation method.

The depreciation expense for each of the next three years would be $15 000 in year 1 (50 per cent of $30 000), $7 500 in year 2 (50 per cent of ($30 000 − $15 000)), and $3 750 in year 3 (50 per cent of ($30 000 − ($15 000 + $7 500))). Employing diminishing balance depreciation, the annual depreciation is higher in earlier years relative to later years. The asset's carrying value at the end of the third year is $3 750, being its cost price of $30 000 less the accumulated depreciation of $26 250.

The **units of production depreciation** method charges depreciation expense based on the activity or output in the reporting period relative to the asset's total expected activity or output. Units of production depreciation is calculated using the equation below.

$$\text{Depreciation expense (for the period)} = \frac{(\text{Cost of asset} - \text{Expected residual value})}{\text{Total estimated units}} \times \text{Units in the period}$$

Suppose that the asset used in this illustration is a machine with a useful life of 100 000 units of production. The depreciation charge each year would be a function of the yearly units produced. Assume the machine produces 50 000, 30 000 and 20 000 units in years one to three respectively. Using the units of production method, the depreciation expense in the statements of profit or loss for the next three reporting periods would be $13 500 in year 1 calculated as (($30 000 − $3 000)/100 000) × 50 000 units; $8 100 in year 2 calculated as (($30 000 − $3 000)/100 000) × 30 000 units; and $5 400 in year three calculated as ([$30 000 − $3 000]/100 000) × 20 000 units. The asset's carrying value at the end of the third year is $3000, being its cost price of $30 000 less the accumulated depreciation of $27 000 in years 1, 2 and 3.

Table 4.2 presents a comparison of annual and total depreciation expense of the three methods. Given that the depreciation expense differs according to the depreciation method employed, the estimated useful life and estimated residual value, the reported profit or loss in a particular reporting period will vary according to these selections and estimations as will the carrying value of the assets subject to depreciation.

TABLE 4.2　Comparison of depreciation methods

	Year			Accumulated depreciation
	1	2	3	
Straight-line				
Asset carrying value at start of year	30 000	21 000	12 000	
Annual depreciation expense	9 000	9 000	9 000	27 000
Asset carrying value at end of year	21 000	12 000	3 000	
Diminishing balance				
Asset carrying value at start of year	30 000	15 000	7 500	

Continued

	Year			Accumulated depreciation
	1	2	3	
Annual depreciation expense	15 000	7 500	3 750	26 250
Asset carrying value at end of year	15 000	7 500	3 750	
Units of production				
Asset carrying value at start of year	30 000	16 500	8 400	
Annual depreciation expense	13 500	8 100	5 400	27 000
Asset carrying value at end of year	16 500	8 400	3 000	

Figure 4.1 compares the depreciation patterns over the three years by showing the carrying value of the asset at the end of each of the three years for different depreciation methods. Under the straight-line method, with an equal depreciation expense each year, the asset's carrying value reduces evenly over each of the three years. Under the diminishing balance method, with higher depreciation expense in earlier than in later years, the carrying value reduces at a faster rate in earlier years relative to the outcome of straight-line depreciation. Under the units of production method, with the depreciation expense varying with the usage each year, the reduction in carrying value each year is dependent on the asset's usage that year.

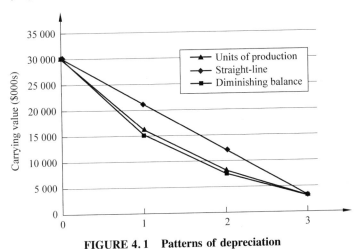

FIGURE 4.1   Patterns of depreciation

As just demonstrated through the depreciation example, an entity's accounting choices, estimates and judgements will affect the profit or loss figure. This also has implications for balance sheet items. For example, depreciation expense affects accumulated depreciation, which in turn affects the carrying amount of the asset.

Other examples of estimations that affect the magnitude of expenses recognised in the statement of profit or loss in a particular reporting period, and balance sheet items, include estimating any impaired accounts receivable, estimating costs associated with a well-planned and well-documented business restructure, and estimating the expense in a particular period associated with employee benefits (e.g. long service leave and sick leave).

Quality of earnings

Given that preparers of financial statements have discretion with respect to accounting policies and estimations, it is necessary to consider the quality of the profit or loss figure, often referred to as the quality of earnings. Are the earnings persistent? Earnings derived from the entity's repetitive operations are regarded as persistent or sustainable, or core earnings. Are the earnings being managed? Earnings management refers to managers' use of accounting discretion via accounting policy choices and/or estimations to portray a desired level of profit in a particular reporting period. Reported profits are used in entities' contractual arrangements and to value entities and are therefore an important financial number.

Managers' choices may be determined by their desire to portray the economic reality of the entity in the statement of profit or loss; however, the choices may also be driven by self-interest. A particular profit range may be desirable for a number of reasons including to avoid breaching loan covenants, to maintain the share price or to maximise salary bonuses. The independent audit of financial statements provides assurance that, based on the audit evidence, the financial statements give a true and fair view of the entity's financial position and performance and comply with required accounting standards. In a demonstration of good corporate governance, the Chief Executive Officer (CEO) and Chief Financial Officer (CFO) may be required to sign a declaration certifying the accuracy of the financial statements.

Earnings management often occurs via the accruals process. In chapter 5, we will examine the statement of cash flows. This financial statement details the net cash inflows and outflows for an entity during the reporting period. It is useful to compare an entity's profit or loss with its cash flows from operations. This is synonymous with comparing profit or loss under accrual accounting with profit or loss calculated under cash accounting. Remembering that timing differences associated with accrual accounting even out over the life of the entity, such a comparison enables the user to determine any unusual trends in accruals that may suggest the profit figure reported is being managed.

4.4 Measuring financial performance

Recall that the Conceptual Framework discussed in chapter 4 identifies the objective of financial reporting, assumptions underlying financial statements and the qualitative characteristics of financial statements, and defines the elements of financial statements (assets, liabilities, equity, income and expenses) and the recognition criteria applied to the elements. In the next sections, we will discuss the definition and recognition criteria applicable to income and expenses.

"Profit or loss" is not formally defined in the Conceptual Framework, but instead is identified as being measured as the difference between income and expenses in a reporting period. To measure the profit or loss of an entity, it is therefore necessary to identify and measure all income and expense items attributable to the reporting period. This necessitates an understanding of what attributes a transaction requires in order to be classified as an item of income or expense.

The Conceptual Framework specifies definition criteria for income and expenses. It also discusses the recognition process that applies to these elements. A transaction must satisfy the definition and recognition criteria to be included in the statement of profit or loss. We will see that the definitions of income and expenses are integrally linked with assets and liabilities.

Income

To be recorded as income in a particular reporting period, the income definition criteria must be satisfied. These criteria are examined in the following sections.

Income definition

Income is defined in the proposed Conceptual Framework (para. 4.48) as:

Income is increases in assets or decreases in liabilities that result in increases in equity, other than those relating to contributions from holders of equity claims.

Recall that income comprises both revenue and gains, with revenue arising in the ordinary course of an entity's activities. Gains also represent increases in economic benefits, but they may or may not arise in the ordinary course of an entity's activities.

Income must be associated with an increase in assets or decrease in liabilities. When deciding if the income definition criteria are satisfied, it is necessary to ascertain whether a new asset exists or an existing asset has increased, or whether an existing liability has been reduced. Recalling the duality principle, an increase in an asset or a reduction in a liability must be accompanied by an increase in equity. Thus, income increases equity.

Consider a retail operation that is making credit and cash sales. A cash sale would satisfy the definition of income, as it results in an inflow or increase of economic benefits — the entity has increased its cash at bank. Similarly, a credit sale also satisfies the income definition criteria, as it results in the creation of an accounts receivable — representing a present economic resource. The transaction in which the customer settles the account by paying cash to the business does not satisfy the income definition. While the retail operation has more cash, due to the customer paying, assets have not increased in total because another asset — accounts receivable — has been extinguished and therefore offsets the increase in cash. Thus, there is no increase in assets as a result of this latter transaction.

If a transaction involves a contribution by owners or contributed capital (such as a cash injection to the business from the owner's personal account), the income definition criteria is not satisfied. For example, the owners of a retail business contribute $100 000 to the business to fund a store refurbishment. The receipt of the $100 000 will not be recorded as income by the business (to be reported in the statement of profit or loss), because it results from a transaction with the owners of the business. Instead, cash (an asset) will increase and capital contributions (an equity item) will increase.

Income classification

Income arising in the ordinary course of an entity's activities (i.e. revenue) is generated from various activities; typically these include providing goods and services, investing or lending, and receiving contributions from parties other than owners. As well as diversity in income-generating activities, there are diverse income types such as sales, fees, commissions, interest, dividends, royalties, rent and non-reciprocal transfers. Most companies have revenue from the sale of goods and services as its main revenue source. There is also "other income" but no details are provided as to what type of income is included in this category.

Expenses

As with income, definition criteria must be satisfied before an expense is recorded in the statement of profit or loss. The following sections discuss these criteria.

Expense definition

Expenses are defined in the proposed Conceptual Framework (para. 4.49) as:

> *Expenses are decreases in economic benefits during the accounting period in the form of outflows or depletions of assets or incurrences of liabilities that result in decreases in equity, other than those relating to distributions to equity participants.*

The word "expenses" refers to expenses arising in the ordinary course of the entity's activities, as well as losses (both realised and unrealised). When deciding if the expense definition criteria are satisfied, it is necessary to ascertain that assets have been reduced or that liabilities have increased. A reduction in an asset or an increase in a liability must be accompanied by a reduction in equity for the definition to be satisfied. Thus, expenses decrease equity. The qualification to this definition is that the transaction does not involve a distribution to owners (i.e. a dividend distribution or return of capital to equity participants). The qualification eliminates dividend distributions or capital returns to owners being recognised as expenses.

Consider a retail operation. The main expense incurred by the business is the cost of sales. In order to sell goods and generate revenue, the entity must purchase goods for resale.

Remembering that financial statements are prepared using accrual accounting, the cost of sales expense comprises the entity's purchases during the reporting period and the change in the inventory balance from the beginning to the end of the reporting period (calculated using the equation below).

Cost of sales = Inventory at beginning of period + Purchases − Inventory at end of period

Imagine that the entity purchases goods on credit from a supplier on 15 June. For the reporting period ended 30 June, the purchases would be included in the cost of sales determination, even though no cash has been paid to the supplier by 30 June.

The critical feature of an expense is that an asset has been reduced or a liability increased, with a consequent reduction in equity. In the transaction described, the entity has an obligation to pay the supplier, so a liability is increased (accounts payable). The dual side of the transaction is that an expense, purchases, increases and thereby reduces equity. When the supplier is paid, the liability account (accounts payable) is reduced and an asset account (cash) is also reduced, with no corresponding reduction in equity. Hence, the payment does not involve the recognition of an expense.

Other expenses associated with selling goods include advertising, sales staff salaries, store displays and wrapping materials. Generally, the expense will arise as a result of the payment of cash (asset reduction) or the recognition of an accrued expense or accounts payable (liability increase). Expenses are also associated with administrative functions, and investing and financing activities. Administrative expenses include items such as rent, office wages and salaries, utility charges and supplies. Finance-related expenses include interest on borrowings, lease payments and bank charges.

The acquisition of certain assets (such as items of property, plant and equipment) is not an expense of the reporting period, as there is no reduction in equity associated with the transaction. If the asset is acquired for cash, cash at bank is reduced but the reduction is offset by an increase in another asset class — property, plant and equipment. Such items are expected to provide the entity with future economic resources over a period extending beyond the current reporting period, so it would be inappropriate to recognise the acquisition as an expense in the period it occurs. What is periodically recognized as an expense is the depreciation of such assets. The carrying amount (book value) (which is the dollar value assigned to the asset in the balance sheet) of the asset must be allocated over the asset's useful life, representing future economic benefits of the asset that have been consumed during the reporting period. Further, when the value of the asset is lower than its carrying amount, the asset is impaired. In such circumstances, the asset must be written down to its recoverable amount, and the write-down would be recognised as an impairment expense in the reporting period in which it occurs.

Expense classification

Entities have a choice as to how they display and classify expenses in the statement of profit or loss. Smaller entities will often list all their expenses in the statement of profit or loss, whereas larger entities will aggregate their expenses into certain classes for reporting purposes. Entities required to comply with accounting standards must classify their expenses by nature or function. For example, if an entity classifies expenses by nature, expense categories in its statement of profit or loss might include employee benefits expense and depreciation and amortisation expense. If the entity classifies expenses by function, expense categories in its statement of profit or loss might include distribution, marketing, occupancy and administrative expenses, and borrowing costs expense.

4.5 Applying recognition criteria to income and expenses

The term recognition refers to recording items in the financial statements with a monetary value assigned to them. Therefore, "income recognition" or "expense recognition" means that the income or expense is recorded and appears in the statement of profit or loss. Central to the recognition principle is that items can be measured in monetary terms. This is referred to as the monetary concept. As money is the language used to quantify items recognised in the financial statements, if items cannot be assigned a monetary value, then they cannot appear in the financial statements.

It is recognition that links the elements in the balance sheet (assets, liabilities and equity) and statement of profit or loss (income and expenses). Given the definitions of income and expenses, the recognition of one of these elements requires the recognition of an equal amount of another element. For example, recognizing income simultaneously requires recognising an increase in asset or decrease in liability. Similarly, recognising an expense simultaneously requires recognising a decrease in assets or increase in liabilities. For example, recognising tennis fee income for Appreciation Basketball Coaching (ABC) requires recognising an increase in an asset (e.g. cash at bank if the fees are paid in cash or accounts receivable if the fees are outstanding). Recognising an expense for ABC, such as paying court hire, requires simultaneously recognizing a decrease in an asset (e.g. cash). Recognising a mobile phone expense that is due but has not been paid requires simultaneously recognising an increase in a liability (accrued expense or payables).

As discussed in the previous chapter 3, there are no definitive rules to assist the decision of whether an item should be recognised. The recognition decision requires judgement. The overarching considerations when deciding to recognise an income or an expense (and any related asset or liability) are whether the recognition provides financial statement users with relevant information about the asset or the liability and about any income, expenses or changes in equity, whether it is a faithful representation of the asset or the liability and of any income, expenses or changes in equity, and whether the information results in benefits exceeding the cost of providing that information.

The factors to consider when making a recognition decision, framed in terms of whether an asset or liability is recognized are uncertainty, probability and measurement uncertainty.

If the uncertainty surrounding existence is high, the probability of inflows or outflows of economic benefits is low or measurement uncertainty is high, then it is less likely that the asset or liability, and hence income or expense, will be recognised.

Income (revenue) recognition

The determination of when an increase in assets or reduction in liabilities has arisen, and hence when income can be recognised, can be difficult and demands consideration of relevance assessed with reference to uncertainty, probability and measurement. Consider the following transactions:

(1) a customer made a 50 per cent non-cancellable deposit for goods worth $5 000;

(2) a customer made a $10 cancellable deposit for goods worth $5 000. The inflow of economic benefits associated with collecting the remaining cash for the $5 000 of goods sold are less likely to have arisen in the scenario of the customer paying a $10 deposit. For income recognition purposes, the first transaction would result in income of $5 000 being recognised in the statement of profit or loss for the reporting period, but the probability factor would be unlikely to be satisfied in the second transaction.

It is difficult to be prescriptive as to the appropriate point in time when income should be recognised. In fact, accounting standard setters have been grappling with producing a standard on revenue recognition. Instances of earnings management where income has been recognised in earlier rather than later reporting periods (to increase earnings) have focused regulators' attention on the income recognition policies used by entities. To determine whether income should be recognised, consideration should be given to the following.

- Does an agreement for the provision of goods and services exist between the entity and a party external to the entity?
- Has cash been received, or does the entity have a claim against an external party that is for a specified consideration and is unavoidable without penalty?
- Have all acts of performance necessary to establish a valid claim against the external party been completed?
- Is it possible to reliably estimate the collectability of debts?

A positive response to all of these questions would result in income being recognised in the statement of profit or loss. However, it is not necessary for all the suggested tests to be satisfied for income to be recognised — it depends on the circumstances of the situation.

Expense recognition

Recognising an expense involves determining if a decrease in assets or an increase in liabilities is required, paying due attention to relevance as assessed considering the factors of uncertainty, probability and measurement uncertainty. In many instances, this is straightforward (e. g. goods to a known value have been sold, or an invoice for advertising expenses has been received). Other transactions involve greater uncertainty about the occurrence and measurement of the outflow of economic benefits (e. g. employee benefits expense and asset impairments).

As a result of the economic climate, many entities have suffered impairment losses. The accounting rules require entities to write down the carrying amount of their assets if the carrying amount is higher than the asset's recoverable amount. The recoverable amount is the higher of the asset's value in use and net selling price. The reality check "Orica's $1.65 billion write-down a disappointing but decisive action, CEO Alberto Calderon says" illustrates a decision that has been made to recognise an expense (an impairment loss) based on the need to reduce the carrying value of an asset, and how this has impacted on the entity's reported profit.

REAL WORLD

Orica's $1.65 billion write-down a disappointing but decisive action, CEO Alberto Calderon says

The company significantly downgraded profit expectations, telling the market it expected its net profit after tax would be 10 to 15 per cent below current consensus forecasts of $490 million. The market reacted with Orica's shares tumbling 12 per cent — down $2.28 to $16.58 when the market opened.

Orica, the world's largest explosives maker, announced a massive $1.65 billion asset write-down associated with declining fortunes in mining and a global oversupply of ammonium nitrate.

The decision, in response to a changed operating environment, saw asset write-downs across all Orica key business units.

The impairment charge against its ground support business— which focuses on underground mining — will be in the range of $730 to $870 million.

Ammonium nitrate manufacturing assets based in Indonesia and Peru will be written down by up to $600 million, while another $120 million to $180 million impairment charges will be taken across the business to reflect changed "longer-term operating conditions".

Source: Letts, S 2015, "Orica"s $1.65 billion write-down a disappointing but decisive action, CEO Alberto Calderon says. ABCNews, 7. August, www.abc.net.au/news/2015-08-07/orica27s-24165-billion-write-down/6680272.

Prior to the Conceptual Framework and the definitions of income and expense contained in it, considerable emphasis was placed on the matching principle when recognising income and expenses in a reporting period. The matching principle required matching the income earned with the expenses incurred in a reporting period. Applying the income and expense definition and recognition criteria will generally involve a matching of income and expenses. This occurs when:

- items of income and expense result directly and jointly from the same transaction (e.g. the concurrent recognition of sales and cost of sales).
- income is matched with progressive performance (e.g. a borrower will recognise the interest expense associated with a loan throughout the loan's life even if all the interest is to be paid at the loan's maturity).
- expenses are matched with the entity's productivity (e.g. the recognition of depreciation on a systematic basis according to the asset's useful life is allocating the depreciation expense according to asset productivity).

4.6 Presenting the statement of profit or loss

In chapter 3, the difference in appearance of the balance sheet depending on the type of entity and the choice of the entity was explored. Nonetheless, the balance sheet has common elements such as assets, liabilities and equity. Similarly, the appearance of the statement of profit or loss differs depending on whether the statement is being prepared for internal or external reporting purposes, and whether the preparing entity is required to comply with accounting standards. For example, the statement of profit or loss presented for ABC, a non-reporting small business in example 4.1, looks quite different from that presented for a listed company. While the two statements of profit or loss have common elements such as income, expenses and profit, listed company's statement of profit or loss contains more aggregated data with greater detail in the notes to the accounts. The following sections examine other presentation and content requirements for the statement of profit or loss, with a focus on requirements for entities required to comply with accounting standards.

Prescribed format for general purpose financial statements

As discussed in chapter 3, some entities are legally required to prepare financial statements in accordance with approved accounting standards. IFRS include a standard that specifies the presentation of financial statements. Income and expenses may be presented in a variety of ways, with the aim being to make the presentation consistent and relevant to external users. We will now explore some of the presentation issues.

The statement of profit or loss for the previous reporting period in addition to the current reporting period is presented. Known as comparative information, it allows users to see how the entity's financial performance in the current period differs from that of the previous period. When comparing the figures for the current and previous period, users should familiarise themselves with the entity's accounting policies to ensure that a change in accounting policy is not the reason for the change in the reported figures.

The presentation of the numbers in the statement of profit or loss in whole dollars, or thousands or millions of dollars, is at the discretion of the entity, but the entity should clearly identify on the statement the monetary value reported. In the situation where the entity has investments in other entities, the statement of profit or loss for the group is presented. The concept of group (consolidated) accounts is explored in chapter 3.

The accounting standard governing the presentation of the statement of profit or loss requires the following to be presented on the statement of profit or loss:

- revenue
- cost of sales (if revenue from sales is disclosed)
- finance costs
- share of profit or loss of associates and joint ventures if equity accounted
- tax expense
- profit or loss.

If an entity has discontinued part of its operations during the reporting period, the entity must segregate profit or loss from continuing operations and discontinued operations. This allows users of the financial statements to better analyse the financial performance — past, current and future.

Entities are permitted to disclose additional line items, headings and subtotals in the statement of profit or loss if it is relevant to users in assessing the financial performance of the entity.

Material income and expenses

To enhance the usefulness of information for decision making, entities are required to separately disclose any item of income or expense that is material or significant. The determination of whether an item is material is based on the size and/or nature of the item, and whether its non-disclosure could influence users' decision making. This disclosure can occur via the notes to the accounts or in the statement of profit or loss.

It is important to identify and separately disclose material items, as this helps users to identify permanent versus transitory earnings charges and thereby better predict future earnings. Situations that may result in material items of income and expenses are disposals of property, plant and equipment, asset impairments and restructuring activities.

Format for entities not required to comply with accounting standards

Entities not required to prepare general purpose financial statements complying with accounting standards have freedom in the presentation of the statement of profit or loss. While the presentation and classification of items can exhibit great diversity, the purpose of the statement of profit or loss does not change: to report the profit or loss for the entity for the reporting period. As was shown in example 4.1, the statement of profit or loss for an entity not required to comply with accounting standards is usually more detailed and less aggregated than that prepared in accordance with accounting standards, as the statement is typically prepared for internal rather than external users. For example, consider example 4.2.

In the statement presented the entity has grouped income into sales-related and other income. The entity's other income could consist of items such as dividends received, interest revenue and royalties. Entities may choose to list other income items individually. Expenses have been grouped into six categories: cost of sales, warehousing, distribution, selling and marketing, administration and finance. Entities can elect to aggregate or disaggregate expenses as there are no fixed formatting requirements.

EXAMPLE 4.2

Statement of profit or loss format for an entity not required to comply with accounting standards

× × × Ltd Statement of profit or loss for ended 31 December 2019		
Income		
Sales		$500 000
Cost of sales		275 000
Gross profit		**225 000**
Other income		5 000
Operating expenses		
Warehouse	$32 000	
Distribution	10 000	
Finance	5 000	
Selling and marketing	3 000	
Administration	30 000	80 000
Profit before tax		150 000
Income tax expense		45 000
Profit after tax		$105 000

The cost of sales for a retailer represents the opening inventory value, plus purchases, less closing inventory value. For a manufacturing operation, such as Coconut Plantations Pty Ltd, the cost of sales represents the opening value of finished goods, plus the cost of goods manufactured (which is the cost of materials, labour and overhead used in manufacturing the goods), less the closing value of finished goods.

Typical items included in "warehouse" expenses could be warehouse rent, wages and salaries of warehouse staff, insurance for stored inventory, depreciation of warehouse plant and equipment, and utilities (e. g. electricity, telephone, gas) consumed by the warehouse. Distribution expenses could include courier fees, fleet management costs, and postage and handling. Selling and marketing expenses could include advertising, sales staff salaries and promotional events. Items that comprise administrative expenses could include general staff costs and head office expenses such as stationery, utilities, rates, depreciation of office furniture and equipment, and general insurance. Finance costs could include interest on borrowings, bank fees and lease charges.

Financial performance measures

We saw earlier that the statement of profit or loss complying with accounting standards must disclose a number of required profit figures such as profit before and after tax. There are additional profit figures that may be referenced in the financial statements or referred to in the financial press. The following sections introduce these profit figures.

Gross profit

Gross profit refers to revenue less the cost of sales, and is applicable to manufacturing and retail operations. The gross profit measures the revenue remaining after deducting the cost of sales. An entity cannot be sustainable unless it has a positive gross profit, meaning that it is selling its goods at a price exceeding their cost. Gross profit reflects the percentage by which an entity marks up the cost of its products to sell to its customers. It also reflects an entity's relationship with suppliers and its purchasing power. Both of these are intrinsically linked to the competitiveness of the industry in which it operates.

Profit

Profit is the term commonly given to the gross profit less all other expenses incurred in operating the business. Effectively, it is the entity's income less expenses for the reporting period.

Profit pre-and post-tax

Profit performance measures can be referred to on a pre-and/or post-tax basis. Taxation is an expense of a company, because a company has an obligation to pay tax on business activities. The tax that a company pays is based on taxable income as calculated by applying taxation rules. In contrast, the profit reported in the statement of profit or loss is measured by applying accounting rules. To the extent that the taxation and accounting rules differ, the tax

expense of a company will not be simply the pre-tax accounting profit multiplied by the applicable tax rate. Taxation and accounting rules can diverge due to:
- income not being assessable for taxation purposes.
- expenses not being deductible for taxation purposes.

Consider a company that sold a building in the current reporting period for a $20 000 gain. The building was purchased prior to the introduction of the capital gains tax, although the $20 000 will be included in the determination of accounting profit for the period, it is not assessable income for taxation purposes. Profit before and after tax is used to assess the profitability of an entity. An owner is more interested in the profit after tax, because tax obligations must be satisfied before profits can be distributed as dividends. Conversely, a financial analyst would be interested in the profit before tax, because this reflects the outcomes of the entity's investing and financing activities without the effect of a variable (taxation) that is determined by forces outside the control of the entity, namely by the government.

Profit pre-and post-interest

As previously noted, profit reflects the effects of an entity's investing and financing decisions and the taxation consequences thereof. To isolate the returns associated with the investment decision only, profit before interest and tax is the relevant figure. This is more commonly referred to as **earnings before interest and taxation** (**EBIT**). The interest figure refers to the net effect of finance-related income and expenses. Net finance costs are defined as interest income less interest expense (including finance lease charges). If the entity is a net lender (i.e. a bank) with interest income exceeding interest expense, it will be necessary to subtract the net interest from the profit before tax figure to derive EBIT. If the entity is a net borrower, with interest expense exceeding interest income, it will be necessary to add the net interest to the profit before tax figure to derive EBIT. The steps involved in calculating EBIT are shown in table 4.3.

TABLE 4.3   Calculation of EBIT

Step 1: Identify the entity's profit from continuing operations before income tax but after interest.
Step 2: Calculate the entity's net finance income (cost): Finance income − Finance costs = Net finance income (costs)
Step 3: If the entity has net finance income, deduct the net finance income from profit from continuing operations before tax to give EBIT. If the entity has net finance costs, add the net finance costs to profit before tax to give EBIT.

Profit pre-and post-depreciation and amortisation

Depreciation and amortisation are non-cash expenses included in the statement of profit or loss. **Earnings before interest, tax, depreciation and amortisation** (**EBITDA**) refers to the profit before net interest, taxation and depreciation/amortisation expense. It is a measure of the raw operating earnings of an entity, as it excludes asset diminution in addition to tax and financing charges. EBITDA is used for a number of purposes, including financial statement analysis and credit analysis. It was used traditionally as a substitute for a cash-based profit measure. Because cash flows associated with operating activities are available in the statement of cash flows, the need to approximate cash flows from operations via EBITDA is no longer necessary.

Profit pre-and post-material items

Items of income and expense can be labelled as material (or significant) on the basis of their size or nature. Many users of financial statements are interested in an entity's maintainable earnings. Often this is taken to be the income less expenses from "ordinary" activities, excluding the material items. It is argued that the exclusion of material items from profit provides a better reflection of the trend and sustainability of profit. This does not mean that users should ignore material items. Due consideration should still be given to these items, as interesting trends in relation to them may emerge.

Profit from continuing and discontinued operations

If an entity has sold or plans to sell a part of its business during the reporting period, information must be disclosed that enables users of the financial statements to evaluate the financial effects of the discontinued operations. The entity must disclose separately the profit or loss after tax associated with the discontinued operations from that of the continuing operations. This assists users to better predict future profits.

4.7 The statement of comprehensive income

The statement of profit or loss reports the profit or loss for the reporting period. Entities that are required to comply with accounting standards must also prepare a statement of comprehensive income. In addition to income and expenses recognised in the determination of profit or loss, there are other income and expense items that are required or permitted by some accounting standards to be taken directly to equity rather than recognised in profit or loss, for example non-current asset revaluation surplus, foreign currency rate changed, and a new accounting standard applied.

Such items are included in the determination of an entity's "other comprehensive income" for an accounting period, but they are not taken into account when determining an entity's profit or loss for the period. This is a product of having accounting standards that permit some transactions to bypass the statement of profit or loss. There is no rule or rationale explaining why this is permitted in some circumstances.

Other comprehensive income refers to all changes in equity during the reporting period other than profit or loss in the statement of profit or loss and those resulting from transactions with owners as owners (such as dividends and capital contributions).

Entities can elect to present all items of income and expense in a reporting period in a single statement of comprehensive income or in two statements:

(1) a statement of profit or loss showing the income and expenses associated with the determination of profit (or loss) for the reporting period and

(2) a statement beginning with profit or loss and displaying components of other comprehensive income (statement of comprehensive income).

Table 4.4 shows the **statement of comprehensive income** from the 2019 financial report of a listed company. The company has elected to present a statement of profit or loss showing the profit or loss for the reporting period and a statement of comprehensive income beginning with profit or loss and displaying components of other comprehensive income.

TABLE 4.4 Statement of comprehensive income

× × × Ltd Statement of comprehensive income for the financial year ended 30 June 2019	Consolidated	
	2019 $ '000	2018 $ '000
Profit for the year	136 511	128 447
Other comprehensive income		
Changes in the fair value of cash flow hedges (net of tax)	1	576
Exchange differences on translation of foreign operations	(2 509)	4 728
Other comprehensive income for the year (net of tax)	(2 508)	5 304
Total comprehensive income for the year	134 003	133 751
Total comprehensive income attributable to:		
Owners of the company	134 003	133 663
Non-controlling interests	—	88
	134 003	133 751

4.8 The statement of changes in equity

When assessing the change in an entity's financial position, in addition to users being informed of the profit or loss for the reporting period, users should also be able to identify the change in equity from the start to the end of the reporting period and the reasons for the change. For example, if ABC earned a profit of $6 000 for the 3 month period from 1 October

2020 to 31 December 2020 and Jack, the owner, withdrew $1 000 during that period, the change in equity would be an increase of $6 000. Equity at the end of 2020 would be $42 370 comprising equity at 30 September 2020 ($36 370) plus the increase in equity ($6 000). Table 4.5 shows the statement of changes in equity for ABC, a sole trader, for the year ended 31 December 2020.

TABLE 4.5 ABC statement of changes in equity for 3 months ended 31 December 2020

Statement of changes in equity for the year ended 31 December 2020	
Capital, Jack, as at 1 October 2020	$36 370
Plus: Profit for three months	6 000
Less: Drawings	1 000
Capital, Jack, as at 31 December 2020	$41 370

Entities required to comply with accounting standards must present a **statement of changes in equity**. The statement shows the change in an entity's equity between two reporting periods. Effectively, the statement of changes in equity is showing the impact of all of the changes in assets and liabilities during the reporting period. The statement shows all changes in equity arising from transactions with owners in their capacity as owners (such as equity contributions, dividends paid and shares purchased) separately from non-owner changes in equity (e.g. profit). The purpose is to provide users with better information by requiring aggregation of items with similar characteristics and separation of items with different characteristics.

Table 4.6 shows a listed company statement of changes in equity during 2019. The shareholders' equity balance at 1 July 2019 was $294 633 000 and the closing balance at 30 June 2020 is $343 479 000. Company's statement of changes in equity shows a reconciliation between the opening and closing balance disaggregated by contributed equity, reserves and retained earnings. The illustration shows the following.

- The reconciliation between the opening retained earnings balance at 1 July 2019 ($219 985 000) and the closing balance at 30 June 2020 ($269 322 000). The $136 511 000 profit for the reporting period (as shown in the statement of profit or loss) has increased the retained earnings. The company has paid dividends of $87 174 000 that have reduced the retained earnings balance.
- The reconciliation between the opening reserves balance at 1 July 2019 ($16 265 000) and closing balance as at 30 June 2020 ($17 636 000). Some of the items resulting in a change in reserves are items of other comprehensive income. For example, the foreign currency translation differences, value of employee share payments and the change in the value of cash flow hedges have, as allowed or required by accounting

standards, bypassed the statement of profit or loss and gone directly to reserve accounts in equity.

- The reconciliation between the opening contributed equity at 1 July 2019 ($58 383 000) and closing contributed equity at 30 June 2020 ($56 521 000). The change in contributed equity during the reporting period is due to issuing shares under the entity's share option plan. The company also did a share buy-back during the year.

TABLE 4.6 Statement of changes in equity for the financial year

Consolidated	Contributed equity $'000	Reserves $'000	Retained earnings $'000	Total $'000
Balance at 1 July 2019	58 383	16 265	219 985	294 633
Profit for the year	—	—	136 511	136 511
Cash flow hedges (net of tax)	—	1	—	1
Exchange differences on translation of foreign operations	—	(2 509)	—	(2 509)
Total comprehensive income for the year	—	(2 508)	136 511	134 003
Issue of shares under share option plan	3 125	—	—	3 125
Share buy-back	(4 970)	—	—	(4 970)
Share issue and buy-back costs (net of tax)	(17)	—	—	(17)
Dividends provided for or paid	—	—	(87 174)	(87 174)
Share-based payments — expense		3 508		3 508
Share-based payments — income tax	—	371	—	371
Balance at 30 June 2020	56 521	17 636	269 322	343 479

The link between the financial statements

It is important to understand the relationships between the financial statements, rather than viewing each statement in isolation. We have already seen how the income and expense definitions are linked to the asset and liability definitions. The recognition of income occurs simultaneously with the increase in assets or decrease in liabilities. Similarly, the recognition of expenses occurs simultaneously with the decrease in assets or increase in liabilities. The fundamental purpose of the statement of profit or loss is to present the entity's financial performance for a period of time. The entity's profit or loss for the reporting period belongs to the entity's owners. The profit or loss for the reporting period is added to the undistributed profits from previous periods (**retained earnings**, or **retained profits** or **accumulated profits** are interchangeable terms used to describe undistributed profits in the entity). The retained earnings at the end of the reporting period are the retained earnings at the start of the period, plus the current period's profits, less any distributions (dividends or drawings) made to owners during the reporting period. The retained earnings balance at the end of the reporting period is equity item in the balance sheet. Items of income and expense directly recognised in equity, and transactions with owners as owners (as per the statement of changes in equity), also result in changes in the equity balance from the beginning to the end of the reporting period. This relationship between the main financial statements is illustrated in figure 4.2.

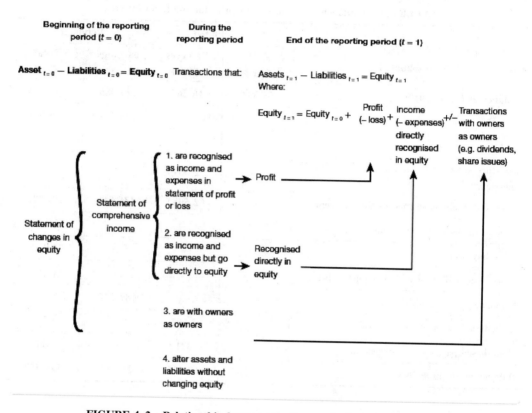

FIGURE 4.2　Relationship between the four main financial statements

SUMMARY

1. Explain the purpose and importance of measuring financial performance.

It is important to measure financial performance periodically so that users, both internal and external, can assess the profitability of the entity. The primary objective of preparing financial statements is to provide information that is useful for decision making. Knowledge of the profit or loss is crucial in assessing past performance and forming an opinion as to expected future performance for a for-profit entity.

2. Explain the reporting period concept and the difference between accrual accounting and cash accounting.

The fundamental concepts underlying the preparation of the statement of profit or loss are the accounting or reporting period, accrual accounting and generally accepted accounting principles. Generally accepted accounting principles (GAAP) are the accounting rules that determine the recognition, measurement and presentation of financial information. The financial performance of an entity is measured over a period of time — the life of the entity is arbitrarily divided into reporting periods. The profit measurement for a reporting period should include all transactions affecting profit in that reporting period. Accrual accounting, as distinct from cash accounting, means that the profit determination is independent of whether cash is received or paid in relation to profit items during the reporting period.

3. Outline the effect that accounting policy choices, estimates and judgements can have on the financial statements.

Even when preparing financial statements in compliance with approved accounting standards, preparers are provided with choices and are required to use estimations and judgements. Therefore, users of financial statements need to appreciate that accounting flexibility and discretion exist, consider the incentives that may affect the choices, estimations and judgements being made, and be aware of the impact of the choices, estimations and judgements on the financial information reported.

4. Describe and calculate the measurement of financial performance.

Profit or loss for a reporting period is measured as the income during the reporting period less the expenses in the reporting period. If income exceeds expenses in a particular reporting period is a profit results. If expenses exceed income, the entity reports a loss for that reporting period.

5. Discuss the definition and classification of income.

Income is defined as increases in economic benefits— in the form of inflows or enhancement of assets or decreases of liabilities of the entity — that result in increases in equity during the reporting period. Contributions by owners are not regarded as income. Income comprises revenue and gains.

6. Discuss the definition and classification of expenses.

Expenses are decreases in economic benefits— in the form of outflows or depletions of assets or increases of liabilities — that result in decreases in equity during the reporting period. Distributions to owners are not expenses. Expenses can be classified according to their nature or function.

7. Apply the recognition criteria to income and expenses.

The term recognition refers to recording items in the financial statements with a monetary value assigned to them. Therefore, "income recognition" or "expense recognition" means that the income or expense is recorded and appears in the statement of profit or loss. It is recognition that links the elements in financial statements — assets, liabilities, equity, income and expenses — and hence the financial statements.

The linkage between the statements arises because the recognition of one element (or a change in one element) requires the recognition of an equal amount in one or more other elements (or changes in one or more other elements) as per the accounting equation. There are no definitive rules to assist the decision of whether an item should be recognised. The recognition decision requires judgement. The overarching considerations when deciding to recognise an asset or a liability (and any related income, expenses or changes in equity) are whether the recognition provides financial statement users with relevant information about the asset or the liability and about any income, expenses or changes in equity, whether it is a faithful representation of the asset or the liability and of any income, expenses or changes in equity, and whether the information results in benefits exceeding the cost of providing that information. Factors of uncertainty and unreliable measurement may result in non-recognition. An entity always has the option to disclose information concerning items not recognised.

8. Identify presentation formats for the statement of profit or loss.

There is an accounting standard governing the presentation of the statement of profit or loss for entities that are required to comply with accounting standards. This standard prescribes the line items that must be disclosed in the statement of profit or loss or in the notes to the accounts, but permits discretion as to the presentation format.

9. Differentiate alternative financial performance measures.

Various profit measures may be used. Gross profit is restricted to revenue less the cost of sales. Other derivations of profit include:

- profit before and after tax
- earnings before interest
- earnings before interest, tax, depreciation and amortization
- profit before and after material items
- profit from continuing and discontinued operations.

10. Explain the nature of the statement of comprehensive income and statement of changes in equity.

Entities required to comply with accounting standards must present a statement of comprehensive income and a statement of changes in equity. The statement of comprehensive income reports profit or loss and other comprehensive income. The statement of changes in equity explains the change in an entity's equity for the reporting period. The statement discloses income and expenses recognised in the statement of profit or loss, income and expenses recognised directly in equity, and transactions with owners as owners.

11. Explain the relationship between the statement of profit or loss, the balance sheet, the statement of comprehensive income and the statement of changes in equity.

The statement of profit or loss reports the profit or loss generated in the reporting period that belongs to the owners of the business. It is added to the retained earnings from previous periods to determine the pool of retained earnings available for distribution to owners. Retained earnings is included in the equity section of the balance sheet as at the end of the period. The statement of comprehensive income details the profit or loss for the period (i.e. the statement of profit or loss) as well as items of income and expense that are not recognised in profit or loss as required as permitted by accounting standards. These items of income and expense bypass the statement of profit or loss and are recorded directly in the equity section of the balance sheet. The statement of changes in equity explains the change in equity from the start to the end of the reporting period. These changes relate to profit or loss for the period, other comprehensive income and transactions with owners as owners. The statements are also related, given that recognising income and expenses involves simultaneously recognizing (or reducing) assets or liabilities.

KEY TERMS

Accrual accounting 权责发生制
Accrued expenses 应计费用
Accrued income 应计收入
Accumulated depreciation 累计折旧
Amortisation 摊销
Carrying amount (book value) 账面值
Cash accounting 现金收付制
Comparative information 对比的信息
Contra account 备抵账户
Cost of goods manufactured 制造企业产品成本
Cost of sales 已售成本
Depreciation 折旧
Diminishing balance depreciation （折旧）余额递减法
Distribution to owners 对股东的分配
Earnings before interest and taxation (EBIT) 息税前利润
Earnings before interest, tax, depreciation and amortisation (EBITDA) 折旧及息税前利润
Earnings management 盈余管理
Expenses 费用
Gains 利得
Gross profit 毛利
Impairment 减值损失
Income 收入(广义)

Income received in advance 预收收入
Integrated reporting 合并报告
Material items 重要事项
Net finance costs 净财务费用
Other comprehensive income 其他综合收益
Prepaid expenses（prepayments） 预付费用
Profit or loss 盈利或亏损
Recoverable amount 可回收金额
Recognition reporting period（accounting period） 确认报告期（会计期间）
Retained earnings（retained profits or accumulated profits） 留存收益
Revenue 收入（狭义）
Statement of changes in equity 所有者权益变动表
Statement of comprehensive income 综合收益表
Statement of profit or loss 损益表
Straight-line depreciation 直线折旧法
Units of production depreciation 工作量折旧法

SELF-EVALUATION ACTIVITIES

4.1 Single choice questions

1. MM company produces monthly accounting reports. The following are all the transactions for October 2020.

Sales	$25 000
Purchase	23 750
Freight outwards	1 250
Inventory, 1 October 2020	12 500
Inventory, 31 October 2020	18 750

The gross profit for the business for October 2020 is(　　)

(a) $7 500；　　(b) $3 750；　　(c) $6 250；　　(d) $5 000；
(e) $2 500.

2. Retailers can possibly classify their expenses into four major categories. Under this system, how would freight outwards be classified?（　　）

　　(a) Financial express；
　　(b) Cost of sales；
　　(c) Selling and distribution expense；
　　(d) Administration and general expense；
　　(e) Either (b) or (c).

3. If estimated bad debts are not properly accounted for in accordance with the matching

convention, the effect on the financial statements is to ( )

    (a) Overstate owner's equity , overstate assets;

    (b) Understate liabilities, overstate profit;

    (c) Overstate expenses, overstate assets;

    (d) Overstate revenues, understate assets;

    (e) Understate profits. overstate assets;

4. Tommy Tucker recently purchased a machine costing $42 000. The machine had an estimated residual value of $2 000 at the end of its useful life of five years . Tommy adopts the reducing-balance depreciation method with a rate of 25% per annum. What will be the written down value of the machine at the end of the fourth year of the machine's life (to the nearest dollar)? ( )

    (a) $10 000   (b) $13 289   (c) $9 967   (d) $13 500

    (e) $10 125

5. Peter's Pies bought a new oven on 1 January 2020 with a total cost of $88 000. Its expected residual value was $8 000; useful life 16 years or 1 600 000 units of production . In the first year of the oven's use (to 31 December 2020), Peter baked 80 600 pies. Using the units of production method, what should be the amount of depreciation expense on the oven to be shown in the Income Statement for the year ended 31 December 2020? ( )

    (a) $4 433;   (b) $5 000;   (c) $12 248;   (d) $4 030;

    (e) $5 500.

4.2 True or false

1. Income measures the outflow of assets or the increase in liabilities that result from business operations.   ( )

2. Gross profit is calculated as the difference between the value of sales and the cost of the goods that were sold.   ( )

3. Inventory cost flow assumptions must match the underlying physical inventory movements as closely as possible.   ( )

4. Expenses are incurred in order to generate income and measure increases in assets or liabilities during a reporting period.   ( )

5. The transaction recognition criteria are based on probability of occurrence and reliability of measurement.   ( )

4.3   Sam operates a retail clothing store. In preparing the financial reports, his accountant has made the following adjustments:

1. Reduced prepaid advertising by $3 000.

2. Increased accumulated depreciation by $2 400.

3. Reduced income received in advance by $4 350.

4. Increased wages expense by $240.

Required

Given double entry accounting, for each of the adjustments explain the corresponding entry and the rationale for the decision to make the adjustment.

Answer to self-evaluation activities

4.1 Single choice questions
1. a   2. c   3. a   4. b   5. d

4.2 True or false
1. F   2. T   3. F   4. F   5. T

4.3 Solution

1. Reduced prepaid advertising by $3 000. The corresponding entry for this adjustment is an increase in advertising expense by $3 000. The adjustment recognises that some of the future economic benefits of advertising paid in advance, and therefore recorded as an asset, have been used up during the period. The adjustment reduces the asset account (Prepaid advertising) and increases the expense account (Advertising expense).

2. Increased accumulated depreciation by $2 400. The corresponding entry for this adjustment is an increase in depreciation expense. Depreciation is the systematic allocation of the cost of an asset over its useful life. The depreciation expense recognises that some of the asset's future economic benefits have been used up in the reporting period.

3. Reduced income received in advance by $4 350. The corresponding entry for this adjustment is an increase in income. Income received in advance is a liability as it represents cash that has been received for services yet to be provided. If this liability account has been reduced, it is due to some of the income having been earned.

4. Increased wages payable by $240. The corresponding entry for this adjustment is an increase in wages expense. At the end of the reporting period, some wages have been incurred but have not been paid. The adjustment recognises the wages expense incurred in the period (increasing wages expense) but not yet paid (increasing a liability account — wages payable).

CHAPTER 5

Statement of Cash Flows

LEARNING OBJECTIVES

After studying this chapter, you should be able to:
5.1 understand the purpose and usefulness of a statement of cash flows
5.2 outline the format and content in the statement of cash flows
5.3 prepare a statement of cash flows and a reconciliation using the indirect method
5.4 explain the statement of cash flows

We had discussed the balance sheet, the statement of profit or loss, statement of comprehensive income, and statement of changes in equity in previous chapters. Now, this chapter will introduce the statement of cash flows. It provides cash flow information to help decision makers to assess an entity's ability to generate cash, meet its obligations and explain why assets and liabilities have changed. So the statement of cash flows keep closely linked with the statement of profit or loss and the balance sheet. Then introduce the general format of cash flow statement. At last discussed is the preparation and interpretation of the statement of cash flows.

5.1 The purpose and usefulness of a statement of cash flows

Cash flows are the lifeblood of the business. Without cash flows a business will wither and die. We have seen many companies and countries during the global financial crisis (GFC) and its aftermath stall or come to a halt due to a cash shortage. Therefore, it makes sense to prepare a report that shows the cash flows of a business. This is the purpose of a statement of cash flows.

As we know the statement of profit or loss shows the income earned and expenses incurred through this cycle under the accrual accounting. But the statement of cash flows shows the actual cash receipts and payments. So it is important that we differentiate between a sale (revenue generated) and cash received; or between a purchase and a payment.

The flows of cash are important for the **working capital** management of an entity. Working capital is needed to fund inventory and accounts receivable while awaiting receipts from sales.

The flow of cash through purchases and payments of inventory and labour to the receipt of cash can be simply depicted as shown in figure 5.1.

The bigger number of times an entity can cycle through this process, generally the more profit it can make. However, cash is very important through the cycle as there is normally an outflow of funds for inventory and wages prior to the inflow from sales. The statement of cash flows helps ascertain the cash generation from this cycle and whether or not the entity is collecting its receipts in a timely manner.

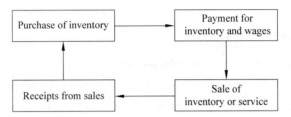

FIGURE 5.1   Flow of cash in business cycle

Difference between cash and accrual accounting

Recall from chapter 4 that reporting entities must calculate their profit or loss using an accrual system of accounting. However, the accrual system focuses on when a transaction takes place (i.e. the sale) and not when the payment for that transaction occurs. In contrast, the statement of cash flows is concerned with cash receipts and payments, and not the timing of the underlying transaction.

This difference is highlighted in example 5.1. The statement of profit or loss reports a profit of $9 400, while the statement of cash flows reports that the net cash provided by operating activities for the reporting period is ($5 000). Why the difference?

EXAMPLE 5.1

Difference in profit and cash position

× × × Pty Ltd Statement of profit or loss for the month of July 2020		
Income		$24 000
Cost of sales		6 600
Gross profit		**17 400**
Expenses		
Rent	$2 000	
Wages	5 000	
Depreciation	1 000	8 000
Profit		**$9 400**

× × × Pty Ltd Statement of cash flows for the month of July 2020			
Beginning cash balance			$2 000
Cash flows			
Receipts from sales		$10 000	
Payments for inventory	($8 000)		
Payments for rent	(2 000)		
Payments for wages	(5 000)	(15 000)	
Net cash flows			(5 000)
Closing cash balance			($3 000)

According to the statement of profit or loss the entity made a profit of $9 400 for the month of July 2020. The statement of profit or loss reflects the transactions for the month, which included sales of products worth $24 000 ($10 000 of which has been collected), rent paid of $2 000 and wages paid of $5 000. The depreciation relates to shop fixtures and fittings the entity has been depreciating over a period of time. The entity also purchased and paid for $8 000 worth of products from its supplier, but the cost of the products sold during the month amounted to $6 600. (The other $1 400 will form part of inventory and be recorded as an asset on the balance sheet.) The statement of cash flows shows that the entity's cash position is negative $3 000 (i.e. the bank account is in overdraft) at the end of July 2020, despite having a $2 000 credit balance at the beginning of the month.

A comparison of the two statements shows that, although the business was quite profitable for the month of July, the business will have trouble meeting its financial obligations. This illustrates the importance of the statement of cash flows: it allows users of the statement to quickly see what money is coming in and how the money is being used. The following statements demonstrate that, although income of $24 000 was generated, only $10 000 of the sales were collected in cash during the period. It also demonstrates that, while depreciation is an expense incurred by the entity, it does not involve an outflow of cash and, as such, is a non-cash item. Business needs to address the collection of debts if the entity is going to survive and meet its financial obligations when they fall due. A quick glance at the statement of cash flows can show a user if an entity has a good cash position or not. In general, for an entity to survive, the net cash flows from operating activities should be positive.

The time between the payments of inventory, wages and so on and the collection of debts is called the operating cash cycle. By minimising this time an entity can save on funding costs (i.e. interest). Prudent companies tightly manage their working capital requirements and their operating cash cycle. Companies such as supermarket have a positive operating cash cycle.

This means they collect funds from sales/accounts receivable prior to paying their accounts payable. So rather than paying funding costs through this period they are earning interest on funds collected prior to paying their accounts payable. This can be a great competitive advantage over rival companies.

> ### REAL WORLD
>
> **Global liquidity crisis**
>
> Cash and access to funding is important for every individual and every business. It is also important for countries. The credit expansion in 2007-2008 and the subsequent global financial crisis in 2009 have highlighted which governments have been managing their country's liquidity and solvency needs. During 2010-2011 the Bank of England, the US Federal Reserve, the Bank of Japan and the European Central Bank borrowed heavily to inject funding into their economies. Bank bailouts were common place and in most of these countries people rioted in the streets against their government's austerity measures that would force sacrifices and a downgrade of living standards on the general population. In 2013, Cyprus's financial crisis saw bank closures and the European Monetary Fund stepping in to help stop contagion to other countries.
>
> Despite the GFC occurring seven years ago, the world's economy still hasn't recovered.

The statement of cash flows is needed as it summarises the cash and types of cash flows coming into and flowing out of the entity. The balance sheet does show the beginning and ending cash balances, but the statement of cash flows shows the various categories of cash flows. For instance, if the entity received cash from bank loans but no cash was coming into the entity through normal operations, it would indicate to a user that it would not be a good business to invest in. Likewise, if ample cash was coming in through the entity's normal operations and it therefore had no need for cash from borrowing, it would indicate to a user that it would be a good entity to invest in.

The importance of cash to the ongoing survival of a business cannot be overstated. An entity needs to have enough ready cash to ensure that it can meet its financial obligations in a timely manner, yet not too much — there are costs associated with keeping a supply of ready cash (e.g. interest payments on debt, or lost investment opportunities). The ability of an entity to manage the flow of cash in and out of the business is critical for success. Paying for supplies, converting sales into cash and paying for assets are central to managing a business. Entities can be quite profitable and yet still falter due to poor cash management.

5.2　The main features of the statement of cash flows

The statement of cash flows is a summary of the cash receipts and payments over the period concerned. All payments of a particular type, for example cash payments to acquire additional non-current assets or other investments, are added together to give just one figure that appears in the statement. The net total of the statement is the net increase or decrease of the cash (and cash equivalents) of the business over the period.

The statement is basically an analysis of the business's cash (and cash equivalents) movements for the period.

A definition of cash and cash equivalents

Cash is defined as notes and coins in hand and deposits in banks and similar institutions that are accessible to the business on demand. **Cash equivalents** are short-term, highly liquid investments that are readily convertible to known amounts of cash and which are subject to an insignificant risk of changes of value. Cash equivalents are held for the purpose of meeting short-term cash commitments rather than for investment or other purposes.

For example a bank deposit and an overdraft on the business's bank current account would be included in the figure for cash and cash equivalents. Although the overdraft has negative amount of cash. If a company acquired some ordinary shares in Stock Exchange because the company has a temporary cash surplus and its directors believed that the share represents a good short-term investment. The funds invested will need to be used in the short term for operating purposes. This is nota cash equivalent. Although the investment was made as part of normal cash management, there is a significant risk that the amount expected when the shares are sold may not actually be forthcoming.

Whether a particular item falls within the definition of cash and cash equivalent depends on two factors:
- the nature of the item;
- why it has arisen.

The relationship between the main financial statements

The financial statements comprise:

1. the statement of profit or loss and statement of comprehensive income — which show the results of an entity's performance for the reporting period.

2. the balance sheet — which shows the entity's financial position at a particular point in time.

3. the statement of changes in equity — which shows the change in an entity's equity between two reporting periods

4. the statement of cash flows — which shows the entity's cash inflows, outflows and net cash flow for the reporting period.

The statement of cash flows was introduced because the statement of profit or loss and balance sheet did not provide a complete picture of an entity's economic activities. That is, a statement of profit or loss summarised the entity's income and expense transactions but did not identify the flow of funds relating to those transactions; and a comparison of successive balance sheets would show the change in cash position from one point in time to another, but would not expose the cash flows associated with that change. Cash flows refer to the movement of cash resulting from transactions with external parties. As discussed in chapter 3, the balance sheet lists the assets (investing decisions) and the liabilities and equity (financing decisions) of the entity. The statement of cash flows also helps to identify changes in balance sheet items. For example, the sale or purchase of an asset for cash would have an effect on both the balance sheet and the statement of cash flows. Similarly, borrowing money and paying a dividend to the owners of the entity are examples of transactions that affect both statements.

The statement of cash flows along with the income statement and the statement of financial position, as a major financial statement. The relationship between the three statements is shown in figure 5.2.

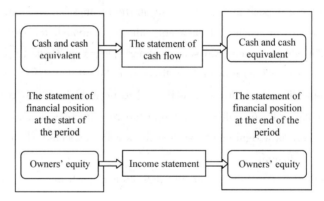

FIGURE 5.2 The relationship between the statement of financial position, the income statement and the statement of cash flows

So, the purpose of a statement of cash flows is to give information additional to that provided by the other statements. Generally, the information provided should assist decision makers in assessing an entity's ability. Together, the statement of profit or loss and the balance sheet (based on accrual accounting) and the statement of cash flows provide a rich source of information regarding the profitability, liquidity and stability of an entity.

The classification of cash flows

Cash flows from operating activities

This is the net inflow or outflow from trading operations, after tax payments (or receipts)

and cash paid to meet financing costs. It is equal to the sum of cash receipts from trade receivables, and cash receipts from cash sales where relevant, less the sums paid to buy inventories, to pay rent, to pay wages and so on. From this are also deducted payments for interest on the business's borrowings, corporation tax and dividends paid.

Note that it is the amounts of cash received and paid during the period that feature in the statement of cash flows, not the revenue and expenses for that period. It is, of course, the income statement that deals with the revenue and expenses. Similarly the tax and dividend payments that appear in the statement of cash flows are those made in the period of the statement. Companies normally pay tax on their profits in four equal installments. Two of these are during the year concerned, and the other two are during the following year. As a result, by the end of each accounting year, one half of the tax will have been paid and the remainder will be a current liability at the end of the year, to be paid off during the following year. During any particular year, therefore, the tax payment would normally equal 50 per cent of the previous year's tax charge and 50 per cent of that of the current year.

The net figure for this section is intended to indicate the net cash flows for the period that arose from normal day-to-day trading activities after taking account of the tax that has to be paid on them and the cost of servicing the finance (equity and borrowings) needed to support them.

Cash flows from investing activities

This section of the statement is concerned with cash payments made to acquire additional non-current assets and with cash receipts from the disposal of non-current assets. These non-current assets will tend to be the usual items such as buildings and machinery. They might also be loans made by the business or shares in another company bought by the business.

This section also includes cash receipts arising from financial investments (loans and equities) made outside the business. These receipts are interest on loans made by the business and dividends from shares in other companies that are owned by the business.

Cash flows from financing activities

This part of the statement is concerned with the long-term financing of the business. So here we are considering borrowings (other than very short term) and finance from share issues. This category is concerned with repayment/redemption of finance as well as with the raising of it. It is permissible under IAS 7 to include dividend payments made by the business here, as an alternative to including them in "Cash flows from operating activities" (above).

This section shows the net cash flows from raising and/or paying back long-term finance.

Net increase or decrease in cash and cash equivalents

The total of the statement must, of course, be the net increase or decrease in cash and cash equivalents over the period concerned.

TABLE 5.1　Activity classification in the statement of cash flows

	Cash inflows	Cash outflows	Link to other statements
Operating activities	• Receipts from customers • Interest received • Dividends received	• Payments to suppliers and employees • Interest paid • Taxes paid	• Revenue and expense items in the statement of profit or loss and current assets and current liabilities in the balance sheet
Investing activities	• Sale of property, plant and equipment • Receipt of loan payments • Sale of other businesses	• Purchase of property, plant and equipment • Making loan repayments • Purchase of other businesses	• Non-current assets in the balance sheet
Financing activities	• Borrowing cash • Proceeds from issuing shares	• Repaying borrowed cash • Payments to acquire or redeem the entity's shares • Payment of dividends	• Non-current liabilities and equity in the balance sheet

The normal direction of cash flows

Various activities of the business each have their own effect on its cash and cash equivalent balances, either positive (increasing them) or negative (reducing them). The net increase or decrease in the cash and cash equivalent balances over a period will be the sum of these individual effects, taking account of the direction (cash in or cash out) of each activity.

Normally "operating activities" provide positive cash flows, that is, they help to increase the business's cash resources. In fact, for most businesses, in most time periods, cash generated from day-to-day trading, even after deducting tax, interest and dividends, is overwhelmingly the most important source of new finance.

If a company show a negative cash flow from operating activities in its statement of cash flow, what could be the reason for this and should the business's management be alarmed by it?

The two reasons are:

- The business is unprofitable. This leads to more cash being paid out to employees, to suppliers of goods and services, for interest and so on, than is received from trade receivables in respect of sales. This would be particularly alarming, because a major expense for most businesses is depreciation of non-current assets. Since depreciation does not lead to a cash flow, it is not considered in "net cash inflows from operating activities". This means that, a negative operating cash flow might well indicate a very much larger trading loss — in other words, a significant loss of the business's wealth; something to concern management.

- The other reason might be less alarming. A business that is expanding its activities (level of sales revenue) would tend to spend quite a lot of cash relative to the amount of cash coming in from sales. This is because it will probably be expanding its assets (non-current and current) to accommodate the increased demand. For example, a business may well need to have inventories in place before additional sales can be made. Similarly staff have to be employed and paid. Even when the additional sales are made, those sales would normally be made on credit, with the cash inflow lagging behind the sale. All of this means that, in the first instance, in cash flow terms, the business would not necessarily benefit from the additional sales revenue. This is particularly likely to be true of a new business, which would be expanding inventories and other assets from zero. It would also need to employ and pay staff. Expansion typically causes cash flow strains for the reasons just explained. This can be a particular problem because the business's increased profitability might encourage a feeling of optimism, which could lead to lack of attention being paid to the cash flow problem.

Investing activities typically cause net negative cash flows. This is because many types of non-current asset wear out, and many that do not wear out become obsolete. Also, businesses tend to seek to expand their asset base. When a business sells some non-current assets, the sale will give rise to positive cash flows, but in net terms the cash flows are normally negative with cash spent on new assets outweighing that received from disposal of old ones.

Financing activities can go in either direction, depending on the financing strategy at the time. Since businesses seek to expand, there is a general tendency for this area to lead to cash coming into the business rather than leaving it.

REAL WORLD

The summarised statement of cash flows of Tesco plc, the UK-based supermarket.

Like many larger companies, Tesco produces summary versions of its financial statements for users who do not want all of the detail. The summary statement of cash flows for the business for the year ended 28 February 2009 shows the cash flows of the business under each of the headings described above.

Tesco plc Summarised statement of cash flows for the year ended 28 February 2009	
Cash generated from operations	$4 978
Interest paid	(562)

	Continued
Corporation income tax paid	(456)
Net cash from operating activities	**3 960**
Net cash used in investing activities	**5 974**
Cash flows from financing activities	
Dividends paid	(883)
Other net cash flows from financing activities	4 498
Net cash from financing activities	**3 615**
Net increase in cash and cash equivalents	$1 601

Source: *Tesco Annual Review* 2009, p. 24, *www.tescocorporate.com*.

Presentation of the statement of cash flows

The statement of cash flows can be completed by bringing together all the sections and calculating the net increase or decrease in cash for the reporting period and ending cash balance for the year. The ending cash balance should equate with the cash amount appearing in the balance sheet. The statement of cash flows contains:

- net cash flows from operating activities
- net cash flows from investing activities
- net cash flows from financing activities
- total net cash flow (increase or decrease in cash held for the period)
- the beginning cash balance
- the ending cash balance
- comparative figures from the previous year.

5.3 Preparing the statement of cash flows

The statement of cash flows can be prepared by analysing the cash receipts and payments records or by evaluating the statement of profit or loss and balance sheet.

Normally, an entity will collect information regarding its business transactions based on the accrual method of accounting. The reasons for this generally relate to the appropriate recognition of all transactions affecting income, expenses, assets, liabilities and equity for a given period. Recording transactions in this way helps in the preparation of the statement of profit or loss and the balance sheet. Given that the statement of cash flows is concerned with when receipts and payments are made and not with the recognition of income and expense transactions, there will need to be some adjustments made to the information collected.

Therefore, in preparing the statement of cash flows there needs to be a conversion from the accrual basis to the cash basis. This conversion can be approached in one of two ways. These are the direct method or the indirect method.

The direct method discloses major classes of gross cash receipts and gross cash payments. It is an analysis of the cash records of the business for the period, picking out all payments and receipts relating to operating activities. These are summarised to give the total figures for inclusion in the statement of cash flows.

The indirect method adjusts profit or loss for the effects of transactions of a non-cash nature and deferrals or accruals of operating revenue and expenses. The International Financial Reporting Standards (IFRS) give an entity a choice between presenting cash flows from operating activities using the direct or indirect methods.

Deducing net cash flows from operating activities

Within a particular accounting period, profit for the year will not normally equal the net cash inflows from operating activities. When sales are made on credit, the cash receipt occurs some time after the sale. This means that sales revenue made towards the end of an accounting year will be included in that year's income statement, but most of the cash from those sales will flow into the business, and should be included in the statement of cash flows, in the following year. Fortunately it is easy to deduce the cash received from sales if we have the relevant income statement and statements of financial position, as we shall see in example 5.2.

EXAMPLE 5.2

Reconciliation using indirect method

The relevant information from the financial statements of Dio plc for last year is as follows:

	$
Profit before taxation (after interest)	**122**
Depreciation charged in arriving at profit before taxation	34
Interest expense	6
At the beginning of the year:	
Inventories	15
Trade receivables	24
Trade payables	18
At the end of the year:	
Inventories	17

	Continued
	$
Trade receivables	21
Trade payables	19
The following further information is available about payments during last year:	
	$
Taxation paid	32
Interest paid	5
Dividends paid	9
The cash flow from operating activities is derived as follows:	
	$
Profit before taxation (after interest)	122
Depreciation	34
Interest expense	6
Increase in inventories (17 – 15)	(2)
Decrease in trade receivables (21 – 24)	3
Increase in trade payables (19 – 18)	1
Cash generated from operating activities	**164**
Interest paid	(5)
Taxation paid	(32)
Dividends paid	(9)
Net cash from operating activities	**118**

The indirect method of deducing the net cash flow from operating activities is summarized as following formula:

Net cash from operating activities = Profit or loss after tax + Non-cash expenses +/ – Changes in non-current assets and liabilities

Note that:
- Increase in current assets means a reduction in cash
- Decrease in current assets means an increase in cash
- Increase in current liabilities means an increase in cash
- Decrease in current liabilities means a decrease in cash

Deducing the other areas of the statement of cash flows

Now we can go on to take a look at the preparation of a complete statement of cash flows through example 5.3.

EXAMPLE 5.3

Preparing the cash flow statement by indirect method

Tesco plc's income statement for the year ended 31 December 2020 and the statements of financial position as at 31 December 2020 and they are as follows:

Tesco plc Income statement for the year ended 31 December 2020	
Revenue	$576
Cost of sales	(307)
Gross profit	**269**
Distribution expenses	(65)
Administrative expenses	(26)
	178
Other operating income	21
Operating profit	**199**
Interest receivable	17
	216
Interest payable	(23)
Profit before taxation	**193**
Taxation	(46)
Profit for the year	**147**

Tesco plc Statements of financial position as at 31 December 2019 and 2020		
	2019	2020
Assets		
Current assets		
Trade receivables	$121	$139
Inventories	44	41
Total current assets	**165**	**180**
Non-current assets		
Plant, property and equipment		
Land and buildings	241	241

Continued

	2019	2020
Plant and machinery	309	325
Total non-current assets	**550**	**566**
Total assets	**715**	**746**
Current liabilities		
Borrowings (all bank draft)	68	56
Trade payables	55	54
Taxation payables	16	23
Total current liabilities	**139**	**133**
Non-current liabilities		
Borrowings-Loan notes	400	250
Total non-current liabilities	**400**	**250**
Total liabilities	**539**	**383**
Equity		
Contributed equity	150	200
Reserves-share premium	0	40
Retained earnings	26	123
Total equity	**176**	**363**

During 2020, the business spent $95 million on additional plant and machinery. There were no other non-current asset acquisitions or disposals. A dividend of $50 million was paid on ordinary shares during the year. The interest receivable revenue and the interest payable expense for the year were equal to the cash inflow and outflow respectively. The statement of cash flows would be as follows:

Tesco plc	
Statement of cash flows for the year ended 31 December 2020	
Cash flow from operating activities	
Profit before taxation	$193
Adjustment for:	
Depreciation[1]	79
Interest receivable	(17)
Interest payable	23

	Continued
Increase in trade receivables (139 – 121)	(18)
Decrease in trade payables (55 – 54)	(1)
Decrease in inventories (44 – 41)	3
Cash generated from operations	**262**
Interest paid	(23)
Taxation paid[2]	(39)
Dividend paid	(50)
Net cash from operating activities	**150**
Cash flows from investing activities	
Payments to acquire tangible non-current assets	(95)
Interest receivable	17
Net cash from investing activities	**(78)**
Cash flows from financing activities	
Payment of loan notes (250 – 400)	(150)
Issue ordinary shares (200 + 40 – 150)	90
Net cash from financing activities	**(60)**
Net increase in cash and cash equivalents	**12**
Cash and cash equivalents at 1 January 2020[3]	**(68)**
Cash and cash equivalents at 31 December 2020	**56**

Notes:

1. Since there were no disposals, the depreciation charges must be the difference between the start and end of the year's plant and machinery (non-current assets) values, adjusted by the cost of any additions.

Carrying amount at 1 January 2020	$309
Additions	95
	404
Depreciation (balancing figure)	(79)
Carrying amount at 31 December 2020	325

2. Taxation is paid by companies 50 per cent during their accounting year and 50 per cent in the following year. As a result the 2020 payment would have been half the tax on the profit (that is, the figure that would have appeared in the current liabilities at the end of 2019), plus half of the 2020 taxation charge (that is, $16 + (1/2 \times 46) = 39$). Probably the easiest way to deduce the amount paid during the year to 31 December 2019 is by following this approach:

Taxation owed at start of the year (from the statement of financial position as at 31 December 2019)	$16
Taxation charge for the year (from the income statement)	46
	62
Less Taxation owed at the end of the year (from the statement of financial position as at 31 December 2020)	(23)
Taxation paid during the year	39

3. There were no "cash equivalents", just cash (though negative).

5.4 Explanation of the statement of cash flows

The statement of cash flows tells us how the business has generated cash during the period and where that cash has gone. Since cash is properly regarded as the lifeblood of just about any business, this is potentially very useful information.

Tracking the sources and uses of cash over several years could show financing trends that a reader of the statements could use to help to make judgements about the likely future behaviour of the business.

Looking specifically at the statement of cash flows for Tesco plc, in example 5.3, we can see the following:

- Net cash flow from operations was strong, much larger than the profit for the year figure, after taking account of the dividend paid. This would be expected because depreciation is deducted in arriving at profit. Working capital has absorbed some cash, which would be unsurprising if there had been an expansion of activity (sales revenue) over the year. From the information supplied, however, we do not know whether there was an expansion or not. (We have only one year's income statement.)
- There were net outflows of cash for investing activities, but this would not be unusual. Many items of property, plant and equipment have limited lives and need to be replaced with new ones. The expenditure during the year was not out of line with the depreciation expense for the year, which is not unusual for a business with a regular replacement program for non-current assets.
- There was a fairly major outflow of cash to redeem some borrowings, partly offset by the proceeds of a share issue. This presumably represents a change of financing strategy. Together with the ploughed-back profit from trading, there has been a significant shift in the equity/borrowings balance.

Generally, an analysis of the statement of cash flows would include an identification of cash-flow warning signals. These would include the following.

- Cash received is less than cash paid. Overall the cash inflows should be greater than

the cash outflows, otherwise there would be a depletion of cash on hand over time.
- Operating outflows. The cash flows from operating activities represent the cash flows from normal business operations. This is an important measure to gauge the entity's ability to generate cash, meet its obligations, carry on as a going concern and to expand. If an entity has negative cash flows from operations, it might have difficulty in meeting its finance and investing obligations.
- Cash receipts from customers are less than cash payments to suppliers and employees. This could indicate that insufficient cash is being generated from the entity's operations. Possible reasons for this situation include the entity under pricing its goods, having too few sales, or not being paid by its customers. In any case, immediate action is warranted for the entity's long-term survival.
- Net cash from operating activities is lower than profit after tax. Profit includes non-cash items such as depreciation, so generally cash from operating activities should be higher.
- Proceeds of share capital are used to finance operating activities. Once again, this indicates that the entity might be having difficulty meeting its financial obligations.
- Inflows from investing activities are inconsistent. Generally, spending cash on investments (outflow) indicates a healthy growth entity. It is these investments that will generate future cash flow. Inconsistent inflows from investing activities would mean that the entity is selling off major assets, indicating that it is downsizing or needing to sell assets to pay debts.
- Proceeds from borrowing are continually much greater than the repayment of borrowings. If proceeds from borrowings are significantly greater than the repayment of borrowings over a long period, it might indicate that borrowings are continually being used to finance investment and operations. Again, it is important for the cash flow from operations to be positive to ensure the entity's long-term survival.

SUMMARY

1. Assess the purpose and usefulness of a statement of cash flows.

The purpose of a statement of cash flows is to show the cash flows of an entity over a set period, in order to assess an entity's ability to generate cash and to meet future obligations. The heightened awareness of the management of earnings in the statement of profit or loss has elevated the importance of reviewing the statement of cash flows in conjunction with the statement of profit or loss.

2. Outline the format and the classification of cash flows in the statement of cash flows.

The statement of cash flows presents the beginning and ending cash balances and the cash inflows and outflows of a reporting period. The cash inflows and outflows are classified into operating, investing and financing activities. A reconciliation of cash from operating activities with the profit in the statement of profit or loss is presented in a note to the accounts.

3. Produce a statement of cash flows using the direct method and a reconciliation using the indirect method.

Cash flows from operating activities are determined by examining the income and expenses in the statement of profit or loss and the non-current assets and non-current liabilities in the balance sheet. Cash flows from investing activities are determined from changes in balance sheet items dealing with non-current assets. Cash flows from financing activities are determined from changes in balance sheet items associated with non-current liabilities and equity.

KEY TERMS

Cash 现金
Cash equivalents 现金等价物
Cash flows 现金流
Cash inflows 现金流入
Cash on hand 库存现金
Cash outflows 现金流出
Direct method 直接法
Financing activities 融资活动
Indirect method 间接法
Investing activities 投资活动
Operating activities 经营活动
Statement of cash flows 现金流量表
Working capital 营运资金

SELF-EVALUATION ACTIVITIES

5.1　Single choice questions

1. Which of the following events would have different immediate effects on cash and profits? (　　)

　　(a) Repayment of a loan;
　　(b) Making a share issue for cash;
　　(c) Depreciating a non-current asset;
　　(d) Making a sale on credit;
　　(e) All of the above.

2. The payment of borrowings interest would be an example of (　　)

(a) An investing activity;
(b) An operating activity;
(c) A financing activity;
(d) A non-cash financing activity;
(e) None of the above.

3. The primary purpose of a Cash Flow Statement is to (   )

(a) Provide information about cash receipts and cash outflows during an accounting period;
(b) Give a more accurate picture of profitability than that able to be shown by an Income Statement;
(c) Computer what the net profit would have been if the firm had used cash-basis, rather than accrual-basis, accounting;
(d) Present the cash flow per share for the company;
(e) None of the above.

4. Calculate wages paid for the year ended 30 June 2020 if unpaid wages at 30 June 2019 and 30 June 2020 are $10 080 and $15 120, respectively, and wages expense for the year ended 30 June 2020 is $201 600. (   )

(a) $206 640;
(b) $176 400;
(c) $196 560;
(d) $226 800;
(e) None of the above.

5. Cash Flow Statement provides information that allows user to make more detailed judgements about (   )

(a) Liquidity;
(b) Financial performance;
(c) Financial position;
(d) Financial stability;
(e) None of the above.

5.2 True or false

1. Profit does not generally equate to net cash generated due to the application of accrual accounting principles.   (   )

2. Purchasing inventory for cash has the effect of decreasing cash, but has no immediate effect on profit.   (   )

3. Cash Flow Statement are primarily useful for assessing the profitability of a business.
                                                                                                                                                                                               (   )

4. For the purposes of the Cash Flow Statement, the concept of "cash" includes both cash and cash equivalents.   (   )

5. Collections of interest revenue are classified as operating activity inflows.   (   )

5.3 Listed below are transactions that occurred in the current financial year for a company. Classify each transaction into an operating, investing or financing activity, or a non-cash transaction. If it is a cash transaction, indicate whether it is a cash inflow or a cash outflow.

a. Paid dividend of $10 million to shareholders.

b. Collected $356 000 from a major accounts receivable.

c. Recorded depreciation of $32 000 for some equipment.

d. Paid $150 000 to a supplier.

e. Acquired a parcel of land in exchange for some shares.

f. Received a dividend from an investment in another company.

g. Paid yearly insurance by cash.

h. Purchased a new truck for $50 000 cash.

i. Sold a major piece of equipment for cash.

j. Paid salaries and wages.

Answer to self-evaluation activities

5.1 Single choice questions

1. e   2. b   3. a   4. a   5. a

5.2 True or false

1. T   2. T   3. F   4. T   5. T

5.3 Solution

Transaction	Classification	Inflow/outflow
a. Paid dividend of $10 million to shareholders	Financing	Outflow
b. Collected $356 000 from a major account receivable	Operating	Inflow
c. Recorded depreciation of $32 000 for some equipment	Non-cash	Not recorded
d. Paid $150 000 to a supplier	Operating	Outflow
e. Acquired a parcel of land in exchange for some shares	Non-cash	—
f. Received a dividend from an investment in another company	Investing/operating	Inflow
g. Paid yearly insurance by cash	Operating	Outflow
h. Purchased a new truck for $50 000 cash	Investing	Outflow
i. Sold a major piece of equipment	Investing	Inflow
j. Paid salaries and wages	Operating	Outflow

CHAPTER 6

Analysis of Financial Statements

LEARNING OBJECTIVES

After studying this chapter, you should be able to:
6.1 explain different requirements of information users to the financial statements
6.2 describe the nature and purpose of financial analysis
6.3 apply the major analytical methods of horizontal, trend, vertical and ratio analysis
6.4 define, calculate and interpret the financial ratios of profitability, efficiency and liquidity
6.5 calculate and interpret the key ratios that measure capital structure and market performance
6.6 discuss the limitations of ratio analysis.

In earlier chapters, the various financial statements were introduced. A fundamental purpose of preparing these statements is to provide useful information to assist users in their decision making. The financial data in these statements are expressed in monetary terms, with corresponding figures for the comparative year provided. To better understand the consequences of an entity's operating, investing and financing decisions, it is necessary to analyse the relationships between the numbers in the financial statements, rather than relying on the absolute values in one particular period or a particular statement.

Fundamental analysis refers to analysing many aspects of an entity to assess the entity. Fundamental analysis involves reviewing the state of the industry in which the entity operates, as well as the entity's financial statements, its management and governance, and its competitive positioning. While fundamental analysis is conducted on historical data and current information, the purpose of the analysis is to make predictions about the entity's future.

Financial analysisis major aspect of fundamental analysis. Financial analysis uses the reported financial numbers to calculate and interpret financial ratios. When interpreting a ratio, it is important to understand what the ratio is measuring and to compare it to an appropriate benchmark. This chapter describes an entity's profitability, efficiency, liquidity, capital structure and market performance with a real listed company, JB Ltd's financial statements.

6.1 Assist financial statements users to make decisions

Users and their decision making

The users of financial statements can be classified as resource providers (e.g. creditors, lenders, shareholders and employees), recipients of goods and services (e.g. customers and debtors), and parties performing an overview or regulatory function (e.g. the taxation office, corporate regulators, or a statistical bureau). It is important that different user groups are interested in different aspects of the entity, and various information sources are available to interested parties to facilitate their decision making.

Various information sources include the financial press, trade-related magazines, research reports from broking houses, industry publications, online databases, and government statistics. Another important source of information is financial statements. With a knowledge and understanding of information contained in financial statements, financial analysis can provide information specific to the users' needs. Financial analysis is an analytical method in which reported financial numbers are used to form opinions as to the entity's past and future performance and position.

The decisions that users make vary. For example, creditors would be interested in the entity's ability to pay the debts within the credit period provided. A financial institution contemplating a loan to an entity would be interested in the ability of the entity to generate cash flows to settle the loan over the loan period. A shareholder or potential investor is interested in the ability of an entity to generate profits that allow it to distribute dividends and/or retain the profits to invest, with the expectation of capital appreciation in its share price. Employees are concerned about being paid for services rendered and long-term job security, so they would be interested in the entity's liquidity and profitability. Although the rules for determining taxable income and accounting profit differ, the Taxation Office relies on financial numbers generated from the accounting information system in its assessments of tax payable. Management also uses financial statements in their day-by-day decision-making.

Statement users generally share a common objective: to evaluate past decisions and make informed decisions about future events. In this sense, reported financial numbers have a role to play. Financial analysis is an important decision-making tool for evaluating the historical health of an entity and predicting an entity's future financial wellbeing. The reality check "Weekly recommendation, target price, earnings forecast changes" discusses the role of financial analysis in share recommendation decisions.

> **REAL WORLD**
>
> **Weekly recommendation, target price, earnings forecast changes**
>
> FN Arena monitors recommendations for shares by eight leading stockbrokers on a daily basis. The following are examples of the weekly reporting of share recommendation upgrades and downgrades.
>
> Myer was upgraded to Buy from Hold, with Deutsche Bank lifting its call on the belief that the market still had a steady appetite for discretionary retailer stocks. In this case, Myer represented the best opportunity, given a reasonable valuation and strong, free cash flow. The company was also delivering like-for-like sales growth and was addressing structural issues, said Deutsche. Macquarie lifted its recommendation on Qantas from Hold to Buy. Qantas was lifted on an improving capacity outlook, the broker having more confidence in the industry outlook and believing that earnings margins were moving back to a more normal rate. Virgin Australia was also upgraded, the broker suspecting that Virgin was increasingly challenging Qantas's position in the business class and regional markets. Sentiment was positive for both.
>
> National Australia Bank was upgraded to Buy by Macquarie, but downgraded to Hold from Sell by CIMB. Macquarie noted that institutional and corporate borrowing appeared to be improving in the mining states, with signs of improving demand for equipment finance. Macquarie believed that access to credit might become easier in the second half of the year, which would mean higher earnings. Meanwhile, CIMB was taking a look at bank sector net interest margins for FY13 – 15 and found that risks remained skewed to the downside. While NAB's dividend yield to the Australian government bond yield was supportive, the broker thought that the more fundamental valuations, like NAB's, looked stretched.
>
> Orton Group (ORL) was cut to Hold from Buy by Credit Suisse. The half-year results were below Credit Suisse's forecasts and the outlook appeared more challenging than previously expected. The earnings outlook was affected mainly by the loss of the Ralph Lauren licence. Credit Suisse estimated an $18 million negative earnings impact in FY14. Sentiment moved to neutral on the downgrade.
>
> *Source*: Nelson, A 2013, "Weekly recommendation, target price, earnings forecast changes", FN Arena (Australia), 2 April.

Nature and purpose of financial analysis

Financial analysis involves expressing reported numbers in financial statements in relative terms. Relying on the absolute values contained in the financial statements is not meaningful when trying to evaluate an entity's past decisions and predict future rewards and risks. For example, if you are examining an entity's statement of profit or loss and note that the profit figure has increased from $200 000 in the previous year to $300 000 in the current year, does this mean that the entity has become more profitable? Similarly, if the entity's interest-bearing liabilities have increased from $1 million to $2 million, does this mean that the entity has become more reliant on external funding? The answer to both of these questions is "not necessarily". The entity's absolute dollar values of profit and external debt have increased, but this does not necessarily mean that the entity is more profitable or more reliant on debt. For example, if the entity's asset base increased twofold over the comparative period — from $2 million to $4 million — then the profit generated when expressed per dollar of investment in assets would have fallen. Likewise, if an increase in assets of $2 million was funded by only $500 000 of interest-bearing liabilities, the entity's reliance on external debt relative to equity would have fallen.

Similar analogies can be drawn when comparing two entities. For example, just because Entity A reports a profit of $50 000 and Entity B reports a profit of $10 000, this does not necessarily make Entity A more profitable relative to Entity B. Entity A's absolute dollar value of profit is indeed larger, but it is not possible to make an informed judgement on the relative profitability without comparing the profit generated to the resources available to generate it (e.g. the investment in assets).

These examples emphasise the need to express the reported numbers in relation to other numbers, enabling relationships to be revealed and the financial statements to describe the entity's financial health. Therefore the comparing figures are necessary. It includes the equivalent figures from previous years and other related figures in the financial statements. The process of comparison can be categorised as horizontal analysis, trend analysis, vertical analysis and ratio analysis.

6.2 Analytical methods

This section introduces the analytical techniques of horizontal, trend, vertical and ratio analysis. This chapter focuses on ratio analysis, but horizontal, trend and vertical analysis are important complementary tools to ratio analysis. All analytical methods involve comparing one item in the financial statements with another.

Horizontal analysis

Horizontal analysis compares the reported numbers in the current period with the equivalent numbers for a previous period, usually the immediate preceding period. Financial statements are usually presented in a two-column format containing the figures for the current reporting period and the figures for the comparative reporting period. This permits the user to readily calculate the absolute dollar change and the percentage change in the reported numbers between periods. The percentage change is calculated as shown in the following equation:

Current period's number less previous period's number/Previous period's number × 100

The percentage change cannot be calculated if the equivalent reported figure for the previous year was zero. Care must also be exercised when ascertaining and interpreting the direction of the change. For example, if expenses or cash outflows are greater in the current year than in the previous year, the direction of the change is upwards, but this has a negative rather than a positive impact on reported profit or cash flows.

The 2020 and 2019 balance sheets, statement of profit or loss and statements of cash flows for JB Ltd are provided in table 6.1 to 6.3 respectively. (The statements of comprehensive income and statements of changes in equity have not been provided in this chapter.) Note that JB Ltd's annual reports are available from the company's website. Information in these statements and supporting notes will be used throughout the chapter to illustrate concepts as they are introduced. The columns headed A and B are the absolute dollar figures in the financial statements. The column headed C shows the change in the absolute dollar amount from 2014 to 2015, and the column labeled D represents the percentage change in the reported amounts from 2014 to 2015. From an inspection of the financial statements, it is easy to identify which reported numbers have increased or decreased. By performing horizontal analysis, the magnitude and significance of the dollar changes becomes apparent.

We can see in table 6.1, JB Ltd's total assets increased by $35.2 million (4 per cent), total liabilities decreased by $13.7 million (2 per cent), and equity increased by $48.9 million (17 percent). There are some items that in absolute dollar terms appear to have changed significantly, but the percentage change is relatively small. Similarly, there are some items that in percentage terms appear to have changed significantly, but the absolute dollar change is relatively small. Columns C and D provide insights not easily revealed by columns A and B. The horizontal analysis reveals that JB Ltd was holding more cash and cash equivalents as at 30 June 2020 than at the same time in 2019 (up $5.7 million, 13 per cent) and more trade and other receivables (up $10.7 million, 15 per cent), while the change in most other asset classes were less than 5 per cent. Trade and other payables increased by $22.6 million (7 per cent). JB Ltd reduced its reliance on borrowings in 2020 relative to 2019, with borrowings down $40.2 million (22 per cent). As shown, horizontal analysis identifies significant changes between reporting periods, alerting the user to matters that warrant further investigation.

TABLE 6.1 JB Ltd balance sheet

	Consolidated		Change	
	A 2020 $'00	B 2019 $'000	C $'000	D %
Current assets				
Cash and cash equivalents	49 131	43 445	5 686	13
Trade and other receivables	81 480	70 745	10 735	15
Inventories	478 871	458 625	20 246	4
Other current assets	7 416	5 332	2 084	39
Total current assets	**616 898**	**578 147**	**38 751**	**7**
Non-current assets				
Plant and equipment	176 208	181 564	(5 356)	(3)
Deferred tax assets	17 363	14 909	2 454	16
Intangible assets	84 541	85 218	(677)	(1)
Other financial assets	3	3	0	0
Total non-current assets	**278 115**	**281 694**	**(3 579)**	**(1)**
Total assets	**895 013**	**859 841**	**35 172**	**4**
Current liabilities				
Trade and other payables	325 604	302 979	22 625	7
Provisions	40 585	36 840	3 745	10
Other current liabilities	4 566	4 111	455	11
Current tax liabilities	9 474	8 184	1 290	16
Other financial liabilities	107	79	28	35
Total current liabilities	**380 336**	**352 193**	**28 143**	**8**
Non-current liabilities				
Borrowings	139 461	179 653	(40 192)	(22)
Provisions	6 073	8 699	(2 626)	(30)
Other non-current liabilities	25 664	24 638	1 026	4
Other financial liabilities	0	25	(25)	(100)
Total non-current liabilities	**171 198**	**213 015**	**(41 817)**	**(20)**
Total liabilities	**551 534**	**565 208**	**(13 674)**	**(2)**
Net assets	**343 479**	**294 633**	**48 846**	**17**
Equity				
Contributed equity	56 521	58 383	(1 862)	(3)
Reserves	17 636	16 265	1 371	8
Retained earnings	269 322	219 985	49 337	22
Total equity	**343 479**	**294 633**	**48 846**	**17**

Source: Adapted from JB Ltd 2020, *preliminary final report*, p. 58.

TABLE 6.2 JB Ltd statement of profit or loss

	Consolidated		Change	
	A 2020 $'00	B 2019 $'000	C $'000	D %
Revenue	3 652 136	3 483 775	168 361	5
Cost of sales	(2 853 883)	(2727 794)	126 089	5
Gross profit	798 253	755 981	42 272	6
Other income	631	520	111	21
Sales and marketing expenses	(374 084)	(355 694)	18 390	5
Occupancy expenses	(160 216)	(148 969)	11 247	8
Administrative expenses	(27 711)	(27 600)	111	1
Other expenses	(35 414)	(32 716)	2 698	8
Finance costs	(5 927)	(8 845)	(2 918)	(33)
Profit before tax	195 532	182 677	12 855	7
Income tax expense	(59 021)	(54 230)	4 791	9
Profit for the year	136 511	128 447	8 064	6
Attributable to:				
Owners of the company	136 511	128 359	8 152	6
Non-controlling interests	—	88	88	100
	136 511	128 447	8 064	6
Earnings per share				
Basic (cents per share)	137.91	128.39	9.52	7
Diluted (cents per share)	136.46	126.89	9.57	8

Source: *Adapted from JB Ltd* 2020, *preliminary final report*, *p.* 56.

Columns C and D of table 6.2 respectively show the dollar change and percentage change for items affecting JB Ltd's profit.

Analysing the change in the numbers reported in the cash flow statement (table 6.3) reveals that JB Ltd's cash at the end of the 2020 year was $5.7 million higher (up 13 per cent) than it was at the start of the year. Net cash flows from operating activities increased by $138.6 million (335 percent). Investing activities used net cash in 2020 of $44.4 million compared to $38.2 million in 2019, an increase of $6.1 million (16 per cent). JB Ltd's payments for property, plant and equipment were higher in 2020 relative to 2019. The company's financing activities in 2020 resulted in a net outflow of $129.6 million compared to a net outflow in 2019 of $27.6 million (up $102.0 million). This increase in outflow relates to the repayment of borrowings.

TABLE 6.3 JB Ltd statement of cash flows

	Consolidated		Change	
	A 2020 $'00	B 2019 $'000	C $'000	D %
Cash flows from operating activities				
Receipts from customers	4 012 120	3 832 979	179 151	5
Payments to suppliers and employees	(3 767 211)	(3 723 982)	43 229	1
Interest and bill discounts received	552	402	150	37
Interest and other costs of finance paid	(5 689)	(7 496)	(1 807)	(24)
Income taxes paid	(59 886)	(60 577)	(691)	(1)
Net cash inflow from operating activities	**179 896**	**41 326**	**138 570**	**335**
Cash flows from investing activities				
Acquisition of non-controlling interest	(2 400)	(3 000)	(600)	(20)
Payments for property, plant and equipment	(42 466)	(35 914)	6 552	18
Proceeds from sale of plant and equipment	496	674	(178)	(26)
Net cash (outflow) from investing activities	**(44 370)**	**(38 240)**	**6 130**	**16**
Cash flows from financing activities				
Proceeds from issues of equity securities	3 125	21 523	(18 398)	(85)
Proceeds/(repayment) of borrowings	(40 113)	54 063	(94 176)	(174)
Payments for debt issue costs	(484)	(64)	(420)	(656)
Payments for shares bought back	(4 970)	(25 830)	20 860	80
Share issue and buy-back costs	(24)	(118)	(94)	(80)
Dividends paid to owners of the company	(87 174)	(77 183)	9 991	(13)
Net cash (outflow) from financing activities	**(129 640)**	**(27 609)**	**102 031**	**370**
Net increase (decrease) in cash and cash equivalents	5 886	(24 523)	30 509	124
Cash and cash equivalents at the beginning of the financial year	43 445	67 368	(23 923)	(36)
Effect of exchange rate changes on cash and cash equivalents	(200)	600	(800)	(133)
Cash and cash equivalents at the end of year	49 131	43 445	5 686	13

Source: *Adapted from JB Ltd* 2020, *preliminary final report*, p. 60.

Trend analysis

Trend analysis tries to predict the future direction of various items on the basis of the direction of the items in the past. To calculate a trend, at least three years of data are required. A public company often provides a historical summary of various financial items in its annual report. The sales revenue, earnings before interest and taxation (EBIT), and profit after tax data for JB Ltd for 2010 to 2020 are provided in table 6.4. To identify the trends in these data over the six-year period, it is useful to convert the numbers into an index. Using 2015 as the base year, and setting the base year at an index of 100, every subsequent figure is expressed relative to the base year (i.e. relative to 2015). For example, to calculate the trend in sales revenue, the following calculations are made.

Step 1: Set 2015 as the base year, assigning it a commencing index value of 100.

Step 2: Divide the 2016 revenue by the 2015 revenue, and express this as an index by multiplying the answer by 100:

$$\$2\,959.3 \text{ million} / \$2\,731.3 \text{ million} \times 100 = 108$$

Step 3: Divide the 2017 revenue by the 2015 revenue, and express this as an index by multiplying the answer by 100:

$$\$3\,127.8 \text{ million} / \$2\,731.3 \text{ million} \times 100 = 115$$

Step 4: Each subsequent year's sales revenue is divided by the 2015 sales revenue and expressed as an index by multiplying the answer by 100.

Analysing the trend figures in table 6.4 identifies that sales revenue has increased each year during 2015 – 2020. In 2016 and 2017, EBIT and profit after tax declined, but have since trended upwards.

TABLE 6.4 Trends in sales revenue, EBIT and profit after tax figures for JB

Absolute figures $m	2020	2019	2018	2017	2016	2015
Sales revenue	$3 652.1	$3 483.8	$3 308.4	$3 127.8	$2 959.3	$2 731.3
EBIT	189.6	191.5	178.2	161.4	162.6	175.1
Profit after tax	136.5	128.4	116.6	104.6	109.7	118.7
Trend analysis						
Sales revenue	134	128	121	115	108	100
EBIT	108	109	102	92	93	100
Profit after tax	115	108	98	88	92	100

Trend figures can be graphed to visually depict the direction and magnitude of financial items of interest. For example, the graph of the trends in JB Ltd's sales revenue, EBIT and profit after tax for the period 2015 to 2020 is shown in figure 6.1. As we will see later in the chapter, examining trends in financial ratios — instead of focusing only on trends calculated on absolute dollar values — is an important analytical tool as such trends are useful in formulating predictions. For example, the graph in figure 6.1 depicts that the growth in sales revenue outstrips the growth in EBIT and profit after tax. This suggests that JB Ltd's sales volume and revenue has not increased at a greater rate than the increase in the operating and financing costs of the business and hence the trend in profits is not as positive as the trend in sales.

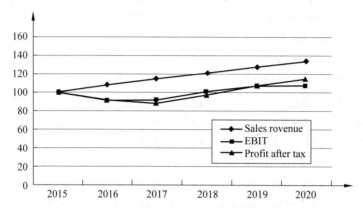

FIGURE 6.1   Graph of trends in JB Ltd sales revenue, EBIT and profit after tax for 2015-2020

Vertical analysis

Vertical analysis is another method of converting the absolute dollar values in financial statements into more meaningful figures. Whereas horizontal analysis compares reported figures over time, vertical analysis compares the items in a financial statement to other items in the same financial statement. When expressed in this way, the financial statements are often referred to as "common size" statements. This involves using a reported item as an anchor point against which other items are compared.

When performing vertical analysis on the statement of profit or loss, the anchor point is the revenue figure, and every item in the statement of profit or loss is expressed as a percentage of the income item. When performing vertical analysis on the balance sheet, the anchor point is the total asset figure, and every item in the balance sheet is expressed as a percentage of the total asset figure. The concept of vertical analysis is illustrated in table 6.5 and 6.6 for JB Ltd.

TABLE 6.5   Vertical analysis of a balance sheet: JB Ltd

	Notes	Consolidated	
		2020 $'000	% relative to total assets
Current assets			
Cash and cash equivalents		49 131	5
Trade and other receivables	9	81 480	9

Continued

	Notes	Consolidated	
		2020 $'000	% relative to total assets
Inventories	10	478 871	54
Other current assets	14	7 416	1
Total current assets		616 898	69
Non-current assets			
Plant and equipment	12	176 208	20
Deferred tax assets	13	17 363	2
Intangible assets	14	84 541	9
Other financial assets		3	0
Total non-current assets		278 115	31
Total assets		895 013	100
Current liabilities			
Trade and other payables	15	325 604	36
Provisions	16	40 585	5
Other current liabilities	17	4 566	1
Current tax liabilities		9 474	1
Other financial liabilities		107	0
Total current liabilities		380 336	42
Non-current liabilities			
Borrowings	18	139 461	16
Provisions	19	6 073	1
Other non-current liabilities	20	25 664	3
Other financial liabilities		0	0
Total non-current liabilities		171 198	19
Total liabilities		551 534	62
Net assets		343 479	38
Equity			
Contributed equity	21	56 521	6
Reserves	22	17 636	2
Retained earnings		269 322	30
Total equity		**343 479**	**38**

Source: Adapted from *JB Ltd* 2020, *preliminary final report*, p. 58.

TABLE 6.6 Vertical analysis of a statement of profit or loss: JB Ltd

	Note	Consolidated 2020 $'000	% Relative to revenue
Revenue	3	3 652 136	100
Cost of sales		(2 853 883)	78
Gross profit		798 253	22
Other income		631	1
Sales and marketing expenses		(374 084)	10
Occupancy expenses		(160 216)	4
Administrative expenses		(27 711)	1
Other expenses		(35 414)	1
Finance costs	4	(5 927)	1
Profit before tax		**195 532**	5
Income tax expense	5	(59 021)	1
Profit for the year		**136 511**	4

Source: Adapted from JB Ltd 2020, preliminary final report, p. 56.

The vertical analysis of the statement of profit or loss highlights the importance of an item relative to the revenue figure. Each item in the statement is divided by the revenue figure and expressed as a percentage of that figure. In table 6.6, the anchor point for the vertical analysis of the statement of profit or loss is revenue ($3 652.1 million). The gross profit and profit before tax are 22 per cent and 5 per cent respectively, suggesting that every dollar of sales generates on average 22 cents of gross profit and 5 cents of profit before tax. Aside from the cost of sales, the main expenses of the entity are sales and marketing expenses, constituting 10 per cent of revenue. This suggests that JB Ltd spends around 10 cents of every sales dollar on sales and marketing.

Ratio analysis

Ratio analysisis an important aspect of the financial analysis. A ratio is simply a comparison of one item in a financial statement relative to another item in a financial statement— one item is divided by another to create the ratio. **Ratio analysis** examines the relationship between two quantitative amounts with the aim of expressing the relationship in ratio or percentage form.

The amounts compared do not necessarily have to be in the same statement, because it is often meaningful to compare items in the statement of profit or loss or statement of cash flows to those in the balance sheet. However, comparisons between these statements are not always straight forward, because the statement of profit or loss and statement of cash flows involve **flow items** that are generated over a period of time, whereas the balance sheet reports **stock items** at a point in time. For example, consider an entity that generated a profit of $50 000. The entity's investment in assets is $500 000 for the majority of the reporting period, but rises to $1 000 000 following the purchase of an asset close to reporting year-end. For the majority of the year, the entity had investments of $500 000 from which to generate profit. If the $50 000 profit generated over the year is compared to the assets at the end of the year (i.e. $1 000 000), the profit per dollar of investment will be understated and not reflect the fact that the $1 000 000 investment existed for only a small portion of the year. As a result, when calculating ratios involving a comparison of a "stock" and a "flow" item, the average of the "stock" item during the year is often used instead of the year-end figure. To calculate the average, the beginning year value and ending year value are added, with the sum being divided by 2. The ratio calculations in this chapter use average balances when comparing stock and flow items. For simplicity, often the year-end balance of stock items is used in ratio analysis.

Ratio analysis is a three-step process.

1. Calculate a meaningful ratio by expressing the dollar amount of an item in a financial statement by the dollar amount of another item in a financial statement.

2. Compare the ratio with a benchmark.

3. Interpret the ratio and seek to explain why it differs from previous years, from comparative entities or from industry averages.

The purpose of ratio analysis is to express a relationship between two relevant items that is easy to interpret and compare. In this chapter, the ratios will be categorised into five groups:

- profitability ratios. The profitability ratios inform users as to the profit associated with their equity investment.
- efficiency ratios. The efficiency ratios shed light on management's effectiveness in managing the assets entrusted to it.
- liquidity ratios. An entity's ability to meet its short-term commitments is indicated by liquidity ratios, while its long-term stability and financing decisions are reflected in capital structure ratios.
- capital structure ratios.
- market performance ratios or market test ratios. It generally requires share price data. For this reason, they are usually confined to listed companies, relating the company's financial numbers to its share price, and indicate the market's sentiment towards the company.

Benchmarks

Just as a financial number expressed as an absolute dollar amount is limited for decision-making purposes, a ratio is of limited usefulness unless it is compared to a relevant benchmark.

Ratios are useful when the returns and risks for entities over time are compared with those of entities in different industries or with those of entities in the same industry. Comparing the ratio with a benchmark enables the favourableness or otherwise of the ratio to be assessed. The various comparisons that can be made include the following.

1. *A comparison of the entity's ratios over time to identify trends.* This permits users to assess the stability and/or directional changes in the ratios over time. Unfavourable trends should be investigated by financial statement users.

2. *A comparison of the entity's ratios with those of other entities operating in the same industry, referred to as intra-industry analysis.* For example, a potential investor who wishes to invest in banking shares has identified four entities operating in that economic industry sector. The investor can use ratios to compare their respective returns and risks.

3. *A comparison of the entity's ratios with the industry averages.* An industry norm is a relevant benchmark that enables a user to assess a particular entity's return and risk relative to its competitors, to determine if it is outperforming or lagging behind its peers. Industry averages for various economic industry sectors are available through commercial databases.

4. *A comparison of the entity's ratios with those of entities operating in different industries or with the norms of other industries, referred to as inter-industry analysis.* Caution is needed when such an analysis is being undertaken as differences in industry structures will affect the ratios.

5. *A comparison of the entity's ratios with arbitrary standards.* It is not possible to specify what a ratio should be, but users operate on rules of thumb that serve as crude points of initial assessment. For example, a rule of thumb may be that a debt to equity ratio should not exceed 100 per cent. However, given that the 100 per cent is arbitrary, if an entity has a higher ratio than this, it cannot be concluded that the ratio is unsatisfactory and the entity is in financial distress.

When comparing an entity's ratios over time or across industries, it is assumed that industry and entity risk remain constant. If risk changes, returns should also change. Caution needs to be exercised when comparing entities within the same industry, as no two entities have identical products and product markets. Similarly, caution is needed when judging the favourableness of an entity's ratio with that of entities in other industries as industry characteristics affect ratios. For example, a supermarket's gross profit generated per dollar of sales revenue would be substantially lower than that of a car manufacturer.

Financial ratios are also affected by an entity's accounting policy choices and assumptions. Before comparing the ratios for different entities, the consistency in the accounting policies and assumptions of the entities should be reviewed. Similarly, before comparing an entity's ratios over time, the consistency of that entity's accounting policy choices and assumptions should be checked. For example, an entity that revalues its property, plant and equipment (PPE) may generate lower returns from its assets relative to an entity that measures its PPE at cost, presuming that the value of PPE assets is increasing.

In the remainder of this chapter, we will calculate these ratios with 2015 JB Ltd financial statements, compare them with relevant benchmarks, and interpret the ratios. The comparative benchmark will be the ratio for the previous year. Other comparisons could include competitors' ratios such as those of other listed companies operating in the consumer retail industry, or industry averages. Through the ratio analysis comes from interpreting and interrelating the ratios to answer the "why" questions — for example, why did profitability decline? Why has liquidity improved? Why is the entity's efficiency declining?

6.3 Profitability analysis

An entity's ability to generate profits and return on investment is one of the prime indicators of its financial health.

Return on equity

Owners are interested in the return that the entity is generating for them. This test of an entity's performance is the **return on equity** (**ROE**). The return on equity, expressed as a percentage, is computed by relating the profit that the entity has generated for its owners during the period to the owners' investments in the entity. For a non-company entity, the ROE is the profit available to the owners divided by the owners' equity in the business. When calculating the ROE for a company, we are interested in the profit available to the ordinary equity holders of the parent entity relative to the ordinary shareholders' equity in the company. The equity comprises any capital invested, retained earnings and reserves.

$$\text{Profit available to owners/Average equity} \times 100 = x\%$$

Profit is the current year's profit available for distribution to the owners. The numerator, profit, is obtained from the statement of profit or loss. The denominator, equity, is obtained from the equity section of the balance sheet. When analysing a company, some analysts exclude the impact of significant items, which can distort the ratio by their size or nature and so distort the trends in the ratio over time. It is also necessary to exclude any dividends due to preference shareholders (should they exist), as the preference shareholders are entitled to receive their dividends before any distributions of profit can be made to ordinary shareholders. The equity figure before minority interests and preference capital is obtained from the balance sheet. As the numerator of this ratio is a flow item and the denominator is a stock item, the stock item is averaged by summing the balance at the start and end of the reporting period and dividing this by 2. This assumes that any change between opening and closing balances occurred evenly throughout the reporting period.

The ROE indicates the annual return that the entity is generating for owners for each dollar of owners' funds invested in the entity. It is advantageous for this ratio to show an upward trend overtime. However, a sustained high ROE will attract new competitors to the industry and eventually erode excess ROE. The adequacy of the ROE is assessed by comparing it with the returns on alternative investment opportunities (of equivalent risk) available to owners. An inability to generate an adequate ROE will restrict an entity's capacity to attract new capital investment and adversely affect its ability to be sustainable in the long term.

The ROE is a ratio that reflects an entity's profitability, efficiency and capital structure. Changes in the ratio over time, and differences in the ratio across entities, will reflect the direction of an entity's profitability, asset efficiency and capital structure.

Return on assets

The **return on assets (ROA)** is a profitability ratio that compares an entity's profit to the assets available to generate the profits. Effectively, the ratio reflects the results of the entity's ability to convert sales revenue into profit, and its ability to generate income from its asset investments. In the numerator, profit or the EBIT figure can be used. For the purpose of our analysis, the profit figure is used. The ratio can be calculated including (or excluding) the effect of significant items from the profit figure. The ratio is calculated as:

$$\text{Profit (loss)/Average total assets} \times 100 = x\%$$

Given that the ROA reflects an entity's profitability (ability to convert income dollars into profit) and asset efficiency (ability to generate income from investments in assets), the change in the ROA can be explained by changes in the entity's profitability and asset efficiency. The profitability ratios that reflect the ability of the entity to generate profits from income include the gross profit margin and the profit margin, as discussed below.

Profit margin ratios

Ratios that relate profit to sales revenue generated by the entity include the gross profit margin and the profit margin. The gross profit margin compares an entity's gross profit to its sales revenue, reflecting the proportion of sales revenue that results in gross profit. Given that gross profit is sales revenue less cost of sales, 100 per cent less the gross profit margin is the cost of sales as a percentage of sales revenue. The gross profit margin calculation is:

$$\text{Gross profit/ Sales revenue} \times 100 = x\%$$

Both the numerator and denominator are sourced from the statement of profit or loss. The gross profit margin reflects the gross profit (in cents) generated per dollar of sales revenue and reflects an entity's pricing strategy. It is not possible to specify a gross profit range that would be desirable. This is because the gross profit is interrelated with sales volume. Entities with high (low) turnover tend to have smaller (larger) gross margins. For example, the gross margin for a supermarket is between 2 and 5 per cent. This is sustainable given the high volume turnover of a supermarket. However, a gross profit margin of between 2 and 5 per cent would not be satisfactory for a manufactory, as the volume of trade would not justify such a low margin.

An entity must meet all other expenses from its gross profit. The comparison of sales revenue and profit is referred to as the **profit margin**. This ratio reveals what percentage of sales revenue dollars results in profit (loss). As with the ROA, it is not uncommon to see the profit margin computed with EBIT rather than profit (loss) as the numerator. Any change in the profit margin over time must be attributable to changes in the gross profit margin and/or changes in the expenses as a percentage of sales (**expense ratios**). The ratio is calculated as:

$$\text{Profit (loss)/Sales revenue} \times 100 = x\%$$

This ratio measures the relative amount of cash flow generated by each sales revenue dollar. It is useful to compare this ratio with the equivalent accrual-based ratio, namely, the profit margin. The ratio is calculated as:

$$\text{Cash flow from operating activities/Sales revenue} \times 100 = x\%$$

Analysis of profitability

In this section we will show the profitability ratios for JB Ltd for the 2020 and 2019 reporting periods, interpret the information that they convey and comment on their adequacy. The profitability ratios for JB Ltd for 2019 and 2020 are presented in table 6.7.

TABLE 6.7 Analysis of JB Ltd's profitability (all numbers are in $000s)

	2020 (%)	2019 (%)
Return on equity (ROE)	42.79	47.71
Return on assets (ROA)	15.56	15.08
Gross profit margin	21.86	21.70
Profit margin	3.74	3.69
Cash flow to sales	4.93	1.19
Expense ratios		
Sales and marketing	10.24	10.21
Occupancy	4.39	4.28
Administrative	0.76	0.79
Finance	0.16	0.25
Other	0.97	0.94
Total expenses	16.52	16.47

The profitability ratios for JB Ltd show improvement from 2019 to 2020 even with expense ratios trending up. As shown in table 6.7, in 2020 relative to 2019, the ROE declined to 42.79 per cent from 47.71 per cent. While the numerator, profit, was higher in 2020 relative to 2019, the denominator, equity, was larger in 2020 than 2019. An investment of $1 of shareholders' equity in 2020 returned 42.79 cents of earnings available for distribution to shareholders. In 2019, an equivalent investment generated 47.71 cents of earnings available for distribution to shareholders. The decline in the ROE is not due to a decline in the ROA. JB Ltd generated 15.56 cents of profit per dollar of investment in assets in 2020; its profit-generating ability was lower in 2019 when $1 of investment in assets generated 15.08 cents of profit. Increased profitability and asset efficiency can contribute to an ROA improvement.

In terms of profitability, JB Ltd's gross profit margin was higher than 20 per cent in both years. This reflects the company's low pricing strategy. The gross profit margin for JB Hi-Fi Ltd increased slightly, with $1 of sales revenue in 2020 resulting in 21.86 cents of gross profit (21.70 cents in 2019). If $1 of sales revenue resulted in 21.86 cents (21.70 cents) of gross profit in 2020 (2019), the cost of sales must therefore have accounted for 78.14 cents of each sales dollar in 2020 (78.30 cents in 2019). This suggests that either input prices decreased, and/or JB Ltd increased selling prices more in 2020 than in 2019. The change in the gross margin could also reflect a change in the mix of products sold by JB Ltd. Some product categories would have higher margins relative to those of other product categories. Selling a higher proportion of higher margin products would be beneficial to JB Ltd's gross profit margin. For example, the establishment of their online store could have changed the product mix.

JB Ltd converted $1 of sales revenue into 3.69 cents of profit in 2019, and this increased to 3.74 cents in 2020. Users would have been pleased with this improved profit margin. The profit margin for an entity is a function of the industry it operates in. Low-volume businesses have higher profit margins while high-volume businesses tend to operate with lower profit margins. The increase in profit margin reflects the company's higher gross profit margin in 2020 relative to 2019. The profit margin is also affected by expense ratios, so attention now turns to these.

An entity's expenses (excluding the cost of sales) can be expressed (in aggregate or individually) as a percentage of sales revenue to determine which expenses have increased or decreased relative to sales revenue. From JB Ltd's statement of profit or loss (table 6.2), the sum of the entity's sales and marketing, occupancy, administration, significant items and other expenses totaled $603 352 000 in 2020 ($573 824 000 in 2019). Expressed relative to sales revenue, these expenses represent 16.52 cents of every sales dollar in 2020 (16.47 cents in 2019). This analysis identifies that JB Ltd's costs were a higher proportion of revenue in 2020 relative to 2019. All expense ratios increased in 2020 relative to 2019 except for administrative and finance expenses. The increase in the occupancy expense ratio reflects the growth in the number of stores. JB Ltd also spent a higher percentage of sales revenue on sales and marketing expenses in 2020 compared to 2019, reflecting the competitive nature of this industry. The decrease in the finance expense ratio, with finance costs representing 0.16 cents (0.25 cents) of $1 of revenue in 2020 (2019), was due to lower borrowings as well as lower interest rates.

The cash to sales ratio for JB Ltd suggests that every dollar of sales revenue generated 4.93 cents of net operating cash flows in 2020, compared to 1.19 cents in 2019. Any improvement in this ratio is favourable, although cash flow timing affects this ratio.

6.4 Asset efficiency analysis

Asset turnover ratio

Entities invest in assets in anticipation that the investment will generate returns. **Asset efficiency ratios** measure the effectiveness of an entity in generating sales revenue due to investments in current and non-current assets. An entity's overall efficiency in generating income per dollar of investment in assets is referred to as the **asset turnover ratio**. The asset turnover ratio is calculated as:

$$\text{Sales revenue/Average total assets} = x \text{ times}$$

An entity's asset efficiency, as depicted by the asset turnover, will depend on the efficiency with which it manages its current and non-current investments. A large component of an entity's investments in assets that requires significant management is inventory and accounts receivable. It is therefore useful to assess management's efficiency in managing these assets, and this is done by calculating the entity's inventory and accounts receivable turnover. The accounts receivable turnover is also referred to as the debtors turnover. A largely cash-based service business, such as Advantage Tennis Coaching introduced earlier in the text, does not have inventory and debtors to manage, so these ratios are not as applicable to such an entity.

Days inventory and days debtors ratios

The days inventory indicates the average period of time it takes for an entity to sell its inventory. The days debtors indicates the average period of time it takes for an entity to collect the money from its trade-related accounts receivable. Funds invested in inventory and accounts receivable are earning a zero rate of return, so it is advantageous for an entity to turn over its inventory and accounts receivable as quickly as possible (i.e. convert them into sales revenue and receive the cash). Accordingly, lower days inventory and days debtors generally reflect better management efficiency. However, lower days inventory could also suggest that the entity is carrying insufficient levels of inventory. The calculation of these ratios is as follows.

Days inventory: (Average inventory/Cost of sales) $\times 365 = x$ days

Days debtors: (Average trade debtors/Sales revenue) $\times 365$ days $= x$ days

It is common to calculate the number of times per annum that the inventory (times inventory turnover) and trade debtors (times debtors turnover) are turned over, rather than the number of days this occurs. The calculations are as follows.

Times inventory turnover: Cost of sales/ Average inventory $= x$ times

Times debtors turnover: Sales revenue/Average trade debtors $= x$ times

The higher the times turnover ratios, the more efficient an entity would appear to be in converting inventory and accounts receivable to cash. It should be noted that dividing the times inventory turnover and times debtors turnover into the number of days per annum (365) will yield the days inventory ratio and days debtors ratio respectively. For the purpose of our analysis, we will refer to the turnover in days rather than times.

It is not possible to prescribe what an appropriate days inventory ratio is, as it will vary according to the type of inventory being sold. For example, a supermarket would have a significantly faster inventory turnover than an exclusive car store. Remember, however, that a supermarket's gross margin would be significantly lower than that of the car store.

Similarly, the appropriateness of the days debtor turnover depends on the credit terms offered by the entity. Accounts receivable arise as a result of credit sales. Note that sales revenue from both cash and credit sales is used in the ratio calculation, as entities do not disclose the cash and credit components of sales. It would be expected that an entity offering its customers 30-day settlement terms would have a longer days debtors compared with an entity offering credit terms of only ten days. A 30-day settlement term means that the customer is expected to pay within 30 days of the end of the purchase month. If purchasing goods on the first day of the month, the customer effectively receives 60 days' credit. As an arbitrary rule of thumb, the days debtors is expected to be around 1.3 times the settlement terms offered by the entity. When analysing an entity's efficiency in managing its debtors and inventory, concerns would be raised if the ratios showed an upward trend.

The days inventory and days debtors turnovers in conjunction to reflect the entity's activity cycle (also referred to as the operating cycle). If an entity sells only on credit terms, then summing the days inventory and days debtors will reflect the average period of time it takes to convert inventory into cash (the activity cycle). As inventory can be purchased on credit terms, there is often a delay between receiving the inventory and paying for the inventory (this is referred to as days creditors). This is why the activity cycle is longer than the cash cycle.

A period of time elapses between an entity paying for the inventory, selling the inventory, and receiving cash for the inventory. This period is the cash cycle. During this time, the entity is effectively financing the investment in inventory and incurring negative cash flows. Suppose that an entity's days inventory is 45 days, with days debtors of 55 days and days creditors of 25 days. Its activity cycle (example 6.1) and cash cycle are 100 days and 75 days, respectively. The length of the activity and cash cycle will have a significant impact on the entity's liquidity position. Given that the entity has to finance the investment in inventory and debtors, the shorter the activity cycle, the better the entity's efficiency and liquidity.

EXAMPLE 6.1

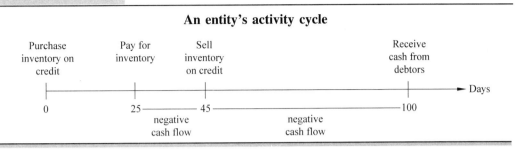

Analysis of asset efficiency

Asset efficiency ratios measure the efficiency with which an entity manages its current and non-current investments and converts its investing decisions into sales dollars. The ratios for JB Ltd are presented in table 6.8.

JB Hi-Fi Ltd's ability to convert a dollar investment in assets into sales revenue dollars has marginally declined over the two years. In 2020, an investment of $1 in assets generated $4.16 of sales revenue, compared to $4.09 in 2019.

TABLE 6.8 Analysis of JB Ltd's assets efficiency

	2020	2019
Asset turnover ratio	4.16 times	4.09 times
Days inventory	60 days	59 days
Days debtors	8 days	7 days

Note: The inventory includes the current portion of finished goods, raw materials and work in progress.

When calculating the days debtors, only the gross value of current trade-related debtors should be included in the numerator. Recall that the gross value of debtors is the value prior to the deduction of the allowance for impairment losses. In 2020, JB Ltd took on average 60 days to sell its inventory items — one day more than the average days taken in 2019. The suitability of this ratio needs to be considered in light of the industry average. JB Ltd is a high-volume business and the company relies on turning over its inventory quickly. A quick turnover of inventory is imperative for a business that sells perishable inventory such as fresh items. While this same imperative does not exist for JB Ltd, it requires high turnover to maintain low margins and to ensure that its inventories do not become obsolete.

JB Ltd's business is predominantly cash based and so the management of trade receivables is not as critical as it would be for a business that sells on credit terms. Calculating the debtors turnover (days) using gross trade receivables rather than trade and other receivables, the turnover of eight days in 2020 and seven days in 2019 highlights the predominance of cash sales in the business. As stated in the notes to the company's accounts, JB Ltd does sell some goods on credit with a 30-day credit period and no interest charged on trade receivables. With inventory turning over on average every 60 days and most sales being cash sales, JB Ltd asset efficiency is strong and its activity cycle is relatively short. A short activity cycle provides liquidity to the business.

6.5　Liquidity analysis

An entity's inability to pay its debts when they fall due can result in creditors taking legal action against the entity to recover their monies. The survival of the entity therefore depends on its ability to pay its debts when they fall due. This ability to discharge short-term cash flow obligations is referred to as an entity's liquidity. A number of ratios can be calculated to determine an entity's liquidity. Because liquidity is a measure of events over the short term, the ratios concentrate on an entity's current assets and current liabilities. The excess from current assets and current liabilities is referred to as an entity's working capital. An entity must have sufficient working capital to satisfy its short-term requirements and obligations. However, excess working capital is undesirable because the funds could be invested in other assets that would generate higher returns.

Current ratio and quick ratio

The current ratio and quick ratio are commonly used to assess an entity's liquidity position. The ratios are calculated as follows.

Current ratio: Current assets/Current liabilities = x times

Quick ratio: (Current assets – inventory)/Current liabilities = x times

The **current ratio** (also referred to as the working capital ratio) indicates the dollars of current assets the entity has per dollar of current liabilities. It is undesirable to have a ratio that is too low, as this suggests that the entity will have difficulty in meeting its short-term obligations. However, a high current ratio is not necessarily good, as it could be due to excess investments in unprofitable assets — cash, receivables or inventory.

The **quick ratio** (also referred to as the acid-test ratio) measures the dollars of current assets available (excluding inventory) to service a dollar of current liabilities. It is a more stringent test of liquidity, as it excludes current inventory from the numerator. Inventory is excluded because it is the current asset that takes the longest period of time to convert to cash.

The difference between the current and quick ratios will be significant for manufacturing and retail entities with large inventory holdings, but insignificant for entities that are in service-related industries.

When assessing the current ratio, an arbitrary rule of thumb is that it should be around $1.50 of current assets for every $1 of current liabilities. The arbitrary benchmark ratio for the quick ratio is around $0.80 of current assets (excluding inventory) for every $1 of current liabilities. In calculating the quick ratio, bank overdrafts can be deducted from the denominator. This is done in recognition that bank overdrafts are permanent sources of funding to an entity, but are classified as current because they are repayable on demand. Similarly, prepayments can be deducted from the numerator because they will not produce a cash inflow. A ratio that is higher (lower) than the arbitrary ratios should not be interpreted as a positive (negative) signal. The adequacy of the liquidity ratios needs to be assessed in conjunction with the entity's activity cycle. A short activity cycle will support a lower level of liquidity, whereas a longer activity cycle will require more liquidity.

Cash flow ratio

Another ratio that helps to assess liquidity is the cash flow ratio. Based on net cash flows from operating activities, the cash flow ratio indicates an entity's ability to cover its current obligations from operating activity cash flows. The higher the ratio, the better the position of the entity to meet its obligations. It is argued that the cash flow ratio is a better measure of liquidity than the current ratio, because it uses cash flows generated over a whole reporting period rather than the current assets at a particular point in time. The ratio is calculated as follows:

Net cash flows from operating activities/Current liabilities = x times

Analysis of liquidity

JB Ltd's current ratio, quick ratio and cash flow ratio (liquidity) for 2020 and 2019 are presented in table 6.9.

JB Ltd had $1.64 of current assets for every $1 of current liabilities in 2019. This decreased to $1.62 of current assets for every $1 of current liabilities in 2020. As JB Ltd has a relatively short activity cycle, the company can operate with lower levels of liquidity. Given that JB Ltd has a large investment in inventories, the quick ratio should be significantly lower than the current ratio. The quick ratio is 0.34 times and 0.36 times in 2019 and 2020 respectively. This suggests that JB Ltd had approximately $0.36 of current assets excluding inventory for every dollar of current liabilities. For a retail operation, this is not unusual. In 2020, JB Ltd had $0.47 of net operating cash flows for every $1 of current liabilities. This significantly increased from $0.12 of net operating cash flows for every $1 of current liabilities in 2019, suggesting that the company has capacity to meet its current obligations from its net operating activities cash flows.

TABLE 6.9 Analysis of JB Ltd's liquidity

	2020	2019
Current ratio	1.62 times	1.64 times
Quick ratio	0.36 times	0.34 times
Cash flow ratio (liquidity)	0.47 times	0.12 times

6.6 Capital structure analysis

An entity's **capital structure** is the proportion of debt financing relative to equity financing, and reflects the entity's financing decision. As per the accounting equation, an entity's assets equal its liabilities plus equity. Investments in assets are funded externally by liabilities, or internally by owner's equity. Expressing any of these three items — assets, liabilities and equity — relative to each other will reveal how an entity has used debt relative to equity to finance assets. **Capital structure ratios** (also referred to as gearing ratios) depict the proportion of debt to equity funding, and are useful when assessing an entity's long-term viability. Achieving a balance between debt and equity funding affects the entity's ROE. The use of debt can be advantageous, as debt funding is cheaper than equity funding. The lower cost of debt reflects:

- the lower returns required by debt holders, given the lower risk borne by debt holders relative to equity holders
- the tax deductibility of interest expense.

However, excessive debt levels can be burdensome for an entity if the cost of servicing the debt exceeds the return generated by investments in assets (i.e. the cost of debt exceeds the return on assets), and this will depress the return on equity. If the debt is being used profitably, and the return on assets financed with debt exceeds the cost of borrowing, then the benefit accrues to the owners in the form of higher returns on equity.

Capital structure ratios

The ratios that reflect an entity's use of debt relative to equity to finance assets are as follows.

Debt to equity ratio: Total liabilities /Total equity × 100 = x%
Debt ratio: Total liabilities /Total assets × 100 = x%
Equity ratio: Total equity/Total assets × 100 = x%

It is necessary to calculate only one of the above three capital structure ratios, as they all indicate the entity's use of debt relative to equity to finance its investments in assets. We will focus on the debt ratio, which indicates how many dollars of liabilities exist per dollar of assets. If this exceeds 50 per cent, then the entity finances its investments in assets by relying more on debt relative to equity. If the debt ratio is less than 50 per cent, then the entity finances more of its assets with equity than with debt. The debt to equity ratio indicates how many dollars of debt exist per dollar of equity financing. If this ratio exceeds 100 per cent, then the entity is more reliant on debt funding than equity funding. The equity ratio suggests the dollars of equity per dollar of assets. If this ratio is less than 50 per cent, then the entity is more reliant on debt funding than equity funding.

Example 6.2 shows these ratios for an entity with $100 million of assets, $70 million of debt and $30 million of equity on its balance sheet. The entity is more reliant on debt relative to equity, as indicated by the ratios. The debt ratio indicates that the entity uses $2.33 of debt per dollar of equity. Other ways of expressing this are: the debt ratio tells us that the entity funds every $1 of assets with $0.70 of debt; and the equity ratio indicates that every $1 of assets is financed by $0.30 of equity. The debt ratio divided by the equity ratio gives the debt/equity ratio, and the sum of the debt ratio and equity ratio equals 100 per cent.

EXAMPLE 6.2

Capital structure ratios measuring the use of debt relative to equity funding

$$\text{Assets} = \text{Liabilities} + \text{Equity}$$
$$\$100 \text{ m} = \$70 \text{ m} + \$30 \text{ m}$$

Capital structure ratios

$$\text{Debt/equity ratio} = 70/30 = 233\%$$
$$\text{Debt ratio} = 70/100 = 70\%$$
$$\text{Equity ratio} = 30/100 = 30\%$$
$$\text{Debt ratio} + \text{equity ratio} = 100\%$$

What is the appropriate level of debt funding relative to equity funding? Debt funding increases an entity's financial risk and the variability of cash flows to equity holders. The ability of an entity to absorb financial risk depends on the variability of its cash flows, which in turn is influenced by the entity's business risk. An entity that operates in a seasonal or risky industry will experience greater variability in its cash flows from operations, and therefore have less ability to assume large financial risk. It is common to find variations in capital structure ratios across industries, but entities within an industry tend to operate at similar gearing levels.

An arbitrary benchmark that is used for a debt ratio is 50 per cent — an entity should use equal portions of debt and equity to finance its assets. This is not to say that a ratio exceeding 50 per cent proves that the entity's long-term financial viability is jeopardised. Many mature entities have debt ratios larger than 50 per cent.

When looking at how an entity has financed assets, the extent of current borrowings should also be examined. An entity that relies on current borrowings needs to refinance on a regular basis, and may face the situation when the current debt is due of the financing not being available or only being available at a higher cost. For example, the global financial crisis made it more difficult for entities to access debt, and entities with short-term debt maturing had difficulty refinancing.

Capital structure ratios (as well as interest coverage ratios) are often used in lending contracts as a means of protecting the lender's wealth. For example, a loan contract could include a covenant specifying that the entity's debt ratio must not exceed 70 per cent. If the entity breaches this covenant by allowing its debt to assets to exceed 70 per cent, the lender has the right to withdraw the loan facility and demand that the entity repay the loan. This illustrates how accounting numbers are used in entities' contractual arrangements. Users should focus on the trend in the ratio as an increasing reliance on debt over a number of years would be of concern. When analysing an entity's capital structure, it is also relevant to examine the type of interest-bearing debt the entity is using, the breakdown of the debt into short and long term, and the maturity structure of the long-term debt.

Interest coverage ratio

The financial risk of the entity can also be assessed using the interest coverage ratio (also referred to as times interest earned). This ratio measures the number of times an entity's EBIT covers the entity's net finance costs. It indicates the level of comfort that an entity has in meeting interest commitments from earnings. The calculation is:

EBIT / Net finance costs = x times

The interest coverage ratio is inversely related to an entity's financial risk. A ratio less than 1 suggests that an entity's net finance costs exceed its EBIT — a situation that is unsustainable in the long run. The interest coverage ratio will exceed 1 so long as the EBIT is greater than net finance costs. As an arbitrary guide, the interest coverage ratio should not be below three times.

Debt coverage ratio

Debt needs to be serviced from cash flow, so it is useful to relate the entity's cash generating capacity to its long-term debt. The debt coverage ratio links the cash flows from operating activities with long term debt, and is found by dividing non-current liabilities by cash from operating activities. It is also a measure of an entity's ability to survive in the longer term and remain solvent, as it indicates how long it will take to repay the existing long-term debt commitments at the current operating level. The ratio is calculated as:

Non-current liabilities / Net cash flows from operating activities = x times

Analysis of capital structure

Table 6.10 reports the capital structure ratios for JB Ltd for 2020 and 2019. It shows that JB Ltd funded every $1 of assets with 62 cents of debt in 2020, compared to 66 cents of debt in 2019. Funding approximately 60 per cent of the assets with debt reflects a medium reliance on debt and suggests that the entity's exposure to financial risk is not high. During recent past years, JB Ltd has pursued a debt reduction strategy with declining long-term borrowings. As revealed by the statement of cash flows, the company was a net borrower in 2019 (cash proceeds from borrowings are shown as $54 062 000), whereas in 2020 JB Ltd repaid more debt than it borrowed (cash repayments associated with borrowings are shown as $40 113 000).

The EBIT of JB Ltd adequately covers its net finance costs, suggesting the company does not have interest-bearing debt that is a financial strain. The interest coverage is a function of interest-bearing liability levels, interest rates and profitability levels. The less reliance on borrowings, combined with higher EBIT, has increased the interest coverage ratio from 21.65 times in 2019 to 34 times in 2020. This means that JB Ltd's EBIT covers its net finance costs about 34 times over, representing more than an adequate safety margin.

TABLE 6.10   Analysis of capital structure ratios for JB Ltd

	2020	2019
Debt ratio	61.62%	65.73%
Interest coverage ratio	34 times	21.65 times
Debt coverage ratio	0.95 times	5.15 times

The cash debt coverage ratio for 2015 indicates that, if JB Ltd maintains its net operating cash flows, it would take the company on average less than one year of operating cash flows to repay its non-current liabilities. This is less than the 5.15 years indicated by the 2014 ratio.

Entities complying with accounting standards disclose further details about their borrowings such as the weighted average interest rate, overdraft facilities and other secured debt. This provides users with further information about entities' debt funding and the facilities available to the entities.

6.7   Market performance analysis

Market performance ratios (also referred to as market test ratios) are most applicable to companies listed on organised securities exchanges as the ratios relate reported numbers to the number of shares on issue or the market price of the share. The ratios we will introduce are ratios that are commonly referred to in the financial press.

Earnings, cash flow and dividend per share

A measure of the profit generated for each ordinary share on issue is the earnings per share. **Earnings per share** (EPS) is the entity's profit expressed relative to the number of ordinary shares on issue. Companies seek to achieve growth in earnings per share as this signals to the market the company's earning ability. Companies are required to disclose their earnings per share at the bottom of their statement of profit or loss, as well as the numerator and denominator used in the calculation. In recognition of the importance of cash flows, the operating **cash flow per share** (CFPS) can be calculated. This ratio reflects the net cash flows from operating activities that are available to pay dividends to shareholders and fund future investments. The difference in the EPS and CFPS highlights the differences that arise from preparing accounts on an accrual rather than a cash basis.

An investment in shares can generate returns in the form of dividends and/or share price appreciation. The dividend per share (DPS) is the former measure of return and indicates the distribution of the company's profits in the reporting period via dividends expressed relative to the number of ordinary shares on issue. Like the EPS, the DPS is reported in a company's financial statements. The formulae below detail the basic calculations for these ratios.

Earnings per share:

$$\frac{\text{Profit available to ordinary shareholders}}{\text{Weighted number of ordinary shares on issue}} = \text{x cents/share}$$

Operating cash flow per share:

$$\frac{\text{Net cash flows from operating activities-Preference dividends}}{\text{Weighted number of ordinary shares on issue}} = \text{x cents/share}$$

Dividend per share:

$$\frac{\text{Dividends paid or provided to ordinary shareholders in the current reporting period}}{\text{Weighted number of ordinary shares on issue}}$$
$$= \text{x cents/share}$$

Dividends can be distributed from current profits or from previous years' profits. Most companies pay a similar dividend each year or distribute a constant percentage of EPS as dividends. Expressing the DPS as a percentage of EPS results in the dividend payout ratio, which indicates the proportion of current year's profits that are distributed as dividends to shareholders. The profit not distributed remains in the entity for reinvestment.

Price earnings ratio

The **price earnings ratio** (PER) is a market value indicator that reflects the number of years of earnings that investors are prepared to pay to acquire a share at its current market price. The formula for the PER is:

$$\frac{\text{Current market price}}{\text{Earnings per share}} = \text{x times}$$

If a company's current market price is $15.00 and its latest reported EPS is $2.50, the reported PER would be six times. This suggests that market participants are prepared to pay six years of current earnings to acquire the company's shares. Price earnings ratios fluctuate as share prices change. The ratios vary across industries and are normally higher for high-growth companies. It is useful to compare the PER of a company with that of its competitors as this highlights the market's assessment of the company's future performance relative to its peers. As a general rule, price earnings ratios for industrial companies are commonly between 10 and 15 times, although this alters according to the strength of the equity market.

Analysis of market performance

Because the market performance ratios are often available in the annual report of listed companies, as well as in the financial press, we will not calculate the past five years ratios for JB Ltd in table 6.11.

TABLE 6.11 Market performance ratios for JB Ltd

	2020	2019	2018	2017	2016	2015
NTAB per share	$2.62	$2.12	$1.61	$1.07	$0.75	$1.93
EPS	$1.36	$1.27	$1.17	$1.06	$1.01	$1.08
Gross cash flow per share	$1.81	$1.67	$1.59	$1.45	$1.52	$1.33
DPS	$0.90	$0.84	$0.72	$0.65	$0.77	$0.66
Dividend payout ratio	65.42%	66.20%	61.53%	61.40%	62.16%	60.87%
PER	14.28	14.42	14.37	8.37	16.88	17.59
Year-end share price	$19.48	$18.30	$16.81	$8.86	$17.07	$19.07

Source: Morningstar 2020, *FinAnalysis of JB Ltd*, www.morningstar.com.au.

The trends in the market performance ratios for JB Ltd are generally positive. The EPS has gone from $1.08 in 2015 to $1.36 in 2020. It is worth noting that JB Ltd repurchased shares in 2016. A reduction in the number of shares on issue will improve any ratio that involves the number of shares in the denominator, all else being equal. The EPS disclosed by JB Ltd at the bottom of its statement of profit or loss is based on the weighted average number of shares on issue during the year as opposed to the number of shares on issue at the end of the year (as in table 6.1). The gross cash flow per share is higher than the EPS, but the gross cash flow ratio reported may not be restricted to operating cash flows only. Cash flow ratios are also generally higher than profit-based ratios because cash flows do not include depreciation and amortisation as these are non-cash flow expenses.

The company's dividend payout ratio hovers around 60 per cent. JB Ltd is distributing more than half of its current reporting period's profit as dividends to its shareholders. The consistency in the payout ratio reflects the company's preference to not significantly vary dividends each year even if profits vary. The price earnings ratio suggests that investors in 2020 were prepared to pay 14.28 years of earnings to acquire a share in JB Ltd. With the exception of 2017, this is lower than the PER in any other year and reflects factors such as lower market sentiment. JB Ltd's share price increased from $19.07 in 2015 to $19.48 in 2020; a recovery on the $8.86 the shares were trading for at the end of June 2012. The total return to shareholders from any share investment is the capital growth plus dividends.

6.8 Ratio interrelationships

Financial analysis is used to assess an entity's financial health, both past and future. The value of conducting ratio analysis, a key tool of financial analysis, is in interpreting ratios and explaining why the ratios may be different from those of previous years, competitors, industry averages and entities in unrelated industries.

Ratio analysis is a convenient starting point for isolating and explaining reasons for differences. Understanding what each ratio is measuring, and how the ratios interrelate, helps users to answer the "why" questions. For example, as demonstrated in the previous sections, any change in an entity's ROE will be attributable to changes in the entity's ROA and its financial risk. To analyse the underlying reason for the change in ROE, it is necessary to examine what has happened to an entity's ROA and its financial risk. Similarly, an entity's ROA reflects its asset efficiency and profitability; explaining why the ROA has changed therefore necessitates an examination of profitability ratios and asset efficiency ratios.

Figure 6.2 illustrates the disaggregation of the ROA. It can be seen that the ROA is the product of the profit margin and the asset turnover ratio. An entity's profit margin is affected by its gross profit margin and expense ratios. An entity's asset efficiency significantly depends on the efficient management of inventory and debtors.

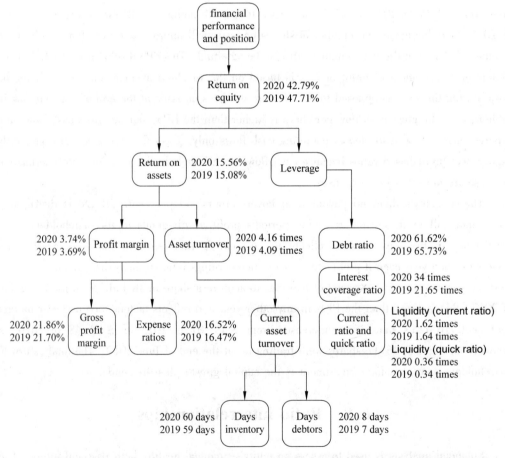

FIGURE 6.2 The interrelationship between ratios using JB Ltd as the example

The interrelationships between ratios are depicted in figure 6.2. This provides a useful template to use when conducting ratio analysis or structuring a report on an entity's financial position and performance. For the purpose of illustration, the ratios for JB Hi-Fi Ltd have been included in this diagram.

It is important to remember, however, that ratios can be affected by the individual accounting policies applied to a company's financial data, or by significant changes to accounting standards. For example, the implementation of IFRS distorted PER ratios due to significant changes in rules for determining certain revenue and expense items.

Ratio analysis, in conjunction with other considerations, is an important input to the process of valuing an entity or business. Analysts' reports, prepared to inform investors' investment decisions and other user decisions, always refer to the financial analysis that has been conducted on the entity as well as other factors that influence the likely success of the entity in the future. The reality check "JB profit falls, earnings outlook subdued" presents a report summarising JB Hi-Fi Ltd's financial position and performance after the first six months of 2015.

REAL WORLD

JB profit falls, earnings outlook subdued

JB has reported a small fall in first-half profit, posting $88.5 million of net earnings in the six months to December. That was down 1.9 per cent on the same period last year, despite a 1.3 percent rise in total sales, an 11 basis point rise in gross margins and a 1.8 per cent increase in gross profit. However, comparable store sales were down 0.7 per cent, showing that it was only the opening of new stores driving the modest revenue growth.

JB's chief executive Richard Murray said the first quarter of this financial year had been weak, and there had been one-off factors boosting the previous comparable result. "We executed the key Christmas trading period well, maintaining our price leadership and keeping costs well controlled while investing for future growth in HOME, commercial and online," he noted in the report.

JB continued to rollout expanded stores that also sell appliances and white goods, its HOME format, opening three more in the half-year and converting 14 existing stores. The retailer said it had 39 HOME format stores by December 31, 2014; in the current half-year JB Hi-Fi expects to convert a further 11 stores and open two new shopfronts in the HOME format.

Mr Murray said the retailer had got off to a good start to 2015, with January sales up 8.9 per cent and comparable sales 7 per cent, and year to date sales now

> up 2.2 per cent and comparable sales edging up 0.2 per cent. "January sales and operational earnings are ahead of the same period last year and year to date comparable sales growth is now positive," he said. "This gives us confidence on our momentum for the second half."
>
> However, not confidence that JB will beat 2014's full-year result. It is forecasting annual sales of $3.6 billion and a net profit in the range of $127 - 131 million, compared with last financial year's $128 million profit.
>
> **Source**: *Janda, M* 2015, *"JB profit falls, earnings outlook subdued"*, *ABC News*, 2 February.

Limitations of ratio analysis

There are a number of limitations of ratio analysis. Some limitations relate to the nature of the financial statements and the data disclosed (or not disclosed), while others are inherent in the nature of the financial ratios themselves. The limitations of the analytical process need to be considered when interpreting and relying on the ratios to form an opinion about an entity's financial health, past, present and future.

Ratio analysis relies on financial numbers in financial statements. Accordingly, the quality of the ratios calculated is dependent on the quality of an entity's financial reporting. The quality may be affected by inadequate disclosures and details in an entity's financial statements and/or in its accounting policy choices and estimations. Financial statements often aggregate numbers, with some separate figures reported in the notes to the accounts. The information needed to calculate a particular ratio may not be available, so an alternative financial number will have to be used instead. There exists a variety of ways to account for some transactions (e.g. the measurement of property, plant and equipment). If ratios are being calculated for different entities, it is important to establish that the entities account for transactions in the same manner. If the entities adopt different methods of accounting, the ratios may not be comparable. We have also seen that many of the reported accounting numbers involve estimations (e.g. doubtful debts), so it is important to consider how such estimations affect the ratios.

Many of the ratios that calculated relied on asset, liability or equity numbers reported in the balance sheet. Remember that this statement reflects the financial position of an ongoing entity at a particular date and may not be representative of the financial position at other times of the year. For example, an entity may sell (buy) substantial assets close to the end of the reporting period. Using the figures at year-end will therefore overstate (understate) the return on assets, all else being equal. We have tried to compensate for this by using average balances when comparing stock and flow items. However, such an averaging process is an approximation, and for assets sold (purchased) close to year-end, the averaging process used will understate (overstate) the "real" average asset balance.

Financial statements are historical statements reflecting past transactions. Often, the past is a good guide to the future, but the use of information outside the financial statements needs to be considered when forming predictions as to an entity's financial health. For example, what are the technological advances, swings in consumer tastes and changes in economic conditions that may affect an entity's future operations? Financial data alone cannot adequately reflect the intricacies of an entity's operations. Effective analysis and interpretation of financial statements generally requires a comprehensive analysis of an entity, its management, its competitors, its location and the industry in which it operates, and the surrounding economic conditions.

Users are also becoming more concerned about non-financial aspects of a business, particularly sustainability aspects. An entity's environmental and social performance is often factored into users' assessments of the entity. Many entities prepare a sustainability report either in addition to or contained within the annual report. Often the sustainability report contains non-financial ratios designed to provide users with information on how effectively the entity manages the environmental and social impact of its business activities. Some entities have developed environmental targets and publicly report against those targets.

There is a movement to reshape reporting by entities to make reports more useful to users. In July 2011, the International Integrated Reporting Committee (IIRC) released a discussion paper titled "Towards integrated reporting — communicating value in the 21st century". The concept of integrated reporting is that the reports should be strategically focused, connect information, be future oriented and be responsive and inclusive of all stakeholders, and the information should be concise, reliable and material. The reality check "Integrated reporting at the crossroads?" discusses the movement to transform business reporting and the challenges it faces.

SUMMARY

1. Explain why different user groups require financial statements to be analysed and interpreted.

The financial statements assist users in their decision making. The decisions being made by users vary. For example, the decision may involve whether to advance credit to an entity, purchase or sell an ownership stake in an entity, or lend money to an entity to acquire assets. Irrespective of the decision being made, an analysis of an entity's financial statements can inform the decision-making process. Analysing the past financial performance and position of an entity is useful in predicting an entity's future performance and profitability. Such analysis allows users to detect changes in an entity's performance, to gain an insight as to why the changes have occurred, and to assess the entity's performance and position relative to its peers, industry averages or unrelated entities.

2. Describe the nature and purpose of financial analysis.

Financial analysis refers to the assessment of an entity's financial position and profitability. Conducting financial analysis gives the user an enhanced understanding and appreciation of an entity's financial health. The reported numbers are of limited usefulness, given that they are in absolute dollar amounts. By expressing the numbers in relative terms, the financial statements become more meaningful and useful in evaluating an entity's past decisions and predicting future rewards and risks.

3. Apply the analytical methods of horizontal, trend, vertical and ratio analysis.

A reported number or ratio on its own is of limited usefulness. The analytical methods of horizontal analysis, trend analysis, vertical analysis and ratio analysis are designed to add a comparative dimension to the number or ratio. Using horizontal analysis, the current reporting period's number or ratio is compared with that in previous years, permitting the absolute dollar change and percentage change to be computed. If the comparative period extends further, trends can be depicted. Such a comparison is referred to as trend analysis. Alternatively, the reported numbers in the statement of profit or loss (or in the balance sheet) can be expressed as a percentage of a base number in the statement of profit or loss (or in the balance sheet). Items in the balance sheet are expressed as a percentage of total assets, and items in the statement of profit or loss are expressed as a percentage of sales revenue. Ratio analysis involves expressing one item in the financial statements relative to another item in the financial statements to add meaning to the reported numbers. Through ratio analysis, users can explore relevant relationships between reported financial numbers and gain a better understanding of an entity's financial health.

4. Define, calculate and interpret the ratios that measure profitability.

Profitability refers to an entity's performance during the reporting period or over a number of reporting periods. Profitability is not identical to profit. Profitability relates an entity's profit to the resources (assets or equity) available to generate profits, and to an entity's effectiveness in converting income to profits. In comparison, profit is an amount measured in absolute dollars. The distinction is important because one entity can generate less profit than another entity but be more profitable than that other entity. Assessing an entity's historical profitability helps users to form an opinion about its expected future profitability. The ratios that measure an entity's profitability include the return on equity, the return on assets, gross profit margin, profit margin and expense ratios.

5. Define, calculate and interpret the ratios that measure asset efficiency.

Asset efficiency refers to the effectiveness of an entity's investment in assets to generate income. The ratios in this category typically relate a particular class of assets to income. The asset turnover is calculated as income divided by total assets, and reveals the average sales dollars generated for every dollar invested in assets. The asset efficiency ratios that are commonly referred to are the days debtors and days inventory. The former measures the average period of time it takes to collect the cash from debtors, while the latter reflects the average length of time the inventory is in stock before it is sold. A lower days ratio is desirable, as it reflects a quicker turnover of debtors and inventory.

6. Define, calculate and interpret the ratios that measure liquidity.

Liquidity refers to the ability of an entity to meet its short-term commitments. Creditors and employees expect to be paid for services and goods provided, and liquidity ratios indicate the likelihood that an entity will be able to make such payments. The two common liquidity measures are the current ratio and quick ratio. Expressing current assets relative to current liabilities indicates the dollar value of current assets available per dollar of current liabilities. Recognising that inventory is the least liquid current asset, the quick ratio removes inventory from current assets when comparing current assets to current liabilities.

7. Define, calculate and interpret the ratios that measure capital structure.

To be viable in the long term an entity must be able to satisfy its long-term commitments. The ability to do so depends on an entity's financial risk and profitability. An entity must finance its investments in assets using new equity, retained earnings or debt. An entity's capital structure refers to the entity's relative use of debt and equity funding to finance assets. Capital structure ratios relate the proportion of debt funding relative to equity funding in financing an entity's assets. Financial risk increases as the proportion of debt funding relative to equity funding increases. The debt ratio expresses the total liability figure relative to total assets, thereby reflecting the entity's reliance on debt to finance investments in assets. Variations of this ratio include expressing equity as a proportion of assets or debt as a proportion of equity. The ability of an entity to absorb interest costs associated with borrowings is measured using the interest coverage ratio. This ratio indicates an entity's ability to meet interest commitments from its current year's profits.

8. Define, calculate and interpret the ratios that measure market performance.

Market performance ratios are relevant only for entities listed on organised securities exchanges, as they relate reported numbers to the number of shares on issue or the market price of the share. The common market performance ratios that were introduced in this chapter include net tangible asset backing per share, earnings per share, dividend per share, the dividend payout ratio and the price earnings ratio. It is common practice to compare these ratios with those of the entity's competitors, and to assess the trend in the ratios.

9. Explain the interrelationships between ratios and use ratio analysis to discuss the financial performance and position of an entity.

Calculating a ratio and ascertaining how it varies (compared with previous years or other entities) raises the question of why the variation occurs. Recognising that various ratios are interrelated enables a user to explore why the variation occurs. For example, in explaining why the ROE has improved or declined, the user can see what has happened to the entity's ROA and financial risk. Explanations as to why the ROA has changed can be explored by calculating the profit margin and asset efficiency ratios. Appreciating the interrelationships enriches explanations and understanding of an entity's financial circumstances. Rather than focusing solely on what the ratio is and how it has changed, analysing the interrelationships between ratios helps to better explain why the variations occurred.

10. Discuss the limitations of ratio analysis.

Ratio analysis provides valuable insights into the financial position and performance of an entity, but the process has its limitations. Due consideration must be given to such limitations when interpreting and relying on the ratios to form an opinion about an entity's financial health, both past and present. The limitations can relate to the quality of the financial statements and the data disclosed (or not disclosed). Comprehensive and effective fundamental analysis considers information beyond, and in addition to, reported financial numbers. In particular, social and environmental performance is becoming increasingly important.

KEY TERMS

Activity cycle (operating cycle) 经营周期

Asset efficiency ratios 资产效率指标

Asset turnover ratio 资产周转率

Capital structure 资本结构

Capital structure ratios 资本结构比率

Cash cycle 现金回收周期

Cash flow ratio 现金流比率

Cash flow to sales ratio 销售收入收现比

Current ratio (working capital ratio) 流动比率(营运资金比率)

Days debtors 应收账款周转天数

Days inventory 存货周转天数

Debt coverage ratio 长期负债与经营活动现金流比率

Debt ratio 债务比率

Debt to equity ratio 债务占权益比率

Dividend payout ratio 股利支付比率

Dividend per share (DPS) 每股股利

Earnings per share (EPS) 每股盈余

Efficiency ratios 效率指标

Equity ratio 权益比率

Expense ratio 费用比

Financial analysis 财务分析

Flow item 流量

Fundamental analysis 基础分析

Gross profit margin 边际毛利

Horizontal analysis 水平分析

Interest coverage ratio（times interest earned） 利息偿还比率（利息赚取倍数）

Liquidity 流动性

Liquidity ratios 流动比率

Market performance ratios（market test ratios） 市场业绩指标

Net tangible asset backing（NTAB）**per share** 每股有形净资产

Operating cash flow per share（CFPS） 每股经营活动现金流

Price earnings ratio（PER） 股价与收益比率

Profit margin 边际利润

Profitability 盈利能力

Profitability ratios 盈利能力指标

Quick ratio（acid-test ratio） 速冻比率（酸性测试比率）

Ratio analysis 比率分析

Return on assets（ROA） 总资产收益率

Return on equity（ROE） 净资产收益率

Stock item 存量

Trend analysis 趋势分析

Vertical analysis 垂直分析

Working capital 营运资金

SELF-EVALUATION ACTIVITIES

6.1　The balance sheet of AAA Ltd is presented as follows.

AAA Ltd Balance sheet as at 31 December		
	2019	**2018**
CURRENT ASSETS		
Cash and cash equivalents	$23 092	$18 952
Account receivable	29 588	25 750
Inventories	18 966	25 094
Prepayments	11 740	14 600
Other current assets	21 000	17 530
Total current assets	**104 386**	**101 926**
NON-CURRENT ASSETS		
Property, plant and equipment	87 174	71 722

	2019	2018
Agricultural assets	53 748	49 368
Intangible assets	32 970	40 904
Total non-current assets	**173 892**	**161 994**
Total assets	**278 278**	**263 920**
CURRENT LIABILITIES		
Account payable	34 738	27 156
Short-term borrowings	44 000	56 000
Current tax liabilities	29 250	25 086
Total current liabilities	**$107 988**	**$108 242**
NON-CURRENT LIABILITIES		
Long-term borrowings	$92 500	$78 000
Deferred tax liabilities	43 316	49 748
Total non-current liabilities	**135 816**	**127 748**
Total liabilities	**243 804**	**235 990**
Net assets	**34 474**	**27 930**
EQUITY		
Issued capital	21 000	17 000
Retained earnings	13 474	10 930
Total equity	**$34 474**	**$27 930**

Required:

(a) Prepare a horizontal analysis;

(b) Prepare a vertical analysis of the balance sheets.

6.2 Selected information for two companies competing in the retail clothing industry is presented below.

	X	Y
Sales revenue	$2 000 000	$1 000 000
Cost of sales	(1 410 000)	(420 000)
Gross profit	590 000	580 000
Less: Expenses	(315 000)	(327 000)
Profit	$275 000	$253 000
Total assets	490 000	$475 000

Required

(a) Analyse and compare the profitability of X and Y company. Provide calculations to support your analysis.

(b) From your calculations in part (a), explain the different business approaches the two companies have adopted.

(c) Explain how increasing the proportion of debt to assets can affect profitability ratios.

Answer to self-evaluation activities

6.1

a. Horizontal analysis

	AAA Ltd Balance sheet as at 31 December			
			Change	
	2019	2018	$	%
CURRENT ASSETS				
Cash and cash equivalents	$23 092	$18 952	4 140	21.84
Account receivable	29 588	25 750	3 838	14.90
Inventories	18 966	25 094	(6 128)	(24.42)
Prepayments	11 740	14 600	(2 860)	(19.59)
Other current assets	21 000	17 530	3 470	19.79
Total current assets	**104 386**	**101 926**	**2 460**	**2.41**
NON-CURRENT ASSETS				
Property, plant and equipment	87 174	71 722	15 452	21.54
Agricultural assets	53 748	49 368	4 380	8.87
Intangible assets	32 970	40 904	(7 934)	(19.40)
Total non-current assets	**173 892**	**161 994**	**11 898**	**7.34**
Total assets	**278 278**	**263 920**	**14 358**	**5.44**
CURRENT LIABILITIES				
Account payable	34 738	27 156	7 582	27.92
Short-term borrowings	44 000	56 000	(12 000)	(21.43)
Current tax liabilities	29 250	25 086	4 164	16.60
Total current liabilities	**107 988**	**108 242**	**(254)**	**(0.23)**
NON-CURRENT LIABILITIES				
Long-term borrowings	92 500	78 000	14 500	18.59
Deferred tax liabilities	43 316	49 748	(6 432)	(12.93)
Total non-current liabilities	**135 816**	**127 748**	**8 068**	**6.32**
Total liabilities	**243 804**	**235 990**	**7814**	**3.31**
Net assets	**34 474**	**27 930**	**6 544**	**23.43**
EQUITY				
Issued capital	21 000	17 000	4 000	23.53
Retained earnings	13 474	10 93	2 544	23.28
Total equity	**$34 474**	**$27 930**	**6 544**	**23.43**

b. Vertical analysis

AAA Ltd Balance sheet as at 31 December				
	2019	% to assets	2018	% to assets
CURRENT ASSETS				
Cash and cash equivalents	$23 092	8	$18 952	7
Account receivable	29 588	11	25 750	10
Inventories	18 966	7	25 094	10
Prepayments	11 740	4	14 600	6
Other current assets	21 000	8	17 530	7
Total current assets	104 386	38	101 926	39
Total assets	278 278	100	263 920	100
NON-CURRENT ASSETS				
Property, plant and equipment	87 174	31	71 722	27
Agricultural assets	53 748	19	49 368	19
Intangible assets	32 970	12	40 904	15
Total non-current assets	173 892	62	161 994	61
CURRENT LIABILITIES				
Account payable	34 738	12	27 156	10
Short-term borrowings	44 000	16	56 000	21
Current tax liabilities	29 250	11	25 086	10
Total current liabilities	107 988	39	108 242	41
NON-CURRENT LIABILITIES				
Long-term borrowings	92 500	33	78 000	30
Deferred tax liabilities	43 316	16	49 748	19
Total non-current liabilities	135 816	49	127 748	48
Total liabilities	243 804	88	235 990	89
Net assets	34 474	12	27 930	11
EQUITY				
Issued capital	21 000	8	17 000	6
Retained earnings	13 474	5	10 930	4
Total equity	$34 474	12	$27 930	11

6.2

(a) calculation ratios

	X	Y
Return on assets	$275 000/ $490 000 = 56.1%	$253 000/ $475 000 = 53.3%
Profit margin	$275 000/ $2 000 000 = 13.75%	$253 000/ $1 000 000 = 25.3%
Asset turnover	$2 000 000/ $490 000 = 4.08 times	$1 000 000/ $475 000 = 2.1 times

(b) Both companies are similar in the return on assets that they generated. However, X seems to have a high turnover, low profit margin approach. X has a much lower profit margin than Y, indicating that it is making less profit per dollar of sales. X, however, has a much more efficient use of assets to generate revenue as evidenced by the asset turnover.

(c) Increasing the gearing ratio can have a positive effect on the ROE. If the ROA exceeds the cost of borrowing, then borrowing to finance assets will have a positive impact. However, if the borrowed funds are used to finance assets and the ROA is less than the cost of borrowings, then the impact will not be favourable.

Part 2

Management Accounting

CHAPTER 7

Costing and pricing

LEARNING OBJECTIVES

After studying this chapter, you should be able to:
7.1 define a cost object and explain the usefulness of business cost information
7.2 classify costs for common cost objects
7.3 discuss the allocation process for indirect costs
7.4 calculate the full cost of a cost object
7.5 pricing methods.

It is a fundamental task for a business to look at how an entity can determine the costs incurred for specific objects, such as products, services, or business departments, because costs are important for cost management and decision making. Cost information is useful for price setting, profitability analysis and performance evaluation. In this chapter, we will look at the inventoriable product cost (the inventory value of manufactured products) which is used for financial reporting purposes. As well as costs, managers and accountants also have to considerate the price charged for products and services. It is key elements that the price is both competitive and allows for profit maximisation. At last we will look at different pricing of goods and services.

7.1 Role of cost information

A cost is a resource, commonly measured in monetary terms, used to achieve a particular objective. So management requires cost information that is both timely and accurate, and includes the performance of all the firm's products, services and activities. Cost information can assist in the more effective and efficient use of all resources.

In previous chapters, we looked at the financial accounting responsibilities of an entity, where costs are classified as either expenses in the statement of profit or loss or assets in the balance sheet. However, costs recorded in the financial statements are aggregated and do not provide sufficiently detailed information to assist in both day-to-day management and strategic management. It is important for an entity to understand why costs are incurred as the allowed costs to be managed and also leads to more informed decision making. This requires the costs to be assigned to the specific objects of interest to management.

Whatever it is that an entity requires a separate measurement of cost for is called a **cost object**. Examples of cost objects are products, services, activities, departments, business units and geographic regions. Although an entity can view costs through these different views, the total costs of the entity do not change. Costs will only change if management takes action to alter the level of costs incurred by the cost object.

The accounting information system used by entities to collect and report the cost of resources used by particular cost objects is known as a **costing system**. Traditionally, costing systems focused on determining the inventory value of manufactured products (the inventoriable product cost) for external financial reporting. Such systems focused on production costs only and ignored other non-production costs such as information technology and human resources that also support the production process. So, due to an increasingly competitive business environment, coupled with an increase in the level of costs common to many cost objects, entities were forced to take a more contemporary view when developing costing systems. To remain competitive, entities now needed to understand the costs incurred at all stages of the internal value chain—from research and development, design, production and distribution, to customer service. This internal value chain represents all the linked activities undertaken within an entity—from the inception of the product or service, to the final delivery to customers.

Costing systems were developed to support internal management rather than simply to measure the inventoriable product cost. These costing systems take a more contemporary approach by enabling an entity to capture costs at any stage in the value chain, and are suitable for measuring the cost of any cost object. The focus is on aligning the cost to activities in the first instance and then to cost objects. For example, consider an entity that follows the traditional approach of allocating salary costs to individual departments. While this provides management with information about total departmental salary cost, it gives no insight into why the costs have been incurred. Such salary costs represent the employee effort in undertaking a variety of activities. For accounts payable staff, these activities would include processing invoices, assessing credit and reconciling payments against the bank account. More insight into the cost of these activities will be gained if the salary costs are assigned to the activities that make use of the costs rather than to the department.

It is necessary to discuss how to develop a costing system to measure the **full cost** (direct costs plus allocated indirect costs) of a cost object. Before we do this, we will understand the classification of costs under different cost object of interest.

7.2 Classification of costs

Outlay and opportunity costs

Outlay costs involve actual financial expenditure to obtain goods and services. The basic household task of paying cash for groceries in the supermarket is an example of actual financial expenditure. In the case of a restaurant, the goods and services would also include food ingredients obtained from a supermarket or wholesale supplier.

Opportunity costs do not represent financial expenditures, but they are measures of the loss of benefits from a forgone alternative. For example, the cost you reading this chapter may be viewed as the loss of one hour's leisure time. When you want to purchase a residence you may be considering: one alternative is a unit in the city close to transport and the other is a suburban house away from public transport. What are the benefits of each and what are the opportunities you forgo if you choose the unit in the city location? Therefore opportunity costs will be important concept in decision making.

Direct and indirect costs

Direct costs are those costs that are capable of being identified with, or traced to, an activity—known as a "cost object". A **cost object** is any activity or segment of a firm for which costs are accumulated. The cost object is usually the product or service. The product costs are accumulated by:
- raw materials
- labour
- overhead charges

These costs that can be directly traced increases the accuracy of the costs for the cost object.

Note that the product costs are reported above the gross profit in the income statements and the **period costs** (costs charged to revenue in the period in which they are incurred) are reported below the gross profit figure in the financial reports.

Indirect costs (also referred to as **overheads**) are those costs not readily identifiable or traceable to a specific cost object. An indirect cost has a relationship to many cost objects. Figure 7.1 shows the relationship between an indirect cost and the many cost objects that consume the resource. These costs may be directly traceable to an individual cost object, but such an exercise may not always pass the cost/benefit test. For example, what would be involved in collecting information about the number of nails used in the construction of a particular house if the builder is constructing 20 houses at the same time, or the amount of glue used to laminate individual office desks? Clearly, the benefits of calculating these costs would be outweighed by the cost of doing so. The question then arises as to how these indirect costs can be allocated to the many cost objects that have made use of the resources. We will interpret this issue in the 7.3 section.

The classification of a cost as either direct or indirect will depend on the specific cost object that has been identified as the focus for the cost analysis, as well as on a cost/benefit assessment of tracing the cost. The total cost of a cost object is

Total cost of a cost object = direct costs + indirect costs

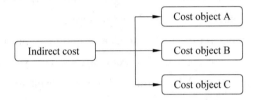

FIGURE 7.1 Relationship of indirect cost to multiple cost objects

Example 7.1 explores the classification of costs as direct or indirect in relation to a cost object.

EXAMPLE 7.1

Classifying costs as direct or indirect

SHE is a local rock group. Costs incurred by the group during August are listed below. Note the classification of each cost as either direct or indirect in relation to a show.

1. Rehearsal room hires to practice for the shows in August (indirect cost).

2. Petrol costs incurred to go to rehearsals and the shows in August (no record of kilometers travelled; indirect cost).

3. Wages of a sound engineer for each show (direct cost).

4. Advertising brochures for the shows during August (indirect cost).

5. Interest payment on loan for musical instruments (indirect cost).

6. Payments to band members for each show (direct cost).

7. Guitar strings—new set needed for each show (direct cost).

The cost object in the SHE example is the show held in August. Only those costs that were incurred directly for this particular show would be classified as direct costs—items 3, 6 and 7. All other costs (items 1, 2, 4 and 5) would be classified as indirect because the expenditure is for the benefit of all shows held in August.

Variable and fixed costs

Variable and fixed costs are classified according to the behavior of the cost type. We will discuss the details of them in the following chapter 8 cost-volume-profit analysis.

7.3 Cost allocation

As indirect costs are incurred for the benefit of multiple cost objects, determining the full cost of a particular cost object will require assigning such costs to the many cost objects that have received the benefit of the resources. Cost allocation refers to the process of allocating indirect costs to the cost objects that make use of the resource.

Cost allocation base and cost driver

When allocating the indirect costs to individual cost objects, an appropriate allocation base (or driver) needs to be identified to establish the link between the indirect cost and the many cost objects that make use of the resource. A **cost allocation base** is simply a variable used to allocate costs from a cost pool to a cost object—there may not be a causal relationship. But a **cost driver** provides a measure of activity that explains the cost object's use of the indirect cost. The accuracy of the cost allocation is increased if there is a cause and effect relationship between the cost driver (allocation base) and the indirect cost. That is, a change in the use of the cost driver should cause a corresponding change in the amount of cost incurred. Criteria that can be used in the selection of an appropriate cost driver include:

- cause and effect—choosing the variables that cause resources to be consumed (e.g. allocating machine costs based on the cost object's use of machine time)
- benefits received—identifying the beneficiaries of the outputs of the cost object (e.g. allocating advertising costs based on the cost object's increase in income)
- fairness or equity—selecting the costs that appear reasonable and fair
- ability to bear—allocating costs in proportion to the cost object's ability to bear them (e.g. allocating indirect costs based on a cost object's level of profit or level of income)
- behavioural—selecting a cost driver to modify behaviour (e.g. using direct labour hours to encourage a reduction in the use of labour hours).

Cost drivers can be classified as either volume drivers, resource drivers or activity drivers. **Volume drivers** use a measure of output (or volume) to assign the indirect costs, for example, labour hours, machine hours or units of output. It is assumed that indirect costs are consumed by the cost object in relation to its use of the volume driver.

Resource drivers are factors that measure resource consumption by activities. Such drivers enable costs to be assigned to activities. For example, the accounting system will have costs collected in accounts for electricity, rent, rates and so on. In the case of electricity, costs may be allocated to activities based on kilowatt hours and rent based on the metres of floor space where the activity takes place.

Activity drivers are then used to assign the costs from the activities to the cost object.

Activity drivers represent the attributes of the individual activities and recognise that factors other than volume cause indirect costs to be used by cost objects. For example, rather than using machine hours as the cost driver, further investigation of the processes might reveal that other factors cause the consumption of indirect costs. Such factors could be the time taken to set up the machine, the number of machine set-ups, the type of labour used, or the type of material or packaging used.

When developing a costing system based on activities, reference to an activity hierarchy can assist in identifying the most appropriate type of cost driver. The **activity hierarchy** is a framework that describes how indirect costs change with various activities. For a manufacturing entity, the hierarchy would include:

- unit level costs—costs incurred for each unit of output (e.g. the cost of electricity to operate machines)
- batch level costs—costs incurred for the benefit of a group of products simultaneously (e.g. the cost of setting up machines to manufacture batches of product)
- product level costs—costs incurred for the benefit of a specific product family (e.g. the cost of designing specific products)
- facility level costs—costs incurred for the benefit of the entire entity (e.g. the cost of operating the entity's headquarters).

Costs allocation process

To determine the full cost for any cost object, direct costs are traced and indirect costs are allocated based on the cost object's usage of the chosen cost allocation base (or drivers). The indirect cost allocation formula is used to calculate the rate at which indirect costs will be assigned:

$$\frac{\text{Indirect costs to be allocated}}{\text{Total cost driver usage}} = \text{Indirect cost rate per unit of cost driver}$$

The allocation process involves three phases.

1. Structure the indirect cost allocation formula. This requires identifying the indirect costs to be allocated, and selecting the cost driver that will link the indirect cost to the cost object.

2. Calculate the indirect cost rate. This is done by dividing the indirect costs by the total cost driver usage.

3. Allocate the indirect cost to the cost object. This is calculated by multiplying the indirect cost rate by the cost object's use of the cost driver.

Once the cost driver (or allocation base) has been identified for each cost pool, the total use of the cost driver for the financial period under investigation will need to be determined. Cost driver usage will be based on either the budgeted or actual usage to match the type of indirect costs to be allocated. By dividing the total indirect costs by the total use of the cost driver, a measure of the cost per unit of the cost driver will be calculated. The determination of this indirect unit cost rate allows the indirect costs to be allocated to the many cost objects that have made use of the resource. Allocation will be based on each cost object's use of the cost driver.

Determination of full cost

The indirect cost pools and related cost drivers enable the determination of the full cost for the desired cost object. Figure 7.2 further refines the simple system, with the changes being seen in the breaking up of the indirect costs into multiple cost pools (including electricity, rent and insurance).

Note that this process can be used to cost any cost object. The determination of a full cost using business units as the cost object of interest is demonstrated in example 7.2. This highlights the cost assignment process. Examples 7.3 and 7.4 show the structure of a costing system used in manufacturing entities to determine the inventoriable product cost for financial reporting purposes.

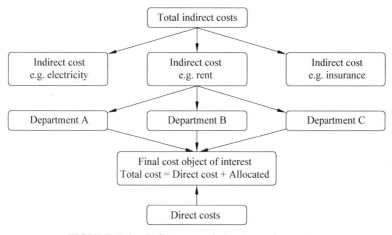

FIGURE 7.2 Refinement of simple costing system

EXAMPLE 7.2

Determination of full cost—cost objects (business units)

Partridge Insurance Company has three service departments—finance, personnel, and computer services—each providing services to the entity's three operating departments: home insurance, car insurance, and life insurance. Partridge's management wants to determine the full cost of each operating department to assist in the pricing of insurance premiums for the various policies issued by the entity. An investigation by the accounting department identified the direct costs for each department (both service and operating) and appropriate cost drivers to allocate the service department costs to the operating departments. (Remember the costs of the service departments are indirect costs of the operating departments.) There were also a number of other cost categories (rent, electricity, and general administration) that were deemed indirect as the resources were used for the benefit of all departments.

The first stage allocation involves the allocation of costs sourced from the accounting system to the cost objects, which in this stage are the departments. (Note: In this example it is assumed that the service departments do not share resources. Further study of service departments sharing resources can be found in more advanced texts.)

An overview of the relationships between the costs and cost objects in the first stage allocation is shown in figure 7.3. You will notice the direct costs are traced directly to each department.

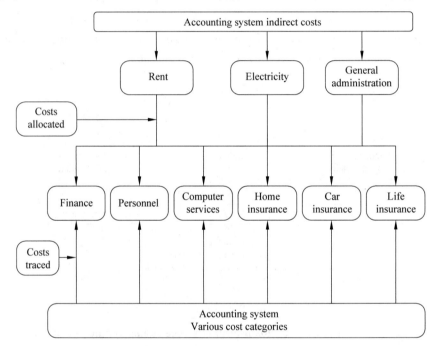

FIGURE 7.3 First stage cost allocation—relationship between costs and cost objects

After analysis of the accounting records, the following indirect costs were identified, and a suitable resource driver (allocation base) was selected.

Indirect cost category	Cost	Resource driver
Rent	$200 000	Metres floor space
Electricity	199 500	Kilowatt hours
General administration	300 000	Number of employees
Total	**$699 500**	

Therefore, to calculate the full cost of each department, the indirect costs (rent, electricity, and general administration) need to be allocated to each department (both service and operating). To assist with the allocation, the accounting staffs have undertaken a study to identify the most appropriate resource driver and have measured the total usage of the resource driver. The resource driver selected and the use of the resource driver by each department are shown below.

Departments	Resource driver usage		
	Metres floor space m²	Kilowatt hours	Number of employees
Finance	500	10 000	10
Personnel	500	10 000	5
Computer services	1 000	20 000	10
Home insurance	500	10 000	20
Car insurance	500	10 000	25
Life insurance	200	10 000	10
Totals	3 200	70 000	80

With the above data it is now possible to calculate the indirect cost rate for each indirect cost category to enable the indirect cost to be allocated to each department. Remember the allocation formula is the cost to be allocated divided by the total amount of the cost driver.

Indirect cost category	Allocation formula	Indirect cost rate
Rent	$200 000/3200 m²	$62.50 per m²
Electricity	$199 500/70 000 kilowatt hrs	$2.85 per kilowatt hr
General administration	$300 000/80 employees	$3750 per employee

The indirect cost rate calculated can now be used to allocate the indirect costs to each department based on its use of the resource driver. For example, we can see that the finance department was charged electricity costs ($28 500) based on its use of kilowatt hours (10 000 hours) multiplied by the indirect cost rate ($2.85 per kilowatt hour).

Departments	Resource driver usage			Total cost allocated
	Rent—metres floor space m	Electricity — kilowatt hours	General administration — number of employees	
Finance	$31 250 (500 × $62.50)	$28 500 (10 000 × $2.85)	$37 500 (10 × $3 750)	$97 250
Personnel	$31 250 (500 × $62.50)	$28 500 (10 000 × $2.85)	$18 750 (5 × $3 750)	78 500

Continued

Departments	Resource driver usage			Total cost allocated
	Rent—metres floor space m	Electricity — kilowatt hours	General administration — number of employees	
Computer services	$62 500 1000 × $62.50	$57 000 (20 000 × $2.85)	$37 500 (10 × $3 750)	157 000
Home insurance	$31 250 500 × $62.50	$28 500 (10 000 × $2.85)	$75 000 (20 × $3 750)	134 750
Car insurance	$31 250 500 × $62.50	$28 500 (10 000 × $2.85)	$93 750 (25 × $3 750)	153 500
Life insurance	$12 500 (200 × $62.50)	$28 500 (10 000 × $2.85)	$37 500 (10 × $3 750)	78 500
Total allocated	**$200 000**	**$199 500**	**$300 000**	**$699 500**

The full cost for each department can now be calculated. As mentioned, the accounting staffs were able to trace the direct costs to the departments, and from our calculations above we have allocated the indirect costs. Therefore, the total cost for each department is as follows.

Departments	Indirect cost (allocated)	Direct cost (traced)	Total costs
Finance	$97 250	$52 750	$150 000
Personnel	78 500	41 500	120 000
Computer services	157 000	143 000	300 000
Home insurance	134 750	365 250	500 000
Car insurance	153 500	246 500	400 000
Life insurance	78 500	221 500	300 000
Total allocated	**$699 500**	**$1 070 500**	**$1 770 000**

The second stage of the allocation process is to allocate the service department costs to the operating departments. In this second stage allocation, the service department costs (being the indirect cost pools) need to be allocated to the cost objects, which are the operating departments. The activity cost drivers (allocation bases) chosen for allocation of the service department costs to the operating departments are: the number of invoices for the finance department; the number of employees for the personnel department; and the number of computers for the computer services department. The following information details the total cost for each service department and the total usage of the cost drivers selected to allocate service department costs.

Cost		Cost driver	
Finance	$150 000	Number of invoices	5 000
Personnel	120 000	Number of employees	100
Computer services	300 000	Number of computers	60
Home insurance	500 000		
Car insurance	400 000		
Life insurance	300 000		
Total costs	**$1 770 000**		

The cost driver usage by the three operating departments follows.

	Invoices	**Employees**	**Computers**
Home insurance	1 500	50	25
Car insurance	2 000	30	25
Life insurance	1 500	20	10
Totals	**5 000**	**100**	**60**

The above information highlights that each operating department requires the three service departments to provide services such as invoice processing, personnel services and information technology support.

The steps involved in allocating the service department costs to the three operating departments are outlined below.

Step 1: Overview of cost assignment—identifying cost objects, cost pools and cost drivers

Before commencing any calculations, it is important to understand the costing system that will be used to determine the full cost for each operating department. The first step is identifying the relevant cost objects, the number and type of cost pools, and the appropriate cost drivers by which to allocate the indirect costs. The cost objects are the three operating departments: home insurance, car insurance, and life insurance. Therefore, we have three indirect cost pools classified on a departmental basis measuring costs on an actual basis.

The cost drivers identified to allocate the indirect costs are the number of invoices (finance department), the number of employees (personnel department), and the number of computers (computer services department). The actual usage of the cost driver is used to allocate indirect costs. The next stage in the allocation process is calculating the indirect cost rate for each cost pool.

Step 2: Determining indirect cost rates for each cost pool

In this example, there are three cost allocation formulas—one for each of the three service department cost pools. Each allocation formula will require determination of the cost to be allocated for the accounting period, and the total use of the cost drivers. The indirect cost rate can then be calculated, and the indirect costs allocated according to the use of the cost driver by the individual cost objects, which in this example are the operating departments.

For the finance department, the total costs are $150 000, with 5 000 invoices being processed in the current accounting period. Each invoice paid by the finance department will lead to a $30 charge being assigned to the operating department to cover such costs as finance staff salaries, stationery and telephone costs. Using the same rationale for the personnel department costs and the computer services costs, charges of $1 200 per employee and $5 000 per computer will be used to assign costs to these operating departments.

Department (cost pool)	Allocation formula	Indirect cost rate
Finance	$150 000/5 000 invoices	$30 per invoice
Personnel	$120 000/100 employees	$1 200 per employee
Computer services	$300 000/60 computers	$5 000 per computer

Step 3: Allocating indirect costs to the cost objects

Now that the indirect cost rate has been determined, allocation of the indirect costs can be undertaken by applying the indirect cost rate to the cost object's use of the cost driver. For Partridge Insurance Company, indirect costs are allocated according to the cost object's actual use of the cost driver. For example, the indirect cost rate for the finance department is $30 per invoice. The home insurance department raises 1 500 invoices per year and so will be allocated $45 000 (1500 invoices × $30) to cover its share of the costs incurred by the finance department.

Indirect costs are assigned to individual cost objects by multiplying the indirect cost rate by the cost object's use of the cost driver.

	Home insurance	Car insurance	Life insurance
Finance	$45 000 (1 500 invoices × $30)	$60 000 (2 000 invoices × $30)	$45 000 (1 500 invoices × $30)
Personnel	$60 000 (50 employees × $1 200)	$36 000 (30 employees × $1 200)	$24 000 (20 employees × $1 200)
Computer services	$125 000 (25 computers × $5 000)	$125000 (25 computers × $5 000)	$50 000 (10 computers × $5 000)
Indirect costs	$230 000	$221 000	$119 000

Step 4: Determining the full cost of each cost object

The full cost for each of the cost objects can now be determined. You will notice that the total cost of $1 770 000 (refer to original information) has now been assigned to the three cost objects—the operating departments.

	Home insurance	Car insurance	Life insurance	Total costs
Indirect costs	$230 000	$221 000	$119 000	$570 000
Direct costs	500 000	400 000	300 000	1 200 000
Full cost	**$730 000**	**$621 000**	**$419 000**	**$1 770 000**

This example highlights the different lenses that have been used to view the costs—the total cost for the entity, the costs of the individual departments, and the full cost of each operating department.

Partridge Insurance Company can now use the data from the allocation process in many ways, for example:

- to determine the full cost of each operating unit
- to review current premiums on insurance policies
- in strategic management—making decisions about which insurance policies to offer in the future based upon the profitability analysis of each type of policy
- in cost management—if individual operating department managers believe that the charges are too high, they will pressure the service departments to lower costs.

The above process for determining the full cost of the operating departments can be used to determine the full cost of any cost object. Obviously there may be different cost pools and different cost drivers; however, the process will be the same. In the following section we illustrate how the costing system is structured to meet the requirements of the accounting standards for determining inventory valuation for manufacturing entities.

7.4 Product cost of inventories

An important cost object reported in a manufacturing entity's financial reports is the inventory value of manufactured products. **Inventoriable product cost** represents the cost of converting raw material into a finished product. Accounting standards guide the preparation of financial statements and the valuation of inventory. Any costs incurred to support entity activities that are non-manufacturing in nature—such as office salaries, administration expenses, and depreciation of office equipment—are treated as **period costs** (i.e. non-manufacturing costs for the current period) and expensed in the current reporting period. Therefore, the indirect costs used to calculate the inventoriable product cost are limited to indirect manufacturing (production) costs. Remember that the indirect manufacturing costs are a direct cost for the manufacturing department, but indirect in relation to the individual products being manufactured.

When products are sold, the inventoriable product cost is expensed as a cost of sales. For products still remaining in inventory (i.e. unsold), the inventoriable product cost is carried into the next reporting period as a current asset (either as work-in-process inventory for incomplete goods, or finished goods inventory for completed goods) on the statement of financial position (balance sheet).

The type of the costing system selected to determine the inventoriable product cost is influenced by an entity's product range and processes. If an entity's products are mass produced, or if there is only one product manufactured, the entity will use a process costing system (see figure 7.4). In the **process costing system**, direct costs are considered the raw materials, and the indirect costs represent the labour and other indirect manufacturing costs (the two costs are grouped into one cost pool and described as **conversion costs**). The indirect cost is allocated by averaging the indirect costs used in the process for the period. This is done by dividing the total costs by the number of units of output.

When an entity manufactures products to different customers' specifications, the costing system will need to capture the differences in resource consumption. A **job costing system** (see figure 7.5) is used when the costs need to be assigned to jobs on an individual basis. Direct costs include labour, which is used directly in the production process, and raw materials that are converted into the finished product. Indirect manufacturing costs are all the other costs incurred in the factory.

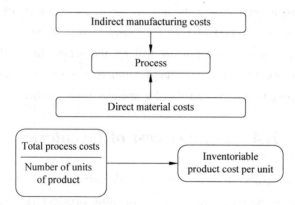

FIGURE 7.4 Overview of a process costing system

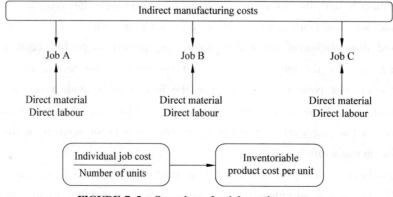

FIGURE 7.5 Overview of a job costing system

Illustrative examples 7.3 and 7.4 demonstrate the use of both costing systems by a manufacturing entity.

EXAMPLE 7.3

Determination of inventoriable product cost—single product (process costing)

Jone (Jo) established a private company, Coconut Plantations Pty Ltd, to manufacture and sell a range of sustainable coconut-based products such as soaps, candles and detergents. The company commenced operations in September 2019. Assume that Jone made a cautious, risk-averse decision to manufacture only soaps initially to reduce production complexity, and planned to increase the range of products gradually as feedback was obtained on production processes.

In the first four months of operation, Coconut Plantations Pty Ltd produced 15 000 soaps, of which 12 500 were sold. The following costs were recorded:

Direct material	$180 000
Direct labour	100 000
Manufacturing overhead	50 000
Total manufacturing costs	**$330 000**
Warehouse and distribution expenses	$42 000
Selling and marketing expenses	3 000
Administrative and finance expenses	35 000
Total non-manufacturing	**$80 000**

Determining the inventoriable product cost for Coconut Plantations Pty Ltd is relatively simple as the company produced only one product, soap. A process costing system is therefore suitable as all manufacturing costs will be consumed in the same way by all units of output. The total manufacturing costs incurred in the production process for the first four months were $330 000, being direct material, direct labour, and manufacturing overhead. This amount excludes the selling and administrative expenses, in line with the IFRS, as they are not "costs" of the inventory.

The determination of the unit cost enables Coconut Plantations to value cost of sales and inventory on hand at the end of the period as follows: $275 000 (12 500 units × $22) will be expensed to cost of sales; and $55 000 (2 500 units × $22) will be recorded as a current asset (inventory). (Further discussion of the effect of opening and closing inventories on the determination of inventoriable product costs in a process costing system can be found in management accounting texts.)

Assume that Coconut Plantations extended its range of products in 2020 to include candles as well as soaps. The choice of costing system now depends on how resources are consumed by each product. If the indirect costs are consumed differently, an averaging approach to product costing will no longer be appropriate. In order to recognise the difference in resource consumption, Coconut Plantations would have to adopt a job costing system to determine the inventoriable product cost for each product. Example 7.4 illustrates how the costing system would change for Coconut Plantations with the introduction of the new product line and candles which consumes resources differently to the existing product, soaps.

EXAMPLE 7.4

Determination of inventoriable product cost—multi-product (job costing)

Coconut Plantations Pty Ltd has extended its product range, and now manufactures both soaps (30 000 units) and candles (20 000 units).

	Soaps	Candles
Units	30 000	20 000
Direct costs	$613 125	$276 875
Labour hours per unit	0.25	0.125
Machine hours per unit	1	1.5

Indirect costs are allocated on a departmental basis. Actual costs and relevant cost driver information for each department follows.

	Production Department A	Production Department B
Indirect costs	$60 000	$62 500
Cost driver	Machine hours	Labour hours
Usage of cost driver	60 000 machine hours	10 000 labour hours

To recognize the increased complexity in the process, the manufacturing section has now been separated into two departments: Department A, where the soaps and candles are moulded; and Department B, where the products are finished and wrapped. The use of departmental cost pools recognizes that different cost drivers cause resource consumption in each department. Department A is machine intensive, so the use of machine hours has been identified as the appropriate cost driver; while in Department B, the process is labour intensive, with labour hours being the appropriate cost driver. To illustrate the job costing system, we will now calculate the inventoriable product cost for each product.

Step 1: Understand the structure of the costing system

The first step is to understand the job costing system. Figure 7.6 outlines how costs are to be allocated to the individual products—soaps and candles. The manufacturing operation has been divided into two departments—Department A and Department B. All costs incurred by both departments are direct costs of those departments and of the manufacturing operation. Remember that the costs can be classified as direct to the manufacturing operation because there have been no costs allocated from the non-manufacturing departments.

There are two direct cost pools—direct labour and direct material—which can be directly traced to the individual products. Indirect costs will be allocated based on the products' use of the cost drivers identified as causing resource consumption in Department A and Department B. The next step is to determine the indirect cost rate.

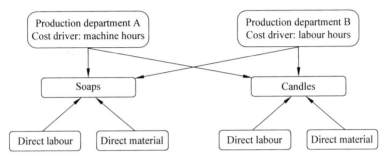

FIGURE 7.6 Overview of a job costing system

Step 2: Determine the departmental indirect cost rates

The products consume indirect costs differently, so there is more than one indirect cost pool to capture the difference in resource consumption.

For products passing through Department A, indirect costs will be allocated based on the use of machine hours. In Department B, the indirect costs will be allocated to the individual products based on the use of labour hours. The accuracy of the cost assignment will depend on the strength of the cost driver to explain resource consumption.

Department A	Department B
$\dfrac{\$60\,000}{60\,000}$ machine hours	$\dfrac{\$62\,500}{10\,000}$ labour hours
$1.00 per machine hour	$6.25 per labour hour

Step 3: Allocate indirect costs

Multiplying the products' use of the cost driver by the indirect cost rate will complete the allocation process. For example, the soap product uses 1 hour of machine time per unit and, given the total output of 30 000 units, would have used 30 000 machine hours. Overhead will be applied at the rate of $1 per machine hour. Therefore, 30 000 machine hours at $1 per hour will result in $30 000 being applied to the soap product. These calculations are summarized below.

	Soaps (30 000 units)	Candles (20 000 units)
Department A	$30 000 ($1 × 1 machine hours) × 30 000 units	$30 000 ($1 × 1.5 machine hours) × 20 000
Department B	$46 875 ($6.25 × .25 labour hours) × 30 000 units	$15 625 ($6.25 × .125 labour hours) × 20 000 units
Total indirect costs	**$76 875**	**$45 625**

Does a variance need to be identified? No, because actual indirect costs incurred and actual usage of the cost driver were used for cost determination. Variances need to be identified only if budgeted costs are used in the allocation process and they differ from actual costs. (A detailed look at the calculation of variances can be found in management accounting texts.)

Step 4: Determine inventoriable product cost

The determination of the inventoriable cost for each product is now possible by adding the direct cost and the allocated indirect cost. The unit cost can be calculated by dividing the total inventoriable product cost by the number of units of output. The total cost of the soap product is $690 000 (direct material plus direct labour plus allocated indirect costs) divided by 30 000 units, giving a unit cost of $23.00 per unit of soap. The unit cost for candles is $16.125. These costs are summarized below.

Cost category	Soap (30 000 units)	Candles (20 000 units)
Total indirect costs	$76 875	$45 625
Direct costs	613 125	276 875
Inventoriable product cost (direct costs + indirect costs)	$690 000	$322 500
Unit cost (inventoriable product cost / # units)	$23.00	$16.125

The degree of accuracy of the inventoriable product cost is influenced by the use of a cost driver that explains resource consumption. If we look at the soap product, we can see that in example 7.3 the unit cost was $22.00 per unit in 2019, yet in example 7.4 the unit cost has changed to $23.00. The difference relates to the introduction of a new product, changes in input prices or production efficiencies, and the change in the design of the cost system. This difference could indicate that the costing system design is not appropriate for the entity. The current design assumes that products consume resources in the same manner in each department. Also, as a volume cost driver has been selected, the higher volume products will always be burdened with more of the indirect costs. This could suggest a need for the entity to look more closely at the selection of cost pools and cost drivers.

How will Coconut Plantations use this unit cost information?
- If the pricing policy is cost plus mark-up, the unit cost can be increased by the desired mark-up to set the selling price. However, what would be the impact if an incorrect cost driver had been used to allocate costs?
- The unit cost enables inventory valuation for financial reporting—manufacturing costs incurred for the accounting period can be divided between ending work-in-process inventory and finished goods. When goods are sold, the unit cost enables the calculation of the cost of sales.
- Coconut Plantations can determine the contribution of each product to the company's profits. This information will assist with decisions regarding product mix, production promotion and cost management strategies to improve profitability.

Example 7.4 demonstrates the determination of an inventoriable product cost using volume-based cost drivers. If products do not consume resources in relation to volume, then cross-subsidisation between products will result. To obtain a more accurate inventoriable product cost, an entity could classify the indirect manufacturing costs into activity costs pools and assign costs using activity-based cost drivers. The activity view of costs recognises that factors other than labour hours or machine hours influence resource consumption.

As mentioned, the inventoriable cost is primarily used to satisfy financial reporting requirements. The question could be asked whether this cost is appropriate for internal decision making. For more informed decision making, the determination of a full product cost would be more suitable. This would require both manufacturing and non-manufacturing costs to be assigned to the product. The process for determining the full cost of a cost object was explained earlier in this chapter; this requires the indirect cost pools to include non-manufacturing costs.

7.5 Pricing methods

As we have learned from earlier chapters, an entity's profit is determined by income less expenses (costs that have been consumed). So far in the chapter we have examined issues in relation to cost determination. Let's now focus on how an entity sets its pricing policy for the determination of the individual product/service price in order to calculate sales revenue. To maximise profits, an entity should charge customers the highest price possible, but not such a high price that the customers will buy from a competitor or decide not to purchase at all. There are two common methods of pricing—cost-based and market-based.

Cost-based pricing applies a mark-up to some calculations of the product or service cost. The cost base can be calculated in several ways. For example, some entities may use a variable cost base, or an average cost that includes both fixed and variable costs. Mark-ups can originate from general industry practice, be based on previous entity practices, or be chosen so that the entity can earn a target rate of return on investment. Therefore, cost-based pricing will vary significantly across entities.

Market-based pricing is based on some measure of customer demand. The market price is influenced by the degree of product differentiation and competition in the market. Managers would attempt to identify what price customers are willing to pay for a product or service. An entity with many competitors will set the price at what customers would pay to any entity offering such a product or service. With less competition, where the entity is selling a more unique good or service, the entity will set the price at the maximum the market will bear.

Which pricing method is more suitable? Cost-based pricing ignores customer demand and therefore prices could be either higher or lower than what customers are willing to pay. However, one of its major benefits, at least initially, is its simplicity, as prices can be calculated from readily available data. In contrast, market-based pricing allows managers to make better decisions about sales volumes and whether to sell products or services, leading to more success in entity strategies. A disadvantage is that estimating market demand and prices is often difficult; however, this is being addressed with the use of more sophisticated information systems.

To illustrate the different pricing methods, let's return to Coconut Plantations Pty Ltd. From our costing exercise we were able to calculate the unit cost of the soap in 2020 to be $23.00 and the candle product to be $16.125. We could apply a cost-based pricing policy whereby we add 50 per cent mark-up to cost. However, given the differences in the two products, is a 50 per cent mark-up across both products appropriate? It could be that soap is a product available from competitors and, as such, the price should be in line with competitors' pricing. However, if candles were not available from competitors, Jone, the manager of Coconut Plantations Pty Ltd, would want to maximise the price to be charged for this product.

Regardless of the method chosen, there are other factors that can influence the setting of product prices of individual entities or in specific circumstances.

- **Peak load pricing**—different prices are charged at different times to reduce capacity restraints. For example, cinemas charge less for movies shown early in the day or on quieter days.
- **Price skimming**—a higher price is charged for a product or service when it is first introduced. For example, when DVD players were first introduced into the market they were around $1 000, whereas today we can purchase a unit for as little as $20.
- **Penetration pricing**—prices are set low when new products are introduced to increase market share. For example, Microsoft reduced the price of their Xbox to match its competition. It should be noted that an entity is not free to establish any price they wish; some pricing practices are illegal. In most countries, illegal practices include price discrimination, predatory pricing, collusive pricing and dumping. A brief discussion of these follows.

- **Price discrimination**—the practice of setting different prices for different customers.
- **Predatory pricing**—the deliberate act of setting prices low to drive competitors out of the market and then raising prices once competition is removed.
- **Collusive pricing**—two or more organisations conspire to set prices above a competitive price.
- **Dumping**—a foreign-based entity sells products overseas at prices below the market value in the local country where the product is produced, and the price could harm the country industry.

REAL WORLD

Taxi fees set to fall after ACCC action against Cabcharge

Taxi card processing fees are likely to fall with Cabcharge now allowing other in-taxi payment terminals to process its cards.

The move comes in a court enforceable undertaking to the Australian Competition and Consumer Commission (ACCC) and resolves a long-running legal battle by the regulator to introduce competition into the taxi card processing sector.

Cabcharge originally had a monopoly on the industry, and charged a processing fee that was 10 per cent of the taxi fare.

Some states have passed legislation limiting that fee to 5 per cent of the fare, however the ACCC's chairman Rod Sims believes that fares could fall further with more competition.

"We'd hope that when you move from what has been a traditional monopoly by Cabcharge to where you've got competition for these processing machines that you will get charges reflecting normal retail levels," he said.

In most shops, a typical credit card surcharge is around 1-2 per cent, however Mr Sims did not express a view that taxi card payment surcharges would fall to those levels.

The undertaking by Cabcharge is to allow other terminal operators to be able to process payments made using Cabcharge cards, which are widely used by many medium and large businesses and public agencies.

"All cabs have got a Cabcharge terminal because only that Cabcharge terminal could process all forms of payment," explained Mr Sims.

"Now that other terminals can also process Cabcharge payments, they can also cover all forms of payment, and so taxi drivers now may be able to at least have competition between which terminal they want in their cab and that competition we think should see a reduction in fares."

> Many taxis now have two terminals, a Cabcharge one and a rival terminal for processing credit cards, however soon that second terminal should be able to process all forms of card-based payment.
>
> Cabcharge shares were down 2.9 per cent to $3.73, although the broader market was down around 2.2 per cent. Cabcharge was forced to pay $15 million in penalties and costs in 2010 after the ACCC's initial action against it for refusing to engage with certain firms and engaging in predatory pricing.
>
> *Source*: Janda, M 2015, "*Taxi fees set to fall after ACCC action against Cabcharge*", *ABC News*, 29 June, www. abc. net. au/news/2015-06-29/cabcharge-fees-likely-to-fall-after-accc-action/6581500.

SUMMARY

1. Define a cost object and explain how cost information is used.

A cost object is anything for which a separate measurement of cost is required. Examples are customers and individual business units. Cost information is used for a variety of purposes to assist in day-to-day management and strategic management—in determining inventory values, analysing product profitability, identifying relevant costs for outsourcing decisions and so on.

2. Classify costs into direct costs and indirect costs for individual cost objects.

A direct cost is traceable to a particular cost object. The tracing is made possible by the implementation of a tracking system to link the cost to the cost object. An indirect cost is used for the benefit of multiple cost objects, and the cost is linked to the individual cost objects by the identification of an appropriate cost driver.

3. Discuss the allocation process for indirect costs.

An indirect cost is used for the benefit of multiple cost objects. Therefore, an allocation of costs is necessary to enable the cost to be assigned to the many cost objects that make use of the resource. By allocating indirect costs, an entity is able to determine the full cost of the cost object.

4. Calculate the full cost of a cost object.

Full cost is equal to direct costs plus indirect costs. The accuracy of the cost is strengthened by the choice of cost driver for indirect cost allocation. Cost drivers can be based on either volume or activity. Volume drivers assign indirect costs based on some measure of the volume of output; for example, units of output, direct labour hours or machine hours. In contrast, activity drivers recognise that factors other than volume will cause indirect costs to be consumed; for example, number of invoices processed, number of orders processed, or time taken to set up machines.

5. Calculate an inventoriable product cost.

An inventoriable product cost is calculated by manufacturing entities to satisfy the requirements of having an inventory value in the financial reports, in line with International Financial Reporting Standards (IFRS). An inventoriable product cost includes only manufacturing costs. All non-manufacturing costs are expensed in the current accounting period.

6. Discuss pricing methods.

An entity has the option of applying either a cost-based or market-based pricing strategy for its products or services. A cost-based price will add a markup to a calculated cost of the product or service. A market-based price will be set at the highest possible price that a customer will pay and this will be dependent on the degree of product differentiation and competition.

KEY TERMS

Activity drivers　作业动因
Activity hierarchy　作业等级
Allocation base　分摊基础
Collusive pricing　合谋定价
Conversion costs　转换成本
Cost resource　成本资源
Cost allocation base　成本分摊基础
Cost-based pricing　成本定价法
Cost/benefit test　成本收益测算
Cost driver　成本动因
Cost object　成本对象
Cost pool　成本池
Costing system　成本核算系统
Direct costs　直接成本
Dumping　倾销
Full cost　完全成本
Indirect cost rate　间接成本率
Indirect costs (overheads)　间接成本(制造费用)
Inventoriable product costs　可列入存货的成本
Job costing system　作业成本体系
Market-based pricing　市场定价法
Opportunity costs　机会成本
Outlay costs　付现成本
Peak load pricing　分时定价法
Penetration pricing　渗透定价法

Period costs　期间费用

Predatory pricing　掠夺定价法

Predetermined indirect cost rate　预计间接成本率

Price discrimination　价格歧视

Price skimming　撇脂定价法

Process costing system　分步成本法

Resource drivers　资源动因

Variance　（预算成本与实际成本间的）差异

Volume drivers　数量动因

SELF-EVALUATION ACTIVITIES

7.1 Single choice questions

1. Where the units of output are not identical, we normally separate costs into two categories：(　　)

  (a) fixed and variable;　　　　　　(b) avoidable and unavoidable;
  (c) product and period;　　　　　　(d) full and marginal;
  (e) direct and indirect.

2. Which of the following overhead would not normally be related to time? (　　)

  (a) rent;　　　　　　　　　　　　(b) lighting;
  (c) loan interest;　　　　　　　　(d) non-compliance fine;
  (e) depreciation.

3. Another label for indirect costs is(　　)

  (a) marginal costs;　　　　　　　　(b) absorbed costs;
  (c) overhead costs;　　　　　　　　(d) product costs;
  (e) period costs.

4. Manufacturing overhead costs would not include：(　　)

  (a) indirect labour;
  (b) indirect material;
  (c) depreciation of manufacturing plant;
  (d) electricity charged to manufacturing;
  (e) sales commissions.

5. In practice, what is the most popular method of allocating overhead costs to individual products or services? (　　)

  (a) machine hours;　　　　　　　　(b) units produced;
  (c) direct material cost;　　　　　(d) direct labour cost;
  (e) the selling price of output.

7.2 True or false

1. If a business is trying to set price for its output which will lead to the business making a profit, the prices charged must cover marginal costs.

2. Pricing output is one of the major uses to which cost information is put.

3. Full cost is the total amount of resources sacrificed to achieve a particular objective.

4. Fixed costs are not the same as overhead costs.

5. In allocating overhead costs to products, we must identify something observable and measurable about the costs unit that we feel provide a reasonable basis for distinguishing between one cost unit and the rest.

Answer to self-evaluation activities

7.1 Single choice questions
1. e   2. d   3. c   4. e   5. d

7.2 True or false
1. F   2. T   3. T   4. T   5. T

CHAPTER 8

Cost-volume-profit Analysis

LEARNING OBJECTIVES

After studying this chapter, you should be able to:
8.1　define fixed, variable and mixed costs
8.2　apply the contribution margin ratio to CVP calculations
8.3　discuss the uses of break-even data
8.4　outline the concept of operating leverage
8.5　understand outsourcing and special order operational decisions.

In this chapter we will learn a technique cost-volume-profit (CVP). CVP analysis helps us to understand how profits will change in response to changes in sales volumes, costs and prices, and it can help to answer queries such as the following.

- How many units need to be sold, or services performed, to break even (earn zero profit)?
- What is the impact on profit of a change in the mix between fixed and variable costs?
- How many units need to be sold, or services performed, to achieve a particular level of profit?
- Which products or services are contributing best to the entity's profit performance?

In order to answer these questions, management needs to apply CVP analysis. Conducting CVP analysis requires an understanding of the nature of fixed costs and variable costs. We then identify the relevant revenues (the term "revenues" is used to refer to income from ordinary activities) and costs to assist with short-term decision making. In particular, we look at the financial and non-financial considerations in relation to an entity assessing either a special order or the decision to outsource a business activity to another entity.

8.1　Cost behavior

Examining cost behavior enables us to consider the way in which costs change, and the main factors that influence those changes. Understanding of these is important for basic **cost-volume-profit analysis** whereby we investigate the change in profits in response to changes in sales volumes, costs and prices.

Fixed, variable and mixed costs

The nature of fixed and variable costs relates to whether such costs are likely to alter in total with changes in activity. **Fixed costs** are commonly identified as those that remain the same in total (within a given range of activity and timeframe), irrespective of the level of activity. Typically, fixed costs include such costs as facility-sustaining costs (e. g. rent costs and depreciation expenses). When levels of activity are thought of in terms of units of output, total fixed costs remain the same but the fixed costs per unit will decrease as the number of units produced increases. This is illustrated in figure 8.1.

Variable costs are commonly identified as those that change in total as the level of activity changes. Typically, variable costs include such costs as ingredients for a food manufacturer or fuel costs for a courier. Just as we did for fixed costs, we can consider variable costs on a total or unit basis. The difference is illustrated in figure 8.2.

The traditional definition of fixed and variable costs relates to the concept of the relevant range. The relevant range is the range of activity over which the cost behavior is assumed to be valid. If the activity level goes outside the relevant range, the expected behavior of costs may change.

Of course, the classification of costs as fixed or variable is not simple. Indeed, some costs may appear to possess fixed and variable characteristics, in which case the costs would be classified as mixed costs (sometimes referred to as "semi-fixed costs" or "semi-variable costs"—see reality check "mixed costs in practice"). The mixed cost relationship is evident in figure 8.3, which illustrates a mixed cost for television advertising based on a fixed amount of $10 000 to generate the advertisement and a $500 charge each time it is aired.

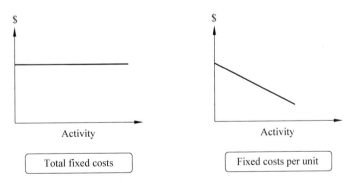

FIGURE 8.1 Fixed cost behavior

In order to split costs into their fixed and variable components, there are a number of techniques that are available, ranging from an approach where managers can use their business knowledge to split costs to the use of more complex statistical analysis. To gain an understanding

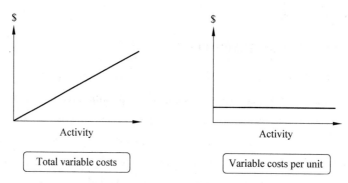

FIGURE 8.2 Variable cost behavior

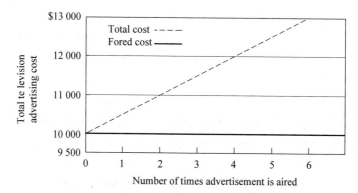

FIGURE 8.3 Mixed cost behavior

of how costs can be separated let's consider the following example.

Carry Pty Ltd established an online shop to increase sales of its products. Carry, the manager, is taking a conservative approach to online selling and is initially only offering a single product. He is planning to analyze profitability of the online shop before offering a wider range of products. The following information relating to internet activity and internet charges was extracted from his accounts and the sales database.

	3 months to 31 March 2020	3 months to 30 June 2020
Number of online sales orders	5 000	5 500
Total internet charges	$150 000	$155 000

Before CVP analysis can be undertaken, we need to split the total costs into their fixed and variable components. We know that fixed costs stay the same regardless of the level of activity and total variable costs increase in proportion to output. Therefore, the variable cost behavior can explain why the costs of Carry Pty Ltd have increased by $5 000 for an increased activity level of 500 online sales orders. To calculate the variable cost per order we divide the difference in cost by the difference in activity level as follows.

Change in internet charges	$5 000
Change in online orders	500 online orders
Variable cost per unit	$10 per online order

We know that total costs are equal to total fixed costs plus total variable costs. Therefore, to calculate the total fixed costs we have to deduct the total variable costs, which will be equal to the number of sales orders times $10, from the total costs. From the calculations below we have calculated total fixed costs to be $100 000.

For 5 000 online orders = $150 000 − (5 000 online sales × $10) = $100 000

For 5 500 online orders = $155 000 − (5 500 online sales × $10) = $100 000

Now Carry Pty Ltd can use this cost behavior knowledge to determine total costs for any level of online orders within the relevant range. Carry will know that costs will increase at the rate of $10 per online order due to the variable cost behavior, and that fixed costs will remain constant at $100 000. For example, if Carry wanted to know the total cost at 5 100 online orders, he would determine the variable cost (5 100 × $10) and then add the fixed cost ($100 000), which would give a total cost of $151 000.

An understanding of fixed and variable costs is necessary in order to explore break-even analysis

REAL WORLD

Mixed costs in practice

Communication and utility costs are good examples of a mixed cost. Telephone and internet costs are usually a mix of a fixed component (e.g. rental or access charges) and a variable component (e.g. usage relating to calls or levels of internet traffic). Cost of utilities (e.g. gas and electricity) will include a supply charge, which is fixed, and a variable component based on usage.

8.2 Break-even analysis

Break-even analysis relates to the calculation of the necessary level of activity required in order to break even in a given period. Break-even occurs when total revenue and total costs are equal, resulting in zero profit. There are a number of ways in which the break-even calculation can be made. (Example 8.1 explores the more popular of these.)

Break-even analysis draws on the traditional understanding of fixed and variable costs to introduce the concept of the contribution margin. The contribution margin is calculated by deducting total variable costs from the total revenue. To determine contribution margin per unit the variable cost per unit is deducted from the revenue per unit. We can think of the contribution margin as that amount of revenue that contributes in the first instance towards fixed costs with any excess contributing to profit. Alternatively, if the contribution margin does not cover fixed costs, the entity is in a loss-making situation. At break-even point, the total contribution margin is equal to the fixed costs.

We will now calculate break-even for single-product and multi-product entities and highlight the differences in calculations for each.

Break-even analysis is an important tool for entities such as airlines to understand the financial impact of changing cost structures.

EXAMPLE 8.1

Break-even analysis for a single product

Jack, the owner of Appreciation Basketball Coaching (ABC), is planning to take a team to join a match. The match will be held at another city. Players will be transported in a bus (48 seat capacity) and ABC will engage an additional coach to support the athletes during the match. ABC will award each player a kit bag embossed with the event and their name. Lunches will be provided.

Participation charge (parents to pay)	$150 per player
Nomination fees	$25 per player
Embossed kit bag	$35 per player
Lunches	$30 per player
Support coach	$1 200 for the event
Bus rents	$600 for the event

The break-even calculation (in units or players) can be expressed as:

$$\frac{\text{Fixed costs } \$}{\text{Contribution margin per unit (or player) } \$} = x \text{ break} - \text{even (units or players)}$$

where the contribution margin (per unit or player) is equal to the selling price (participation charge) per player less variable costs per player. For ABC, the contribution margin per player would be equal to:

Selling price (participation charge) per player		$150
Variable costs per unit (or player):		
Nomination fees	$25	
Embossed kit bag	35	
Lunches	30	90
Contribution margin per unit		$60

The break-even point for ABC in numbers of players attending the match is:

$$\text{Break-even for ABC} = \frac{\text{Fixed costs}}{\text{Contribution margin per unit}}$$

$$= \frac{\$(1\,200 + 600)}{\$60}$$

$$= \frac{\$1\,800}{\$60}$$

$$= 30 \text{ players}$$

CVP analysis may also be viewed in graphical form as shown in figure 8.4.

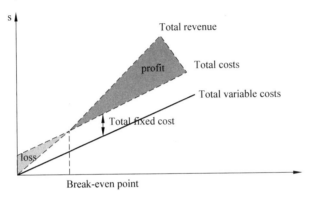

FIGURE 8.4 A graphical representation of CVP

Figure 8.5 below shows the CVP graph for ABC at break-even number of players.

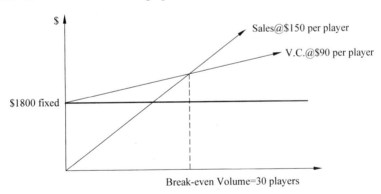

FIGURE 8.5 Graphical presentation—ATC break even

Clearly, as soon as ABC increases the number of players above 30, it begins to make a profit. It is possible to build a desired profit level into the above analysis and thereby calculate the units (or players) required to be sold to achieve a particular profit. The formula for this calculation is:

$$\frac{\text{Fixed cost} + \text{desired profit}(\$)}{\text{Contribution margin per unit}(\$)} = x \text{ sales units to earn a desired profit}$$

For example, if ABC sets a desired profit level (prior to any income tax consideration) of

$600, then the number of units (or players) required can be calculated as:

$$\frac{(\text{Fixed costs} + \text{desired profit})}{\text{Contribution margin per unit(or players)}} = \frac{\$(1\,800+600)}{60} = 40 \text{ units (or players)}$$

Figure 8.6 illustrates the number of units (or players) required to be sold (or to attend) to earn the $600 profit in a CVP graph.

Another way to view this is that an additional $600 of contribution margin is required to earn the desired profit. Given that the contribution margin per unit (or player) is $60, an additional 10 units (or players) are required ($600/$60) to earn $600 profit on tournament attendance.

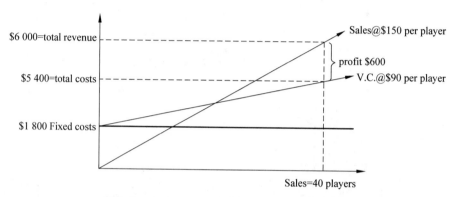

FIGURE 8.6 Break-even graph showing profit

Once the basic calculations have been made, it is possible to consider alternative scenarios. For example, what if ABC did not provide players with lunches, then variable costs would reduce to $60 per player and if the selling price (participation charge) is reduced to $100 per player? This would alter the contribution margin per player to $40 ($100 less $60), and the break-even for ABC would then be:

$$\frac{\$1\,800}{\$40} = 45 \text{ players}$$

If ABC made changes as outlined that would decrease variable costs and reduce the selling price (participation charge) to $100, it would increase the break-even number of players from 30 to 45 players.

CVP can be used in an equation form or as a ratio. In some circumstances, the unit data may not be available, or the aim may be to calculate the break-even in total sales dollars. In such circumstances, the contribution margin ratio can be used. This issue is explored in the following unit.

The break-even calculation can be viewed as an equation in the following form.

$$s(x) = vc(x) + fc \quad \text{for break-even and}$$
$$s(x) = vc(x) + fc + p \quad \text{for meeting a desired profit}$$

where:

s = selling price per unit

x = number of units

vc = variable cost per unit

fc = fixed costs

p = desired profit

We have explored only the very basics of CVP analysis here. Each entity would need to find its own application of the concepts outlined. CVP analysis provides the opportunity for spreadsheet analysis, including "what if" and sensitivity analysis. Indeed, some entities use quite complex modelling to identify break-even points. Moreover, some entities adapt the basics outlined here to suit their own environment. For example, transport entities speak of break-even kilometres or miles and hotels speak of break-even occupancy rates. While each of these calculations will be made at a more complex level, they still require an understanding of the fundamentals outlined here.

Another measure that can be used to assess risk associated with sales is the margin of safety. The margin of safety is commonly regarded as the excess of revenue (or units of sales) above the break-even point. It provides an indication of how much revenue (sales in units) can decrease before reaching the break-even point, and may be calculated as:

Margin of safety in units = Actual or estimated units of activity − Units at break − even point

Margin of safety in revenues = Actual or estimated revenues − Revenues at break − even point

If the margin of safety is small, managers may put more emphasis on reducing costs and increasing sales to avoid potential loss. A larger margin of safety gives managers more confidence in making plans such as incurring additional fixed costs.

8.3 Contribution margin ratio

In lots of circumstances, there may be insufficient data to calculate the number of units of the break-even point, or it may not be feasible to calculate the number of units. In these circumstances, executing CVP analysis by using the contribution margin per unit is of little use. What we can use instead is the contribution margin ratio. The contribution margin ratio is the percentage by which revenue exceeds variable costs (or, alternatively, the contribution margin expressed as a percentage of revenue). It is particularly useful when seeking the total sales dollars required to break even or earn a desired profit, rather than a specific number of units. The contribution margin ratio can be calculated as:

$$\frac{\text{Contribution margin per unit}}{\text{Selling price per unit}} \times 100 = X\%$$

$$\frac{\text{Total contribution margin}}{\text{Total sales}} \times 100 = X\%$$

The contribution margin provides a measure of the contribution of every dollar of sales or fees to cover fixed costs and generate profit. This is demonstrated in example 8.2.

EXAMPLE 8.2

Contribution margin ratio

Referring back to the data for Appreciation Basketball Coaching (ABC) in illustrative example 8.1, the contribution margin ratio would be calculated as:

$$\frac{(\$150 - \$90)}{\$150} = 0.40 \text{ or } 40\%$$

Break-even sales can then be calculated as total fixed costs/contribution margin ratio. In ABC's case this is:

$$\frac{\$1\ 800}{0.40} = \$4\ 500 \text{ in sales (total parents' contributions)}$$

We can confirm this result, as the break-even units (players) in example 8.1 were 30. At a selling price (or parent contribution) of $150, this gives total sales of $4 500 (30 units or players × $150).

The contribution margin ratio can be particularly useful when individual unit price and cost data are not available, or when the focus is on calculating the sales dollars required to break even. It can also be used to analyse the impact of a change in sales revenue on profit. Consider the following independent data.

	Product A	Product B	Total
Sales revenue	$20 000 000	$10 000 000	$30 000 000
Variable costs	8 000 000	5 000 000	13 000 000
Contribution margin	$12 000 000	$5 000 000	$17 000 000
Contribution margin ratio	0.60[1]	0.50[2]	0.567[3]
Fixed costs			$9 000 000

[1] 0.60 = $12 000 000/ $20 000 000
[2] 0.50 = $5 000 000/ $10 000 000
[3] 0.567 = (($20 000 000/ $30 000 000) ×0.6) + (($10 000 000/ $30 000 000) ×0.5)

The break-even level of sales will be equal to:

$$\frac{\$9\ 000\ 000}{0.567} = \$15\ 873\ 015$$

At this level of sales revenue, the contribution margin will be equal to the fixed costs.

We can use the contribution margin ratio data to consider the impact on profit of a 5 per cent increase in sales revenue. Using the example above, a 5 per cent increase in sales revenue would be (30 000 000 ×0.05) = $1 500 000. With an average contribution margin of 0.567, the additional contribution margin (and profit) would be ($1 500 000 ×0.567) or $850 500.

CVP assumptions

CVP analysis and break-even analysis are underpinned by a range of important assumptions. Key assumptions include the following.
- The behaviour of costs can be neatly classified as fixed or variable.
- Cost behaviour is linear (see figures 8.1 and 8.2).
- Fixed costs remain "fixed" over the time period and/or a given range of activity (often referred to as the relevant range).
- Unit price and cost data remain constant over the time period and relevant range.
- For multi-product entities, the sales mix between the products is constant.

If the conditions and environment for the entity fall outside the assumptions (e.g. not all costs can easily be classified as fixed or variable), then such analysis is of little benefit.

Using break-even data

Break-even data can be used to assist with a variety of decision situations, including:
- identifying the number of products or services required to be sold to meet break-even or profit targets
- allocating resources, by focusing on those products that contribute more to profits
- determining the impact on profit of changes in the mix of fixed and variable costs
- pricing products.

An interesting issue relating to break-even calculations is: what do you do if the break-even units are too high for the period in question? In other words, how does an entity reduce its risk and lower its break-even point? A range of possibilities exists.
- Are the assumptions and forecasts relating to costs reliable?
- Can costs be lowered?
- Can anything be done about price(s)?
- What would the impact be of increasing some costs (e.g. marketing) in order to achieve higher sales levels?
- Can the cost mix be altered (i.e. changing the mix between fixed and variable costs)?

8.4 Operating leverage

Operating leverage refers to the mix of fixed and variable costs in the cost structure of an entity. A knowledge of operating leverage helps in understanding the impact of changes in sales on profit. Those entities with a higher proportion of fixed costs than variable costs within their cost structure are often classified as having high operating leverage. Such entities are commonly thought to be more risky, as fluctuations in sales will produce higher fluctuations in profit for entities with high operating leverage than they would for entities with lower operating leverage.

The reason for this is that higher fixed costs lead to a higher contribution margin; however, more sales need to be achieved to cover the fixed costs.

During the global financial crisis and the swine flu outbreak airlines were struggling to break even due to their high fixed-cost structure. Passenger loads being achieved about 71 per cent, and above 73 per cent is considered necessary for flights to be profitable. Another example was in 2012 when the Indian Pacific railway commenced its usual low season service two months earlier than normal due to increasing competition from low-cost airlines and ships. The reason given for the earlier than expected "low season" was to remain financially viable by reducing services in a period of lower demand. Train travel has a high level of fixed costs such as hiring the locomotives, hiring the track and employment of staff, all of which occur before welcoming one paying guest.

In the Appreciation Basketball Coaching (ABC) example, it illustrated the impact of different cost structures. ABC has variable costs that include $30 per player for providing lunch for the players. Then there is a catering service that is offered to prepare lunches for a fixed fee of $1 200 per match regardless of the number of players. If this proposal was accepted, it would lead to a change in the cost structure as the lunch costs would be reclassified from a variable cost to a fixed cost. The change in cost structure would also change the contribution margin as under existing arrangements the contribution margin per player is $60, whereas with the proposed lunch arrangement the contribution margin would increase to $90 per player due to the higher fixed costs. Given the different cost structures, Jack, the owner of ABC, has a choice of which option to go with. To determine the best option, we need to work out the number of sales (or players) where ABC is indifferent to either option for providing lunch to the players. This point of indifference is the sales level (or number of players) where profits are the same for both options. To calculate this level, we divide the $1 200 fixed lunch charge by the $30 variable lunch cost, which gives us the sales level (or number of players) where the lunch costs are the same. Therefore, the sales level (or number of players) at which ABC would be indifferent to the lunch options is 40 units or players. To prove this, we can prepare a statement of profit or loss for both options.

Lunch provided @ $30 per player		Contract lunch @ $1 200 permatch	
Fee (40 players × $150)	$6 000	Fee (40 players × $150)	$6 000
Less: Variable costs(40 players × $90)	3 600	Less: Variable costs(40 players × $60)	2 400
Contribution margin		Contribution margin	
($60 per player)	$2 400	($90 per player)	$3 600
Less: Fixed costs	1 800	Less: Fixed costs	3 000
		($1 800 + 1 200)	
Profit	$600	Profit	$600

The statement of profit or loss show that at a sales level (number of players) of 40, ABC would be indifferent to either lunch strategy as profits are identical. However, if the sales level changed, ABC's preference would change due to the difference in the contribution margin offered by each option. For example, if sales (number of players) fell below 40, ABC would prefer to go with the per player lunch option as profits would fall by only $60 per player due to the lower contribution margin. However, beyond 40 units (or players), ABC would prefer the contract lunch option as profits would increase by $90 per unit (player) due to the higher contribution margin. The change in profit is able to be explained by the change in contribution margin.

The reality check "Cost structure at General Motors" highlights the issues in relation to high operating leverage due to high fixed cost structure. For General Motors to grow profits, high volumes of output were necessary and unfortunately General Motors was unable to use nearly a third of its production capacity.

REAL WORLD

Cost structure at General Motors

The demise of General Motors (GM) had been expected for some time. While the global financial crisis impacted heavily on industries and companies around the world, it brought to a head the problems confronting the motor vehicle industry and in particular those confronting GM. GM was placed into bankruptcy protection in the United States in June 2009 triggering the largest industrial bankruptcy in history. At the time, GM had assets of US $82.2 billion and liabilities of US $172 billion. While a range of factors were used to explain the demise of GM, a number of observations can be made which are relevant to issues in this chapter.

The initial plan for GM was to emerge from bankruptcy after eliminating 14 factories, 2 400 dealers, 21 000 hourly-paid jobs, 8 000 white-collar jobs and US $79 billion in debt. Government monetary assistance was necessary to facilitate this. These significant actions suggest that over the years GM (along with other car manufacturers) had added levels of capacity and bureaucracy that were unsustainable in the longer term. Combined with what appears to have been a focus on wide-of-the-mark car design, changing market conditions and a dynamic competitive environment, GM had a cost structure that made it difficult to generate profits at any level of production, which highlights the operating leverage problem.

The industry needed to downsize. At the time of the GM bankruptcy, it was estimated that there was enough global capacity in the industry to produce 90 million vehicles per year; yet annual demand was around 6 0 million vehicles . Much of this oversupply in capacity was likely to be represented in the form of fixed costs. Consequently, as demand fell there was relatively little alteration in costs. GM had to reduce its break-even point. GM's chief financial officer stated, "We do need to bring down our break-even level".

By 2010 and 2011, GM was able to generate profits of US $4.7 billion and US $7.6 billion respectively. Parts of its operations (e.g. Europe) were still unprofitable, but its outlook was brighter, and it was hoping to achieve profits again in Europe by 2016. Today, GM continues to address challenges associated with its cost structure. The company, which is still owned 32 per cent by the US government, appears to be on the right track to recovery—at least for now.

Sources: *Adapted from Buckley, C 2009, "General Motors losses hit $6bn as cash burn grows", Times Online, 7 May, www.timesonline.co.uk; The Economist 2009, "The decline and fall of General Motors: Detroitosaurus wrecks", 4 June, www.economist.com; The Economist 2009, "A giant falls: the bankruptcy of General Motors", 4 June, www.economist.com; Reed, J & Bond, B 2012, "GM earnings hit record $7.6bn in 2011", Financial Times, 16 February, www.ft.com; "GM posts its best U.S. October sales since 2007", GM media release, October 2014, media.gm.com/media/us/en/gm/news.detail.../1001-gm-plan.html.*

DECISION-MAKING

Improving the break-even level of sales

SITUATION A tollway opening in 2015 forecasted that 200 000 vehicles would use the tollway daily. However, in 2019, fewer than 150 000 trips were being made and at the time industrial analysts advised that at least 156 000 trips a day were needed to cover the monthly interest bill. By 2020, daily trips were on average 186 332, still well below the original forecasts. Using CVP concepts, how do you think management respond to this situation?

DECISION Connect management focused on cost efficiencies and, as a result, the cost per trip dropped from $1.72 in 2019 to $1.28 in 2020. Cost efficiencies were gained by upgrading the image processing system, which led to a reduction in manual processing, and through technical improvements to the web and contact centre channels with the expectation that customers would elect to use self-service options. However, the actions taken were not sufficient and in 2021 the tollway was sold to foreign investors.

8.5 Relevant concepts for decision making

Business decisions usually involve the selection of one alternative over another. An entity may need to choose whether to accept or reject a one-off customer order, or whether to make a product or deliver an activity in-house or purchase it externally (known as make or buy or outsourcing). It is important that decisions are based on the right information, and this requires identifying relevant costs and income. **Relevant costs** and **relevant income** are those that differ among alternative courses of action, with the focus being on identifying **incremental income** and **incremental costs**, which represent the additional income/costs resulting from an alternative course of action. It is also important to identify if there is an opportunity cost (i.e. what is given up if one alternative is chosen over another) as a result of the decision. For example, if an entity can lease space that has become empty due to outsourcing a production activity, the loss of rental income would be considered an **opportunity cost** if the outsourcing did not take place. However, remember that the financial analysis is only one input into the decision-making process and together with relevant qualitative factors forms the information package to be used by those within the entity. Relevant qualitative information may include risk-related factors such as:

- an assessment of how existing customers will react to an entity selling one-off orders at a lower price
- the quality of service delivery by the outsourced provider
- the ability for the outsourced provider to deliver when required
- the financial stability of the outsourced provider.

When both the quantitative and qualitative analyses have been considered, an informed decision can then be made to ensure the best outcome for the entity. In the next section we will further explore these issues by looking at two operational decisions made by entities—outsourcing and special orders.

Outsourcing decisions

An outsourcing decision (also refer to a product) will require an entity to choose whether to continue producing a product component or providing a service in-house. Many entities today have chosen to outsource activities or to have a component part manufactured by an external entity. For example, some universities outsource the teaching of particular industry-based software to industry experts who have up-to-date practical experience in using that software. Similarly, major car companies outsource the manufacture of many of their vehicle component parts such as seat belts, windscreens and engines. Other services commonly outsourced by entities include building maintenance, office cleaning and security.

When considering an outsourcing decision, it is important to identify both avoidable costs (those that will no longer be incurred if the decision is made to buy) and unavoidable costs (those that will still be incurred under either option). Therefore, it is necessary to identify those costs that will change as a result of a business decision. Costs that do not change are unavoidable and will be incurred regardless of the decision taken.

Example 8.3 provides the financial input into the decision by a service entity of whether it should outsource a business activity to an external provider.

EXAMPLE 8.3

Outsourcing a business activity

Giant Accounting Services (Giant) is an accounting business that provides services to local entities. Its services include the maintenance of accounting records, the preparation of financial statements and tax returns, and the provision of consulting services. Due to the increasing demand for consulting services, Giant is considering concentrating more on this service area. In order to staff the consulting activities, Giant is considering outsourcing the maintenance of clients' accounting records to a local bookkeeper. The following relevant information has been collected to assess this proposal.

- 1 600 billable hours per year are currently being charged to clients for bookkeeping services provided.
- The charge-out rate is $200 per hour for Giant's consulting services, and $50 per hour for its bookkeeping services.
- An external bookkeeper has quoted $2 000 per week for 52 weeks.
- An analysis of the overhead costs identified that $500 could be avoided each week if the bookkeeping activity was outsourced.

The question could be asked as to why Giant is considering outsourcing the bookkeeping service. Given the increasing demand for consulting services, Giant is faced with the issue of how best to enable the capacity to provide these services. By outsourcing the bookkeeping activity, capacity is made available to pursue the new business opportunity without eliminating the bookkeeping service currently provided to clients. As part of the decision process, it will be necessary to undertake a financial analysis to identify the revenue and costs that will be affected by the outsourcing decision.

Relevant costs and revenue	
Increase in revenue	
Billable hours 1 600 hours × $150 per hour ($200 − $50)	$240 000
Avoidable overhead costs ($500 × 52 weeks)	26 000
	266 000
Increase in cost	
Bookkeeping fee ($2 000 × 52 weeks)	104 000
Net benefit to outsource	**$162 000**

The switch in billable hours from bookkeeping services to consulting services has enabled the charge-out rate to increase from $50 to $200 per hour, giving rise to a $150 increase in revenue per billable hour. An analysis of the overhead expenditure has identified that the outsourcing will decrease costs by $500 each week, with a total saving of $26 000 over the year. The financial benefits gained from the outsourcing must be offset by the increase in costs resulting from the contract fee of $2 000 per week. All other income and costs are irrelevant because they will not change with either choice.

This example indicates that the outsourcing will be favorable for the entity from a financial perspective, as it is expected that profits will increase by $162 000. However, Giant will also need to consider any qualitative factors that may affect the decision. For example: How reliable is the contract bookkeeper? Does the person have the necessary experience? Can the bookkeeper complete the assigned tasks within the timeframe expected by clients? Will all billable hours currently charged to bookkeeping be taken up with consulting?

In an out-sourcing decision particularly considered with the management of risk-related factors. Example 8.4 looks at the decision, Bee, a manufacturing entity should make or buy a special flashing light needed in the manufacture of a mobile phone.

EXAMPLE 8.4

Make or buy decision—outsourcing a component part

Bee manufacture produces mobile phones specifically for hearing-impaired people. One of the components is a special flashing light that alerts the user to a call. The unit cost of making this light is as follows:

Variable costs per unit	
Direct material	$0.80
Direct labour	0.20
Indirect	0.10
Total variable costs	$1.10
Total fixed costs	
Various	$60 000

Flag Ltd has offered to supply 100 000 units of the light for $1.40. If the offer is accepted, $10 000 of the fixed costs can be eliminated. Wang Industrial has offered to lease the factory space currently used to produce the flashing light from Bee for $560 per week.

The decision for Bee is whether to outsource production of the special flashing light component to Flag Ltd and lease the factory space to Wang Industrial, or continue to manufacture the light in-house. Of the fixed costs, $50 000 is irrelevant to the decision as it is a cost that will be incurred regardless of the decision made by Bee. For example, the $50 000 would represent allocated costs such as factory rent, equipment depreciation and maintenance. If the $50 000 was included in the analysis it would need to be assigned to both the make and buy option. The income from leasing the factory will be an opportunity cost if the flashing light is not outsourced, so it is relevant to this decision and reduces the cost of outsourcing the component part.

Identification of relevant costs	
Cost to make	
Variable manufacturing costs ($1.10 × 100 000 units)	$110 000
Avoidable fixed costs	$10 000
Total relevant costs to make	**$120 000**
Cost to outsource	
Purchase price ($1.40 × 100 000 units)	140 000
Less: Lease income ($560 per week × 52 weeks)	(29 120)
Total relevant costs to outsource	**$110 880**

The financial analysis indicates that outsourcing will benefit Bee by decreasing costs by $9 120 ($120 000 - $110 880) and thereby increasing profits by $9 120. Other factors to consider would be whether Flag Ltd:

- can deliver the lights when required
- manufacture to the same quality as that of Bee Industries
- guarantee supply when required
- be financially stable enough to enable ongoing supply.

Focusing on full costs, the financial analysis would be as follows (you will notice that the $50 000 unavoidable cost is also now included in the outsource option):

Cost to make	
Variable manufacturing costs ($1.10 × 100 000 units)	$110 000
Fixed costs	60 000
Total costs to make	**$170 000**
Cost to outsource	
Purchase price ($1.40 × 100 000 units)	140 000
Unavoidable fixed costs	50 000
Less: Lease income ($560 per week × 52 weeks)	(29 120)
Total costs to outsource	**$160 880**
Additional costs to make	**$9 120**

The decision to outsource can be motivated by many factors such as the need to reduce costs, the desire to free up capacity to pursue other ventures, or a decision to focus on core activities. Many entities today outsource the routine aspects of their accounting needs, maintenance, payroll and recruitment. The reality check "Outsourcing trend continues but with warnings" provides two recent examples of likely outsourcing decisions but also highlights the dangers.

REAL WORLD

Outsourcing trend continues but with warnings

Outsourcing (and offshoring) has become huge over the last 25 years and in many ways has transformed the way organisational activity is conducted. While it may be pursued for a variety of reasons, organisations are often seeking to reduce costs and focus their internal activities on what they believe to be their value-adding activities. Two recent Australian examples relate to the likelihood of outsourcing finance and accounting jobs at Virgin Australia and Fairfax Media. The combination of reasons includes increased flexibility and cost-reduction objectives. While the risks associated with outsourcing these types of support service tasks may be relatively low, this is not always the case. For example, when Boeing outsourced a lot of the work on its 787 Dreamliner, they ran into all sorts of problems such as parts not fitting together and contractors subcontracting some of the work to other companies, the end result being that Boeing had to assume control of some of the previously contracted work.

Sources: "*The trouble with outsourcing: outsourcing is sometimes more hassle than it is worth*" 2011, *The Economist*, 30 July, www.economist.com/node/21524822? zid = 292&ah = 165a5788fdb0726c01b1374d8e1ea285; King, A 2015, "*Fairfax, Virgin look to outsource finance teams*", *The Sydney Morning Herald*, 28 April, www.smh.com.au/business/accounting/fairfax-virgin-look-to-outsource-finance-teams-20150422-1mqhxz.html.

Special order decisions

A special order will require the entity to consider whether it would be willing to supply goods or services at a reduced price or with special features, or a combination of both. As its name, it is an order which is different from an entity's "normal" customer orders. The answer as to whether the order should be accepted will depend on many factors, including whether the entity has unused capacity or the opportunity exists to have a long-term relationship with the customer. The time period for such decisions is short term (i.e. during the current financial period), so existing fixed costs can be considered irrelevant because any unused capacity will be within the relevant range. It is unlikely that the level of fixed-cost expenditure will be altered in the short term. Therefore, only incremental fixed costs will be relevant for such a decision.

In assessing a special order, it is important to identify the entity's available capacity. **Available capacity** (also referred to as **idle capacity**) indicates the amount of capacity an entity has available to increase output. For example, a manufacturing entity that can produce a maximum of 100 000 units (100 per cent capacity) might be producing only 90 000 units (90 per cent capacity). This indicates that the entity has available capacity of 10 000 units (10 per cent). Any order up to 10 000 units can be accepted without affecting current production or altering the existing level of fixed costs. However, what would be the effect if the special order required 20 000 units? To accept the special order in full, the entity would need to make use of the 10 000 units available, as well as directing 10 000 units from the normal production to the special order. The loss of contribution margin from the 10 000 units of normal production would be considered an opportunity cost and a relevant cost of the special order.

Furthermore, how would the entity's normal customers react if their deliveries were affected? Management would need to make judgment about the potential effect of the decision to forgo 10 000 units of normal sales for the special order. Normal customers may react negatively to late deliveries or the knowledge that other customers were getting a better deal. An entity could increase production capacity by working overtime hours so that normal production would not be affected, but this would lead to increased costs for the special order.

Example 8.5 demonstrates the assessment of a special order for an entity with idle capacity.

EXAMPLE 8.5

Special order with idle capacity

Blue manufacture is a popular range of sportswear. Due to increase in customer orders over the next few years, the entity has recently expanded its production capacity by 20 000 suits. Its current output is 100 000 suits that are sold in the market for $75 each. The current costs are as follows.

Variable costs	
Direct material	$800 000
Direct labour	1 200 000
Indirect	750 000
	$2 750 000
Fixed costs	1 500 000
Total costs	$4 250 000

Based on current sales, Blue is generating a profit of $3 250 000. The statement of profit or loss, therefore, would be as follows.

Statement of profit or loss (contribution margin format)	
Revenue	$7 500 000
Less: Variable costs	2 750 000
Contribution margin	**4 750 000**
Less: Fixed costs	1 500 000
Profit	**$3 250 000**

A localfashion shop has requested the supply of 500 suits manufactured to its own design, and has offered to pay $70 per suit. The order will increase direct labour by 10 per cent and direct material by 20 per cent. In addition, $5 000 will be charged to program the machinery to cut the fabric for the new design.

Blue is interested in this special order, as it has available capacity of 20 000 units due to its recent expansion to meet future customer demand. Therefore, the 500 suits requested by the fashion shop can be satisfied by the available capacity. The financial analysis will consider the incremental income and incremental costs. Existing fixed costs are irrelevant as the 500 suits are within the relevant range. The unit cost for the regular suits is as follows.

Variable cost per suit	
Direct material ($800 000/100 000 units)	$8.00
Direct labour ($1 200 000/100 000 units)	12.00
Indirect ($750 000/100 000 units)	7.50
Variable cost per unit	**$27.50**

Increasing production will increase expenditure only on variable costs. The variable costs for the special order will increase to $30.30 (see calculations following). The total variable costs will increase by $15 150, with an additional $5 000 required to program the machine specifically to manufacture the suits. As this is a one-off order, it is assumed that the machinery will not be used for other purposes, and therefore full cost recovery is required from income generated by the special order.

Relevant costs and income of special order		
Incremental income		
500suits × $70		$35 000
Incremental costs		
Variable manufacturing costs		
Direct material (500 suits × $9.60[1])	$4 800	

Continued

Relevant costs and income of special order		
Direct labour (500 suits × $13.20²)	6 600	
Indirect manufacturing (500 suits × $7.50)	3 750	15 150
Incremental fixed costs		
Programming of machinery		5 000
Total incremental costs		**20 150**
Benefit of special order (increase in profit)		**$14 850**

¹ Increase of 20% = $8 × 1.2
² Increase of 10% = $12 × 1.1

The financial analysis of the special order indicates that Blue manufacture can increase its current profits by $14 850. The statement of profit or loss incorporating the special order would be as follows:

Statement of profit or loss (contribution margin format)		
	with existing sales	with existing orders
Revenue		
100 000 units × $75	$7 500 000	$7 500 000
500 units × $70		35 000
Total revenue	**$7 500 000**	**$7 535 000**
Less: Variable costs		
100 000 units × $27.50	$2 750 000	$2 750 000
500 units × $30.30		15 150
Total variable costs	**$2 750 000**	**$2 765 150**
Contribution margin	**$4 750 000**	**$4 769 850**
Less: Fixed costs	$1 500 000	$1 500 000
Additional fixed costs		$5 000
	$1 500 000	$1 505 000
Profit	**$3 250 000**	**$3 264 850**

However, the qualitative factors also need to be considered. How will existing customers react if they discover the fashion shop is purchasing these suits at a lower price? Will the shop be a potential long-term customer after this order? A final decision cannot be made until such factors are considered.

Example 8.6 demonstrates the assessment of a special order for an entity without idle capacity.

EXAMPLE 8.6

Special order with no idle capacity

The fashion shop has now placed another order with Blue, asking for the same contractual arrangements as last time. Despite the time difference, all income and costs have remained the same. However, Blue anticipated new customer orders have now fully used its additional production capacity of 20 000 suits. Should the order be accepted this time? The last order increased Blue' profits by $14 850. However, this new order has created an opportunity cost, which is the contribution margin of forgone regular sales. As the production capacity is fully utilised, the only option available to satisfy the order is to reduce current sales by 500 units. The financial analysis of the new order calculates a loss of $8 900 for Blue if this order is accepted.

Relevant costs and income of special order	
Benefit of special order (refer to example8.5)	$14 850
Opportunity cost	
Contribution margin forgone on 500 suits × ($75 – $27.50)	(23 750)
Loss generated from special order	**$(8 900)**

Therefore, Brooks Enterprises should not accept the fashion shop' offer. The difference between the first order (which generated a profit of $14 850) and the second order (which would result in a loss of $8 900) is due to the lack of available capacity for the second order. The statement of profit or loss would change as follows:

Statement of profit or loss (contribution margin format)		
	with existing sales	with existing orders
Revenue		
120 000 units × $75	$9 000 000	
119 500 units × $75		$8 962 500
500 units × $70		35 000
Total revenue	$9 000 000	$8 997 500
Less: Variable costs		
120 000 units × $27.50	$3 300 000	
119 500 units × $27.50		$3 286 250
500 units × $30.30		15 150

Continued

Statement of profit or loss (contribution margin format)		
	with existing sales	with existing orders
Total variable costs	$3 300 000	$3 301 400
Contribution margin	$5 700 000	$5 696 100
Less: Fixed costs	$1 500 000	$1 500 000
Additional fixed costs		5 000
	$1 500 000	$1 505 000
Profit	$4 200 000	$4 191 100

SUMMARY

1. Define fixed, variable and mixed costs.

Fixed costs are commonly identified as those that remain the same in total (within a given range of activity and timeframes), irrespective of the level of activity. Variable costs are commonly identified as those that change in total as the level of activity changes. Mixed costs are those that appear to possess fixed and variable characteristics.

2. Prepare a break-even analysis for single-product entities.

CVP analysis commonly requires the use of the contribution margin concept to calculate the breakeven number of units. Data are needed on fixed and variable costs in order to execute the calculation.

3. Apply the contribution margin ratio to CVP calculations.

The contribution margin ratio can be used to perform break-even calculations by focusing on the ratio of the contribution margin to sales. This can be particularly useful when seeking the total break-even sales dollars, rather than the per unit numbers.

4. Explain the key assumptions underlying CVP analysis.

The key assumptions underlying CVP analysis include the assumption that the behavior of costs can be neatly classified as fixed or variable—which may not be the case, as some costs do not behave as expected; cost behavior is generally assumed to be linear (see figures 8.1 and 8.2); fixed costs are believed to remain "fixed" over the time period and/or a given range of activity (often referred to as the relevant range); unit price and cost data are assumed to remain constant over the time period and relevant range; and, for multi-product entities, the sales mix between the products is assumed to be constant.

5. Discuss the uses of break-even data.

Break-even data can be used in a number of ways, including identifying the number of products or services required to be sold to meet break-even or profit targets; planning products and allocating resources by focusing on those products that contribute more to profitability; determining the impact on profit of changes in the mix of fixed and variable costs; and pricing products.

6. Outline the concept of operating leverage.

The margin of safety is commonly regarded as the excess of revenue (or units of sales) above the break-even point. It provides an indication of how much revenue (sales in units) can decrease before reaching the break-even point. Operating leverage refers to the mix between fixed and variable costs in the cost structure of an entity. A knowledge of operating leverage helps in understanding the impact of changes in revenue on profit.

7. Assess relevant costs and income for decision making.

Relevant costs and relevant income are those that differ among alternative courses of action, with the focus being on identifying incremental income and incremental costs, which represent the additional income/costs as a result of taking an alternative course of action. It is also important to identify if there is an opportunity cost (i.e. what is given up if one alternative is chosen over another) as a result of the decision.

8. Analyse an outsourcing decision.

Whether it is for cost savings or other factors, an entity may decide to outsource a product or business activity to an external provider. To assess such a decision, the entity would need to compare the in-house costs with those of the external provider. Costs that will be incurred regardless of the decision taken are unavoidable and therefore irrelevant.

9. Analyse a special order decision.

An entity may be requested by a new or existing customer to provide a modified product or provide an existing product at a lower cost. The motivation could be driven by a need for cash flow or a strategic move to develop relationships with new customers. In such a decision the entity would need to compare the incremental income with the incremental cost. An opportunity cost should be considered if there is no idle capacity.

KEY TERMS

Available capacity(idle capacity) 闲置产能
Avoidable costs 可避免成本
Break-even analysis 保本点分析
Contribution margin 边际贡献
Contribution margin per unit 单位边际贡献
Contribution margin ratio 边际贡献率
Cost-volume-profit analysis 本—量—利分析
Fixed costs 固定成本
Incremental costs 增量成本

Incremental income 增量收入
Margin of safety 安全边际
Mixed costs 混合成本
Operating leverage 经营杠杆
Opportunity cost 机会成本
Outsourcing 外包
Outsourcing decision 外包决策
Relevant costs 相关成本
Relevant income 相关收入
Relevant range 相关范围(产能)
Special order 特殊订单
Unavoidable costs 不可避免的成本
Variable costs 变动成本

SELF-EVALUATION ACTIVITIES

8.1 Single choice questions

1. Which of the following costs would most likely be classified as variable rather than fixed in a bread shop? (　　)

(a) Advertising
(b) Rent of premises
(c) Flour
(d) Equipment lease payment
(e) Depreciation of ovens

2. Telephone costs with a rental charge per quarter plus a charge per call would be(　　).

(a) Fixed cost
(b) Variable cost
(c) Direct cost
(d) Semi-variable cost
(e) Opportunity cost

3. which of the following equations is the break-even unit formula represented by? (　　)

(a) Fixed costs/(sales revenue per unit-variable cost per unit)
(b) Total revenue-all costs
(c) Fixed cost/([unit selling price-unit variable cost]/[unit selling price])
(d) (Fixed cost + desired profit)/contribution margin per unit
(e) All of the above

4. What are the monthly break-even sales, when(　　)?

Fixed cost per quarter　　$2 700
Variable costs per unit　　$22
Selling price per unit　　$31

(a) 400 units
(b) $12 400
(c) $3 100
(d) $49 600
(e) 1 600 units

5. When the activity level increase, ( ).
   (a) Variable cost per unit declines
   (b) Variable cost in total declines
   (c) Fixed cost per unit increases
   (d) Variable cost per unit increases
   (e) Fixed cost per unit declines

8.2 CVP analysis

Selling price/unit	Variable costs/unit	Units sold	Contribution margin(total)	Fixed costs	Profit (loss)
$40	?	5 000	?	$60 000	$40 000
55	$25	?	$30 000	?	0
44	22	?	?	115 000	(5 000)
?	75	2 500	72 500	28 000	?
100	?	1 000	?	60 000	(20 000)

Required Show your understanding of basic CVP analysis by finding the missing numbers.

8.3 Break-even analysis

	Business A	Business B
Sales ($)	320 000	480 000
Contribution margin ratio	40%	35%
Fixed costs ($)	80 000	120 000
Units sold (#)	2 000	1 600

For each business compute the following

	Business A	Business B
(a) Contribution margin/unit ($)		
(b) Variable cost per unit ($)		
(c) Break-even sales ($)		
(d) Profit or loss ($)		

Answer to self-evaluation activities

8.1 Single choice questions
1. c 2. d 3. a 4. c 5. e

8.2 The solution of CVP analysis

Selling price/unit	Variable costs/unit	Units sold	Contribution margin(total)	Fixed costs	Profit (loss)
$40	$20	5 000	$100 000	$60 000	$40 000
55	25	1 000	30 000	30 000	0
44	22	5 000	110 000	115 000	(5 000)
104	75	2 500	72 500	28 000	44 500
100	60	1 000	40 000	60 000	(20 000)

8.3 The solution of Break-even analysis

	Business A	Business B
(a) Contribution margin/unit ($)	64	105
(b) Variable cost per unit ($)	96	195
(c) Break-even sales ($)	200 000	342 857
(d) Profit or loss ($)	48 000	48 000

CHAPTER 9

Budgeting

LEARNING OBJECTIVES

After studying this chapter, you should be able to:
9.1 understand the link and difference between planning and budgeting
9.2 explain the key steps in the budgeting process and the types of budgets
9.3 prepare a master budget and cash budget
9.4 outline the use of budgeting in management control

In this chapter, we will explore one of the key issues associated with planning—budget. Planning relates to looking ahead in some kind of formal process. Budgets are an important tool for management planning and control. Budgeting process is formal and regular in different entities. An entity will have developed its strategic plans that need to be drawn up and put into operation. Now what we focus is how this occurs in the budgeting area, rather than a study of strategic planning itself.

9.1 Strategic planning and budgeting

As individuals, we often look ahead and plan various aspects of our future. A business also holds its overall direction and converts the objective into short-term or long-term plans. **Strategic planning** relates to longer term planning (such as three to five years) of the entity's activities. It is usually carried out by senior management, and commonly relates to broader issues such as business takeovers, expansion plans and deletion of business segments. The way in which the strategic planning process is conducted depends upon a range of issues, including the industry and culture of the entity. For example, larger entities will use a rather formal process, while more creative or smaller entities may choose a less formal process. Nevertheless, the outcomes from the process are the strategic plans of the entity, and these will guide shorter term planning such as budgeting.

Budgeting is a process that focuses on the short term, commonly one year, and results in the production of budgets that set the financial framework for that period. The planning process evaluates whether there will be sufficient resources available to achieve the strategic plan, and most importantly whether the strategy leads to profits and thereby creates value for the entity. Budgets, therefore, operationalise the strategic plan and allow those in operational areas to understand how their work effort contributes to the entity's strategic objectives. Once the budget has been prepared, it is also used as a control tool to monitor actual results, to investigate differences between actual and budget, and to evaluate and reward performance.

REAL WORLD

ABC Shops to be closed, jobs to go as retailer moves online

ABC Shops around the country will be phased out and closed as the national broadcaster moves to an online retail model. The ABC currently has 50 stores around the country and 78 ABC Centers in other retail outlets as part of its bricks and mortar portfolio. ABC Shops largely rely on the sale of CDs, DVDs and some books. That content is now migrating to digital downloads. Last year, the ABC Shops were operating at a loss, and experts have advised it will not be possible for the ABC to run the stores profitably in the future. The ABC will continue to deliver the ABC Shop online, and will look to find partnerships with other retailers to include ABC branded sections in their stores. The move by the ABC comes as "digital disruption" continues to rock the retail environment as consumers spend their money through subscription services, downloads and purchase goods online. The accelerating switch to online purchases means the ABC's costs of maintaining its current retail network has become unviable and that it is no longer possible to sustain its network of stores. "Customers are now getting that content through digital downloads and so all our advice is that the shops are now not making money," the ABC's managing director Mark Scott told AM. "They've made a lot of money over the years but they're not making money now. "It's very hard to project them making significant money in the future and we can't cross subsidise a retail business by taking money out of broadcasting and investing it to prop up a retail business anymore."

Source: "*ABC Shops to be closed, jobs to go as retailer moves online*" 2015, *ABC News*, 23 *July*, www.abc.net.au/news/2015-07-23/abc-shops-to-be-phased-out-and-closed/6641476.

In the above real world, it relates to strategic repositioning of the ABC Stores which sell branded merchandise. The increasing competition from online retailers and customers' preference for online purchases has made the current shopfront store model unviable. Coupled with this is funding cuts of $254 million to the national broadcaster. With fewer resources, ABC management had to make decisions as to how best to allocate funds between the different divisions—for example, should they direct funds from broadcasting activities to the ABC Stores?

This example highlights the need for both strategic planning and budgeting in such decision making, as management have to determine how to make best use of the available resources so that the focus is on those activities that will allow the business to remain viable into the future. Moreover, it reminds us of the link between the decision made and its future impact on the budgeting process.

Short-term plans commonly involve setting goals and targets in financial terms and referred to as a budget. In doing so, entities will engage in a planning process which, among other things, requires involvement in a budgeting process. The process relates to an entity's operational plans, including short-term goals and targets. These goals and targets can be stated in financial or non-financial terms.

9.2 Budgeting progress and types

A **budget** is simply the quantitative expression of an entity's plans. The nature of the entity will determine the type of budget that might be prepared, as a minimum, it would be expected that the financial statements be prepared in budgeted form. Budgeting and the associated planning can assist in a decision-making context in a variety of ways, including:

- assessing the feasibility of strategic plans, thus creating value for the entity
- setting targets for managers
- identifying resource constraints in the budget period
- identifying periods of expected cash shortages and excess cash holdings
- assisting with short-term planning decisions, such as capacity utilisation
- providing profit forecasts and other financial data to the capital markets
- forecasting data such as sales or fees, which set the level of activity for the budget period
- helping determine required inventory levels and purchasing requirements for raw materials
- planning labour and other inputs
- determining the ability of the entity to meet financing commitments.

The budgeting process

The **budgeting process** will commonly involve a series of steps, including:
1. consideration of past performance
2. assessment of the expected trading and operating conditions
3. preparation of initial budget estimates
4. adjustment to estimates based on communication with, and feedback from, managers
5. preparation of the budgeted reports and any sub-budgets
6. monitoring of actual performance against the budget over the budget period

7. making any necessary adjustments to the budget during the budget period.

Communication and coordination is important in budgeting progress. Throughout the process, communication with managers who are affected by the budgets should occur. These managers are commonly responsible for a segment of the entity, such as a division, a department or a branch. These segments may be referred to as responsibility centers, and may form part of the entity structure. The level of communication in the budgeting process will vary from entity to entity, as will the level of participation sought from managers of responsibility centers in the budgeting process. In larger entities, there will be a budget committee that coordinates the preparation of the budget. Committee membership will include the managing director, treasurer, chief accountant, and management personnel from each of the major areas of the company, such as sales, production and research.

The process is strengthened by considering the interrelationship between profit, cash and return on investment. The three wheels (cash, profit and return on investment) are interlocking and turn simultaneously. For example, the entity may be able to generate more sales in the coming year. However, will there be enough cash flow to acquire the inventory to support sales or acquire other necessary resources? Will the increased sales lead to higher profits, which in turn will enable investment in assets that should lead to higher sales and more profits? The higher profit will lead to an increase in the return on owner's investment.

Departments within the entity should work together to develop the profit plan for the coming year. The sales manager provides important information about the potential sales levels for the coming year and the operational personnel will assess whether there are the necessary resources required to achieve these sales or alternatively recommend process changes to achieve the sales goal. The financial personnel will assess both the cash flow resulting from the plans to assess the need for cash to cover day-to-day operations and the profitability of the planned activities. Overall, the interaction of the various personnel enables them to understand the impact of their decisions and to assess whether value is created for the entity.

Types of budgets

The nature of the entity will determine the types of budgets prepared. Nevertheless, budgets commonly prepared include the following.

- **Sales or fees budget**, which also serves as an important input variable for other budgets and is, therefore, often referred to as the "cornerstone" of the budgeting process. The sales or fees budget is commonly used to set the expected level of activity for the budget period. The expected level of activity is an important consideration for many of the other budgets. This central role of the sales or fees budget is further underpinned in three wheels of planning.
- **(Operating) expenses budget**, which is commonly an aggregation from functional, sectional or departmental expense budgets, and which also serves as an input variable

to other budgets. For example, the expenses budget relating to the operation of the accounting department is used, along with other (e.g. marketing) departmental budgets to build the overall operating expenses budget. It is sometimes simply called the cost budget.

- **Production and inventory budgets**, which are necessary in manufacturing environments for planning production levels and managing inventory levels. There are usually sub-budgets relating to direct materials, direct labour (if any) and indirect manufacturing overhead costs.
- **Purchases budget**, for both merchandising and manufacturing entities, which will set the required level of inventory/direct materials purchases based on data from the sales budget, and possibly from the production and inventory budgets as well.
- **Manufacturing overhead budget**, which is concerned with estimating the overheads or expenses associated with production activities.
- **Budgeted statement of profit or loss**, which is essentially an aggregation of many of the other subbudgets, including the sales budget and operating expenses budget.
- **Cash budget**, which focuses on cash in the same way that the statement of cash flows does, and may be viewed as a statement of the expected future cash receipts and cash payments.
- **Budgeted balance sheet**, which shows what the entity's financial position is expected to be as at the end of the period.
- **Capital budget**, which deals with expenditure relating to long-term investments.
- **Program budget**, which focuses on costs associated with a specific program. This is a budget form commonly used in the government and not-for-profit sector.

The budget structure that an entity will use depends on a range of factors. Table 9.1 provides a sample list of possible budgets for different entity settings. These budgets are commonly arranged under the umbrella of a master budget.

TABLE 9.1 Applicable budgets for sample entities

Manufacturer	Service	Professional services	Government department
Sales budget	Sales budget	Fees budget	Labour-related budget
Production budget	Labour budget	Labour budget	Expenses budget
Direct materials budget	Expenses budget	Expenses budget	Departmental/functional budgets
Direct labour budget	Departmental budgets	Departmental budgets	Cash budget
Manufacturing Overhead budget	Cash budget	Cash budget	Program budget
Non-manufacturing expenses budget	Budgeted statement of profit or loss	Budgeted statement of profit or loss	

Continued

Manufacturer	Service	Professional services	Government department
Departmental budgets	Budgeted balance sheet	Budgeted balance sheet	
Cash budget			
Budgeted statement of profit or loss			
Budgeted balance sheet			

9.3 Master budget

A **master budget** is a set of interrelated budgets for a future period. It provides a framework for viewing the relevant budgets of an entity. While the nature of the budgets prepared will vary according to the nature of the entity and its operating environment, the master budget is commonly classified into operating budgets and financial budgets. The **operating budgets** usually include the sales budget and operating expenses budget, while the **financial budgets** commonly include the broader budgeted statement of profit or loss, the budgeted balance sheet, the cash budget and the capital budget. The plans developed for the master budget are summarised in a set of budgeted financial statements.

Because budgets are based on forecasts about the future, complete accuracy is impossible and variances will inevitably arise. A **variance** is the difference between actual and budget results, and it can be either favourable or unfavourable. A favourable variance occurs when actual revenues are larger than budgeted, or actual costs are lower than budgeted. Conversely, an unfavourable variance arises when actual revenues are lower than budgeted, or actual costs are greater than budgeted. Determining the underlying reasons for a budget variance is not a straightforward exercise. For example, a favourable cost variance could be obtained by an efficient use of resources, or by the use of lower quality, low-cost resources. Each entity determines the level of variance that will be tolerated before investigations are undertaken to understand the cause. Such investigations will provide the necessary feedback to inform future actions, and may require a revision of the budget.

An illustration of the main components of a master budget is provided in example 9.2. The individual components that make up a master budget are specific to the entity. We illustrate the preparation of the various budgets that make up the master budget for a manufacturing entity. Compared to a service entity, a manufacturing entity will need to prepare additionally budgets of the raw materials purchased and the production costs required to convert the raw materials to a finished product.

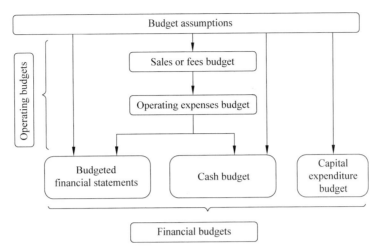

FIGURE 9.1 Master budget illustration

Preparation of operating budgets for a manufacturing entity

Anni is the accountant of Mountain Bikes, a manufacturer of sturdy mountain bikes. The company's managers are forecasting an increase in sales because of the success of their current advertising campaign. They ask Anni to create a master budget for 2018, given the forecasted sales increase.

To gather information needed for the budget, Anni first compiles relevant data about revenues, inventories and production costs from last period's accounting records. Next, she obtains information from every department and meets with senior management to identify changes in sales volumes and prices, production processes, manufacturing costs and support department costs.

Developing the sales budget

First, Anni prepares the sales budget which is derived from the sales forecast. The sales budget represents management's best estimate of sales revenue for the budget period. Obviously, the sales budget will have a direct impact on profit. For example, if the sales forecast is too optimistic, the entity may purchase excessive material inventories and/or overproduce the number of units required. This may lead to additional operating costs due to the need to store more materials, not to mention the unnecessary increase in working capital requirements. Also, if there is an excess of finished goods inventory, the product may need to be sold at reduced prices. In contrast, a too-pessimistic forecast may result in insufficient materials and finished goods inventory, which could lead to a loss of sales revenue and/or a loss of customer goodwill.

The marketing manager has forecasted that 100 000 bikes will be sold in total at a price of $800 each, and due to the seasonal nature of the product the sales will vary per quarter. Anni develops the sales budget detailed in example 9.1 for Mountain Bikes, based on the sales pattern identified by the marketing manager.

EXAMPLE 9.1

Sales budget

Mountain Bikes Sales budget for the year ended 31 December 2019					
	Quarter 1	Quarter 2	Quarter 3	Quarter 4	Total
Expected sales (units)	30 000	20 000	10 000	40 000	100 000
Units selling price	× $800	× $800	× $800	× $800	× $800
Total sales revenue	$24 000 000	$16 000 000	$8 000 000	$32 000 000	$80 000 000

Developing the production budget

Second, Anni develops the production budget (example 9.2). Production will be required to meet the need for both ending finished goods inventory of the mountain bikes and sales for the period. However, not all of these units will need to be manufactured as the entity has opening finished goods inventory to offset some of these required units. According to the accounting records, beginning finished goods inventory consists of 2 500 bikes. Given the anticipated increase in sales volume, the inventory manager wants to increase finished goods inventory to 3 500 units per quarter. Anni calculates the number of bikes that will be manufactured each period, factoring in the sales forecast and both beginning and targeted ending finished goods inventory levels.

EXAMPLE 9.2

Production budget

Mountain Bikes Production budget for the year ended 31 December 2019					
	Quarter 1	Quarter 2	Quarter 3	Quarter 4	total
Expected unit sales (refer sales budget)	30 000	20 000	10 000	40 000	
Add: Desired ending inventory	3 500	3 500	3 500	3 500	
Total required units	33 500	23 500	13 500	43 500	
Less: Beginning inventory	2 500	3 500	3 500	3 500	
Required production units	**31 000**	**20 000**	**10 000**	**40 000**	**101 000**

It is estimated that 101 000 mountain bikes will need to be produced in 2019. This production level highlights the influence of inventory policy and sales requirements on production output. The production budget, in turn, provides the basis for determining the budgeted costs for each manufacturing cost element, as explained below.

Developing the materials budget

Once the production output has been estimated, Anni can determine the amount of materials that must be purchased for use in the manufacturing process and to meet the desired finished goods inventory. The entity carries inventory of the materials used in the manufacture of the bike, and the beginning materials inventory is $700 000. After discussions with the material requisitions manager, Anni was advised that the cost per unit of materials per bike to be purchased from suppliers this year is expected to be the same as last year, which was $140 per bike. Management has determined that due to the expected sales increase they want ending materials inventory per quarter to be $840 000.

Given these assumptions, Anni prepares the following materials budget (example 9.3), which shows that a total of $14 280 000 of material will be purchased during the year.

EXAMPLE 9.3

Materials budget

Mountain Bikes
Materials budget for year ended 31 December 2019

	Quarter 1	Quarter 2	Quarter 3	Quarter 4	Total
Units to be produced (refer production budget)	31 000	20 000	10 000	40 000	101 000
Material cost per bike	× $140	× $140	× $140	× $140	
Cost of materials required for production	$4 340 000	$2 800 000	$1 400 000	5 600 000	$14 140 000
Target ending materials inventory	840 000	840 000	840 000	840 000	
Total materials required	5 180 000	3 640 000	2 240 000	6 440 000	
Less: Beginning materials inventory	700 000	840 000	840 000	840 000	
Total cost of material purchases	$4 480 000	$2 800 000	$1 400 000	$5 600 000	$14 280 000

Developing the labour budget

Fourth, to develop the labour budget Anni met with both the production manager and the human resource manager. Based on production requirements, she was advised of the labour hours required to meet the production and the type of employee skills required to undertake the tasks. Wage rates were then sourced from the payroll manager. Based on these discussions, Anni identified that the quantity and cost of labour per mountain bike are expected to be two hours per bike at $20 per hour. Anni prepares the labour budget (example 9.4), which forecasts the number of total labour hours and the total labour costs required per quarter to produce the 101 000 bikes.

EXAMPLE 9.4

Labour budget

Mountain Bikes Labour budget for the year ended 31 December 2019					
	Quarter 1	Quarter 2	Quarter 3	Quarter 4	total
Units to be produced (refer production budget)	31 000	20 000	10 000	40 000	101 000
Labour time per bike	×2	×2	×2	×2	×2
Total required labour hours	62 000	40 000	20 000	80 000	202 000
Labour cost per hour	× $20	× $20	× $20	× $20	× $20
Total labour cost	$1 240 000	$800 000	$400 000	$1 600 000	$4 040 000

Developing the production overhead budget, the selling and administrative expense budget

Fifth, in addition to the costs of labour and material, other production and support department costs need to be included in the budgetary process. Information collected from last year's budget and updated for current prices assists in preparing the production overhead budget (example 9.5) and the selling and administrative expense budget (example 9.6).

EXAMPLE 9.5

Production overhead budget

Mountain Bikes Production overhead budget for the year ended 31 December 2019					
	Quarter 1	Quarter 2	Quarter 3	Quarter 4	total
Depreciation	$1 000 000	$1 000 000	$1 000 000	$1 000 000	$4 000 000
Supplies	1 000 000	500 000	250 000	250 000	2 000 000
Indirect labour	1 500 000	1 000 000	750 000	250 000	3 500 000
Miscellaneous	200 000	200 000	200 000	200 000	800 000
Total production overhead	$3 700 000	$2 700 000	$2 200 000	$1 700 000	$10 300 000

EXAMPLE 9.6

Selling and administrative expense budget

Mountain Bikes
Selling and administrative expense budget for the year ended 31 December 2019

	Quarter 1	Quarter 2	Quarter 3	Quarter 4	total
Administration	$4 000 000	$4 000 000	$4 500 000	$4 000 000	$16 500 000
Marketing	4 000 000	2 000 000	3 000 000	1 000 000	10 000 000
Distribution	1 250 000	1 250 000	1 250 000	1 250 000	5 000 000
Customer service	375 000	375 000	375 000	375 000	1 500 000
Total production overhead	$9 625 000	$7 625 000	$9 125 000	$6 625 000	$33 000 000

At last, Anni will review the budget with the entity's financial controller and the budget documents will then be presented to the CEO and other department heads for consideration.

9.4 Cash budget

Cash is king so cash budget is very important. A **cash budget** is a statement of expected future cash receipts and cash payments, and enables the calculation of expected cash balances. A cash budget prepared on a month-by-month basis over the budget period is preferable as it provides more timely information and enables closer monitoring of the cash position. The cash budget is a key component of the master budget and assists decision making by:
- documenting the timing of all estimated cash receipts and cash payments
- helping to identify periods of expected cash shortages, so corrective action can be taken
- helping to identify periods of expected cash surpluses, so short-term investments can be considered
- identifying suitable times for the purchase of non-current assets
- assisting with the planning and use of borrowed funds
- providing a framework for "what if" analysis.

The cash budget focuses on cash-related items. Cash is often referred to as the lifeblood of any entity. Consequently, the use of the cash budget as a planning tool is critical in terms of providing direction, and setting financial targets and the benchmarks against which performance will be evaluated. When prepared on spreadsheets, the cash budget allows alternative scenarios on the cash position of the entity to be considered. The preparation of a cash budget will identify any liquidity issues and ensure that the entity always has access to cash either through cash from operating activities or, if needed, financing.

Queen Ltd is a wholesale business. Example 9.7 demonstrates the preparation of a cash budget for the business.

EXAMPLE 9.7

Preparation of a cash budget

Queen Ltd's budgeted income statements for each of the next six months are as follows.

	January $'000	February $'000	March $'000	April $'000	May $'000	June $'000
Sales	52	55	55	60	55	53
Cost of goods sold	30	31	31	35	31	32
Salaries and wages	10	10	10	10	10	10
Electricity	5	5	4	3	3	3
Depreciation	3	3	3	3	3	3
Other overhead	2	2	2	2	2	2
Total expenses	50	51	50	53	49	50
Net profit	2	4	5	7	6	3

The business allows all of its customers one month's credit (this means, for example, that cash from January sales will be received in February). Sales revenue during December totalled £60 000.

The business plans to maintain inventories at their existing level until sometime in March, when they are to be reduced by £5 000. Inventories will remain at this lower level indefinitely. Inventories purchases are made on one month's credit. December purchases totalled £30 000. Salaries, wages and "other over-heads" are paid in the month concerned. Electricity is paid quarterly in arrears in March and June. The business plans to buy and pay for a new delivery van in March. This will cost totally £15 000, but an existing van will be traded for £4 000 as a part of the deal. The business expects to have £12 000 in cash at the beginning of January.

The cash budget for the six months ending in June will look as follows:

	January $'000	February $'000	March $'000	April $'000	May $'000	June $'000
Receipts[1]	60	52	55	55	60	55
Payments[2]	30	30	31	26	35	31
Salaries and wages	10	10	10	10	10	10

Continued

	January $'000	February $'000	March $'000	April $'000	May $'000	June $'000
Electricity			14			9
Other overhead	2	2	2	2	2	2
Van purchase	-	-	11	-	-	-
Total payments	42	42	68	38	47	52
Cash surplus	18	10	(13)	17	13	3
Opening balance	12	30	40	27	44	57
Cash balance[3]	30	40	27	44	57	60

Note:

1. The cash receipts from trade receivables lag a month behind sales because customers are given a month in which to pay for their purchases. So, Sales in december will be paid for in January, and so on.

2. In most months, the purchases of inventories will equal the cost of goods sold. This is because the business maintains a constant level of inventories. For inventories to remain constant at the end of each month, the business must replace exactly the amount that has been used. During March, however, the business plans to reduce its inventories by £ 5 000. This means that inventories purchases will be lower than inventories usage in that month. The payments for inventories purchases lag a month behind purchases because the business expects to be allowed a month to pay for what it buys.

3. Each month's cash balance is the previous month's figure plus the cash surplus (or minus the cash deficit) for the current month. The balance at the start of January is £ 12 000 according to the information provided earlier.

Depreciation does not give rise to a cash payment. In the context of profit measurement (in the income statement), depreciation is a very important aspect. Here, however, we are interested only in cash.

Budgets variance

The preparation of the cash budget is an important part of the planning process. Once prepared, the cash budget can be used for monitoring cash performance, which is sometimes referred to as part of the control process. A cash budget prepared on a month-by-month basis is much more useful for this purpose than one prepared on a quarterly or yearly basis.

As each month passes, the actual cash numbers can be compared to the budget numbers. The difference between the two is called **variance**. A variance report is shown in example 9.8, with "u" representing unfavourable and "f" favourable variances. This example indicates that there are problems with the entity's estimate of its operating expenses with the majority of the actual expenses resulting in an unfavourable variance compared to budgeted amounts. The other concern for the entity is the significantly lower value of actual cash received from its customers. The current budget estimates will need to be revised in the light of these changed conditions. It will also impact upon possible investment options as the "surplus" cash identified in the original budget may not now eventuate.

EXAMPLE 9.8

Variance report

Cash budget variance report for month ending 31 January			
	January budget	**January actual**	**Variance**
Cash receipts Receipts from accounts receivable	$285 300	$208 200	$77 100 (u)
Total cash receipts	285 300	208 200	77 100 (u)
Cash payments			
Payments to suppliers	$120 000	$114 500	$5 500 (f)
Direct labour	20 000	22 550	2 550 (u)
Manufacturing overhead	6 500	7 800	1 300 (u)
Warehouse and distribution expenses	4 000	4 400	400 (u)
Sales and marketing expenses	5 600	5 100	500 (f)
Administrative expenses	3 250	3 500	250 (u)
Total cash payments	159 350	157 850	1 500 (f)
Net cash flow	125 950	50 350	75 600 (u)
Bank balance at start of month	59 310	59 310	
Bank balance at end of month	$185 260	$109 660	$75 600 (u)

Note: Actual receipts from accounts receivable is a reflection of the fees, which must be lower than expected unless there has been a change in the collections pattern.

At last, we should know making any adjustments to budget in light of any variances identified. This might result in a reconsideration of the budget numbers for the remaining budget period. Remember that the variance report is an example of the control process, the results of which may assist with further planning.

Improving cash flow

The cash budget identifies periods of expected cash shortages. In such situations, corrective action can restore the cash position.

Cash inflow may be increased by:
- improving the collections of cash from accounts receivable—perhaps the entity needs to review its invoicing and follow-up procedures, offer incentives for prompt payment or charge interest on overdue accounts.
- seeking ways to improve sales or fees—increasing advertising campaigns, or changing features of the product/service to increase fees.
- reducing unnecessary inventory levels—discounting obsolete inventory will generate cash.
- arranging external finance—bank overdraft, accounts receivable factoring, invoice discounting.
- receiving an extra capital contribution from the owners, or considering a change in

ownership suitable.
- selling excess non-current assets—a sale and leaseback arrangement may be more suitable.

Cash outflow may be reduced by:
- cutting expenses by identifying areas of waste, duplication or inefficiency
- making use of terms of credit—where purchases are made on credit, there is some benefit in using the full extent of the credit terms
- keeping inventory levels to only what is required, as excess inventory ties up cash and often adds to storage and handling costs
- deferring capital expenditures—it may be necessary to delay the acquisition of any non-current assets
- reducing the carbon footprint, which may reduce resource use and cash outflows.

The following real world, "Iron ore price tumbles", highlights the need for entities to review budget estimates during the budget period, particularly in light of changing circumstances beyond their control.

REAL WORLD

Iron ore price tumbles

Iron ore is a major input into the iron smelting and steel manufacturing industries. Prior to 2012/2013 increased steel production in developing countries, such as China and India, led to strong demand for iron ore and as a consequence high iron ore prices. During this time the price of iron ore peaked at over US $200 per tonne. In 2014/2015 the situation changed with the price dropping to below US $50 per tonne. Many factors have led to this dramatic price decrease including increased production from Australia and Brazil that has flooded the market and decreased demand from China.

Accountants working in the iron smelting and steel manufacturing industries probably did not anticipate the size of the price decrease when they developed their company's budget. If you work in an industry using/selling a commodity such as iron ore, what can you do when prices are in such decline and also tend to fluctuate? The original master budget would not be an appropriate tool for monitoring performance in such a volatile market, and from the sellers' perspective the accountants would need to revise cost and revenue budgets, and search for ways to use resources more efficiently or increase sales volume, as there would be no opportunity to change the selling price.

Like all decision-making processes, budgeting is affected by human attitudes and assumptions.

SUMMARY

1. Understand the link and difference between planning and budgeting.

Planning is needed to ensure that what happens today supports the future direction of the entity. Strategic planning relates to long-term planning while budgeting focuses on the short term (usually one year). The planning process evaluates whether the strategy leads to profits, thereby creating value.

2. Explain what a budget is and describe the key steps in the budgeting process.

A budget is a set of short-term goals and targets in financial terms. The key steps in the budgeting process are a consideration of past performance, an assessment of the expected trading and operating conditions, preparation of initial budget estimates, adjustments to estimates based on communication with and feedback from managers, preparation of the budgeted financial statements and any sub-budgets, monitoring of actual performance against the budget over the budget period, and, where necessary, adjusting the budget during the budget period.

3. Explain the different types of budgets.

Commonly prepared budgets include the sales or fees budget, the operating expenses budget, the production and inventory budgets, the purchases budget, the budgeted statement of profit or loss, the cash budget, the budgeted balance sheet and the capital budget.

4. Outline the components of a master budget and prepare a master budget.

A master budget may be viewed as a set of interrelated budgets for a future period. The master budget is commonly classified into a set of operating budgets and financial budgets.

5. Prepare a schedule of cash budget.

Cash budget focuses on expected future cash receipts and payments, and the expected cash levels at the end of each month, quarter or year. The planning aspect relates to operationalising plans and developing budget estimates and targets. The control aspect is evident in the comparison of budget with actual performance.

KEY TERMS

Budget 预算
Budgeting 预算编制
Budgeting process 预算程序
Cash budget 现金预算
Financial budgets 财务预算
Master budget 总预算
Operating budgets 经营预算

Strategic planning　战略规划
Variance　偏差(预算数与实际数之间的差额)

SELF-EVALUATION ACTIVITIES

9.1　Single choice questions

1. What is the correct order of the following steps to the building progress? (　　)
   ① identify the key or limiting factor;
   ② communicate budget guidelines to relevant managers;
   ③ review and coordinate the budgets;
   ④ establish who will take responsibility for the budget setting progress;
   ⑤ prepare budget for the area of limiting factor;
   ⑥ prepare draft budgets for all other areas;
   ⑦ communicate the budgets to all interested parties;
   ⑧ prepare master budget.
   (a) ①②③④⑤⑥⑦⑧
   (b) ④②⑤①③⑥⑧⑦
   (c) ④②①⑤⑥③⑧⑦
   (d) ⑧⑦⑥⑤④③②①
   (e) ①②④⑤⑥③⑧⑦

2. The master budget includes: (　　)
   (a) sales budget;
   (b) cash budget;
   (c) production budget;
   (b) expense budget;
   (e) budget statement of financial performance.

3. Budgets are generally regarded as having four areas of usefulness. Which of the following is not one of these? (　　)
   (a) They tend to promote forward thinking and possible identification of short-term problems;
   (b) They can be used to help co-ordination between various sections of the business;
   (c) They can motivate managers to better performance;
   (d) They can be used in allocating direct expenses;
   (e) They can provide a basis for a system of control.

4. Which of the following would not normally be a practical reason associated with an adverse labour efficiency variance? (　　)
   (a) poor supervision;
   (b) a low skill grade worker taking longer to do the work than was envisaged for the correct skill grade;
   (c) lower grade material leading to high levels of scrap and wasted labour time;
   (d) change in labour market conditions between setting the standard and the actual event;

(e) dislocation of material supply leading to workers being unable to process with production.

5. Which of the following is not a potential limitation of control through variance analysis? ( )

(a) Vast areas of most business and commercial activities do not have the same direct relationship between inputs and output;

(b) Standards can quickly become out of date as a result of both technological change and price change;

(c) Sometime factors are outside the control of the manager and can affect the calculation of the variance for which the manager is held accountable;

(d) In practice, creating clear lines of demarcation between the areas of responsibility of various managers is a simple task;

(e) None of the above.

9.2 True or false

1. Long-term plans would define the general direction of the business over the next five or so years.

2. The sale volume variance measures the effect on profit of a change in sales volume.

3. Budget is not prepared with the objective of affecting the attitudes and behavior of managers.

4. Significant favourable variance should probably be investigated as they may mean that targets have been set unrealistically.

5. A budget committee is formed to supervise and take responsibility for the budget setting progress.

9.3 Development of budget

From the following data for Ox Services, complete a schedule of receipts from accounts receivable for the three months ending 30 June 2017.

Credit sales are normally settled according to the following pattern: 40 per cent in the month of sale, 30 per cent in the month following the sale, and 25 per cent in the second month following the sale. Five per cent of accounts are never collected.

	Actual		Estimated		
	February	March	April	May	June
Credit sales	$134 000	$126 000	$108 000	$110 000	$128 000

Answer to self-evaluation activities

9.1 Single choice questions

1. c   2. e   3. d   4. d   5. d

9.2 True or false
1. T   2. T   3. F   4. T   5. T

9.3 Development of budget
Solution:

		April	May	June
February	$134 000	$33 500		
March	126 000	37 800	$31 500	
April	108 000	43 200	32 400	$27 000
May	110 000		44 000	33 000
June	128 000			51 200
Total		$114 500	$107 900	$111 200

Part 3

Financial Management

CHAPTER 10

Capital Investment

LEARNING OBJECTIVES

After studying this chapter, you should be able to:
- 10.1 understand the nature of investment decisions
- 10.2 describe and apply the concept of the accounting rate of return (ARR)
- 10.3 explain and use the payback period (PP) method
- 10.4 discuss and calculate net present values (NPV) and apply the decision rule
- 10.5 discuss and calculate internal rates of return (IRR) and apply the decision rule
- 10.6 explain some of the practical issues in making investment decisions

How entities make decisions to invest in new assets or new projects? Both a listed company and a small business should make decisions about investments in new product markets, new stores or new fixtures and fittings. Even so investments may be small or large, but the principles that underlie the decisions about whether to make the investments are the same, no matter the absolute size of the investment or the type of entity investing.

In this chapter we will introduce four principal methods to evaluate whether an investment in assets or projects should proceed. They are the accounting rate of return (ARR), payback period (PP), net present value (NPV) and internal rate of return (IRR). Finally, sometimes there are practical difficulties and complications in calculating and applying numerical decision-support tools.

10.1 The nature and scope of investment decisions

Investment decisions are made by managers in all sorts of entities, large and small. Some of the most common features of investments are that they:
- often need large amounts of resources in relation to entity asset bases or turnover,
- involve risk and uncertainty,
- often span long periods of time and returns are received over the long period,
- normally require a relatively large initial cash outlay,
- are often difficult to reverse without the loss of substantial funds.

Let us look at each of these features in turn. Investments in projects, property, plant and equipment often involve large amounts of resources (staff time and funds) in relation to some other measure of the entity's size. JB Ltd, for example, on its 2015 balance sheet had more than $176 million of plant and equipment. The amounts of investments involved are very large and need to be made with the help of appropriate decision-support tools.

Investment decisions normally involve risk and uncertainty, with managers expected to also bear the responsibility for "bad investments". **Risk** in finance is defined as measurable variation in outcomes. **Uncertainty**, on the other hand, is the unmeasurable variation in outcomes. Risk can be measured with some degree of confidence when the same decision is taken many times and the varying outcomes can be analysed, so that a measure of the variation can be made. Thereafter, the decision maker will have a better understanding of how expected outcomes may vary. BMW Group (the German motor cycle and vehicle manufacturer) spends large amounts of funds on research and development activities. The company employs approximately 11 800 employees in its global research and innovation network situated in 12 locations across five countries. The company expenses research costs as they are incurred. Costs on development projects are recognised as intangible assets when it is foreseeable that a product will generate future economic benefits. In 2014, research and development (R&D) costs expensed were £4.6 billion which was a decrease of 4.7 per cent compared to those in 2013. BMW Group undertakes this process to help deliver the best product possible and keep up to date with innovative technologies. This strategy obviously involves risks as there is no guarantee that saleable and successful products will be developed. BMW cannot be certain about the market's desirability for any new products.

Investments normally span long periods of time and require cash outlays initially, with cash inflows being received over a long future period. For example, airlines invest large sums of cash outlaid on new aircraft. Airlines make a choice whether to buy or lease the aircraft. New aircraft require millions of dollars to be spent upfront or as progress payments before delivery. Returns come from the sale of flights to passengers or freight income over several years.

What happens if, part-way through the development of a project, the investors find circumstances have changed and they really would prefer not to be involved? Such unexpected changes might involve major changes in consumer or political values, changes in legislation governing an industry, substantial increases in the infrastructure development costs, or perhaps major reductions in the supply of raw materials. Normally, if projects are suspended before coming to fruition, investors stand to lose most, if not all, of their invested funds. This risk should impose great pressure on analysts and investors when they are investigating the worth of potential investment projects.

The process of decision making

Just as funds are normally a scarce and valuable resource in our personal lives, so to they are for business entities. Hence, entities that are successful in the long term make investment decisions very carefully and follow established decision-support procedures. At any one time, most entities will have many projects or investments available to them, and the decision as to which projects to invest in is based on an assessment of the attractiveness of the returns relative to the risk.

The steps involved in making an investment decision are as follows.

1. Identify all the investment alternatives available at the time.
2. Select a decision-support tool and set the decision rule.
3. Collect the data necessary to make the decision.
4. Analyse the data.
5. Interpret the results in relation to the decision rule.
6. Make the decision.

After making the investment decision, the next step is often to arrange finance (the financing decision) and start the planning and physical implementation of the project or investment.

The investment alternatives available to any entity at any one time normally fit into new investments to increase revenue, new technology to decrease costs or replacement of old assets as they wear out.

The following sections in this chapter deal with the steps in the decision-making process and discuss the decision-support tools available, their data requirements and their decision rules. The final section examines some of the practical issues in applying these decision-support tools. Data and information for an investment decision are given in example 10.1.

EXAMPLE 10.1

The material for a decision—Coconut

Coconut Pty Ltd manufactures sustainable coconut-based products. Jone, the manager, has been successful in securing long-term contracts to supply a variety of retailers with quantities of soaps, candles and detergents packaged under the Eco Friendly label. To ensure the adequate supply of coconut oil, the major raw material for each product, Jone has worked out a remuneration deal for potential suppliers. Each manufacturer is offered a four-year contract to supply certified organic coconut oil. The oil is purchased at $200 per 100 litres as a standard price. Coconut oil that fails the certification process will be accepted at a 20 per cent discount.

Under these arrangements, manufacturers can expect to earn the following net cash returns. The net cash inflows in table 10.1 are net of raw materials, other ingredients, processing costs, manufacturing overhead and delivery. The manufacturer's own labour costs are excluded.

TABLE 10.1

Year	Expected net cash flows ($000)
1	30
2	60
3	50
4	40

Specialised equipment necessary to manufacture certified organic coconut oil is estimated to cost $120 000. The equipment can be sold for $60 000 on the secondhand market after four years of usage. Each supplying manufacturer will use the straight-line method of depreciation. Throughout the chapter, we will use this data and information to arrive at an investment decision for the suppliers of coconut oil using the various techniques as they are explained.

10.2 Accounting rate of return

The **accounting rate of return** (**ARR**) is a simple measure, which has immediate appeal to accountants and managers who are accustomed to dealing with profit figures and asset values. This measure expresses the average profit over the period of the investment as a percentage of the average investment. Thus, it uses the same methodology as the familiar return on assets (ROA) measure, which was discussed in chapter 6. ROA is, of course, a historical measure, while the ARR involves projected future values.

The ARR is calculated as follows:

$$ARR = \frac{\text{Average profit}}{\text{Average investment}}$$

Example 10.2 demonstrates the application of the ARR equation to Coconut Pty Ltd.

EXAMPLE 10.2

Calculating the ARR

The cash flows (net of cash expenses) given in the Coconut information in illustrative example 10.1 are not profits for each year. The cost of using up the value of the equipment or depreciation must be considered. The value of equipment used up is $60 000 ($120 000 − $60 000). Depreciation of $60 000 for the four-year period, or $15 000 per year, must be deducted to arrive at profits before tax. The ARR for the Coconut contract is as follows. (The figures on the top line are in thousands, as are the figures on the bottom line, so we can ignore the thousands in our calculations.) The average investment in the equipment is the average of the values initially, and at the end of four years; that is, the average of $120 000 and $60 000.

$$\text{ARR} = \frac{\text{Average profit}}{\text{Average investment}} = \frac{\dfrac{\$30 + \$60 + \$50 + \$40 - \$60}{4}}{\dfrac{\$120 + \$60}{2}} = \frac{30}{90} = 33.33\%$$

Having calculated this rate of return, manufacturers may think the contract offered by Coconut looks like a pretty good deal. What also must be considered in this case is the opportunity cost of the manufacturers' labour. Opportunity cost is the cost of forgoing benefits that otherwise would be available had the manufacturer not spent time manufacturing the coconut oil. If the manufacturer could earn $20 000, on average, every year for manufacturing other products in this time, or working for other people, the average profit would fall to $10 000 and the ARR to 11.1 per cent.

Decision rule for ARR

The decision rule associated with the ARR varies among entities. Most entities accept the investment with the highest ARR at the time; they set a minimum level (their required rate of return (RRR)), below which they will not consider investing. How the RRR is set varies. Some entities base the level on their own past performance, others look to industry averages, and still others compare the estimated ARR with currently available yields or returns from other investments outside their industries.

Advantages and disadvantages of ARR

The advantages of the ARR measure are that it is:
- simple to calculate
- easy to understand
- consistent with the ROA measure, which entities often try to increase in an attempt to maximise owners' wealth.

The disadvantages of the ARR method are that:
- it ignores the time value of money and the timing of profits
- it ignores the importance of cash as the ultimate resource without which entities cannot survive (entities must have sufficient cash to meet their obligations on time, no matter how asset-rich they are)
- profits and costs may be measured in different ways.

Overall, the ARR is considered by most managers to be too simplistic a measure to be appropriate by itself as a decision-support tool for the application of scarce investment funds. The fact that the timing of cash flows and subsequent profits is ignored is seen as a major deficiency. The method, for example, cannot differentiate between two equally profitable projects but with unequal timing of the profits. (In reality, the project with cash surpluses early in its life is preferable to another project with cash receipts received later in its life.)

10.3 Payback period

Entities invest in order to make profits. Investments normally require the outlay of cash and, as noted above, cash is important to entities that want to survive. Thus, the time it takes to recoup cash expended on investment is important. If two investments were potentially equally profitable, most entities would prefer the investment where the outlaid cash was recouped earlier.

The **payback period** (**PP**) is the period of time necessary to recoup the initial outlay with net cash inflows. Hence, the expected net cash inflows each year are added until the sum is equal to or greater than the initial outlay. The number of years of cash surpluses necessary to be earned to equal the initial investment is the PP. This is demonstrated in example 10.3.

EXAMPLE 10.3

Calculating the payback period

For the Coconut's proposal, we know the initial investment in equipment is $120 000. By the end of year 1, $30 000 net cash flows have been received and, by the end of year 2, a further $60 000 in net cash flows should have been received, making $90 000 in total, with a further $30 000 cash necessary to repay the initial investment. Given that we need $30 000 of the $50 000 in year 3 to pay back the initial investment exactly, we can say the payback period is about 2.6 years (see table 10.2). (Assuming funds are received consistently at about $1 000 surplus each week, it will take 30 weeks or 0.6 years to earn the required $30 000 surplus.)

TABLE 10.2 Payback decision rate

Year	Net cash flow $	Cumulative net cash flow ($)	
0	(120 000)	(120 000)	
1	30 000	(90 000)	
2	60 000	(30 000)	Payback occurs between years 2 and 3
3	50 000	20 000	
4	100 000	120 000	

Decision rule for payback period

The decision rule with PP varies among entities, but most have maximum periods beyond which they would not invest. Just as with ARR standards, the maximum periods might be based on past performance in that individual entity, or on industry averages. The maximum periods generally vary quite markedly. For example, the payback period for a major mining venture is much longer than the payback period built into the pricing and investment decisions related to a newly developed herbicide or fashion. Similarly, the purchase of a new airplane would take several years (and many flights) to pay back its initial purchase price. However, one thing is certain: the longer the PP, the greater the risk, because there is a far greater chance that some of the assumptions on which the investment decision was made will change.

Advantages and disadvantages of PP

The advantages of the PP measure are that it:
- is simple to calculate
- is easy to understand
- provides a crude measure of incorporating awareness of risk into the decision, as projects with relatively high early cash surpluses will have smaller PPs.

The disadvantages of the PP method are that it:
- ignores the time value of money, as the PP method treats all cash inflows equally.
- ignores all cash inflows after payback has occurred, so that inherently more profitable investments may be rejected in favour of less profitable short-term investments given that the time horizon of analysis is restricted to the period up until the initial investment is recouped. For example, with the Coconut Plantations Company no consideration is given to cash flows beyond the payback period.

Similarly to the ARR, the PP is considered to be too simplistic a measure to be used by itself as a decision-support tool. Again, it does not recognise that funds received early in the life of a project are worth more than funds received later.

10.4 Net present value

Ignoring the time value of money is a major defect of both the ARR and PP tools. Discounted cash-flow techniques overcome this problem by specifically recognising that $1 received in the future is worth less than $1 received now. In a case, you invest your $1 000 received today elsewhere and earn a return without taking on much risk, making the future value of the $1 000 higher. Let us say you had invested at 4 per cent, the return of $40 on your $1 000 would have covered the effect of inflation if it was about 3 per cent for the year, and would mean you would have received a net increase in funds as well. Here is a timeline showing this situation:

$1 000 (present value)	$1 040 (future value)
T_0 = now	T_1 = 1 year's time

Here is the formula to do this calculation.

$$FV = PV(1+i)^n$$

Where FV = future value
PV = present value
i = interest rate/period
n = no. of periods.

We could look at this situation from the other end—in one year's time. Which is the present value (PV) of $1 000 in one year's time? Under a discount rate of 4 per cent, the $961.54 is called a discounted cash flow. The discounted cash flow or PV is calculated by dividing the future sum by a discount factor.

$$PV = \frac{FV}{(1+i)^n}$$

$$PV = \frac{1\ 000}{1.04} = 961.54$$

Here, that factor is 1.04 (i.e. 1 + the relevant interest rate for the year). You can check to find if $961.54 is correct by multiplying it by 1.04 to see if you get $1 000. This shows that receiving $1 000 in one year is the equivalent of receiving $961.54 today, assuming a rate of return of 4 per cent.

The reason for calculating the present values of all the cash flows is so that the initial investment may be matched with the expected inflows in terms of the same units of money with the same purchasing power. A dollar that is received now has the same purchasing power as a dollar paid out now. In addition, the cash flows are adjusted for risk and the opportunity cost of capital. The cash flows used in the analysis are the net cash inflows (either positive or negative) for each period. This means that the final net cash inflow also includes any salvage value that might be gained by selling the infrastructure or materials that are left over at the completion of the project. Normally, the initial investment is taken to occur now and its value is thus a PV, unless it is a major project where development spans more than one period.

The investment decision techniques involving discounting cash flows in this chapter are **net present value (NPV)** and **internal rate of return (IRR)**. The PV of a project is the sum of the PVs of all the expected cash flows from all the individual periods. These PVs of the cash flows are calculated just as we saw above. Then, the NPV measure compares the sum of the present values (PVs) of all of the expected cash inflows from the project with the PVs of the expected cash outflows. The NPV is the present value of the net cash flows. The discount rate is the interest rate at which a future cash flow is converted to a present value.

$$PV = CF_1/(1+r) + CF_2/(1+r)^2 + CF_3/(1+r)^3 \ldots CF_n/(1+r)^n$$
$$NPV = CF_1/(1+r) + CF_2/(1+r)^2 + CF_3/(1+r)^3 + \ldots + CF_n/(1+r)^n - INV$$

Where CF = the net cash flow at the end of period n
  r = the selected discount rate per period
  n = the number of periods, and
  INV = the initial investment.

Decision rule for NPV

The investment decision rule based on the financial analysis is to invest in projects (assets) if the NPV is positive (i.e. PV net CF > initial investment). This is because the positive value indicates a project that is potentially able to yield a higher return than the opportunity cost of funds (whose value is incorporated in the discount rate). Calculating NPV is demonstrated in example 10.4.

EXAMPLE 10.4

Calculating net present value

Let us now return to the Coconut Plantations example and assume that potential manufacturers require a 10 per cent investment return. Denominated in thousands of dollars, the NPV is calculated as follows.

$$\begin{aligned} NPV &= CF_1/(1+r) + CF_2/(1+r)^2 + CF_3/(1+r)^3 + \ldots + CF_n/(1+r)^n - INV \\ &= 30/1.1 + 60/(1.1)^2 + 50/(1.1)^3 + 100/(1.1)^4 - 120 \\ &= 27.27 + 49.58 + 37.57 + 68.30 - 120 \\ &= 62.72 \end{aligned}$$

Remember, the $100 000 in year 4 is the $40 000 from the sale of coconut oil, plus the $60 000 from the sale of the secondhand machinery. The result of $62 720 is positive and indicates that, on this measure, the contract to manufacture coconut oil should be undertaken, as it will enhance the manufacturer's wealth. While a positive value for the NPV indicates that the manufacturer would be better off if it took on this project, a negative value, on the other hand, indicates that the project would not generate sufficient surplus and the manufacturer would not increase their wealth through this project.

To solve the NPV equation, with r valued at 10 per cent so that $(1+r)$ equals 1.1, a financial calculator can be used in place of the manual steps above.

Determining the discount rate

1. Inflation

One factor in the determination of r is inflation. Inflation is the increase in the prices of goods and services. The converse is deflation, which often coincides with lower levels of demand in an economy, periods of high unemployment and economic depression. It has been seldom seen in the developed economies in the last several decades. Thus, inflation at greater or lesser levels is the norm. What inflation means for investors is that their invested funds lose purchasing power while those funds are being used by the investee. Hence, an investor placing $1 000 today in any investment and receiving $1 000 back in three years' time will not recover the same amount of purchasing power. For example, if inflation has been on average 3 per cent per annum during those three years, the investor will receive only $915 ($1 000/1.033) of purchasing power in today's terms. In reality, interest rates and other returns offered in financial markets have an inflation component already incorporated. Thus, the investor does not really have to worry about this aspect of interest rates and returns. The opportunity return will take care of the inflationary impact.

REAL WORLD

Inflation versus deflation

Inflation and deflation are important factors for considering in investment projects. In terms of inflation, investment strategies such as shares, bonds and commodities such as gold provide a good method of keeping up with inflationary periods. Property also usually increases in value in inflationary periods. In terms of deflation, entities can invest in bonds, especially government bonds. Shares in industries such as consumer goods will always be better than other industries during periods of deflation. However, if entities do not want to change their investment strategy to meet changes in the economic cycle, a good method is to diversify. Blue-chip shares seem to maintain a constant value and also provide the additional bonus of dividends.

2. Risk

Investment decisions involve risk. Costs may rise above what was expected, returns may fall short. A further concern is the extra element of risk associated with an individual investment. Many single investments carry more risk than groups of investments, especially if those investments have been put together carefully to manage their risk. From an individual investor perspective, a single investment in one company on the share market is likely to carry more risk than, say, a deposit with a local building society, where an individual's funds would be pooled with other monies and spread amongst different investments. Investors who take on more risk demand higher returns as compensation for assuming that risk. Thus, more risky investments will have a risk margin added to their opportunity interest rate, to arrive at a final higher discount rate which in turn lowers the present value.

3. Opportunity cost

Opportunity cost was discussed in relation to a manufacturer supplying coconut oil to Coconut Plantations. Money also has an opportunity cost. If investors can place their funds in alternative investments (which they can), directing their funds to a particular investment has an opportunity cost. The opportunity cost is the cost of forgoing the benefit from that alternative investment. If the alternative investment pays 5 per cent per annum, the opportunity cost in making the given investment is 5 per cent.

Remember, we noted earlier that the cash flows are assumed to have been received and paid at the end of each period. This is a simplifying assumption. In reality, most projects have cash flows received and paid more or less evenly throughout the year. It is possible to incorporate this pattern of cash flows into an analysis by using specially calculated daily discount tables. However, we will not investigate this in this chapter. Just be aware that such a refinement is possible.

Advantages and disadvantages of the NPV method

The advantages of the NPV method are that it takes into account:
- all of the expected cash flows
- the timing of expected cash flows (with cash flows received sooner being more beneficial to the entity)
- cash flows only, so it is not subject to changing accounting rules and standards as profit figures are.

The disadvantages of the NPV method are that:
- the method relies on the use of an appropriate discount factor for the circumstances
- the actual return in terms of the percentage of the investment outlay is not revealed
- ranking of projects in terms of highest NPVs may not lead to optimum outcomes when capital is rationed.
- in some cases, it conflicts with IRR rankings. (There also can be multiple IRRs.)

The last three disadvantages may need further explanation. (The first two of these are discussed here, and the final disadvantage is discussed in the section on the IRR.) Suppose a project's cash returns have been discounted by 10 per cent and the calculated NPV is $23 450. From these data, we do not know if the project can be expected to return 11 per cent, 12 per cent, 13 per cent or 20 per cent. To understand the ranking problem, consider the following data in table 10.3.

TABLE 10.3 Outlays and NPVs for proposed projects

Project	Outlay ($A million)	NPV ($A million)
A	100	8.2
B	80	6.9

Continued

Project	Outlay ($A million)	NPV ($A million)
C	60	4.4
D	40	3.0
E	20	1.6

Is A the best project for the entity to undertake? It does have the highest NPV. However, the answer is "no". Suppose an entity has access to $100 million in finance, it could undertake the A project and earn $8.2 million. Alternatively, it could undertake two projects that together involve an investment not exceeding $100 million. In this case, it could undertake the A project or both the B and the E projects, or the C and the D projects. The NPVs of these groups are $8.2 million, $8.5 million and $7.4 million. Thus, the best decision for the entity would be to undertake both the B and E projects, to earn $8.5 million. So, the project with the highest NPV may not be the best project when capital is limited. Sometimes, entities will invest in a range of different projects with differing NPVs as part of their long-term business strategy.

10.5 Internal rate of return

The IRR is the second of the discounted cash-flow techniques discussed in this chapter. It is widely used by entities in their project appraisal work. The IRR is the rate of return that discounts the cash flows of a project so that the PV of the cash inflows just equals the PV of the cash outflows. The IRR thus gives managers a value for the projected return from any project and allows them to compare the returns from various proposed projects. It also allows them to ascertain if the IRR is higher than their hurdle required rate of return. If so, the decision rule would be to invest in the project.

In many cases, the PV of the cash outflows will be just the initial investment, which often can be assumed to occur at time zero or the present time. The equation used to find the IRR is similar to the NPV equation, except that the left-hand side will equal zero when the IRR value is found.

$$0 = -INV + CF_1/(1+r) + CF_2/(1+r)^2 + CF_3/(1+r)^3 + \ldots + CF_n/(1+r)^n$$

To find the IRR, we have to use the equation and solve for r. With a scientific calculator or the use of discount tables, solving for r is a trial and error problem. On the other hand, with a financial calculator or a computerised spreadsheet, the solution is more easily found.

Decision rule for IRR

The decision rule with IRR is to accept projects where the IRR exceeds the entity's required rate of return (RRR). Normally, that level would be the cost of capital, although some entities have arbitrary RRRs that they have set for various reasons. The RRR may be less than 20 per cent for many entities. Accepting projects that have IRRs greater than the entity's cost of capital means that the entity is making investments that both return the cost of finance and make additional returns. Such entities are thus enhancing the wealth of their owners.

The trial and error method of calculating IRR is examined in example 10.5.

EXAMPLE 10.5

Using the trial and error method of calculating IRR

Remembering the data from the Coconut example (given below), the problem is to find the discount rate that will result in the sum of all the discounted positive cash flows less the value of the initial investment ($120 000) equal zero.

Year	Expected cash flows ($000)
0 (initially)	−120
1	30
2	60
3	50
4	100

Let us go through the trial and error method. In example 10.4 the NPV is a healthy $62 720 at a 10 per cent discount rate, and thus the IRR must be more than 10 per cent, because the NPV is positive and much larger than zero. What happens to our NPV if a 20 per cent rate is used? The NPV will be $23 820, and still considerably larger than zero. From this drop in the NPV, you could deduce that 30 per cent would probably be too much and the NPV would be negative, so try 25 per cent. The NPV is still positive at $8 960. We might now try 28 per cent. At 28 per cent, the NPV is $1 140. A discount rate of 29 per cent is probably too much, but let us try it just for fun. Answer: − $1 290. So, 29 per cent is too high a discount rate and the calculated IRR is 28 per cent. (When using a spreadsheet, you could easily refine this answer to several decimal points of accuracy.)

Having done the calculation, the question then is: what does it mean? An IRR of 28 per cent is likely to exceed the manufacturers' RRR, which may be as low as 10-12 per cent, and thus the project is acceptable on this measure. Manufacturers undertaking this project will have their cost of capital returned, plus extra return, which will increase their wealth.

Advantages and disadvantages of IRR

The advantages of the IRR method are that it takes into account:
- all of the expected cash flows
- the timing of expected cash flows (cash flows received sooner are given higher weight)

- a concept (rate of return) familiar to managers.

The disadvantages are that the method:
- ignores the scale of projects, so it does not focus on the generation of absolute wealth
- in some cases, produces two IRR values (or in some circumstances, no IRR)
- in some cases, conflicts with NPV rankings of projects.

Effects of unconventional cash flows

So far we have discussed projects with conventional cash-flow patterns. That is, there is a large initial cash outflow, followed by many years of net cash inflows. However, there are projects that have so-called unconventional patterns of cash flows. In mining investment projects, the restoration expenses at the completion of a mining project may mean that the final year has net cash outflows rather than net cash inflows. Thus, there will be two years of net cash outflows.

Comparing the NPV and IRR for a project

The NPVs and IRRs for projects that have conventional cash flows always bear the same relationship to each other. When the IRR is zero, the NPV will be at a maximum and positive if the sum of the net cash inflows exceeds the original cost. Think about that. If there is no discounting (i.e. $r = 0$), the cash flows will have their full undiscounted values. As the value of r increases, the value of the NPV must decrease. At some point, the value of r will be such that the NPV is zero, and this is the IRR for the project. Beyond that point, if the value of r increases still further, the NPV for the project will be negative. Figure 10.1 shows this situation graphically.

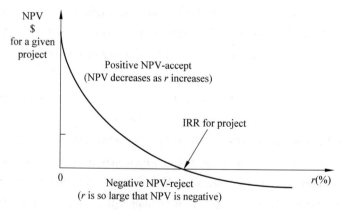

FIGURE 10.1 Relationship of NPV and IRR for a project

Suppose the IRR of the project in figure 10.1 was 15 per cent. Is this acceptable to us as investors? If 15 per cent is above our RRR, we would accept the project on this basis. Similarly, if we had discounted the expected cash flows at any rate less than 15 per cent, we would have calculated positive NPVs, and these values would also support our decision to make the investment. Thus, the two measures in this case have given us the same advice. This is the normal situation with conventional cash flow patterns; but, as noted earlier, it is possible for the two measures to be in conflict.

REAL WORLD

A survey of UK business practice

Senior financial managers at 83 of the UK's largest manufacturing businesses were asked about the investment appraisal methods used to evaluate both strategic and nonstrategic projects. Strategic projects usually aim to increase or change the competitive capabilities of a business, such as introducing a new manufacturing process.

Method	Non-strategic	projects
Net present value	3.682 9	3.975 9
Payback	3.426 8	3.609 8
Internal rate of return	3.329 3	3.707 3
Accounting rate of return	1.986 7	2.266 7

Response scale 1 = never, 2 = rarely, 3 = often, 4 = mostly, 5 = always

We can see that, both for non-strategic and for strategic investments, the NPV method is the most popular. As the sample consists of large businesses (nearly all with total sales revenue in excess of £100 million), a fairly sophisticated approach to evaluation might be expected. Nevertheless, for non-strategic investments, the payback method comes second in popularity. It drops to third place for strategic projects.

The survey also found that 98 per cent of respondents used more than one method and 88 per cent used more than three methods of investment appraisal.

Source: Based on information in "*Strategic capital investment decision-making: a role for emergent analysis tools? A study of practice in large UK manufacturing companies*", F. Alkaraan and D. Northcott, The British Accounting Review, 38, 2006, p. 159.

In US, the similar survey of the chief financial officers (CFOs) of 392 US businesses examined the popularity of various methods of investment appraisal. *The percentage of businesses surveyed that used the four methods is different.* The IRR (76%) and NPV (75%) methods are both widely used and are much more popular than the payback (57%) and accounting rate of return (20%) methods. Nevertheless, the payback method is still used always, or almost always, by a majority of US businesses.

10.6　Practical issues in making decisions

The methods outlined earlier in this chapter make decision making appear relatively easy. However, many things are seldom as easy as they appear. In practice, the investment decision is not normally just a mechanical calculation. There are many other factors that must be taken into consideration. We have already discussed the impact of inflation, risk and opportunity cost. In addition, many decisions and judgements must consider about:
- collecting data
- taxation effects
- finance
- human resources
- goodwill and future opportunities
- social responsibility and care of the natural environment.

Collecting data

Collecting data on costs and returns is often not easy. Think back to the Coconut Plantations' relatively simple coconut oil equipment investment project. In that case, finding the cost of the equipment is simple. Moreover, some of the periodic outflows—such as equipment maintenance and insurance—are relatively easy to cost, but others are not.

The quantity of electricity for running the plant to manufacture the coconut oil, for example, and its total cost are difficult to estimate. There could be unforeseen issues such as poor-quality ingredients that require additional processing to get to the desired end product—certified organic coconut oil! But what about the returns? In order to estimate the cash inflows each year, the manufacturer needs to think about the cost of the ingredients in the process. Ingredients such as unprocessed coconut will fluctuate in price. So, you can see from this simple example that collecting data is not as easy as it looks.

Taxation effects

Taxation impacts on investments. Most, if not all, developed countries have some form of income tax, and many have a form of capital gains tax. Generally, with a 30 per cent flat company tax rate, and marginal taxation rates of up to 46.5 per cent plus a 1 per cent Medicare levy surcharge for businesspeople and investors operating as individuals and in partnerships. Capital gains are taxed at 30 per cent for companies and, under the simplest current regime, at half marginal rates for individuals and investors operating in partnerships. Thus, the impact of taxation for a simple investment by a company is to reduce net cash annual returns by 30 per cent. Complications are introduced into cash-flow analyses with the effect of taxation benefits that stem from non-cash costs such as depreciation.

Finance

Investment appraisals are undertaken on the assumption that finance will be available if the numbers are attractive enough. While this may be true some of the time—even most of the time—it is not true all of the time. Some investments, even though they look good on paper, have trouble attracting venture capital. An infrastructure project partly completed normally represents funds lost, as it is often difficult to recover value, even if the project gains enough funding to regain momentum.

Human resources

As with finance, investment appraisals are undertaken on the assumption that human resources (i. e. employees or consultants with the required skills) will be available on demand. While this may be true for most needs of the more common skills, it may not be true where highly skilled scientists, pilots, artists, computer analysts and others are needed. In addition, sometimes the undertaking of several projects at a time by an entity can overload the capacity of the current skilled workforce to produce the required output of the required quality.

An example of this is an engineering entity that needs to produce specialised parts made from special alloys to very fine tolerances. The trades people with the fine quality skills needed may not be available at the time they are needed. Another example of human resource issues exists in universities. In the last few years, many university departments have significantly changed their course offerings and in doing so have had to look closely at their staff to ensure that they have the appropriate staff numbers and experience to meet the requirements to teach the new courses. In some cases, it has become evident that the university does not have enough staff with a suitable background to teach in these new areas, which has led to the cancellation of some of these new courses or the hiring of additional staff.

Goodwill and future opportunities

Goodwill is built up over time by entities through giving customers the service and quality they demand. Service can mean fast response times, always having the necessary stock on hand, and completing supply contracts on time and at the right price. Quality in relation to goods and services normally means that the goods and services are useful and appropriate, and indeed do the job better than expected.

Entities able to deliver quality service tend to build up loyalty among their customers. The loyalty may have nothing in the way of a reward for past service, but may be merely self-serving on the part of the customers, in that they know they will get what they want, when they want it, and the price they are prepared to pay.

It may be necessary sometimes for an entity to take on projects or investments that it would rather not, but which it does to keep faith with its customers, in the hope that such service will be recognised and that there will be further mutually satisfactory business deals in the future. It is through this sort of behaviour that entities build loyal customer bases, which are assets to the entities, just as much as machinery and skilled employees are.

Social responsibility and care of the natural environment

Social responsibility and care of the natural environment have become important concerns for an increasing proportion of the investor community. Environmental issues, such as the wood chipping of forests and the release of greenhouse gases into the environment, are important issues for both companies and their stakeholders.

Investors should be aware of these issues, the possibility of changes in legislation and the need to consider this source of risk before they commit their funds.

Conclusion—Coconut's investment decisions

Throughout this chapter, we have used the data given in example 10.1 to show how the various decision tools are calculated. Table 10.4 summarises the results of these calculations before discussing the final decision.

TABLE 10.4　Decision tool results

Tool	Result
ARR	33.3% or 11.1% (with the opportunity cost of labour included)
PP	2.6 years
NPV	$62 720 (with 10% discount factor)
IRR	28%

From table 10.4, all the tools seem to indicate that the coconut oil manufacturing project is a reasonably good investment. However, as noted earlier in the chapter, managers make their decisions based on their entity's past performances, their expectations, industry averages or current production in comparable markets. Hence, it is an individual manufacturer's decision as to whether 11.1 per cent is an acceptable return as indicated by the ARR measure. However, in an environment where many manufacturers normally make less than 5 per cent return on their assets, a double-digit return looks acceptable. Moreover, at 2.6 years, the PP tool indicates a project that most managers would probably view as worth giving a second look. Less than three years is a short period to allow for recovery of the initial investment and would be acceptable to many decision makers.

These above tools take little or no account of risk, with the exception that a short PP reduces the period in which adverse factors can develop and manifest themselves. The tools that are able to incorporate risk are the discounted cash flow methods—NPV and IRR.

The NPV of more than $62 000 would be acceptable to many managers, given the initial investment of $120 000 and the fact that the investment is all in readily saleable assets with good second-hand values, no matter what their ages are. The discount factor of 10 per cent incorporates an assessment of inflation, risk and alternative opportunities not taken up by undertaking this project. The IRR backs up the acceptable outcome suggested by the NPV and, at 28 per cent, is quite high without being so high as to suggest that the financial data might not be reliable.

In conclusion, all four tools suggest that the project is worth considering and, if not undertaken immediately, then at least worth further investigation.

SUMMARY

1. **Explain the nature and scope of investment decisions.**

Some of the most common features of investments are that they:
- often involve large amounts of resources in relation to entities' asset bases or turnover
- involve risk and uncertainty
- usually span long periods of time
- normally require a relatively large initial cash outlay, and returns are received over a long period into the future
- are often difficult to reverse without the loss of substantial funds.

2. **Describe and apply the concept of the accounting rate of return (ARR).**

The accounting rate of return is a simple measure which expresses the average profit over the period of the investment as a percentage of the average investment. Decision makers may accept projects where the ARR exceeds a required minimum level.

3. **Explain and use the payback period (PP) method.**

Having sufficient cash is important to entities that want to survive. Thus, the time it takes to recoup cash is important. The payback period is the period of time necessary to recoup the initial outlay with net cash inflows. Investors favour projects with short PPs.

4. **Discuss and calculate net present values (NPV) and apply the decision rule.**

Discounted cash-flow techniques overcome the problem of the time value of money by specifically recognising that $1 received sometime in the future is worth less than $1 received now. The NPV measure compares the sum of the present values (PVs) of all of the expected cash inflows from the project with the PVs of the expected cash outflows. The NPV is the net outcome. Positive NPVs indicate that projects are acceptable. Negative NPVs indicate that projects will not increase wealth.

5. **Discuss and calculate internal rates of return (IRR) and apply the decision rule.**

The IRR is the rate of return, which discounts the cash flows of a project so that the PV of the cash inflows equals the PV of the cash outflows. The equation used to find the IRR is similar to the NPV equation, except that the left-hand side equals zero when the IRR is found.

Investors may accept projects where the IRR exceeds a required rate of return.

6. Explain some of the practical issues in making investment decisions.

The tools outlined cause decision making to appear relatively easy. In practice, there may be difficulties with the following issues:

- collecting data
- taxation effects
- finance
- human resources
- goodwill and future opportunities
- social responsibility and care of the natural environment.

KEY TERMS

Accounting rate of return (ARR)   投资报酬率
Deflation   通货紧缩
Discount rate   折现率
Inflation   通货膨胀
Internal rate of return (IRR)   内含报酬率
Net present value (NPV)   净现值
Opportunity cost   机会成本
Payback period (PP)   回收期
Risk   风险
Time value of money   货币时间价值
Uncertainty   不确定性

SELF-EVALUATION ACTIVITIES

10.1 Single choice questions

1. Capital investment decisions are of crucial importance to the investor because(   ).
    (a) Large amounts of resources are often involved
    (b) The stream of benefits is normally over a restricted period of time
    (c) It is normally inexpensive to "bail-out" of an investment once it has been undertaken
    (d) All of the above
    (e) None of the above

2. The present value of a single future amount equals(   ).
    (a) The amount that could be invested now at the "opportunity investing rate" that would grow to the future value over the specified time period

(b) The future value discounted at the "opportunity investing rate" over the specified time period

(c) The expected amount to be received

(d) All of the above

(e) Both (a) and (b)

3. If the NPV for a projected is zero, the rate of return on the project is(   ).

(a) Nil

(b) Negative

(c) A rate less than the discount rate

(d) A rate equal to the discount rate

(e) A rate greater than the discount rate

4. Which of the following is a problem with using the IRR approach to investment appraisal?

(a) It is difficult to compute manually

(b) Negative cash flows during the life of the project can lead to multiple returns

(c) It does not address the question of wealth creation

(d) It ignores the scale of the project

(e) All of the above are problems with the IRR approach

5. Project A with a internal rate of return of 16% may be preferred to project B with an internal rate of return of 18% when(   ).

(a) A has a longer payback period

(b) B has a lower positive net present value

(c) A has greater cash inflows early in the project's life

(d) A has greater cash inflows later in the project's life

(e) None of the above

10.2　True or false

1. The accounting rate of return calculation is based on cash flows.

2. The payback approach is quick and easy to calculate and can be easily understood by managers.

3. NPV includes all the relevant cash flows irrespective of when they are expected to occur.

4. IRR is the only method of appraisal where the output of the analysis has a direct bearing on the wealth of the business.

5. A project with a positive NPV will have an internal rate of return higher than the hurdle rate.

10.3　Jack Cash of Appreciation Basketball Coaching (ABC) is considering the purchase of a bus to transport players to various tournaments. Purchase of the bus will require an initial outflow of $150 000. As a result of attending the tournaments, Jack believes ABC can generate net cash inflows from sponsorship deals, new player coaching fees and tournament prize money over the next four years of $46 000, $57 500, $46 000 and $69 000 respectively. In addition, the bus is estimated to have a salvage value of $57 500 at the end of year 4. Jack's required rate of return is 10 per cent.

Required: Calculate each of the following measures and comment on their significance.

    a. ARR   b. PP   c. net present value (NPV).

Answer to self-evaluation activities

10.1 Single choice questions
1. a   2. e   3. d   4. e   5. d

10.2 True or false
1. F   2. T   3. T   4. F   5. T

10.3 Solution

a. ARR = Average profit/Average investment
$$= [(\$46 + \$57.50 + \$46 + \$69 - \$92.5)/4]/(\$150 + \$57.50)/2$$
$$= 31.5/103.75$$
$$= 30.36\%$$

This looks like an acceptable return.

b. PP = Initial investment/Net cash inflow

The initial investment is $150 000. This amount will not be recovered until the start of year 4, if cash is received evenly throughout each year. So the PP is 3.007 years. This may or may not be acceptable to the investors.

c. i. NPV $= CF_1/(1+r) + CF_2/(1+r)^2 + CF_3/(1+r)^3 + \ldots + CF_n/(1+r)^n - INV$
$$= 46/(1.1) + 57.5/(1.1)^2 + 46/(1.1)^3 + 126.5/(1.1)^4 - 150$$
$$= 41.82 + 47.52 + 34.56 + 86.40 - 150$$
$$= 60.30 (\$000)$$

With an NPV at $60 300, this project looks highly acceptable.

ii. We can also use the discount table to solve this problem:

NPV $= -150\ 000 + 460\ 000 \times 0.909 + 57\ 500 \times 0.826 + 46\ 000 \times 0.751 + 126\ 500 \times 0.683$
$$= -150\ 000 + 41\ 814 + 47\ 495 + 34\ 546 + 86\ 400$$
$$= 60\ 255$$

CHAPTER 11

Financing the Business

LEARNING OBJECTIVES

After studying this chapter, you should be able to:
11.1　identify the main sources of finance available to a business
11.2　discuss the sources of internal finance and external finance
11.3　outline the ways in which smaller businesses may seek to raise finance.

A major concern for all business entities is the way the entity is financed. In this chapter we shall examine various aspects of financing a business. The sources of internal finance and external finance are discussed in this chapter. The factors to be taken into account when choosing an appropriate source of finance are also considered. Then go on to examine various aspects of the capital markets, including the role of the Stock Exchange, the financing of smaller businesses and the ways in hybrid and international funding.

11.1　Sources of internal finance

When considering the various sources of finance available to a business, it is useful to distinguish between internal and external sources of finance. By **internal sources** we mean sources that do not require the agreement of anyone beyond the directors and managers of the business. Thus, retained profits are considered an internal source because the directors of the business have power to retain profits without the agreement of the shareholders, whose profits they are. Finance from an issue of new shares, on the other hand, is an **external source** because it requires the compliance of potential shareholders.

Within each of the two categories just described, we can further distinguish between long-term and short-term sources of finance. There is no agreed definition concerning each of these terms but, for the purpose of this chapter, **long-term sources of finance** are defined as those that are expected to provide finance for at least one year. **Short-term sources** typically provide finance for a shorter period. As we shall see, sources that are seen as short-term when first used by the business often end up being used for quite long periods.

In practice, businesses tend to look first to internal sources before going outside for new funds. Internal sources of finance usually have the advantage that they are flexible. They may also be obtained quickly—particularly from working capital sources—and need not require the compliance of other parties. The main sources of internal funds are described below and are summarised in figure 11.1.

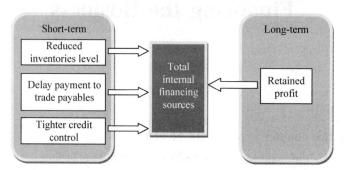

FIGURE 11.1 The major sources of internal finance

Short-term sources of internal finance

Tighter credit control

By exerting tighter control over amounts owed by credit customers, it may be possible for a business to reduce the proportion of assets held in this form and so release funds for other purposes. Having funds tied up in trade receivables represents an opportunity cost in that those funds could be used for profit-generating activities. It is important, however, to weigh the benefits of tighter credit control against the likely costs in the form of lost customer goodwill and lost sales. To remain competitive, a business must take account of the needs of its customers and the credit policies adopted by rival businesses within the industry.

Reducing inventories levels

Reducing the level of inventories is an internal source of funds that may prove attractive to a business. If the business has a proportion of its assets in the form of inventories there is an opportunity cost, as the funds tied up cannot be used for other purposes. If inventories are reduced, funds become available for those opportunities.

However, a business must try to ensure that there are sufficient inventories available to meet likely future sales demand. Failure to do so will result in losing customer goodwill and losing sales revenue.

The nature and condition of the inventories held will determine whether it is possible to exploit this form of finance. A business may have excess inventories as a result of poor buying decisions. This may mean that a significant proportion of the inventories held are slow-moving or obsolete and cannot, therefore, be reduced easily. These issues will be considered in Chapter 12.

Delaying payment to trade payables

By providing a period of credit, suppliers are in effect offering a business an interest free loan. If the business delays payment, the period of the "loan" is extended and funds can be retained within the business. This can be a cheap form of finance for a business, though this is not always the case. If a business fails to pay within the agreed credit period, there may be significant costs. For example, the business may find it difficult to buy on credit when it has a reputation as a slow payer.

These so-called short-term sources are short-term to the extent that they can be reversed at short notice. For example, a reduction in the level of trade receivables can be reversed within a couple of weeks. Typically, however, once a business has established a reduced receivable collection period, a reduced inventories turnover period and/or an expanded payables payment period, it will tend to maintain these new levels.

For the typical business, the level of funds involved with the working capital items is vast. This means that substantial amounts of funds can be raised through exercising tighter control of trade receivables and inventories and by exploiting opportunities to delay payment to trade payables.

Long-term sources of internal finance

Retained profits

Retained profits are an important source of finance for most businesses. If profits are retained within the business rather than being distributed to shareholders in the form of dividends, the funds of the business are increased.

The reinvestment of profits can be a useful way of raising capital from ordinary share investors. An obvious alternative way to increase equity investment is to issue new shares.

Retaining profits will have no effect on the extent to which existing shareholders control the business, whereas when new shares are issued to outside investors there will be some dilution of control.

The decision to retain profits rather than pay them out as dividends to the shareholders is made by the directors. They may find it easier simply to retain profits rather than ask investors to subscribe to a new share issue. Retained profits are already held by the business, and so it does not have to wait to receive the funds. Moreover, there is often less scrutiny when profits are being retained for reinvestment purposes than when new shares are being issued. Investors and their advisers will closely examine the reasons for any new share issue. A problem with the use of profits as a source of finance, however, is that the timing and level of future profits cannot always be reliably predicted.

Some shareholders may prefer profits to be retained by the business, rather than be distributed in the form of dividends. By using profits, it may be expected that the business will expand, and that share values will increase as a result. An important reason for preferring profits to be retained is the effect of taxation on the shareholder. In the UK, dividends are treated as income for tax purposes and therefore attract income tax. Gains on the sale of shares attract capital gains tax. Generally speaking, capital gains tax bites less hard than income tax. A further advantage of capital gains over dividends is that the shareholder has a choice as to when to sell the shares and realise the gain. In the UK, it is only when the gain is realised that capital gains tax comes into play. Research indicates that investors may be attracted to particular businesses according to the dividend/retention policies that they adopt.

11.2 Sources of external finance

Figure 11.2 summarises the main sources of short-term and long-term external finance. We shall now discuss each of the external finance sources identified.

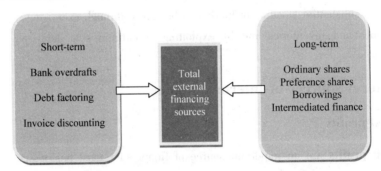

FIGURE 11.2 The major sources of external finance

Short-term sources of external finance

Bank overdrafts

A **bank overdraft** enables a business to maintain a negative balance on its bank account. It represents a very flexible form of borrowing as the size of the overdraft can (subject to bank approval) be increased or decreased more or less instantaneously.

An overdraft is relatively inexpensive to arrange and interest rates are often very competitive, though often higher than those for a term loan. As with all borrowing, the rate of interest charged on an overdraft will vary according to how creditworthy the customer is perceived to be by the bank. An overdraft is normally fairly easy to arrange-sometimes by a telephone call to the bank. In view of these advantages, it is not surprising that an overdraft is an extremely popular form of short-term finance.

Banks prefer to grant overdrafts that are self-liquidating, that is, the funds applied will result in cash inflows that will extinguish the overdraft balance. The banks may ask for a cash budget (projected statement of cash flows) from the business to see when the overdraft will be repaid and how much finance is required. The bank may also require some form of security on amounts advanced. One potential drawback with this form of finance is that the overdraft is repayable on demand. This may pose problems for a business that is short of funds. However, many businesses operate for many years using an overdraft, simply because the bank remains confident of their ability to repay and the arrangement suits the business. Thus the bank overdraft, though in theory regarded as short-term, often becomes a long-term source of finance.

Debt factoring

Debt factoring is a service offered by a financial institution (known as a *factor*). Many of the large factors are subsidiaries of commercial banks. Debt factoring involves the factor taking over the business's debt collection. In addition to operating normal credit control procedures, a factor may offer to undertake credit investigations and to provide protection for approved credit sales. The factor is usually prepared to make an advance to the business of a maximum of 80 per cent of approved trade receivables. The charge made for the factoring service is based on total sales revenue, and is often 2 to 3 per cent of sales revenue. Any advances made to the business by the factor will attract a rate of interest similar to the rate charged on bank overdrafts.

Debt factoring is, in effect, outsourcing the trade receivables control to a specialist subcontractor. Many businesses find a factoring arrangement very convenient. It can result in savings in credit management and create more certainty with the cash flows.

It can also release the time of key personnel for more profitable activities. This may be extremely important for smaller businesses that rely on the talent and skills of a few key individuals. However, there is a possibility that a factoring arrangement will be seen as an indication that the business is experiencing financial difficulties. This may have an adverse effect on the confidence of customers, suppliers and staff. For this reason, some businesses try to conceal the factoring arrangement by collecting debts on behalf of the factor. When considering a factoring agreement, the costs and likely benefits arising must be identified and carefully weighed.

Invoice discounting

Invoice discounting involves a factor or other financial institution providing a loan based on a proportion of the face value of a business's credit sales outstanding (that is, the trade receivables). The amount advanced is usually 75 to 80 per cent of the value of the approved sales invoices outstanding. The business must agree to repay the advance within a relatively short period, perhaps 60 or 90 days. The responsibility for collecting the trade receivables outstanding remains with the business, and repayment of the advance is not dependent on the trade receivables being collected. Invoice discounting will not result in such a close relationship developing between the business and the financial institution as results with factoring. It may be a short-term arrangement, whereas debt factoring usually involves a longer-term relationship.

There are three main reasons for the relative popularity of invoice discounting:

- It is a confidential form of financing that the business's customers will know nothing about.
- The service charge for invoice discounting is generally only 0.2 to 0.3 per cent of sales revenue, compared with 2.0 to 3.0 per cent for factoring.
- Many businesses are unwilling to relinquish control of their customers' records.

Customers are an important resource of the business, and many wish to retain control over all aspects of their relationship with their customers.

Factoring and invoice discounting are forms of **asset-based financing**, as the asset of trade receivables is in effect used as security for the cash advances received by the business.

Long-term sources of external finance

Ordinary shares

Ordinary shares form the backbone of the financial structure of the business. **Ordinary share** capital represents the business's risk capital. There is no fixed rate of dividend and ordinary shareholders can receive a dividend only if profits available for distribution still remain after other investors (preference shareholders and lenders, if any) have received their dividend or interest payments. If the business is wound up, the ordinary shareholders will receive any proceeds from asset disposals only after any lenders (including trade payables) and preference shareholders have received their entitlements. Because of the high risks associated with this form of investment, ordinary shareholders will normally require a comparatively high rate of return.

Although ordinary shareholders have a potential loss liability that is limited to the amount that they have invested or agreed to invest, the potential returns from their investment are unlimited. In other words, their downside risk is limited whereas their upside potential is not. Ordinary shareholders have control over the business, through their voting rights. This gives them the power both to elect the directors and to remove them from office.

From the business's perspective, ordinary shares can be an attractive form of financing, relative to borrowing. At times, it can be useful to be able to avoid paying a dividend. It is not usually possible to avoid paying interest on borrowings.

> **REAL WORLD**
>
> **Under two following circumstances a business generally avoid paying a dividend**
> - An expanding business may prefer to retain funds to help fuel future growth.
> - A business in difficulties may need the funds to meet its operating costs and so may find making a dividend payment a real burden.

A business financed by ordinary shares can avoid making cash payments to shareholders when it is not prudent to do so, the market value of the shares may go down. The cost to the business of financing through ordinary shares may become higher if shareholders feel uncertain about future dividends. On the other hand, for a business which is clearly expanding its operations in a profitable way, share prices are likely to reflect this despite the lack of dividends.

It is also worth pointing out that the business does not obtain any tax relief on dividends paid to shareholders, whereas interest on borrowings is tax-deductible. This makes it more expensive to the business to pay £1 of dividend than £1 of interest on borrowings.

Preference shares

Preference shares offer investors a lower level of risk than ordinary shares. Provided there are sufficient profits available, preference shares will normally be given a fixed rate of dividend each year, and preference shareholders will be paid the first slice of any dividend paid. Should the business be wound up, preference shareholders may be given priority over the claims of ordinary shareholders. The business's own particular documents of incorporation will state the precise rights of preference shareholders in this respect.

Preference shares are no longer an important source of new finance. A major reason for this is that dividends paid to preference shareholders, like those paid to ordinary shareholders, are not allowable against taxable profits, whereas interest on borrowings is an allowable expense. From the business's point of view, preference shares and borrowings are quite similar, so the tax-deductibility of interest on borrowings is an important issue.

Advantages of issuing shares. The secondary market role of the Stock Exchange means that shares and other financial claims are easily transferable. Furthermore, their prices are constantly under scrutiny by investors and skilled analysts. This helps to promote the tendency for the price quoted for a particular business's shares to reflect their true worth at that particular time. These factors can bring real benefits to a business.

Disadvantages of issuing shares. Strict rules are imposed on listed businesses, including requirements for levels of financial disclosure additional to those already imposed by International Financial Reporting Standards. Financial journalists and others tend to monitor closely the activities of listed businesses. Listed businesses are under pressure to perform well over the short term. The costs of obtaining a listing are huge and this may be a real deterrent for some businesses.

> **REAL WORLD**
>
> **The role of the Stock Exchange**
>
> The **Stock Exchange** acts as both an important *primary* and *secondary* capital market for businesses. As a primary market, its function is to enable businesses to raise new finance. As a secondary market, its function is to enable investors to sell their securities (including shares and loan notes) with ease. Thus, it provides a "second-hand" market where shares and loan notes already in issue may be bought and sold.
>
> Despite the problems with IPOs they have been quite popular in terms of the value of funds raised over recent years in China. There are signs that the recession, which began in 2017, is leading to a reduction in IPOs.
>
> **Advantages of a listing**
>
> 1. The secondary market role of the Stock Exchange means that shares and other financial claims are easily transferable. Furthermore, their prices are constantly under scrutiny by investors and skilled analysts. This helps to promote the tendency for the price quoted for a particular business's shares to reflect their true worth at that particular time. These factors can bring real benefits to a business. It is usually the most convenient way of buying or selling shares.
>
> 2. The Stock Exchange can be a useful vehicle for a successful entrepreneur wishing to realise the value of the business that has been built up. By listing the shares on the Stock Exchange, and thereby making the shares available to the public, the entrepreneur will usually benefit from a gain in the value of the shares held and will be able to realise that gain easily, if required, by selling some shares.
>
> **Disadvantages of a listing**
>
> 1. Strict rules are imposed on listed businesses, including requirements for levels of financial disclosure additional to those already imposed by International Financial Reporting Standards (for example, the listing rules require that half-yearly financial reports are published).
>
> 2. Financial analysts, financial journalists and others tend to monitor closely the activities of listed businesses, particularly larger ones. Such scrutiny may not be welcome, particularly if the business is dealing with sensitive issues or is experiencing operational problems.

> 3. It is often suggested that listed businesses are under pressure to perform well over the short term. This pressure may detract from undertaking projects that will yield benefits only in the longer term. If the market becomes disenchanted with the business, and the price of its shares falls, this may make it vulnerable to a takeover bid from another business.
>
> 4. The costs of obtaining a listing are huge and this may be a real deterrent for some businesses.

Borrowings

Most businesses rely on borrowings as well as equity to finance operations. Lenders enter into a contract with the business in which the rate of interest, dates of interest payments, capital repayments and security for the borrowings are clearly stated. In the event that the interest payments or capital repayments are not made on the due dates, the lender will usually have the right, under the terms of the contract, to seize the assets on which their loan is secured and sell them in order to repay the amount outstanding.

Security for a loan may take the form of a fixed charge on particular assets of the borrowing business (land and buildings are often favoured by lenders) or a floating charge on the whole of its assets. A floating charge will "float" over the assets and will only fix on particular assets in the event that the business defaults on its borrowing obligations.

Other Intermediated finance

Entities tend to look to the financial institutions, in the first instance, as suppliers of intermediated finance. While larger entities with standing in the community (or internationally) are able to access the financial markets and financial institutions for funds, smaller entities typically approach one or several financial institutions for long-term funding.

For long-term funding purposes, most financial institutions offer:
- fixed-rate business loans
- variable-rate business loans
- installment loans
- interest-only loans
- lease finance.

Fixed-rate and variable-rate business loans

Fixed-rate business loans are available from most of the major financial institutions. Many institutions prefer loans in the range from $100 000 to $2 million. Terms are usually given for up to 25 years. After the expiry of the initial period, the rate may be fixed for a further period or converted to a variable rate. These loans may be unsecured, secured with entity assets or secured with residential property. The availability of acceptable security naturally affects the interest rates charged. Repayment conditions are negotiated to suit the business conditions of customers. Variable-rate business loans are also available from most of the major financial institutions and amounts available vary up to about $2 million. Terms are available up to 25 years. Interest rates vary in line with changes in the markets and depend on security and loan terms and conditions. The lender will also assess the risk of the entity to determine the excess interest rate the entity is charged over and above a base rate. Many financial institutions offer flexible draw down of the contracted loan amounts and flexible repayment schedules. JB Ltd reported $139.4 million of bank loans secured against its assets for the reporting period ended June 2015.

Installment loans

Installment loans differ from business loans in that fixed repayment schedules are negotiated at the outset. Minimum loan amounts vary among financial institutions and may be as low as $10 000 with some suppliers, and $50 000 from others. The loan periods also vary among suppliers, but are often in the range 1-15 years.

Interest-only loans

Interest-only loans are taken out to finance special situations. During the term of the loan, only interest is paid, while the repayment of the principal amount is made in full at the expiry of the term. These types of loans are suitable for situations where, say, an asset is bought (and used) for a specific period, with the expectation that it will be sold at the end of the period. The sale of the asset then provides funds to repay the loan. Thus, the payment of interest in the intervening period may be considered a holding cost for owning the asset.

Leases

Leasing is a significant form of finance for entities. The major financial institutions provide a full range of leasing options and products to complement their other loans, and to assist entities with financing specific assets such as motor vehicles, construction and manufacturing plant, and IT and office equipment. What is meant by the term lease? A lease is a contract by which an owner of property ("the lessor") allows another person or entity ("the lessee") to use the asset for a specific period in return for rent or lease payments.

Two examples of leases are a novated lease and a hire purchase agreement. A novated lease involves a three-party agreement between an employee, an employer and a financial institution. Novated leases are normally used to provide motor vehicles to employees as part of salary packages. The cost of providing the vehicle is part of the employee's salary, but is paid directly to the financial institution. The employee is able to select the vehicle of choice and to reduce annual taxable income. The financial institution is able to claim from the ATO the GST component of the new price of the vehicle, and this credit effectively reduces the lease payments. Novated leases are normally fully portable among employers, at least from the point of view of the financial institutions.

In this case, the underlying assets are owned by the financier and used by the customer in return for a rental payment. The rental or lease payments are tax deductions for the customer in both cases. There are no tax deductions for interest or depreciation, and there is no guarantee of ownership of the assets at the end of the period by the customer. The fact that there is no such guarantee, however, does not mean that the customer cannot purchase the assets. Often, they do, by paying a final lump sum, "balloon" or residual payment.

In contrast, under a hire-purchase agreement, a financial institution buys equipment required by the customer, then hires it to the customer for use during the agreed period. At the end of the period, the deal is settled by the payment of any outstanding balances and ownership passes to the customer. The payments made by the lessees are treated as ownership costs, and deductions are allowable for interest and depreciation. Consistent with this view, ownership at the expiry of the terms of the agreements resides not with the financial institutions but with the lessees.

All of the forms of leasing discussed earlier may be classified as finance leases. Finance leases are non-cancellable contractual obligations to make payments in return for the use of an asset for the majority of its useful life, and are essentially just one of many forms of financing the use of assets. The lessee party to a finance lease enjoys most of the benefits of ownership and is normally responsible for maintenance and upkeep. Conversely, some leases may be classed as operating leases, which are contractual agreements that are cancellable upon giving notice and tend to be of much shorter term than the useful life of the asset. These include the sorts of agreements that you might enter for the hire of a car for a two-week fly-drive holiday, the hire of a floor-sander or, indeed, the rental of a house.

Reasons must therefore exist for businesses to adopt this form of financing. These reasons are said to include the following:

- Ease of borrowing. Leasing may be obtained more easily than other forms of long-term finance. Lenders normally require some form of security and a profitable track record before making advances to a business. However, a lessor may be prepared to lease assets to a new business without a track record, and to use the leased assets as security for the amounts owing.
- Cost. Leasing agreements may be offered at reasonable cost. As the asset leased is used as security, standard lease arrangements can be applied and detailed credit checking of lessees may be unnecessary. This can reduce administrative costs for the lessor and, thereby, help in providing competitive lease rentals.
- Flexibility. Leasing can help provide flexibility where there are rapid changes in technology. If an option to cancel can be incorporated into the lease, the business may

be able to exercise this option and invest in new technology as it becomes available. This will help the business to avoid the risk of obsolescence.
- Cash flows. Leasing, rather than purchasing an asset outright, means that large cash outflows can be avoided. The leasing option allows cash outflows to be smoothed out over the asset's life. In some cases, it is possible to arrange for low lease payments to be made in the early years of the asset's life, when cash inflows may be low, and for these to increase over time as the asset generates positive cash flows.

REAL WORLD

Finance leasing in a leading airline business

Many airline businesses use finance leasing as a means of acquiring new aeroplanes. The financial statements for British Airways plc (BA) for the year ended 31 March 2008 show that almost 29 per cent (totalling £1 728m) of the net carrying amount of its fleet of aircraft had been acquired through this method.

Source: *British Airways plc Annual Report and Accounts* 2008, *p.* 98.

A finance lease can be contrasted with an **operating lease**, where the rewards and risks of ownership stay with the owner and where the lease is short-term. An example of an operating lease is where a builder hires some earthmoving equipment for a week to carry out a particular job.

Short-term versus long-term borrowing

Having decided that some form of borrowing is required to finance the business, managers must then decide whether it should be short-term or long-term in form. There are many issues that should be taken into account when making this decision. These include the following:

1. *Matching*. The business may attempt to match the type of borrowing with the nature of the assets held. Thus, long-term borrowing might finance assets that form part of the permanent operating base of the business, including non-current assets and a certain level of current assets. This leaves assets held for a short period, such as current assets held to meet seasonal increases in demand (for example, inventories), to be financed by short-term borrowing, because short-term borrowing tends to be more flexible in that funds can be raised and repaid at short notice.

2. *Flexibility*. Short-term borrowing may be a useful means of postponing a commitment to taking on long-term borrowing. This may be seen as desirable if interest rates are high and it is forecast that they will fall in the future. Short-term borrowing does not usually incur penalties if there is early repayment of the amount outstanding, whereas some form of financial penalty may arise if long-term borrowing is repaid early.

3. *Refunding risk*. Short-term borrowing has to be renewed more frequently than long-term borrowing. This may create problems for the business if it is already in financial difficulties or if there is a shortage of funds available for lending.

4. *Interest rates*. Interest payable on long-term borrowing is often higher than short-term borrowing, as lenders require a higher return where their funds are locked up for a long period. This fact may make short-term borrowing a more attractive source of finance for a business. However, there may be other costs associated with borrowing (arrangement fees, for example) to be taken into account. The more frequently borrowings must be renewed, the higher these costs will be.

11.3 Providing long-term finance for small businesses

Although the Stock Exchange provides an important source of long-term finance for large businesses, it is not really suitable for small businesses. The aggregate market value of shares that are to be listed on the Stock Exchange must be huge and, in practice, the amounts are much higher because of the high costs of listing.

Thus, small businesses must look elsewhere for help in raising long-term finance. The more important sources of finance that are available to small businesses are venture capital, business angels and government assistance.

Venture capital

Venture capital is long-term capital provided to small and medium-sized businesses that wish to grow but do not have ready access to stock markets because of the prohibitively large costs of obtaining a listing. The businesses of interest to the venture capitalist will have higher levels of risk than would normally be acceptable to traditional providers of finance, such as the major clearing banks. The attraction for the venture capitalist of investing in higher-risk businesses is the prospect of higher returns.

Many small businesses are designed to provide the owners with a particular lifestyle and with job satisfaction. These kinds of businesses are not of interest to venture capitalists, as they are unlikely to provide the desired financial returns. Instead, venture capitalists look for businesses where the owners are seeking significant sales revenue and profit growth and need some outside help in order to achieve this.

The risks associated with the business can vary in practice. They are often due to the nature of the products or the fact that it is a new business that either lacks a trading record or has new management or both of these.

Venture capitalists provide long-term capital in the form of share and loan finance for different situations, including:

- *Start-up capital*. This is available to businesses that are not fully developed. They may

need finance to help refine the business concept or to engage in product development or initial marketing. They have not yet reached the stage where they are trading.
- *Early-stage capital*. This is available for businesses that are ready to start trading.
- *Expansion capital*. This is aimed at providing additional funding for existing, growing businesses.
- *Buy-out or buy-in capital*. This is used to fund the acquisition of a business either by the existing management team ("buy-out") or by a new management team ("buy-in"). Management buy-outs (MBOs) and buy-ins (MBIs) often occur where a large business wishes to divest itself of one of its operating units or where a family business wishes to sell out because of succession problems.
- *Rescue capital*. To help turn around businesses that are in difficulties. The venture capitalist will often make a substantial investment in the business. It may not be looking for a very quick return, and may well be prepared to invest in a business for five years or more. The return may take the form of a capital gain on the realisation of the investment. Though venture capital is extremely important for some small businesses, the vast majority of small businesses obtain their finance from other sources.

Business angels

Business angels are often wealthy individuals who have been successful in business. They are usually willing to invest, through a shareholding in a start-up business or in a business that is wishing to expand. If larger amounts are required, a syndicate of business angels may be formed to raise the money. Business angels typically make one or two investments over a three-year period and will usually be prepared to invest for a period of between three and five years. They normally have a minority stake in the business, and although they do not usually become involved in its day-to-day management, they tend to take an interest, more generally, in the way that the business is managed.

Business angels fill an important gap in the market as the size and nature of investments they find appealing are often not so appealing to venture capitalists. They can be attractive to small businesses because they may make investment decisions quickly, particularly if they are familiar with the industry in which the new business operates. It can offer useful skills, experience and business contacts. Compared to venture capitalist, business angle accept lower financial returns in order to have the opportunity to become involved in a new and interesting project.

Business angels offer an informal source of share finance and it is not always easy for owners of small businesses to identify a suitable angel. However, numerous business angel networks have now developed to help owners of small businesses find their "perfect partner".

Government assistance

One of the most effective ways in which developed or developing governments assist small businesses is through the Small Firms Loan Guarantee Scheme. This aims to help small businesses that have viable business plans but lack the security to enable them to borrow.

In addition to other forms of financial assistance, such as government grants and tax incentives for investors to buy shares in small businesses, the government also helps by providing information concerning the sources of finance available.

SUMMARY

1. Sources of finance

Internal sources of finance do not require the agreement of anyone beyond the directors and managers of the business, whereas external sources of finance do require the compliance of "outsiders". Long-term sources of finance are not due for repayment within one year whereas short-term sources are due for repayment within one year. The higher the level of risk associated with investing in a particular form of finance, the higher the level of return that will be expected by investors.

2. Internal sources of finance

The major internal source of long-term finance is retained profit. The main short-term sources of internal finance are tighter credit control of receivables, reducing inventories levels and delaying payments to trade payables.

3. External sources of finance

The main external, long-term sources of finance are ordinary shares, preference shares, borrowing, leases, etc.

Ordinary shares are, from the investor's point of view, normally considered to be the most risky form of investment and, therefore, provide the highest expected returns. Lending is normally the least risky and provides the lowest expected returns to investors. Leases and hire-purchase agreements allow a business to obtain immediate possession of an asset without having to pay the cost of acquiring the asset. The main sources of external short-term finance are bank overdrafts, debt factoring and invoice discounting.

When considering the choice between long-term and short-term sources of borrowing, factors such as matching the type of borrowing with the nature of the assets held, the need for flexibility, refunding risk and interest rates should be taken into account.

4. Long-term finance for small businesses

Stock Exchange provides an important source of long-term finance for large businesses, it is not really suitable for small businesses. The more important sources of finance that are available to small businesses are venture capital, business angels and government assistance.

Venture capital is long-term capital for small or medium-sized businesses that are not listed on the Stock Exchange. These businesses often have higher levels of risk but provide the venture capitalist with the prospect of higher levels of return. Business angels are wealthy individuals who are willing to invest in businesses at either an early stage or expansion stage of development. The government assists small businesses through guaranteeing loans and by providing grants and tax incentives.

KEY TERMS

Bank overdraft 银行透支
Business angels 企业(创业)天使基金
Corporate bonds 公司债券
Debentures 信用债券
Debt factoring 债权转让
External sources 外部(融资)渠道
Finance leases 融资租赁
Hire-purchase agreement 租购协议
Installment loans 分期付款
Internal sources 内部(融资)渠道
Invoice discounting 票据贴现
Long-term sources financing 长期融资
Lessee 承租人
Lessor 出租人
novated lease 可变更租赁
Operating leases 经营租赁
Ordinary shares 普通股
Preference shares 优先股
Retained profits 留存收益
Short-term sources financing 短期融资
Stock Exchange 证券交易所
Venture capital 风险投资

SELF-EVALUATION ACTIVITIES

11.1 Single choice questions

1. Which of the following would not be classified as a major internal source of funds? (　　)
　　(a) Retained profit;　　　　　　　　(b) Delay payment to creditors;
　　(c) Reduce inventory levels;　　　　(d) Tighter credit controls;

(e) The sale of fixed assets.

2. Which of the following is not an issue to be taken into account when deciding between long-term and short-term borrowing? (   )

(a) Flexibility;
(b) Security;
(c) Re-funding;
(d) Interest rates;
(e) Matching.

3. Which of the following is not a potential disadvantage for a company to be listed on the Stock Exchange? (   )

(a) The imposition of additional disclosure rules;
(b) The requirement for more frequent financial reporting;
(c) The ready transfer of shares;
(d) The close monitoring by analysts and journalists;
(e) The pressure for short-term results.

4. Which of the following is a long-term source of external finance? (   )

(a) Bank overdraft;
(b) Debt factoring;
(c) Finance leases;
(d) Invoice discounting;
(e) Retained profits.

5. What is the characteristic of a finance lease? (   )

(a) Ownership transfers to the lessee at the inception of the lease;
(b) The risk and rewards incidental to ownership reside with the lessor;
(c) The lease is cancellable;
(d) The lease period covers a significant part of the life of the asset;
(e) It is in essence a form of short-term rental.

11.2　True or false

1. Long-term sources of finance are defined in the text as those which are not due for repayment for at least five years.

2. Preference shares offer investors a lower level of risk than ordinary shares.

3. Invoice discounting is a confidential form of financing which the client's customers will know nothing about.

4. Retained profits are a free source of finance to the business.

5. Interest payable on long-term debt is often lower than short-term debt.

Answer to self-evaluation activities

11.1　Single choice questions
1. e   2. b   3. c   4. c   5. d

11.2　True or false
1. F   2. T   3. F   4. T   5. F

CHAPTER 12

Managing Working Capital

LEARNING OBJECTIVES

When you have completed this chapter, you should be able to:
12.1 Identify the main elements and nature of working capital.
12.2 Discuss the issues with respect to the management of inventories.
12.3 Explain the management of accounts receivable.
12.4 Outline the issues underlying the management of cash.

This chapter considers the factors that must be taken into account when managing the working capital of a business. Each element of working capital will be identified and the major issues surrounding them will be discussed. Working capital represents a significant investment for many businesses and so its proper management and control can be vital.

12.1 Definition of working capital

Working capital is usually defined as current assets less current liabilities. The major elements of current assets are:
- inventories
- trade receivables
- cash (in hand and at bank).

The major elements of current liabilities are:
- trade payables
- bank overdrafts.

The size and composition of working capital can vary among industries. For some types of business, the investment in working capital can be substantial. For example, a manufacturing business will typically invest heavily in raw material, work in progress and finished goods, and will normally sell its goods on credit, giving rise to trade receivables. A retailer, on the other hand, will hold only one form of inventories (finished goods), and will usually sell goods for cash. Many service businesses hold no inventories.

Most businesses buy goods and/or services on credit, giving rise to trade payables. Few businesses operate without a cash balance, though in some cases it is a negative one (a bank overdraft).

Working capital represents a net investment in short-term assets. These assets are continually flowing into and out of the business and are essential for day-to-day operations. The various elements of working capital are interrelated and can be seen as part of a short-term cycle. For a manufacturing business, the working capital cycle can be depicted as shown in figure 12.1.

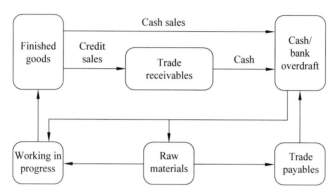

FIGURE 12.1 The working capital cycle

Cash is used to pay trade payables for raw materials, or raw materials are bought for immediate cash settlement. Cash is also spent on labour and other items that turn raw materials into work in progress and, finally, into finished goods. The finished goods are sold to customers either for cash or on credit. In the case of credit customers, there will be a delay before the cash is received from the sales. Receipt of cash completes the cycle.

For a retailer the situation would be as in figure 12.1 except that there would be only inventories of finished goods and no work in progress or raw materials. For a purely service business, the working capital cycle would also be similar to that depicted in figure 12.1 except that there would be no inventories of finished goods or raw materials. There may well be work in progress, however, since many services, for example a case handled by a firm of solicitors, will take some time to complete and costs will build up before the client is billed for them.

Managing working capital

The management of working capital is an essential part of the business's short-term planning process. It is necessary for management to decide how much of each element should be held. As we shall see later in this chapter, there are costs associated with holding either too much or too little of each element. Management must be aware of these costs, which include opportunity costs, in order to manage effectively. Hence, potential benefits must be weighed against likely costs in an attempt to achieve the optimum investment.

The working capital needs of a business are likely to vary over time as a result of changes in the business environment. Managers must try to identify these changes to ensure that the level of investment in working capital is appropriate. This means that working capital decisions are frequently being made.

Some kinds of changes in the business environment might lead to a decision to change the level of investment in working capital. These may include the following:
- changes in interest rates
- changes in market demand
- changes in the seasons
- changes in the state of the economy.

In addition to changes in the external environment, changes arising within the business could alter the required level of investment in working capital. Such internal changes might include using different production methods (resulting, perhaps, in a need to hold less inventories) and changes in the level of risk that managers are prepared to take.

REAL WORLD

Working capital not working hard enough!

According to a survey of 1 000 of Europe's largest businesses, working capital is not as well managed as it could be. The survey, conducted in 2013 by REL Consultancy Group and CFO Europe, suggests that larger European businesses have €865 billion tied up in working capital that could be released through better management of inventories, trade receivables and trade payables. The potential for savings represents a total of 36 per cent of the total working capital invested and is calculated by comparing the results for a particular industry with the results for businesses within the upper quartile of that industry.

Source: www.relconsult.com.

12.2　Managing inventories

A business may hold inventories for various reasons, the most common of which is to meet the immediate day-to-day requirements of customers and production. However, a business may hold more than necessary for this purpose if there is a risk that future supplies may be interrupted or scarce. Similarly, if there is a risk that the cost of inventories will rise in the future, a business may decide to stockpile.

For some types of business, the inventories held may represent a substantial proportion of the total assets held. For example, a car dealership that rents its premises may have nearly all of its total assets in the form of inventories. Inventory levels of manufacturers tend to be higher than in many other types of business as it is necessary to hold three kinds of inventories: raw materials, work in progress and finished goods. Each form of inventories represents a particular stage in the production cycle. For some types of business, the level of inventories held may vary substantially over the year owing to the seasonal nature of the industry. An example of such a business is a greetings card manufacturer. For other businesses, inventory levels may remain fairly stable throughout the year.

Where a business holds inventories simply to meet the day-to-day requirements of its customers and for production, it will normally seek to minimise the amount of inventories held. This is because there are significant costs associated with holding inventories. These include:

- storage and handling costs
- the cost of financing
- the cost of pilferage and obsolescence of the inventories
- the cost of opportunities forgone in tying up funds in this form of asset.

As example 12.1 estimates the financing cost of inventories for four large businesses, We can gain some impression of the level of cost involved in holding inventories.

EXAMPLE 12.1

Inventories financing cost

The financing cost of inventories for each of four large businesses, based on their respective opportunity costs of capital, is calculated below.

Business	Type of operations	Cost of capital	Average inventories held *	Cost of holding inventories	Profit before tax	Cost as a % of profit before tax
		(a)	(b)	(a)x(b)		
		%	$m	$m	$m	%
Rolls-Royce	Engineering	12.75	2 402	306	1 892	16.2
Rexam	Packaging	11.0	503	55	240	22.9
Warehouse	retailer	6.6	187	12.3	124.1	9.9
Kingfisher	Home improvement retailer	7.6	1 702	129.4	395	32.8

* Based on opening and closing inventories for the relevant financial period.

For all of these four businesses, we can see financing costs of inventories are significant in relation to the profits generated. These figures do not take account of other costs of inventories holding mentioned above, like the cost of providing a secure store for the inventories. Clearly, the efficient management of inventories is an important issue for many businesses.

These businesses were not selected because they have particularly high inventory costs but simply because they are among the relatively few businesses that publish their costs of capital.

Source: *Annual reports of the businesses for the financial year ended.*

To try to ensure that the inventories are properly managed, a number of procedures and techniques may be used. These are reviewed below.

Budgeting future demand

One of the best ways to ensure that there will be inventories available to meet future production and sales requirements is to make appropriate plans and budgets. Budgets should deal with each product that the business makes and/or sells. It is important that every attempt is made to ensure that budgets are realistic, as they will determine future ordering and production levels. The budgets may be derived in various ways. They may be developed using statistical techniques such as time series analysis, or they may be based on the judgement of the sales and marketing staff. We considered inventories budgets and their link to production and sales budgets.

Financial ratios

One ratio that can be used to help monitor inventory levels is the average inventory turnover period. This ratio is calculated as follows:

$$\text{Average inventory turnover period} = \frac{\text{Average inventory held}}{\text{Cost of sales}} \times 365$$

The ratio will provide a picture of the average period for which inventories are held, and can be useful as a basis for comparison. It is possible to calculate the average inventory turnover period for individual product lines as well as for inventories as a whole.

Recording and reordering systems

A sound system of recording inventories movements is a key element in managing inventories. There must be proper procedures for recording inventories, purchases and usages. Periodic checks would normally be made in an attempt to ensure that the amount of physical inventories actually held is consistent with what is indicated by the inventory records.

There should also be clear procedures for the reordering of inventories. Authorisation for both the purchase and the issue of inventories should be confined to a few senior staff. This should avoid problems of duplication and lack of co-ordination. To determine the point at which inventories should be reordered, information will be required concerning the **lead time** (that is, the time between the placing of an order and the receipt of the goods) and the likely level of demand.

For example an electrical retailer stocks a particular type of light switch. The annual demand for the light switch is 10 400 units, and the lead time for orders is four weeks. Demand for the light switch is steady throughout the year. At what level of inventories of the light switch should the business reorder, assuming that it is confident of the information given above?

The average weekly demand for the switch is 10 400/52 = 200 units. During the time between ordering new switches and receiving them, the quantity sold will be 4 × 200 units = 800 units. So the business should reorder no later than when the level held reaches 800 units, in order to avoid running out of inventories.

In most businesses, there will be some uncertainty surrounding the above factors and so a buffer or safety inventory level may be maintained in case problems occur. The amount of the buffer to be held is really a matter of judgement. This judgement willdepend on:

- the degree of uncertainty concerning the above factors;
- the likely costs of running out of the item concerned;
- the cost of holding the buffer inventories.

The effect of holding a buffer will be to raise the inventory level (the reorder point) at which an order for new inventories is placed. Assume the same facts as above example (electrical retailer), we are also told that the business maintains buffer inventories of 300 units. At what level should the business reorder?

Reorder point = expected level of demand during the lead time plus the level of buffer inventories
= 800 + 300
= 1 100 units

Carrying buffer inventories will increase the cost of holding inventories; however, this must be weighed against the cost of running out of inventories, in terms of lost sales, production problems and so on.

Levels of control

Senior managers must make a commitment to the management of inventories. However, the cost of controlling inventories must be weighed against the potential benefits. It may be possible to have different levels of control according to the nature of the inventories held. The ABC system of inventories control is based on the idea of selective levels of control.

A business may find that it is possible to divide its inventories into three broad categories: A, B and C. Each category will be based on the value of inventories held, as is illustrated in example 12.2.

EXAMPLE 12.2

ABC system of inventories control

Alics Products plc makes door handles and door fittings. It makes them in brass, in steel and in plastic. The business finds that brass fittings account for 10 percent of the physical volume of the finished inventories that it holds, but these represent 65 percent of its total value. These are treated as Category A inventories. There are sophisticated recording procedures, tight control is exerted over inventories movements and there is a high level of security where the brass inventories are stored. This is economic because the inventories represent a relatively small proportion of the total volume.

The business finds that steel fittings account for 30 percent of the total volume of finished inventories and represent 25 percent of its total value. These are treated as Category B inventories, with a lower level of recording and management control being applied.

The remaining 60 percent of the volume of inventories is plastic fittings, which represent the least valuable items, that account for only 10 percent of the total value of finished inventories held. These are treated as Category C inventories, so the level of recording and management control would be lower still. Applying to these inventories the level of control that is applied to Category A or even Category B inventories would be uneconomic.

Categorising inventories in this way seeks to direct management effort to the most important areas, and tries to ensure that the costs of controlling inventories are appropriate to its importance. Figure 12.2 shows the nature of the ABC approach to inventories control.

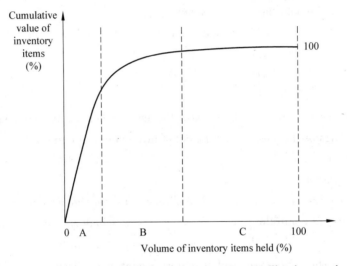

FIGURE 12.2 ABC method of analysing and controlling inventories

Category A contains inventories that, though relatively few in quantity, account for a large proportion of the total value. Category B inventories consists of those items that are less valuable but more numerous. Category C comprises those inventories items that are very numerous but relatively low in value. Different inventory control rules would be applied to each category. For example, only Category A inventories would attract the more expensive and sophisticated controls.

Inventories management models

It is possible to use decision models to help manage inventories. The **economic order quantity** (**EOQ**) model is concerned with answering the question "How much inventories should be ordered?" In its simplest form, the EOQ model assumes that demand is constant, so that inventories will be depleted evenly over time, and replenished just at the point that they run out. These assumptions would lead to a "saw-tooth" pattern to represent inventories movements, as shown in figure 12.3.

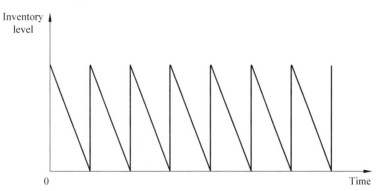

FIGURE 12.3　Patterns of inventory movements over time

Here we assume that there is a constant rate of usage of the inventory item, and that inventories are reduced to zero just as new inventories arrive. At time 0 there is a full level of inventories. This is steadily used as time passes; and just as it falls to zero it is replaced. This pattern is then repeated.

The EOQ model recognises that the key costs associated with inventories management are the cost of holding the inventories and the cost of ordering them. The model can be used to calculate the optimum size of a purchase order by taking account of both of these cost elements. The cost of holding inventories can be substantial, and so management may try to minimise the average amount of inventories held. However, by reducing the level of inventories held and, therefore, the holding costs, there will be a need to increase the number of orders during the period and so ordering costs will rise.

Figure 12.3 shows how, as the level of inventories and the size of inventories orders increase, the annual costs of placing orders will decrease because fewer orders will be placed. However, the cost of holding inventories will increase, as there will be higher average inventory levels. The total cost curve, which is based on the sum of holding costs and ordering costs, will fall until the point E, which represents the minimum total cost. Thereafter, total costs begin to rise. The EOQ model seeks to identify point E at which total costs are minimised. This will represent half of the optimum amount that should be ordered on each occasion. Assuming, as we are doing, that inventories are used evenly over time and that they fall to zero before being replaced, the average inventories level equals half of the order size.

The EOQ model, which can be used to derive the most economic order quantity, is:

$$EOQ = \sqrt{\frac{2DC}{H}}$$

where: D = the annual demand for the inventories item (expressed in units of the inventories item);

C = the cost of placing an order;
H = the cost of holding one unit of inventories for one year.

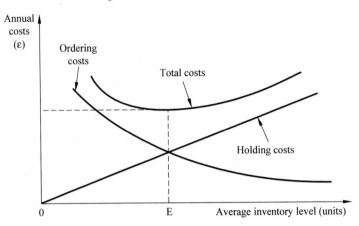

FIGURE 12.4 Holding and order costs of inventories

Small inventory levels imply frequent reordering and high annual ordering costs. Small inventory levels also imply relatively low inventory holding costs. High inventory levels imply exactly the opposite. There is, in theory, an optimum order size that will lead to the sum of ordering and holding costs (total costs) being at a minimum.

EXAMPLE 12.3

Inventories management models (EOQ) calculation

A Ltd sells 2 000 bags of cement each year. It has been estimated that the cost of holding one bag of cement for a year is £ 4. The cost of placing an order for new inventories is estimated at £ 250. Calculate the EOQ for bags of cement.

The answer should be as follows:

$$EOQ = \sqrt{\frac{2 \times 2\,000 \times 250}{4}} = 500 \text{ bags}$$

This will mean that the business will have to order bags of cement four times each year (that is 2 000/500) in batches of 500 bags so that sales demand can be met.

Note that the cost of the inventories concerned, which is the price paid to the supplier, does not directly impact on the EOQ model. The EOQ model is concerned only with the administrative costs of placing each order and the costs of looking after the inventories. Where the business operates an ABC system of inventories control, however, more expensive inventory items will have greater holding costs. For example, Category A inventories would tend to have a lower EOQ than Category B ones. Also, higher-cost inventories tie up more finance than cheaper ones, again leading to higher holding cost. So the cost of the inventories may have an indirect effect on the economic order size that the model recommends.

The basic EOQ model has a number of limiting assumptions. In particular, it assumes that:
- demand for an inventory item can be predicted with accuracy;
- demand is constant over the period and does not fluctuate through seasonality or for other reasons;
- no "buffer" inventories are required;
- there are no discounts for bulk purchasing.

However, the model can be modified to overcome each of these limiting assumptions. Many businesses use this model (or a development of it) to help in the management of inventories.

Materials requirement planning systems

A **materials requirement planning** (**MRP**) system takes planned sales demand as its starting point. It then uses a computer package to help schedule the timing of deliveries of bought-in parts and materials to coincide with production requirements. It is a co-coordinated approach that links materials and parts deliveries to the scheduled time of their input to the production process. By ordering only those items that are necessary to ensure the flow of production, inventory levels are likely to be reduced. MRP is really a "top-down" approach to inventory management, which recognises that inventory ordering decisions cannot be viewed as being independent of production decisions. In recent years, this approach has been extended to provide a fully integrated approach to production planning. The approach also takes account of other manufacturing resources such as labour and machine capacity.

Just-in-time inventories management

In recent years, many businesses have tried to eliminate the need to hold inventory by adopting **just-in-time** (**JIT**) inventory management. This approach was originally used in the US defence industry during the Second World War, but was first used on a wide scale by Japanese manufacturing businesses. The essence of JIT is, as the name suggests, to have supplies delivered to the business just in time for them to be used in the production process or in a sale. By adopting this approach the inventories holding costs rest with suppliers rather than with the business itself. On the other hand, a failure by a particular supplier to deliver on time could cause enormous problems and costs to the business. Thus JIT can save cost, but it tends to increase risk.

For JIT to be successful, it is important that the business informs suppliers of its inventory requirements in advance. Also suppliers, in their turn, must deliver materials of the right quality at the agreed times. Failure to do so could lead to a dislocation of production or supply to customers and could be very costly. Thus a close relationship is required between the business and its suppliers. This close relationship enables suppliers to schedule their own production to that of their customers. This should mean that between supplier and customer there will be a net saving in the amount of inventories that need to be held, relative to that that would not apply JIT in operation.

Adopting JIT may well require re-engineering a business's production process. To ensure that orders are quickly fulfilled, factory production must be flexible and responsive. This may require changes both to the production layout and to working practices. Production flows may have to be redesigned and employees may have to be given greater responsibility to allow them to deal with unanticipated problems and to encourage greater commitment. Information systems must also be installed to facilitate an uninterrupted production flows.

Although a business that applies JIT will not have to hold inventories, there may be other costs associated with this approach. As the suppliers may need to hold inventories for the customer, they may try to recoup this additional cost through increased prices. On the other hand, the close relationship between customer and supplier should enable the supplier to predict its customers' inventory needs. This means that suppliers can tailor their own production to that of the customer. The close relationship necessary between the business and its suppliers may also prevent the business from taking advantage of cheaper sources of supply if they become available.

Many people view JIT as more than simply an inventories control system. The philosophy underpinning this approach is concerned with eliminating waste and striving for excellence. There is an expectation that suppliers will always deliver inventories on time and that there will be no defects in the items supplied. There is also an expectation that, for manufacturers, the production process will operate at maximum efficiency. This means that there will be no production breakdowns and the queuing and storage times of products manufactured will be eliminated, as only that time spent directly on processing the products is seen as adding value. While these expectations may be impossible to achieve, they do help to create a culture that is dedicated to the pursuit of excellence and quality.

REAL WORLD

JIT at Nissan

Nissan Motors UK Limited, the UK manufacturing arm of the world famous Japanese car business, has a plant in Sunderland in the north east of England. Here it operates a fairly well-developed JIT system. For example, Sommer supplies carpets and soft interior trim from a factory close to the Nissan plant. It makes deliveries to Nissan once every 20 minutes on average, so as to arrive exactly as they are needed in production. This is fairly typical of all of the 200 suppliers of components and materials to the Nissan plant.

The business used to have a complete JIT system. More recently, however, Nissan has drawn back from its total adherence to JIT. By using only local suppliers it has cut itself off from the opportunity to exploit low-cost suppliers, particularly some located in China. This has led the business to feel the need to hold buffer inventories of certain inventory items to guard against disruption of supply arising from transport problems of sourcing parts from the Far East.

Source: Information taken from Partnership Sourcing Best Practice Case Study (www.pslcbi.com/studies/docnissan.htm) and "Nissan reviews just-in-time parts policy", C. Tighe, *Financial Times*, 23 Oct 2006.

12.3 Managing receivables

Selling goods or services on credit will result in costs being incurred by a business. These costs include credit administration costs, bad debts and opportunities forgone to use the funds for more profitable purposes. However, these costs must be weighed against the benefits of increased sales resulting from the opportunity for customers to delay payment.

Selling on credit is very widespread and is the norm outside the retail industry. When a business offers to sell its goods or services on credit, it must have clear policies concerning:

- which customers should receive credit;
- how much credit should be offered;
- what length of credit it is prepared to offer;
- whether discounts will be offered for prompt payment;
- what collection policies should be adopted;
- how the risk of non-payment can be reduced.

In the following section, we shall consider each of these issues.

Which customers should receive credit and how much should they be offered? A business offering credit runs the risk of not receiving payment for goods or services supplied. Thus, care must be taken over the type of customer to whom credit facilities are offered and how much credit is allowed. When considering a proposal from a customer for the supply of goods or services on credit, the business must take a number of factors into account. The following **five Cs of credit** provide a business with a useful checklist.

- *Capital.* The customer must appear to be financially sound before any credit is extended. Where the customer is a business, its financial statements should be examined. Particular regard should be given to the customer's likely future profitability and liquidity. In addition, any major financial commitments (for example, capital expenditure, contracts with suppliers) must be taken into account.
- *Capacity.* The customer must appear to have the capacity to pay amounts owing. Where possible, the payment record of the customer to date should be examined. If the customer is a business, the type of business operated and the physical resources of the business will be relevant. The value of goods that the customer wishes to buy on credit must be related to the customer's total financial resources.

- *Collateral.* On occasions, it may be necessary to ask for some kind of security for goods supplied on credit. When this occurs, the business must be convinced that the customer is able to offer a satisfactory form of security.
- *Conditions.* The state of the industry in which the customer operates, and the general economic conditions of the particular region or country, may have an important influence on the ability of a customer to pay the amounts outstanding on the due date.
- *Character.* It is important for a business to make some assessment of the customer's character. The willingness to pay will depend on the honesty and integrity of the individual with whom the business is dealing. Where the customer is a business, this will mean assessing the characters of its senior managers. The selling business must feel satisfied that the customer will make every effort to pay any amounts owing.

It is clear from the above that the business will need to gather information concerning the ability and willingness of the customer to pay the amounts owing at the due dates.

Length of credit period

A business must determine what credit terms are prepared to offer its customers. The length of credit offered to customers can vary significantly between businesses. It may be influenced by such factors as:

- the typical credit terms operating within the industry;
- the degree of competition within the industry;
- the bargaining power of particular customers;
- the risk of non-payment;
- the capacity of the business to offer credit;
- the marketing strategy of the business.

The last point identified may require some explanation. If, for example, a business wishes to increase its market share, it may decide to be more generous in its credit policy in an attempt to stimulate sales. Potential customers may be attracted by the offer of a longer credit period. However, any such change in policy must take account of the likely costs and benefits arising. To illustrate this point, consider example 12.4.

EXAMPLE 12.4

M Ltd produces a new type of golf putter. The business sells the putter to wholesalers and retailers and has an annual sales revenue of $600 000. The business's cost of capital is estimated at 10 per cent a year. The following data relate to each putter produced.

	$
Selling price	40
Variable costs	(20)

Continued

	$
Fixed cost apportionment	(6)
Profit	14

M Ltd wishes to expand the sales volume of the new putter. It believes that offering a longer credit period can achieve this. The business's average receivables collection period is currently 30 days. It is considering three options in an attempt to increase sales revenue. These are as follows:

	Option		
	1	2	3
Increase in average collection period (days)	10	20	30
Increase in sales revenue ($)	30 000	45 000	50 000

To enable the business to decide on the best option to adopt, it must weigh the benefits of the options against their respective costs. The benefits arising will be represented by the increase in profit from the sale of additional putters. From the cost data supplied we can see that the contribution [that is, selling price ($40) less variable costs ($20)] is $20 a putter, that is, 50 per cent of the selling price. So, whatever increase there may be in sales revenue, the additional contributions will be half of that figure. The fixed costs can be ignored in our calculations, as they will remain the same whichever option is chosen.

The increase in contribution under each option will therefore be:

	Option		
	1	2	3
50% of the increase in sales revenue ($)	15 000	22 500	25 000

The increase in trade receivables under each option will be as follows:

	Option		
	1	2	3
	$	$	$
Projected level of trade receivables			
40 × $630 000/365 (Note 1)	69 041		
50 × $645 000/365		88 356	
60 × $650 000/365			106 849

Continued

	Option		
	1	2	3
Current level of trade receivables			
30 × $600 000/365	(49 315)	(49 315)	(49 315)
Increase in trade receivables	19 726	39 041	57 534

The increase in receivables that results from each option will mean an additional finance cost to the business.

The net increase in the business's profit arising from the projected change is:

	Option		
	1	2	3
	$	$	$
Increase in contribution (see above)	15 000	22 500	25 000
Increase in finance cost (Note 2)	(1 973)	(3 904)	(5 753)
Net increase in profits	13 027	18 596	19 247

The calculations show that Option 3 will be the most profitable one.

Notes:

1. If the annual sales revenue totals $630 000 and 40 days' credit is allowed (both of which will apply under Option 1), the average amount that will be owed to the business by its customers, at any point during the year, will be the daily sales revenue (that is, $630 000/365) multiplied by the number of days that the customers take to pay (that is 40). Exactly the same logic applies to Options 2 and 3 and to the current level of trade receivables.

2. The increase in the finance cost for Option 1 will be the increase in trade receivables ($19 726) × 10 percent. The equivalent figures for the other options are derived in a similar way.

Example 12.4 illustrates the way that a business should assess changes in credit terms. However, if there is a risk that, by extending the length of credit, there will be an increase in bad debts, this should also be taken into account in the calculations, as should any additional trade receivable collection costs that will be incurred.

An alternative approach to evaluating the credit decision

It is possible to view the credit decision as a capital investment decision. Granting trade credit involves an opportunity outlay of resources in the form of cash (which has been temporarily forgone) in the expectation that future cash flows will be increased (through higher sales) as a result. A business will usually have choices concerning the level of investment to be made in credit sales and the period over which credit is granted. These choices will result in different returns and different levels of risk. There is no reason in principle why the NPV investment appraisal method, should not be used to evaluate these choices. We have seen that the NPV method takes into account both the time value of money and the level of risk involved.

Approaching the problem as an NPV assessment is not different in principle from the way that we dealt with the decision in example 12.4. In both approaches the time value of money is considered, but in example 12.4 we did it by charging a financing cost on the outstanding trade receivables.

Cash discounts

In an attempt to encourage prompt payment from its credit customers, a business may decide to offer a **cash discount** (or discount for prompt payment). The size of any discount will be an important influence on whether a customer decides to pay promptly.

From the business's viewpoint, the cost of offering discounts must be weighed against the likely benefits in the form of a reduction both in the cost of financing receivables and in the amount of bad debts.

In practice, there is always the danger that a customer may be slow to pay and yet may still take the discount offered. Where the customer is important to the business, it may be difficult to insist on full payment. An alternative to allowing the customer to take discounts by reducing payment is to agree in advance to provide discounts for prompt payment through quarterly credit notes. As credit notes will be given only for those debts paid on time, the customer will often make an effort to qualify for the discount.

Debt factoring and invoice discounting

Trade receivables can, in effect, be turned into cash by either factoring them or having sales invoices discounted. Both are forms of asset-based finance, which involves a financial institution providing a business with an advance up to 80 per cent of the value of the trade receivables outstanding. Both of these methods seem to be fairly popular approaches to managing receivables.

Credit insurance

It is possible for a supplier to insure its entire trade receivables, individual accounts (customers) or the outstanding balance relating to a particular transaction.

Collection policies and reducing the risk of non-payment

A business offering credit must ensure that amounts owing are collected as quickly as possible so that the risk of non-payment is minimised. Various steps can be taken to achieve this, including the following.

Develop customer relationships

For major customers it is often useful to cultivate a relationship with the key staff responsible for paying sales invoices. By so doing, the chances of prompt payment may be increased. For less important customers, the business should at least identify key staff responsible for paying invoices, who can be contacted in the event of a payment problem.

Publicise credit terms

The credit terms of the business should be made clear in all relevant correspondence, such as order acknowledgements, invoices and statements. In early negotiations with the prospective customer, credit terms should be openly discussed and an agreement reached.

Issue invoices promptly

An efficient collection policy requires an efficient accounting system. Invoices (bills) must be sent out promptly to customers, as must monthly statements. Reminders must also be despatched promptly to customers who are late in paying. If a customer fails to respond to a reminder, the accounting system should alert managers so that a stop can be placed on further deliveries.

Monitor outstanding debts

Management can monitor the effectiveness of collection policies in a number of ways. One method is to calculate the **average settlement period for trade receivables** ratio. This ratio is calculated as follows:

$$\text{Average settlement period for trade receivables} = \frac{\text{Average trade receivables}}{\text{Credit sales}} \times 365$$

Although this ratio can be useful, it is important to remember that it produces an average figure for the number of days for which debts are outstanding. This average may be badly distorted by a few large customers who are very slow or very fast payers.

Produce an ageing schedule of trade receivables. A more detailed and informative approach to monitoring receivables may be to produce an ageing schedule of trade receivables. Receivables are divided into categories according to the length of time they have been outstanding. An ageing schedule can be produced, on a regular basis, to help managers see the pattern of outstanding receivables. An example of an ageing schedule is set out in example 12.5.

EXAMPLE 12.5

Ageing schedule of trade receivables

Ageing schedule of trade receivables at 31 December

Customer	Days outstanding				Total
	1 to 30 days	31 to 60 days	61 to 90 days	more than 90 days	
	$	$	$	$	$
A Ltd	20 000	10 000	-	-	30 000
B Ltd	-	24 000	-	-	24 000

Continued

Customer	Days outstanding				Total
C Ltd	12 000	13 000	14 000	18 000	57 000
Total	32 000	47 000	14 000	18 000	111 000

This shows a business's trade receivables figure at 31 December, which totals $111 000. Each customer's balance is analysed according to how long the amount has been outstanding. (This business has just three credit customers.)

Thus we can see from the schedule, for example, that A Ltd has $20 000 outstanding for 30 days or fewer (that is, arising from sales during December) and $10 000 outstanding for between 31 and 60 days (broadly, arising from November sales). This information can be very useful for credit control purposes.

Many accounting software packages now include this ageing schedule as one of the routine reports available to managers. Such packages often have the facility to put customers "on hold" when they reach their credit limits. Putting a customer on hold means that no further credit sales will be made to that customer until amounts owing from past sales have been settled.

Answer queries quickly

It is important for relevant staff to deal with customer queries on goods and services supplied quickly and efficiently. Payment is unlikely to be made by customers until their queries have been dealt with.

Deal with slow payers

It is almost inevitably the case that a business making significant sales on credit will be faced with customers who do not pay. When this occurs, there should be agreed procedures for dealing with the situation. However, the cost of any action to be taken against delinquent credit customers must be weighed against the likely returns. For example, there is little point in taking legal action against a customer, incurring large legal expenses, if there is evidence that the customer does not have the necessary resources to pay. Where possible, an estimate of the cost of bad debts should be taken into account when setting prices for products or services.

12.4 Managing cash

Most businesses hold a certain amount of cash. The amount of cash held tends to vary considerably between businesses. A business decide to hold at least some of its assets in the form of cash. There are three reasons:

1. To meet day-to-day commitments, a business requires a certain amount of cash. Payments for wages, overhead expenses, goods purchased and so on must be made at the due dates. Cash has been described as the lifeblood of a business. Unless it circulates through the

business and is available for the payment of claims as they become due, the survival of the business will be at risk. Profitability is not enough; a business must have sufficient cash to pay its debts when they fall due.

2. If future cash flows are uncertain for any reason, it would be prudent to hold a balance of cash. For example, a major customer that owes a large sum to the business may be in financial difficulties. Given this situation, the business can retain its capacity to meet its obligations by holding a cash balance. Similarly, if there is some uncertainty concerning future outlays, a cash balance will be required.

3. A business may decide to hold cash to put itself in a position to exploit profitable opportunities as and when they arise. For example, by holding cash, a business may be able to acquire a competitor's business that suddenly becomes available at an attractive price.

Although cash can be held for each of the reasons identified, doing so may not always be necessary. If a business is able to borrow quickly, the amount of cash it needs to hold can be reduced. Similarly, if the business holds assets that can easily be converted to cash (for example, marketable securities such as shares in Stock Exchange listed businesses or government bonds), the amount of cash held can be reduced.

The major factors influence cash scale

The decision as to how much cash a particular business should hold is a difficult one. Different businesses will have different views on the subject. Generally, there are major factors that influence how much cash a business will hold. The possible factors are the following:

- The nature of the business. Some businesses, such as utilities (for example, water, electricity and gas suppliers), may have cash flows that are both predictable and reasonably certain. This will enable them to hold lower cash balances. For some businesses, cash balances may vary greatly according to the time of year. A seasonal business may accumulate cash during the high season to enable it to meet commitments during the low season.
- The opportunity cost of holding cash. Where there are profitable opportunities it may not be wise to hold a large cash balance.
- The level of inflation. Holding cash during a period of rising prices will lead to a loss of purchasing power. The higher the level of inflation, the greater the loss.
- The availability of near-liquid assets. If a business has marketable securities or inventories that may easily be liquidated, high cash balances may not be necessary.
- The availability of borrowing. If a business can borrow easily (and quickly) there is less need to hold cash.
- The cost of borrowing. When interest rates are high, the option of borrowing becomes less attractive.
- Economic conditions. When the economy is in recession, businesses may prefer to hold

cash so that they can be well placed to invest when the economy improves. In addition, during a recession, businesses may experience difficulties in collecting trade receivables. They may therefore hold higher cash balances than usual in order to meet commitments.
- Relationships with suppliers. Too little cash may hinder the ability of the business to pay suppliers promptly. This can lead to a loss of goodwill. It may also lead to discounts being forgone.

Controlling the cash balance

Several models have been developed to help control the cash balance of the business. One such model proposes the use of upper and lower control limits for cash balances and the use of a target cash balance. The model assumes that the business will invest in marketable investments that can easily be liquidated. These investments will be purchased or sold, as necessary, in order to keep the cash balance within the control limits.

The model proposes two upper and two lower control limits (see figure 12.5). If the business exceeds an outer limit, the managers must decide whether the cash balance is likely to return to a point within the inner control limits set, over the next few days. If this seems likely, then no action is required. If, on the other hand, it does not seem likely, management must change the cash position of the business by either buying or selling marketable investments.

In figure 12.4 we can see that the lower outer control limit has been breached for four days. If a four-day period is unacceptable, managers must sell marketable investments to replenish the cash balance.

The model relies heavily on management judgement to determine where the control limits are set and the period within which breaches of the control limits are acceptable. Past experience may be useful in helping managers decide on these issues. There are other models, however, that do not rely on management judgement. Instead, these use quantitative techniques to determine an optimal cash policy. One model proposed, for example, is the cash equivalent of the inventories economic order quantity model, discussed earlier in the chapter.

Cash budgets and managing cash

To manage cash effectively, it is useful for a business to prepare a cash budget. This is a very important tool for both planning and control purposes. However, it is worth repeating that these statements enable managers to see how planned events are expected to affect the cash balance. The projected cash budget will identify periods when cash surpluses and cash deficits are expected.

Management sets the upper and lower limits for the business's cash balance. When the balance goes beyond either of these limits, unless it is clear that the balance will return fairly

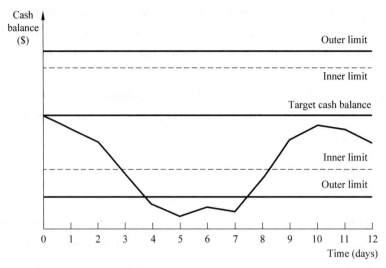

FIGURE 12.5　Controlling the cash balance

quickly to within the limit, action will need to be taken. If the upper limit is breached, some cash will be placed on deposit or used to buy some marketable securities. If the lower limit is breached, the business will need to borrow some cash or sell some securities.

When a cash surplus is expected to arise, managers must decide on the best use of the surplus funds. When a cash deficit is expected, managers must make adequate provision by borrowing, liquidating assets or rescheduling cash payments or receipts to deal with this. Cash budgets are useful in helping to control the cash held. The actual cash flows can be compared with the planned cash flows for the period. If there is a significant divergence between the projected, or forecast, cash flows and the actual cash flows, explanations must be sought and corrective action taken where necessary.

Although cash budgets are prepared primarily for internal management purposes, prospective lenders sometimes require them when a loan to a business is being considered.

Operating cash cycle

When managing cash, it is important to be aware of the **operating cash cycle (OCC)** of the business. For a retailer, for example, this may be defined as the period between the outlay of cash necessary for the purchase of inventories and the ultimate receipt of cash from the sale of the goods. In the case of a business that purchases goods on credit for subsequent resale on credit (for example, a wholesaler), the OCC is as shown in figure 12.6.

The OCC is the time lapse between paying for goods and receiving the cash from the sale of those goods. The length of the OCC has a significant impact on the amount of funds that the business needs to apply to working capital.

Figure 12.6 shows that payment for inventories acquired on credit occurs some time after those inventories have been purchased and, therefore, no immediate cash outflow arises from

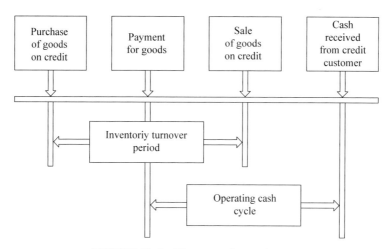

FIGURE 12.6 The operating cash cycle

the purchase. Similarly, cash receipts from credit customers will occur some time after the sale is made and so there will be no immediate cash inflow as a result of the sale. The OCC is the period between the payment made to the supplier for goods concerned and the cash received from the credit customer. Although figure 12.6 depicts the position for a wholesaling business, the precise definition of the OCC can easily be adapted for other types of business.

The OCC is important because it has a significant influence on the financing requirements of the business. Broadly, the longer the cycle, the greater the financing requirements of the business and the greater the financial risks. For this reason, the business is likely to want to reduce the OCC to the minimum possible period.

For the type of business mentioned above, which buys and sells on credit, the OCC can be calculated from the financial statements by the use of certain ratios. It is calculated as shown in figure 12.7.

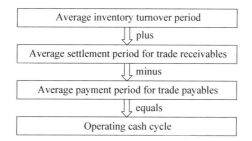

FIGURE 12.7 Calculating the operating cash cycle

EXAMPLE 12.6

Calculate three ratios of the OCC

The financial statements of Q Ltd, a distributor of frozen foods, are set out below for the year ended 31 December last year.

Income statement for the year ended 31 December last year		
	$000	$000
Sales revenue		820
Cost of sales		
Opening inventories	142	
Purchases	568	
	710	
Closing inventories	(166)	(544)
Gross profit		276
Administration expenses		(120)
Distribution expenses		(95)
Operating profit		61
Financial expenses		(32)
Profit before taxation		29
Taxation		(7)
Profit for the year		22

Statement of financial position (balance sheet) as at 31 December last year	
ASSETS	$000
Non-current assets	
Property, plant and equipment	
Premises at valuation	180
Fixtures and fittings at cost less depreciation	82
Motor vans at cost less depreciation	102
	364
Current assets	
Inventories	166
Trade receivables	264
Cash	24
	454
Total assets	818
EQUITY AND LIABILITIES	

Continued

Statement of financial position (balance sheet) as at 31 December last year	
Equity	
Ordinary share capital	300
Retained earnings	352
	652
Current liabilities	
Trade payables	159
Taxation	7
	166
Total equity and liabilities	818

All purchases and sales are on credit. There has been no change in the level of trade receivables or payables over the period.

Required: Calculate the length of the OCC for the business and go on to suggest how the business may seek to reduce this period.

Solution: The OCC may be calculated as follows:

	Number of days
Average inventories turnover period:	
$\dfrac{(\text{Opening inventories} + \text{Closing inventories})/2}{\text{cost of sales}} \times 365 = \dfrac{(142+166)/2}{544} \times 365$	103
Average settlement period for trade receivables:	
$\dfrac{\text{Trade receivables}}{\text{Credit sales}} \times 365 = \dfrac{264}{820} \times 365$	118
Average settlement period for trade payables:	
$\dfrac{\text{Trade payables}}{\text{Credit purchase}} \times 365 = \dfrac{159}{568} \times 365$	(102)
OCC	119

The business can reduce the length of the OCC in a number of ways. The average inventory turnover period seems quite long. At present, average inventories held represent more than three months' sales requirements. Lowering the level of inventories held will reduce this. Similarly, the average settlement period for trade receivables seems long, at nearly four months' sales. Imposing tighter credit control, offering discounts, charging interest on overdue accounts and so on may reduce this. However, any policy decisions concerning inventories and trade receivables must take account of current trading conditions.

Extending the period of credit taken to pay suppliers could also reduce the OCC. However, for reasons that will be explained later, this option must be given careful consideration.

Bank overdrafts

Bank overdrafts are simply bank current accounts that have a negative balance. They are a type of bank loan and can be a useful tool in managing the business's cash flows requirements.

12.5　Managing trade payable

Trade credit arises from the fact that most businesses buy their goods and service requirements on credit. In effect, suppliers are lending the business money, interest free, on a short-term basis. Trade payables are the other side of the coin from trade receivables. One business's trade payable is another one's trade receivable, in respect of a particular transaction. Trade payables are an important source of finance for most businesses. They have been described as a "spontaneous" source, as they tend to increase in line with the increase in the level of activity achieved by a business. Trade credit is widely regarded as a "free" source of finance and, therefore, a good thing for a business to use. There may be real costs, however, associated with taking trade credit.

First, customers who take credit may not be as well treated as those who pay immediately. For example, when goods are in short supply, credit customers may receive lower priority when allocating the goods available. In addition, credit customers may be less favoured in terms of delivery dates or the provision of technical support services. Sometimes, the goods or services provided may be more costly if credit is required. However, in most industries, trade credit is the norm. As a result, the above costs will not apply except, perhaps, to customers that abuse the credit facilities. A business that purchases supplies on credit will normally have to incur additional administration and accounting costs in dealing with the scrutiny and payment of invoices, maintaining and updating payables' accounts and so on.

These points are not meant to imply that taking credit represents a net cost to a business. There are, of course, real benefits that can accrue. Provided that trade credit is not abused, it can represent a form of interest-free loan. It can be a much more convenient method of paying for goods and services than paying by cash, and during a period of inflation there will be an economic gain by paying later rather than sooner for goods and services purchased. For most businesses, these benefits will exceed the costs involved.

In some cases, delaying payment to payables can be a sign of financial problems. One such example is given in Real World.

> ### REAL WORLD
>
> **NHS waiting times**
>
> The National Health Service is delaying paying bills and cutting orders for supplies as it tries to balance its books, according to the trade associations whose members supply the service with everything from scanners to diagnostic tests.
>
> Ray Hodgkinson, director-general of the British Healthcare Trades Association, said that while the picture was highly variable "some of our members are having real trouble getting money out of NHS trusts".
>
> Most had standing orders that said bills should be paid within 30 days, MrHodgkinson said. "But some are not paying for 60 or 90 days and even longer. They are in breach of their standing orders and for a lot of our members who are small businesses this is creating problems with cash flow. There is no doubt there is slow payment on a significant scale."
>
> Doris-Ann Williams, director-general of the British In-Vitro Diagnostics Association, whose members provide diagnostics supplies and tests, said: "We are starting to see invoices not being paid and orders not being closed until the start of the new financial year [in April]... All sorts of measures are being taken to try not to spend money in this financial year."
>
> Having seen orders dry up and bills not paid this time last year as the NHS headed for a £500m-plus financial deficit, she added that this was "starting to seem like an annual event".
>
> *Source*: "*NHS paying bills late in struggle to balance books, say suppliers*", Nicholas Timmins, *FT. com*, 13 *February* 2007.

Taking advantage of cash discounts

Where a supplier offers a discount for prompt payment, the business should give careful consideration to the possibility of paying within the discount period. An example may be useful to illustrate the cost of forgoing possible discounts.

H Ltd takes 70 days to pay for goods from its supplier. To encourage prompt payment, the supplier has offered the business a 2 percent discount if payment for goods is made within 30 days. H Ltd is not sure whether it is worth taking the discount offered.

If the discount is taken, payment could be made on the last day of the discount period (that is, the 30th day). However, if the discount is not taken, payment will be made after 70 days. This means that, by not taking the discount, the business will receive an extra 40 days' (that is, 70 − 30) credit. The cost of this extra credit to the business will be the 2 percent

discount forgone. If we annualise the cost of this discount forgone, we have:
$$365/40 \times 2\% = 18.3\% *$$

We can see that the annual cost of forgoing the discount is very high, and so it may be profitable for the business to pay the supplier within the discount period, even if it means that it will have to borrow to enable it to do so.

* This is an approximate annual rate. For the more mathematically minded, the precise rate is:
$$\{[(1 + 2/98)9.125] - 1\} \times 100\% = 20.2\%$$

Controlling trade payables

To help monitor the level of trade credit taken, management can calculate the average settlement period for trade payables. This ratio is:

$$\text{Average settlement period for trade payables} = \frac{\text{Average trade payables}}{\text{Credit purchase}} \times 365$$

Once again, this provides an average figure, which could be misleading. A more informative approach would be to produce an ageing schedule for payables. This would look much the same as the ageing schedule for receivables described earlier.

12.6 Working capital problems of small businesses

The amounts invested by businesses in working capital are often high in proportion to the total assets employed. It is, therefore, important that these amounts are properly managed. Although this point applies to businesses of all sizes, it may be of particular importance to small businesses. It is often claimed that many small businesses suffer from a lack of capital and, where this is the case, tight control over working capital investment becomes critical. There is evidence, however, that small businesses are not very good in managing their working capital and this has been cited as a major cause of their high failure rate compared to that of large businesses. In this section, we consider the working capital management problems associated with small businesses.

Managing inventories

A lack of financial management skills within a small business often creates problems in managing inventories in an efficient and effective way. The owners of small businesses are not always aware that there are costs involved in holding too much inventories and that there are also costs involved in holding too little. These costs, which were discussed earlier, may be very high in certain industries such as manufacturing and wholesaling, where inventories account for a significant proportion of the total assets held.

It was mentioned earlier in the chapter that the starting point for an effective inventories management system is good planning and budgeting systems. In particular, there should be reliable budgets, that can help with inventories ordering. Not all small businesses prepare these budgets, however. A survey by Chittenden and others (see reference 1 at the end of the chapter) of small and medium-size businesses indicated that only 78 per cent of those replying prepare a sales budget. Inventories management can also benefit from good reporting systems and the application of quantitative techniques (for example, the Economic Order Quantity model) to try to optimise inventories levels. However, the same survey found that more than one-third of small businesses rely on manual methods of inventories control and the majority do not use inventories optimisation techniques. Though the Chittenden survey is now rather old (1998) it represents the most recent reliable evidence available. There is no reason to believe that practices of small businesses have changed much since this evidence was gathered.

Credit management

Small businesses often lack the resources to manage their trade receivables effectively. It is not unusual for a small business to operate without a separate credit control department. This tends to mean that both the expertise and the information required to make sound judgements concerning terms of sale and so on may not be available. A small business may also lack proper debt-collection procedures, such as prompt invoicing and sending out regular statements. This will increase the risks of late payment and defaulting credit customers.

These risks probably tend to increase where there is an excessive concern for growth. In an attempt to increase sales, small businesses may be too willing to extend credit to customers that have high credit risks. Whilst this kind of problem can occur in businesses of all sizes, small businesses seem particularly susceptible.

Another problem faced by small businesses is their lack of market power. They will often find themselves in a weak position when negotiating credit terms with larger businesses. Moreover, when a large customer exceeds the terms of credit, the small supplier may feel inhibited from pressing the customer for payment in case future sales are lost.

The reason for the delay suffered by small businesses probably relates to one of the factors mentioned above, namely the bargaining power of customers. The customers of small businesses may well be larger ones, which can use a threat, perhaps an implied one, of withdrawing custom, to force small businesses to accept later trade receivable settlement.

In most countries the government has intervened to help deal with this problem and the law now permits small businesses to charge interest on overdue accounts. In addition, large companies are now required to disclose in their published financial statements the payment policy adopted towards suppliers in the hope that this will improve the behaviour of those that delay payments. However, it is unlikely that legislation alone will make a significant improvement. Whilst small businesses may be able to charge interest on overdue accounts, they will often avoid doing so because they fear that large customers would view this as a provocative act. What is really needed to help small businesses is a change in the payment culture.

We saw one way of dealing with the credit management problem is to factor the outstanding trade receivables. Under this kind of arrangement, the factor will take over the sales records of the business and will take responsibility for the prompt collection of trade receivables. However, some businesses are too small to take advantage of this facility. The set-up costs of a factoring arrangement often make businesses with a low sales revenue (say, $100 000 a year or less) an uneconomic proposition for the factor.

Managing cash

The management of cash raises similar issues to those relating to the management of inventories. There are costs involved in holding both too much and too little cash. Thus, there is a need for careful planning and monitoring of cash flows over time. The survey found, however, that only 63 percent of those replying prepared a cash budget. It was also found that cash balances are generally proportionately higher for smaller businesses than for larger ones. More than half of those in the survey held surplus cash balances on a regular basis. Though this may reflect a more conservative approach to liquidity among the owners of smaller businesses, it may suggest a failure to recognise the opportunity costs of cash balances.

Managing credit suppliers

In practice, small businesses often try to cope with the late payment of credit customers by delaying payments to their credit suppliers. We saw earlier in the chapter, however, that this can be an expensive option. Where discounts are forgone, the annual cost of this financing option compares unfavourably with most other forms of short-term financing. Nevertheless, the vast majority of small and medium-size businesses are unaware of the very high cost of delaying payment, according to the survey.

SUMMARY

1. The definition and elements of working capital

Working capital is the difference between current assets and current liabilities. That is, working capital = inventories + trade receivables + cash − trade payables − bank overdrafts.

An investment in working capital cannot be avoided in practice—typically large amounts are involved Inventories, trade receivables, cash and trade payables.

2. Managing inventories

There are also costs of not holding sufficient inventories, which include:
- loss of sales and customer goodwill
- production dislocation
- loss of flexibility

- cannot take advantage of opportunities
- reorder costs
- low inventories imply more frequent ordering.

In practice inventories management include identify optimum order size, EOQ models can, keeping reliable inventories records and just-in-time (JIT) inventories management.

3. Managing trade receivables

When assessing which customers should receive credit, the 5 Cs of credit can be used. The practical points on receivables management include:

- establish a policy
- assess and monitor customer creditworthiness
- establish effective administration of receivables
- establish a policy on bad debts
- consider cash discounts
- use financial ratios (for example, average settlement period for trade receivables ratio)
- use ageing summaries.

4. Managing Cash

Issues that entities must manage with regard to cash include the need to have sufficient cash, the timing of cash flows, the cost of cash and the cost of not having enough cash. Entities must have sufficient cash on hand to meet their bills on time. The timing of cash flows may be manipulated to some extent, in order to have sufficient cash at all times and to optimise the returns to cash. The cost of holding cash is the opportunity cost of holding liquid deposits, but the cost of not holding sufficient cash may be the cost of arranging emergency loans, or could be the ultimate penalty, insolvency and business cessation.

Operating cash cycle (OCC) = length of time from buying inventories to receiving cash from receivables less payables payment period (in days). An objective of working capital management is to limit the length of the operating cash cycle, subject to any risks that this may cause.

5. Managing trade payables

Trade payables is a source of short-term finance. Practical points on payables management include establish a policy, exploit free credit as far as possible and use accounting ratios (for example, average settlement period for trade payables ratio).

6. Working capital and small businesses

Small businesses often lack the skills and resources to manage working capital effectively. Small businesses often suffer from large businesses delaying payments for goods and services supplied. Changes in the law designed to help small businesses have had limited success.

KEY TERMS

ABC system of inventory control　ABC 存货控制系统
Ageing schedule of trade receivables　应收账款账龄分析表
Average settlement period for trade payables　应付账款平均周转期
Average settlement period for trade receivables　应收账款平均周转期
Cash discount　现金折扣
Economic order quantity（EOQ）　经济订货批量
Five Cs of credit 5C　信用标准
Just-in-time（JIT）inventory management　存货即时管理系统
Lead time　从发出订货单到收到货物的时间
Materials requirement planning（MRP）system　材料需求计划
Operating cash cycle（OCC）　经营用现金循环周期
Working capital　运营资金

SELF-EVALUATION ACTIVITIES

12.1　Single choice questions

1. Which of the following is not a current asset?

　　(a) Inventories;　　　　　　　　　(b) Prepayments;
　　(c) Accruals;　　　　　　　　　　(d) Accounts receivable;
　　(e) Cash.

2. For category A (of ABC) inventory which of the following controls would not normally be recommended?

　　(a) Sophisticated recording procedures;
　　(b) The use of LIFO cost allocation;
　　(c) Tight control over inventory movements;
　　(d) Individual inventory unit identification;
　　(e) High level security at the inventory location.

3. Which of the following is a limiting assumption of the EOQ model?

　　(a) It assumes that demand for the product can be predicted with accuracy;
　　(b) It assumes that demand is even over the period;
　　(c) It assumes that no buffer stock is required;
　　(d) All of the above;
　　(e) None of the above.

4. Which of the following is an important ingredient to the success of JIT inventory management?

(a) Contract the supplier of inventory needs on the day of production;

(b) The use of contract delivery services;

(c) The establishment of a close relationship between the business and its suppliers;

(d) Ready access to the cheapest sources of supply;

(e) All of the above.

5. Selling goods on credit results in costs being incurred by the business. One of these costs would be:

(a) Discounts received;   (b) Distribution expense;

(c) Depreciation expense;   (d) Goodwill amortisation;

(e) Opportunities.

12.2   True or false

1. In the case of a retailer, inventory levels tend to be higher than for a manufacturer.

2. Inventory lead time is the time between placing of an order and payment for the goods received.

3. The ABC system of inventory control relates to activity based costing.

4. The economic order quantity (EOQ) model is concerned with answering the question, "How much inventory should be held in stock"?

5. An aged schedule of debtors is related to the balance sheet approach of determining bad debts expense.

Answer to self-evaluation activities

12.1   Single choice questions

1. c   2. b   3. d   4. c   5. e

12.2   True or false

1. F   2. F   3. F   4. F   5. T

Appendix

1. Balance Sheet

资产负债表

编制单位：　　　　　　　　　　　　　　　年　月　日　　　　　　　　　　　会企01表
　　　　　　　　　　　　　　　　　　　　　　　　　　　　　　　　　　　　　单位：元

资产	期末余额	年初余额	资产和所有者权益（或股东权益）	期末余额	年初余额
流动资产：			流动负债：		
货币资金			短期借款		
以公允价值计量且其变动计入当期损益的金融资产			以公允价值计量且其变动计入当期损益的金融负债		
应收票据			应付票据		
应收账款			应付账款		
预付账款			预收账款		
应收利息			应付职工薪酬		
应收股利			应交税费		
其他应收款			应付利息		
存货			应付股利		
一年内到期的非流动资产			其他应付款		
其他流动资产			一年内到期的非流动负债		
流动资产合计			其他流动负债		
非流动资产：			流动负债合计		
可供出售金融资产			非流动负债：		
持有至到期投资			长期借款		
长期应收款			应付债券		
长期股权投资			长期应付款		
投资性房地产			专项应付款		
固定资产			预计负债		

续表

资　产	期末余额	年初余额	资产和所有者权益（或股东权益）	期末余额	年初余额
在建工程			递延所得税负债		
工程物资			其他非流动负债		
固定资产清理			非流动负债合计		
生产性生物资产			负债合计		
油气资源			所有者权益（或股东权益）：		
无形资产			实收资本（或股本）		
开发支出			资本公积		
商誉			减：库存股		
长期待摊费用			盈余公积		
递延所得税资产			未分配利润		
其他非流动资产			所有者权益（或股东权益）合计		
非流动资产合计					
资产总计			负债和所有者权益（或股东权益）总计		

Balance Sheet FROM AJI-01

Prepared by： For the Year(or Quarter, Month) Ended Unit：CNY

Assets	Ending	Beginning balance	Liabilities and owners' equity (shareholders' equity)	Ending balance	Beginning balance
Current assets：			**Current liabilities：**		
Monetary fund			Short-term loans		
Financial assets measuring at fair value through profit or loss			Financial liabilities measuring at fair value through profit or loss		
Notes receivable			Notes payable		
Accounts receivable			Accounts payable		
Advances to suppliers			Advances from customers		
Interest receivable			Employee compensation payable		
Dividend receivable			Tax payable		
Other receivable			Interest payable		

Continued

Assets	Ending balance	Beginning balance	Liabilities and owners' equity (shareholders' equity)	Ending balance	Beginning balance
Inventories			Dividend payable		
Non-current assets due within one year			Other payable		
Other current assets			Non-current liabilities due within one year		
Total current assets			Other current liabilities		
Non-current assets:			Total current liabilities		
Available-for-sale financial assets			**Non-current liabilities:**		
Held-to-maturity investments			Long-term loans		
Long-term accounts receivable			Bonds payable		
Long-term equity investments			Long-term payable		
Investment properties			Special payable		
Fixed assets			Accured liabilities		
Construction-in-process			Deferred tax liabilities		
Project materials			Other non-current liabilities		
Disposal of fixed assets			Total non-current liabilities		
Productive biological assets			Total liabilities		
Oil and gas assets			Owners' equity (shareholders' equity):		
Intangible assets			Capital stock		
Developmentexpenditure			Capital reserve		
Goodwill			Less: Treasury Stock		
Long-term deferred expense			Surplus reserve		
Deferred tax assets			Undistributed profit		
Other non-current assets			Total owners' equity (shareholders' equity)		
Total non-current assets					
Total assets			**Total liabilities and owners' equity (shareholders' equity)**		

2. Income Statement

损益表

会企02表

编制单位：　　　　　　　　　　　　　年　月　　　　　　　　　　　　单位：元

项　　目	本 期 金 额	上 期 金 额
一、营业收入		
减：营业成本		
营业税金及附加		
销售费用		
管理费用		
财务费用		
资产减值损失		
加：公允价值变动损益（损失以"－"填列）		
投资收益（损失以"－"填列）		
其中：对联营企业和合营企业的投资收益		
二、营业利润（亏损以"－"填列）		
加：营业外收入		
减：营业外支出		
其中：非流动资产处置损失		
三、利润总额（亏损以"－"填列）		
减：所得税费用		
四、净利润（净亏损以"－"填列）		
五、其他综合收益		
六、综合收益总额		
七、每股收益		
（一）基本每股收益		
（二）稀释每股收益		

Income Statement

Prepared by: For the Year (or Quarter, Month) Ended FORM AJI-02 Unit: CNY

Item	Amount in current period	Amount in last period
Operating revenue		
Less: Operating cost		
Taxes and surcharges		
Selling expenses		
Administrative expenses		
Financial expenses		
Impairment loss on assets		
Add: Gain arising from the change in fair value (loss shown with " - ")		
Investment income (loss shown with " - ")		
Including: investment income from affiliates and joint-ventures		
Operating profit (loss shown with " - ")		
Add: Non-operating income		
Less: Non-operating expenses		
Including: Loss on disposal of non-current assets		
Total profit (loss shown with " - ")		
Less: Income tax expense		
Net profit (loss shown with " - ")		
Other comprehensive income		
Total comprehensive income		
Earnings per share		
Basic earnings per share		
Diluted earnings per share		

3. Statement of Change in Owners' Equity

所有者权益变动表

编制单位：　　　　　　　　　　　　　年度　　　　　　　　　　　　　　　　　　　　　　　　　会企04表
　　　单位：元

项　目	本年金额							上年金额						
	实收资本（或股本）	资本或股本溢价	减：库存股	其他综合收益	盈余公积	未分配利润	所有者权益合计	实收资本（或股本）	资本或股本溢价	减：库存股	其他综合收益	盈余公积	未分配利润	所有者权益合计
一、上年年末余额														
加：会计政策变更														
前期差错更正														
二、本年期初余额														
三、本年增减变动金额（减少以"－"填列）														
（一）综合收益总额														
（二）所有者投入和减少资本														
1. 所有者投入资本														
2. 股份支付计入所有者权益的金额														
3. 其他														
（三）利润分配														
1. 提取盈余公积														
2. 对所有者（或股东）的分配														
3. 其他														

续表

项目	本年金额							上年金额						
	实收资本（或股本）	资本或资本溢价（股本溢价）	减：库存股	其他综合收益	盈余公积	未分配利润	所有者权益合计	实收资本（或股本）	资本或资本溢价（股本溢价）	减：库存股	其他综合收益	盈余公积	未分配利润	所有者权益合计
（四）所有者权益内部结转														
1. 资本公积转增资本（或股本）														
2. 盈余公积转增资本（或股本）														
3. 盈余公积弥补亏损														
4. 其他														
四、本年年末余额														

Statement of Changes in Owners' Equity

For the Year Ended

Prepared by:

From AJI-04
Unit: CNY

Item	Amount of this year							Amount of last year						
	Capital stock	capital or premium on capital stock	Less: Treasury stock	Other comprehensive income	Surplus reserve	Undistributed profit	Total	Capital stock	capital or premium on capital stock	Less: Treasury stock	Other comprehensive income	Surplus reserve	Undistributed profit	Total
Balance at end of last year														
Add: Changes in accounting polices														
Adjustments of prior-year errors														
Balance at beginning of the year														

Continued

Item	Amount of this year							Amount of last year						
	Capital stock	capital or premium on capital stock	Less: Treasury stock	Other comprehensive income	Surplus reserve	Undistributed profit	Total	Capital stock	capital or premium on capital stock	Less: Treasury stock	Other comprehensive income	Surplus reserve	Undistributed profit	Total
Increase (decrease) during this year (decrease shown with " - "														
Total comprehensive income														
Invested/withdrawn capital by owners														
Capital invested by owners														
share-based payments recognized in owners' equity														
Others														
Profit distribution														
Appropriation to surplus reserve														
Distribution to owners (shareholders)														
Others														
Inner transfer in owners' equity														
Capital reserve transferred to capital stock														
Surplus reserve transferred to capital stock														
Surplus reserve used to cover loss														
Balance at end of the year														

4. Statement of Cash Flows

现金流量表

编制单位　　　　　　　　　　　　　　年　月　　　　　　　　　　　　会企03表
　　　　　　　　　　　　　　　　　　　　　　　　　　　　　　　　　　　单位：元

项　　目	本 期 金 额	上 期 金 额
一、经营活动产生的现金流量：		
销售商品、提供劳务收到的现金		
收到的税费返还		
收到的经营活动相关的现金		
经营活动现金流入小计		
购买商品、接受劳务支付的现金		
支付给职工以及为职工支付的现金		
支付的各项税费		
支付与其他经营活动有关的现金		
经营活动现金流出小计		
经营活动产生的现金流量净额		
二、投资活动产生的现金流量：		
收回投资收到的现金		
取得投资收益收到的现金		
处置固定资产、无形资产和其他长期资产收回的现金净额		
处置子公司及其他营业单位收到的现金金额		
收到与其他投资活动有关的现金		
投资活动现金流入小计		
购建固定资产、无形资产和其他长期资产支付的现金		
投资支付的现金		
取得子公司及其他营业单位支付的现金净额		
支付与其他投资活动有关的现金		
投资活动现金流入小计		
投资活动产生的现金流量净额		
三、筹资活动产生的现金流量： 项目	本期金额	上期金额
吸收投资收到的现金		
取得借款收到的现金		

续表

项　　目	本期金额	上期金额
收到其他与筹资活动有关的现金		
筹资活动现金流入小计		
偿还债务支付的现金		
分配股利、利润或偿付利息支付的现金		
支付其他与筹资活动支付的现金		
筹资活动现金流出小计		
筹资活动产生的现金流量净额		
四、汇率变动对现金及现金等价物的影响		
五、现金及现金等价物净增加额		
加：期初现金及现金等价物余额		
六、期末现金及现金等价物余额		

Statement of Cash Flows　　　　　　　　From AJI-03

Prepared by：　　　　For the Year (or Quarter, Month) Ended　　　Unit: CNY

Item	Amount of current period	Amount of last period
Cash flows from operating activities:		
Cash received from sales of goods or offer of services		
Refunds of taxes		
Other cash received relating to operating activities		
Sub-total of cash inflows from operating activities		
Cash paid for goods or receipt of services		
Cash paid to and behalf of employees		
payments of all types of taxes		
Other cash paid relating to operating activities		
Sub-total of cash outflows from operating activities		
Net cash flows from operating activities		
Cash flows from investing activities:		
Cash received from returns of investments		
Cash received from income of investments		
Net cash received from disposals of fixed assets, intangible assets and other non-current assets		

Continued

Item	Amount of current period	Amount of last period
Net cash received from disposals of subsidiaries and other operating entities		
Other cash received relating to investing activities		
Sub-total of cash inflows from investing activities		
Cash paid for purchases fixed assets, intangible assets and other non-current assents		
Cash paid for investments		
cash paid for acquisition of subsidiaries and other operating entities		
Other cash paid relating to operating activities		
Sub-total of cash out flows from investing activities		
Net cash flows from investing activities		
Cash flows from financing activities:		
Cash received from absorption of investments		
Cash received from borrowings		
Other cash received relating to financing activities		
Sub-total of cash inflows from financing activities		
Cash paid for discharges of debts		
Cash paid for distributions of dividends and income or payments of interest		
Other cash paid relating to financing activities		
Sub-total of cash outflows from financing activities		
Net cash flows from financing activities		
Effect of foreign exchange rate changes on cash and cash equivalents		
Net increase in cash and cash equivalents		
Add: Cash and cash equivalents at the beginning of the period		
Cash and cash equivalents at the end of the period		

Main References

[1] Jacqueline Birt, Keryn Chalmers, Suzanne Maloney, Albie Brooks, Judy Oliver. 2017. Accounting: Business Reporting for Decision Making(6e). John Wiley & Sons, Inc.

[2] Craig Deegan. 2016. Financial Accounting(8e). McGraw-Hill Education Pty Ltd.

[3] Atrill, McLaney, Harvey, Jenner. 2009. Accounting: an introduction(4e). Pearson Education Australia.

[4] Jackling, Raar, Williams, Wines. 2008. Accounting: a framework for decision making(2e). McGraw-Hill Education Pty Ltd.

教学支持说明

▶▶ 课件申请

尊敬的老师:

您好!感谢您选用清华大学出版社的教材!为更好地服务教学,我们为采用本书作为教材的老师提供教学辅助资源。该部分资源仅提供给授课教师使用,请您直接用手机扫描下方二维码完成认证及申请。

任课教师扫描二维码
可获取教学辅助资源

▶▶ 样书申请

为方便教师选用教材,我们为您提供免费赠送样书服务。授课教师扫描下方二维码即可获取清华大学出版社教材电子书目。在线填写个人信息,经审核认证后即可获取所选教材。我们会第一时间为您寄送样书。

任课教师扫描二维码
可获取教材电子书目

 清华大学出版社

E-mail: tupfuwu@163.com　　　　　　　网址: http://www.tup.com.cn/
电话: 010-83470332 / 83470142　　　　传真: 8610-83470107
地址: 北京市海淀区双清路学研大厦B座509室　　邮编: 100084